ANTISOCIAL

ANTI

SOCIAL

Online Extremists,
Techno-Utopians,
and the Hijacking of
the American Conversation

ANDREW MARANTZ

VIKING

VIKING

An imprint of Penguin Random House LLC
penguinrandomhouse.com

Portions of this work were previously published in slightly different form in *The New Yorker* as "Trolls for Trump" (October 2016), "Trump and the Truth" (November 2016), "Trump Supporters at the DeploraBall" (February 2017), "Is Trump Trolling the White House Press Corps?" (March 2017), "An Awkward Right-Wing Dance Party" (May 2017), "Behind the Scenes With the Right-Wing Activist Who Crashed 'Julius Caesar'" (June 2017), "Birth of a White Supremacist" (October 2017), and "Reddit and the Struggle to Detoxify the Internet" (March 2018).

"Housekeeping Observation" from *Can't and Won't: Stories* by Lydia Davis. Copyright © 2014 by Lydia Davis. Reprinted by permission of Farrar, Straus and Giroux.

ISBN 9780525522263 (hardcover)
ISBN 9780525522270 (ebook)

Printed in the United States of America
10 9 8 7 6 5 4 3 2 1

Set in MinionPro
Designed by Cassandra Garruzzo

For LBG and the Gid

Morality, if it is to remain or become morality, must be perpetually examined, cracked, changed, made new. . . . Not everything that is faced can be changed; but nothing can be changed until it is faced.

James Baldwin, "As Much Truth As One Can Bear"

Under all this dirt
the floor is really very clean.

Lydia Davis, *Can't and Won't*

Contents

PART THREE

Too Big to Ignore

PART FOUR

The Swamp

ANTISOCIAL, ADJ. (1797)

1. unwilling or unable to associate in a normal or friendly way with other people (*He's not antisocial, just shy*)

2. antagonistic, hostile, or unfriendly toward others; menacing; threatening (*an antisocial act*)

3. opposed or detrimental to social order or the principles on which society is constituted (*antisocial behavior*)

4. *Psychiatry*: of or relating to a pattern of behavior in which social norms and the rights of others are persistently violated

Dictionary.com Unabridged

Based on the *Random House Unabridged Dictionary*, © Random House, Inc. 2019

ANTISOCIAL

Prologue

I landed at the Bob Hope Airport in Burbank, rented a Ford sedan, and asked Google to send me southward on a semiefficient route, scenic but without too much traffic. As I drove, I listened to a nationalist motivational speaker delivering far-right talking points via livestream. I was deprived of the full effect, being unable to see his facial expressions and the comments floating up the left side of my phone's screen, but I figured that the full effect was not worth dying for. "Are you gonna be a passive observer in these extraordinary times, as we fight to save Western civilization, or are you gonna step up?" he asked. "I've decided that I'm stepping up." The 2016 presidential election was approaching, and the institutional gatekeepers in government, business, and media all agreed that the result was inevitable. The nationalist was urging his listeners to question the prevailing narrative, to think the unthinkable, to bend the arc of history. Through my windshield I could see a sliver of the Pacific, picturesque but not all that pacific.

On the Hermosa Beach boardwalk there were longboards and mirrored sunglasses and poke bowls and matcha smoothies. A small film crew from Women.com was shooting a series of woman-on-the-street interviews about sex positivity. On the beach, a crowd had gathered around a drum circle. "Can you feel the Earth's rhythm?" one of the drummers asked, passing around a bucket for donations.

I spotted about a dozen beefy white men, dressed in T-shirts and shorts, milling around near an outdoor bar. In the middle of the scrum was the nationalist motivational speaker. Most people on the boardwalk didn't recognize him, but to his followers, both in person and on the internet, he was something of a hero, or maybe an antihero—an expert at injecting fringe ideas into mainstream discourse. A few months earlier, he had decided, based on no real evidence, that Hillary Clinton was suffering from a grave neurological condition and that the traditional media was covering it up. He turned this conjecture into a meme, which gathered momentum on Twitter, then leaped to the *Drudge Report*, then to Fox News, and then into Donald Trump's mouth. The nationalist had told me, "All the people at each step may or may not know my name, but I'm influencing world history whether they know where their ideas are coming from or not."

He was hosting what he called a free-speech happy hour—a meetup for local masculinists, neomonarchists, nihilist Twitter trolls, and other self-taught culture warriors. About sixty people showed up over the course of the afternoon. Some refused to call themselves alt-right, which had become, in their words, "a toxic brand"; others were happy to own the label. Most were white, most were nationalists, and some were white nationalists—not the old skinhead type but the more polished, just-asking-the-question variety. For years, they'd been able to promote their agenda through social networks like Twitter and Facebook, with almost no restrictions. Now those networks were starting to crack down, banning a few of the most egregious trolls and bigots. "It's straight-up thought policing," one person at the meetup said. "It's *1984*."

A pudgy guy with oversized sunglasses sat at a table by himself. On his T-shirt was a drawing of Harambe, a gorilla who'd recently been shot to death at the Cincinnati Zoo. The incident had resulted in real internet outrage, followed by satirical internet outrage, followed by absurdist metacommentaries on the phenomenon of internet outrage. All afternoon, I saw people pointing at the guy's T-shirt and laughing as they passed by. "Fuck yeah, Harambe," they'd say, or "Dicks out for Harambe." The guy wearing the T-shirt would nod knowingly, as if in solidarity. That was the extent of the interaction.

I sat down next to the guy and asked him to explain the joke. "It's a funny thing people say, or post, or whatever," he said. "It's, like—it's just a thing on the internet." Harambe, of course, was a real animal before he became a meme. Still, I knew what it was like to experience much of life through the mediating effects of a screen. It wasn't hard for me to imagine how anything—a dead gorilla, a gas chamber, a presidential election, a moral principle—could start to seem like just another thing on the internet.

• • •

For as long as the United States has been a country, there have been Americans handing out pamphlets declaring taxation unconstitutional, or standing on soapboxes railing against papist sabotage, or calling C-SPAN to demand that every member of Congress be investigated for treason. (C-SPAN's screeners, if they were doing their jobs, did not put those callers on air.) The First Amendment protected this minority's right to speak, and for a long time it seemed as if the majority were not inclined to listen. "There have always been those on the fringes of our society who have sought to escape their own responsibility by finding a simple solution, an appealing slogan, or a convenient scapegoat," President John F. Kennedy said in 1961. "But in time the basic good sense and stability of the great American consensus has always prevailed."

In 2004 and 2005, a few young men wrote the computer code that would grow into a vast industry called social media—"social" because people could receive information horizontally, from their friends, rather than waiting for gatekeepers to impart it from on high; "media" because information was information, whether it came from a stilted broadcaster, a kid procrastinating during study hall, or a nationalist on a boardwalk. The social media entrepreneurs called themselves disrupters, but they rarely described in much detail what a postdisruption world would look like. When pressed, their visions tended toward hazy utopianism: they expected to connect people, to bring us all closer together, to make the world a better place.

Their optimism wasn't entirely misguided, of course. Millions of people—whistleblowers, citizen journalists, women resisting abuse, dissidents under despotic regimes—did use social media to organize, to reveal abuses of power, to advance the aims of justice. And yet, when the same tools were used to sow disinformation or incite hatred, the disrupters usually responded by saying something vague about free speech and then changing the subject.

The disrupters aimed to topple gatekeepers in dozens of industries, including advertising, publishing, political consulting, and journalism. Within a decade, they had succeeded beyond anyone's expectations. Their social networks had become the most powerful information-spreading instruments in world history. Many traditional media outlets were being dismantled, and no one seemed to have any idea what might replace them. Instead of taking over where the old gatekeepers had left off, the disrupters—the new gatekeepers—refused to acknowledge the expanding scope of their influence and responsibility. They left their gates unguarded, for the most part, trusting passersby not to mess with the padlocks.

Right away, the national vocabulary started to shift, becoming both more liberated and more unhinged. The silent majority was no longer silent. Long-standing fissures furrowed into deep rifts. The disrupters weren't solely responsible for all of this, of course. Like every epochal shift, this one had many preconditions. Political movements mattered; economic structures mattered; geography and demography mattered; foreign wars mattered. Still, only a few years into the unprecedented experiment that was social media, it suddenly seemed quaint to recall that there had ever been such a thing as a great American consensus.

This much was shocking but not quite unthinkable. Then, swiftly, came the unthinkable: smart, well-meaning people unable to distinguish simple truth from viral misinformation; a pop-culture punch line ascending to the presidency; neo-Nazis marching, unmasked, through several American cities. This wasn't the kind of disruption anyone had envisioned. There had been a serious miscalculation.

We like to assume that the arc of history will bend inexorably toward justice, but this is wishful thinking. Nobody, not even Martin Luther King Jr., believed that social progress was automatic; if he did, he wouldn't have bothered marching across any bridges. The arc of history bends the way people bend it. In the early years of the twenty-first century, the internet was full of nihilists and masculinists and ironic neo-Nazis and nonironic neo-Nazis, all working to bend the arc of history in some extremely disturbing directions. Social media feeds were algorithmically personalized, which meant that many people didn't have to see the lurid ugliness online if they didn't want to. But it was there, more and more of it every minute, whether they chose to look at it or not.

•   •   •

In 2012, a small group of former Ron Paul supporters started a blog called *The Right Stuff*. They soon began calling themselves "post-libertarians," although they weren't yet sure what would come next. By 2014, they'd started to self-identify as alt-right. They developed a countercultural tone—arch, antic, floridly offensive—that appealed to a growing cohort of disaffected young men, searching for meaning and addicted to the internet. These young men often referred to *The Right Stuff*, approvingly, as a key part of a "libertarian-to-far-right pipeline," a path by which "normies" could advance, through a series of epiphanies, toward "full radicalization." As with everything the alt-right said, it was hard to tell whether they were joking, half joking, or not joking at all.

The Right Stuff's founders came up with talking points—narratives, they called them—that their followers then disseminated through various social networks. The memes were tailored to the medium. On Facebook, they posted Photoshopped images, or parody songs, or "countersignal memes"—sardonic line "drawings" designed to spark just enough cognitive dissonance to shock normies out of their complacency.* On Twitter, the alt-right trolled and harassed mainstream journalists, hoping to work the referees of the national discourse while capturing the attention of the wider public.† On Reddit and 4chan and 8chan, where the content moderation was so lax as to be almost nonexistent, the memes were more overtly vile. Many alt-right trolls started calling themselves "fashy," or "fash-ist." They referred to all liberals and traditional conservatives as Communists, or "degenerates"; they posted pro-Pinochet propaganda; they baited normies into arguments by insisting that "Hitler did nothing wrong."

When I first saw luridly ugly memes like this, in 2014 and 2015, I wasn't sure how seriously to take them. Everyone knows the most basic rule of the internet: Don't feed the trolls, and don't take tricksters at their word. The trolls of the alt-right called themselves provocateurs, or shitposters, or edgelords. And what could be edgier than joking about Hitler? For a little while, I was able to avoid reaching the conclusion that would soon become obvious: maybe they meant what they said.‡

In October 2018, a white terrorist carried three Glock handguns and an AR-15 into a synagogue in Pittsburgh and started shooting. He had been active on a small social network called Gab, a hermetic bubble of toxicity that billed itself as "the home of free speech online." Two weeks before the shooting, he'd reposted a countersignal meme featuring two stick figures. The first was labeled "Me one year ago" and the second was labeled "Me today." The first stick figure, in a speech

---

*"I'm so brave!!!" said one stick figure, a normie liberal wearing a nose ring. "Parroting the exact same narrative as universities, government departments, schools, the mainstream media, Hollywood, major political parties, and corporations is sooooo anti-establishment."

†Twitter had rules against harassment, and Facebook had rules against terrorist recruitment, but the rules were enforced casually and inconsistently. Techno-libertarian utopianism was ascendant in Silicon Valley, and most social media executives were determined to moderate their networks as lightly as possible. Besides, when the executives vowed to remove terrorist recruiters from their networks, they didn't seem to have white terrorists in mind.

‡"The unindoctrinated should not be able to tell if we are joking or not," the editor of a prominent neo-Nazi site wrote in an internal document that was later leaked to the press. "This is obviously a ploy and I actually do want to gas kikes." For legal reasons, he asked his writers to refrain from openly inciting violence; "however, whenever someone does something violent, it should be made light of." The ultimate goal, he wrote, was to "dehumanize the enemy, to the point where people are ready to laugh at their deaths."

bubble, said, "I believe everyone has the right to live how they want and do what makes them happy." The second one said, "We need to overthrow the government, implement a clerical fascist regime, and begin mass executing these Marxist degenerates." The caption above the drawing: "The libertarian-to-far-right pipeline is a real thing."

• • •

This is not a book arguing that the fascists have won, or that they will win. This is a book about how the unthinkable becomes thinkable. I don't assume that America is destined to live up to its founding ideals of liberty and equality. Nor do I assume that it is doomed to repeat its founding reality of brutal oppression. I can't know which way the arc will bend. What I can offer is the story of how a few disruptive entrepreneurs, motivated by naïveté and reckless techno-utopianism, built powerful new systems full of unforeseen vulnerabilities, and how a motley cadre of edgelords, motivated by bigotry and bad faith and nihilism, exploited those vulnerabilities to hijack the American conversation.

I spent about three years immersing myself in two worlds: the world of the gate-crashers, such as the nationalist on the boardwalk, and the world of the new gatekeepers of Silicon Valley, who, whether intentionally or not, afforded the gate-crashers their unprecedented power. (At the same time, simply by working as a writer at *The New Yorker*, I was immersed in a third world: that of the old gatekeepers, who are increasingly at risk of being disrupted into extinction.) I had breakfast at the Trump Soho with a self-proclaimed "internet supervillain," toured a rural Illinois junkyard with a freelance Twitter propagandist, drank in a German beer hall with a not-quite-Nazi. In Washington, D.C., I shadowed a histrionic far-right troll during his first week as a White House press correspondent. In San Francisco, I sat at a conference table while a group of new gatekeepers, having allowed their huge social network to become overrun with hate speech, opened their laptops and tried to rein in the chaos. I also spent hundreds of hours talking to people who were ensnared in the cult of web-savvy white supremacy, and to a few who managed to get out.

At no point did I start to find Nazi propaganda cute or funny. I did not succumb to the misconception that a journalist must present both sides of every story, or that all interview subjects are owed equal sympathy. I am not of the opinion that we owe Nazis anything. I do believe, however, that if we want to understand what is happening to our country, we can't rely on wishful thinking. We have to look at the problem—at how our national vocabulary, and thus our national character, are in the process of being shattered.

"The left won by seizing control of media and academia," a blogger on *The Right Stuff*, using the pseudonym Meow Blitz, wrote in 2015. "With the Internet, they lost control of the narrative." By "the left," he meant the whole standard range of American culture and politics—everyone who preferred democracy to autocracy, everyone who resisted the alt-right's vision of a white American ethnostate. For decades, Meow Blitz argued, this pluralistic worldview—the mainstream worldview—had gone effectively unchallenged; but now, by promoting their agenda on social media, he and his fellow propagandists could push America in a more fascist-friendly direction. "ISIS became the most powerful terrorist group in the world because of flashy Internet videos," he wrote. "If you're alive in the year 2015 and you don't understand the power of the interwebz you're an idiot."

To the post's intended audience, this was supposed to be invigorating. To me, it was more like a faint whiff of sulfur that may or may not turn out to be a gas leak. The post was called "Right Wing Trolls Can Win." Would the neofascists win? I had a hard time imagining it. *Could* they win? That was a different question. "The culture war is being fought daily from your smartphone," the post continued. On this one point, at least, I had to agree with Meow Blitz. To change how we talk is to change who we are.

PART ONE

DeploraBall

Everyone knows, or ought to know, that there has happened under us a Tectonic Plate Shift. . . . The political parties have the same names; we still have a CBS, an NBC, and a New York *Times*; but we are not the same nation that had these things before.

George W. S. Trow, 1997

CHAPTER ONE

This Is America

The afternoon before Donald Trump was sworn in as president, Cassandra Fairbanks was at home, in a brick duplex twenty minutes north of Washington, D.C., getting dressed for the DeploraBall. She answered the door barefoot, wearing a Stars and Stripes manicure, a necklace made from a rifle casing, and a strapless red ball gown with a plunging neckline. "Sorry about the mess," she said. "Everyone always crashes with me when they come to town." A woman in her twenties and two men, both thirty, sat on a pleather couch, surrounded by a moat of camera equipment, staring silently at their phones.

Fairbanks connected a laptop to her TV and searched YouTube for Bob Dylan. "One of my idols," she said. "One of the last true rebels." She played a clip at random: a radio recording, from 1962, of Dylan performing a folk ballad called "The Death of Emmett Till." Everyone looked up at the TV for a while, even though the image was only a still photograph. "'Cause he was born a black-skinned boy, he was born to die," Dylan sang.

"I'm so paranoid about my dress falling down," Fairbanks said, hoisting up one side of her décolletage, then the other. A minute later, she added, "I need to finish my makeup," and dashed upstairs. She was already wearing a good amount of makeup, but not enough to be camera ready. The DeploraBall would be both a party and a media spectacle; there would be crews from various news outlets, and admirers posting group selfies to Instagram, and several social media demicelebrities, Fairbanks among them, who might at any moment start broadcasting to their followers on YouTube or Periscope or Facebook Live. She was dressing not for the people in the room but for the fans at home.

Fairbanks's puppy, a Yorkie-Chihuahua mix, ran in tight, frantic circles, its paws clacking on the wooden floor. The living room was crowded with knickknacks—hanging lanterns, mirrors in brightly colored frames. A coffee table was strewn with canned Starbucks mochas and packs of American Spirits. The woman on the couch introduced herself as Emily Molli; the two men glanced up briefly, nodded in my general direction, then returned their attention to their phones. I asked their names, to be polite, although I recognized them from YouTube: Luke Rudkowski, lanky and towheaded, and Tim Pool, whose hair I had never seen because he always wore a beanie. Rudkowski and Pool were both one-man media brands, specializing in straight-to-camera punditry and jittery live footage from street demonstrations. (Molli did some camera work for Pool, but he edited, produced, and starred in the videos on his YouTube channel, which he called Timcasts.)

"I'm here to write about Cassandra," I said. "I'm a journalist."

"Oh, cool, I'm a journalist, too," Rudkowski said.

"Yeah, me too," Pool said.

Molli, now eyeing me more warily, exercised her right to remain silent.

"This kind of thing still lives today, in that ghost-robed Ku Klux Klan," Bob Dylan sang.

Fairbanks came downstairs a few minutes later carrying a sequined clutch, a FREE ASSANGE tote bag, and a transparent poncho, "in case the protesters decide to throw paint on me." Antifascist activists—Antifa, they called themselves—had threatened to shut down the event by any means necessary, including violence, and they had circulated a list of "high-value targets" with Fairbanks's name on it. At other far-right events, she said, leftist agitators had thrown jars of urine and socks loaded with batteries. "Normally, I don't mind run-ins with protesters," she said. "But tonight I'm not in the fucking mood."

Unlike the Liberty Ball and the Freedom Ball, official black-tie galas for Republican insiders and campaign bundlers, the DeploraBall was an independent pre-inauguration bash put on by and for the internet trolls and ultranationalists who had, as they liked to put it, "memed Donald Trump into the White House." "It's gonna be all the big names from MAGA Twitter," one of them had told me, using the acronym for Trump's campaign slogan, Make America Great Again. "All the people who joined forces online, all together in a room for the first time." The event would take place at the National Press Club, in downtown D.C., for both symbolic and practical reasons: the Press Club, which held freedom of speech to be sacrosanct, was one of the few venues in town that would accept the organizers' money.

The cohosts of the DeploraBall were Jack Posobiec, Jeff Giesea, and Mike Cernovich, three men whose occupations, like their politics, were impossible to describe in a single word. Posobiec was a wild-eyed navy veteran turned Twitter conspiracy theorist. Giesea, a wealthy entrepreneur who'd once worked for the taciturn libertarian billionaire Peter Thiel, had since become an under-the-table impact investor, funding a clandestine network of pro-Trump trolls. Cernovich, a self-employed lawyer and motivational blogger, had gained a bit of online notoriety for his boorish advice about fitness and pickup artistry. Prior to 2015, he took no interest in electoral politics. Then Donald Trump became the Republican front-runner, and Cernovich, recognizing a kindred spirit, began to amplify Trump's brand of caustic, mendacious rhetoric.

On social media, as on the 1930s burlesque circuit, you've got to get a gimmick if you want to get ahead. Cernovich's gimmick was to liken himself to a gorilla—"a powerful, dominant animal." He wrote *Gorilla Mindset*, a self-help book for aspiring alpha males, and hawked it on Amazon; on his blog, he posted selfies of his hypertrophic upper body, along with a candid account of how he maintained it (green juice, anabolic steroids) and why ("You get more attention from the Bad Ass Bitches").

A friend of Cernovich's named Milo Yiannopoulos, one of the few social media demicelebrities who'd been able to convert online trolling into national fame, affected a very different persona. He fashioned himself a rakish renegade—"the most fabulous supervillain on the internet," as he put it. A Cambridge dropout from Kent, Yiannopoulos was known less for his ideological positions, which were not cogent enough to withstand real scrutiny, than for his genteel British accent, his designer handbags, and his acid one-liners.*

Fairbanks's gimmick was as unoriginal as it was effective. "The only three

---

*Yiannopoulos considered attending the DeploraBall, but declined when he wasn't guaranteed top billing. "He's got once-in-a-generation, Benjamin-Franklin-in-Paris levels of charisma," Cernovich said. "And he's one of the only guys, other than me, who's doing social media right."

things I believe in are the First Amendment, boobs, and WikiLeaks," she once tweeted, with a link to a video in which she wore a low-cut WikiLeaks T-shirt. At the beginning of the video, she said, "This headline, and my shirt, are admittedly clickbait." It worked: the video was viewed half a million times.*

In addition to keeping up her various social media feeds, Fairbanks worked as a political correspondent for Sputnik, an international news agency owned and operated by the Russian government. "She's written for us, too," Rudkowski said. He was using the editorial "we" to refer to *We Are Change*, a blog and YouTube channel that he ran out of his apartment in southern Brooklyn.

Fairbanks, Rudkowski, and Pool didn't agree on a well-developed policy agenda. What they shared was closer to an attitude—an instinctive aversion to anything mainstream. They often expressed this in terms of their antipathy to the establishment wings of the Democratic and Republican parties, but their guiding principles seemed more temperamental than political. Things they liked: energy, scrappiness, rebellion. Things they disliked: institutionalism, incrementalism, the status quo. If something could be described as an emanation of the Man, then they were against it.

"I've been into alternative stuff, fringe stuff, for as long as I can remember," Fairbanks said. "I always felt like, whatever narrative they're forcing down my throat, it's not the whole story." She was thirty-one. Before moving to the D.C. suburbs, she had traveled the country as a sound engineer, an animal-rights activist, and a roadie for punk bands. Her strapless ball gown left visible most of her sixteen tattoos. "I care more about free speech, including for Chelsea Manning and Julian Assange, than almost any other issue," she said. "And now there's censorship from all these other places, not just the government. Silicon Valley? Are you kidding me? People sitting in little rooms, deciding what information we can see? That's not free speech, that's fucking mind control."

In the 2016 presidential primaries, she had supported Bernie Sanders. When she started writing for Rudkowski's site, she said, "I was still a full-on Bernie bro." At the time, she was also a frequent contributor to left-wing clickbait sites such as *US Uncut* and *Addicting Info*. "The job was: find a clip of Trump being an idiot,"

---

*"I fast-forwarded her video and she doesn't show her boobs," one Twitter user commented below Fairbanks's tweet.

  "Thanks for saving me the time," another replied.

she said. "Exaggerate it or take it out of context if you have to, then post it to social with a melodramatic headline and get a gazillion clicks. It was not very hard."

In mid-2016, after Sanders dropped out and Hillary Clinton clinched the Democratic nomination, Fairbanks took another look at Trump. "I knew I could never vote for a Jeb Bush–type Republican, and I knew I could never vote for a Clinton," she said. As a test, she posted "a few things on Twitter that were not completely anti-Trump, and people absolutely lost their shit. I got called a literal Nazi so many times, I eventually went, Fuck it, I'll just go all in." She stopped writing for leftist sites, and her pieces on *We Are Change* became avidly pro-Trump. "I always let her publish all of it," Rudkowski said. "We support free thought."

I sat on the couch next to Pool. "Who'd you say you were with?" he asked.

"*The New Yorker*," I said. "It's a magazine that—"

He cut me off. "I know what it is," he said curtly.

Rudkowski grinned to himself, still looking down at his phone. "*The New Yorker*," he said, in a mock-stentorian voice.

I tried to guess what, specifically, they were reacting to. In many people's minds, *The New Yorker* represented monocled snobbery and Waspy wealth, and there was some truth to this—you don't run Rolex ads unless there's a chance of selling some Rolexes. Some people associated the magazine with bookish pretension, or with center-left politics; others fixated on the magazine's corporate ownership; still others were struck by the length of the articles, or the assiduous fact-checking process, or the droll cartoons. For the people in this living room, I suspected, the mental caricature comprised none of these things in particular, which is to say all of them at once: I worked for the Man.*

I felt a thump against my shin. It was the puppy, head-butting me to get my attention, then looking up at me with wide, expectant eyes.

"Her name is Wiki," Fairbanks said.

"Short for WikiLeaks," Pool said.

"As in, 'It's OK if Wiki leaks, as long as it's in the right spot,'" Rudkowski said. He gestured toward the middle of the room, where there was a square absorbent pad with its borders taped to the floor.

---

*When I'd first texted Fairbanks, asking if I could accompany her to the DeploraBall and write a piece about it for *The New Yorker*, she'd replied, "Is it a hit piece on how the ball is a bunch of Nazis?" She followed this with "haha," either because she was joking or because she thought it tactically prudent to soften her tone.

"I'm trying to train her," Fairbanks said, coaxing the dog toward the absorbent pad. Wikileaks sniffed the pad, circled it a few times, and then peed on it, wagging her tail. "Yay, Wiki!" Fairbanks said, gathering her dress in one hand and crouching to pet the puppy with the other. "What an incredibly good girl you are!"

She stepped outside, lit a cigarette, then changed her mind and stubbed it out. "My boss"—Sputnik's Washington bureau chief—"wants me to write something about the party," she said. "But I just want to relax, maybe have a drink." In any case, she was friends with the event's organizers, and with most of the other social media notables who would be in attendance. "If I need a quote from any of them tomorrow, I'll just text them," she said.

In the living room, Fairbanks switched from Bob Dylan to "Bradley Manning," a song by the rap-rock band Flobots. Manning is transgender, and the song was recorded before she changed her name to Chelsea. "Normally I wouldn't support anything that misgenders her, but it wasn't intentional," Fairbanks said. "Also, it's just a super catchy song." Manning was in federal prison for leaking army secrets; two days prior, Obama, in one of his final acts as president, had commuted Manning's sentence. Asked about this, Fairbanks responded by making a jerking-off motion with her hand. "Too little, too late," she said.

Around three in the afternoon, she turned off the TV and put on a pair of glittery gold high heels. She had volunteered to arrive at the Press Club a few hours early, to help set up. "I'll get an Uber," she said, fishing her phone out of her purse. I insisted on ordering a car for both of us instead. As a journalist, I explained, it would be unethical for me to accept any gifts from her, even a free ride. She narrowed her eyes and looked at me, trying to gauge whether I was joking. When it became clear that I wasn't, she shrugged and put her phone away.

Fairbanks's guests summoned a car of their own, then started stuffing their equipment into camera bags. Pool and Molli discussed their plans for the night:

"Let's hit up the DeploraBall for a bit, see if it's fun, then maybe stop by the Cambridge Analytica party."

"You mean to film? Or just hang out?"

"We could shoot, sure, if something interesting's happening."

On her way out the door, Fairbanks dropped two lapel pins into her purse. One bore the logo of Comet Ping Pong, a pizzeria about five miles away.* The other was a likeness of Pepe, a once-innocuous cartoon frog that had been adopted as a mascot by a growing online confederation of white nationalists, misogynists, belligerent nihilists, and edgy trolls. When the Press Club had agreed to host the DeploraBall, one of its few provisos was that no Pepe iconography was to be worn inside the venue. "Damn the Man," Fairbanks said. "These so-called defenders of the First Amendment are gonna turn around and tell me what to do? Fuck that. This is America."

Our car arrived, and she climbed into the backseat. The driver, an African American man in his twenties, tried to make small talk, asking why she was so dressed up. He met her eyes in the rearview mirror as he waited for her answer. She fidgeted in her seat. "Going to a ball," she said, diverting her attention to her phone.

• • •

"Come have drinks with the biggest names of the season," an online invitation to the DeploraBall read, followed by a list, in bold type, of a dozen VIPs who would be in attendance. Some of them, such as Fairbanks and a YouTube commentator named Lauren Southern, were young independents who had never backed any major-party politician, much less a Republican, before Trump. Others, such as the tabloid blogger Jim Hoft and the amateur podcaster Bill Mitchell, were baby boomers and longtime conservatives who supported every one of Trump's positions, even those that clashed with conservative orthodoxy (or with Trump's other positions). One of the VIPs, an ageless political flack named Roger Stone, had lurked near the periphery of Republican politics for decades, and was called a "dirty trickster" by everyone, including himself. Another name on the list was Alex Jones, a perspiring doomsayer who had made millions of dollars by transfer-

---

*A few weeks earlier, a man had driven from North Carolina to D.C., barged into the restaurant, and fired a semi-automatic rifle; his goal was to "self-investigate" rumors he'd come across online, including the claim that the restaurant's basement was actually a dungeon full of child sex slaves. (Comet Ping Pong does not have a basement.) The rumors were part of a byzantine conspiracy theory known as Pizzagate, according to which many of the country's top entertainers, journalists, financiers, and politicians, including the chairman of Hillary Clinton's presidential campaign and possibly Clinton herself, were pedophiles and human traffickers. The clues were as elaborate as they were unpersuasive: satanic rituals, a secret code involving the words "cheese" and "pizza," a map printed on a handkerchief. The theory had been propagated by some of the internet's most reckless meme hustlers, including Posobiec, Cernovich, and Fairbanks herself.

ring his apocalyptic tirades from public-access cable to the open internet. For more than two decades, Jones had treated almost all politicians with vivid disdain; then, in 2015, he changed his mind and went all in for Trump.

Of all the VIPs on the list, Sheriff David Clarke of Milwaukee was the only African American and the only elected official. He had spoken at dozens of Trump's campaign rallies, warming up the crowds before the main act. Roger Stone was one of Trump's longest-serving political advisers; Alex Jones claimed to talk to Trump on a regular basis, but then again Jones was an inveterate liar. The other VIPs, having emerged recently from apolitical obscurity, had no formal ties to Trump, or to any known political entity. Any one of them, taken alone, might have seemed negligible, a curious by-product of the variegated energies made newly visible by the internet. But together they'd had a decisive impact on the 2016 campaign, and on public opinion more broadly. It was hard to imagine Trump winning without them.

The VIPs shared a common set of enemies—the Clintons, the Bushes, the globalists, the mainstream media—but they didn't agree on everything. Some were more anti-Semitic than others. Some were more openly racist than others. Some emphasized misogyny, whereas others were more passionate about Islamophobia. Still others, rather than committing to any consistent ideology, rotated through evocative tropes about Davos or the Deep State. Each of them espoused opinions that were so politically retrograde, so morally repugnant, or so self-evidently deceitful that no reputable news organization would ever hire them. And yet, in the twenty-first century, they didn't need traditional jobs. Instead, they could mobilize and monetize a following on social media.

They made their names, and in most cases made a good living, by generating what they called content—podcasts, publicity stunts, viral memes—which they peddled across a variety of platforms: a Twitter feed driving traffic to Patreon, a Gab feed soliciting donations through Coinbase, a personal site racking up ad revenue. This insured that, if they got banned from one platform or another, they wouldn't starve, and their message wouldn't be starved of attention. Some of them knew a lot about politics; some knew next to nothing about politics. In every case, their main skill was the same: a knack for identifying resonant images and talking points, and for propelling them from the fringes of the internet into the mainstream. If the old media gatekeepers in New York and D.C. still doubted whether this was a meaningful skill, then this skepticism only worked to the online propagandists' advantage, because it allowed them to be underestimated. They knew that a series of small memetic victories would help them gain ground in a larger informational war.

At bottom, they were metamedia insurgents. They spoke the language of politics, in part, because politics was the reality show that got the highest ratings; and yet their chief goal was not to help the United States become a more perfect union but to catalyze cultural conflict. They took for granted that the old institutions ought to be burned to the ground, and they used the tools at their disposal—new media, especially social media—to light as many matches as possible. As for what kind of society might emerge from the ashes, they had no coherent vision and showed little interest in developing one. They were not, like William Buckley, standing athwart history, yelling "Stop"; they were holding liberal democracy in a headlock, yelling "Stop or I'll shoot!"

When a reporter from CNN requested credentials to the DeploraBall, the organizers posted their response on Twitter: "We question your integrity as an institution of journalism. Therefore, we will not be issuing you press passes." This was retweeted thousands of times. One anonymous Twitter user, whose avatar was a cartoon of a scowling bald eagle, replied with a celebratory meme—a photo of Anderson Cooper, sitting behind a desk in a CNN studio, captioned with the words "Breaking News: The People Don't Believe Our Bullshit Anymore."

"We're the new media," Cernovich told me. "The dinosaur fake-news media—their days are numbered." This may have been Trumpian bluster, but it contained a degree of truth. "It offends their paternalistic, basic-bitch egos to hear it, but, sorry, this is what a truly democratic media looks like. They used to be able to control the narrative. Well, fuck you, motherfuckers. The barbarians are at the gate. Everyone has a voice now."

CHAPTER TWO

Pride

At the Press Club, Cassandra Fairbanks assembled gift baskets for the Deplora-Ball's VIPs and top donors. She laid out a dozen identical piles of tchotchkes (MAGA hat, inauguration-themed chocolate, tiny American flag manufactured in China), arranged every pile inside a wicker basket, and then tied a ribbon around each one. Luke Rudkowski sat nearby, reading Twitter. If any of the event's male organizers were around, I didn't see them offering to help.

"Baskets," Fairbanks said, elbowing me in the ribs. "Get it?"

In September 2016, Hillary Clinton spoke at a campaign fund-raiser in New York City. "To just be grossly generalistic," she said, "you could put half of Trump's supporters into what I call the basket of deplorables." Her audience chuckled. She defined the deplorables as "racist, sexist, homophobic, xenophobic, Islamophobic—you name it," and lamented the fact that her opponent "tweets and retweets their offensive, hateful, mean-spirited rhetoric." The political press immediately characterized Clinton's statement as a gaffe, not because it was untrue—apart from the word "half," it wasn't even disputable—but because it could hurt her politically.

"I regret saying 'half,'" Clinton half apologized the next day. But her infelicitous phrasing (who uses "deplorable" as a noun? who puts people in baskets?) refused to fade from the electorate's memory. A headline in *The Boston Globe*: "With 'Basket of Deplorables' Quip, Clinton Just Made a Meme." Sure enough, the social media ultranationalists immediately flooded Reddit and Twitter with parody images, reclaiming the moniker for themselves.*

---

*A poster for *Les Misérables* became a poster for *Les Déplorables*. An ad for the 2010 ensemble action movie *The Expendables* was transformed, via Photoshop, into *The Deplorables*: Donald Trump, front and center, flanked by a few fallen politicians (Chris Christie, Rudy Giuliani), a few loose-cannon campaign surrogates (Roger Stone,

Fairbanks tied a bow around the last gift basket. With Rudkowski, she walked outside and hailed a cab. The party wouldn't start for another few hours, so she was going to meet her friend Gavin McInnes, another DeploraBall VIP, who was pregaming with a few friends at a luxury condo on K Street, about a mile away. He had offered to escort her later that night, when they made their grand entrance into the Press Club. The idea was to shield her from protesters, and she was eager to take him up on it.

In the cab, Fairbanks opened Instagram, where she'd just posted a photo of herself in her gown. She read a few of the comments aloud: "Looking good"; "Be careful of those Commies"; "Don't give Gavin a heart attack."

Helicopters thumped overhead. Police officers directed traffic, using wooden barricades to block access to the National Mall. On the wide facade of a convention center, artists were projecting the words of a few of the women who had accused Donald Trump of sexual assault.

"El Chapo just got extradited," Rudkowski said, referring to a push notification.

"Dude, let's focus on one country at a time," Fairbanks said.

At the condo building, we took an elevator to the top floor and knocked on a door. A man in his late forties answered. He wore a black bow tie, slicked-back hair, and a full, sculpted beard. He greeted Fairbanks with a kiss on the cheek, then stepped back and gave her a vaudevillian once-over. She giggled and batted her eyes, playing along. "Cleavage looks fantastic, as always," he said.

This was Gavin McInnes. Like the other DeploraBall VIPs, he was a content creator; before becoming an out-and-out Deplorable, he'd come closer than any of the others to a mainstream show-business career. In the 1980s and '90s, he was in a punk band called Anal Chinook, and he later had a bit of success as an actor and a stand-up comic. In 1994, using grant money from the Canadian government and a Haitian nonprofit, he and two friends cofounded *Vice* magazine. The mainstream press dubbed McInnes "the godfather of hipsterdom." After 9/11 he became an outspoken right-winger and a budding Islamophobe; he resigned from Vice Media, signing a lucrative parting settlement that included a non-disparagement clause. He published a salacious memoir, cofounded a boutique

---

Ben Carson), and a few uncategorizable efflorescences of contemporary internet culture (Milo Yiannopoulos, Alex Jones, Pepe the Frog).

advertising firm, and appeared intermittently on Fox News, usually at three in the morning.

In addition to these appearances, McInnes wrote columns for extremist-friendly web publications such as *The American Conservative*, cofounded by Pat Buchanan, and *Taki's Magazine*, founded by Taki Theodoracopulos, a Greek aesthete who seemed to have a soft spot for European fascism.* (McInnes was recruited to write for *Taki's* by its managing editor at the time, a pompous white nationalist named Richard Spencer.) Primarily, though, McInnes presented himself as an internet shock jock. On *The Gavin McInnes Show*, which streamed for an hour and a half every weekday, he told lewd stories, got a butt tattoo live on air, and interviewed comedians, sex workers, and overt white supremacists—not because he endorsed white nationalism, he insisted, but because he wanted to give a fair hearing to all points of view. (He did maintain, however, that women would be happier as housewives, that gender-confirmation surgery was genital mutilation, and that "Muslims are stupid, and the only thing they really respect is violence.") When Donald Trump ran for president, McInnes praised him for being "anti-jihad," "anti-immigration," and "anti-establishment." "Trump is crass and rude and irrational, but that's what we need right now," McInnes said, on Fox Business. "We need hate. We need fearmongering."

In 2016, McInnes announced that he was founding the Proud Boys, an all-male fraternal organization composed of "Western chauvinists who refuse to apologize for creating the modern world." Every few weeks, he gathered dozens of restive young men at a dive bar in Manhattan, gave a vigorous toast about how "the West is the best," and encouraged them to drink heavily; by the time the young men started getting into fistfights with the normies, McInnes had usually slipped away to his wife and sleeping children in Westchester County. Whenever a journalist implied that the Proud Boys were a white-pride organization, McInnes claimed to be shocked and offended: "'Western chauvinist' includes all races, religions, and sexual preferences."

Fairbanks walked through the door and toward the preparty. I started to follow her, but McInnes placed a hand against my chest. "Who's this guy?" he asked, turning over his shoulder to address Fairbanks.

---

*In a 2011 column in *Taki's Magazine*, McInnes wrote, "America's population surge is all Mexican, and I think it's fair to say we're not getting their best and brightest." Four years later, in his presidential announcement speech, Donald Trump said of Mexico, "They're not sending their best."

"He's a journalist, but he's cool," she said. "He's with me."

McInnes, glowering, kept his hand where it was. For the first time, he looked me in the eye. "If you call us Nazis in anything you write," he said, enunciating very clearly, "I'll kick your fucking ass." Then he removed his hand from my chest and stepped aside to let me in, his facial expression changing abruptly to a rictus. "I'm just messing with you!" he said. "Probably. Almost definitely."

He led us through an indoor lounge area and out onto a roof deck, where about a dozen Proud Boys stood in a loose circle, wearing navy blazers and red MAGA hats, drinking bottles of Budweiser. Most of them were younger than McInnes by two decades or more. "Gentlemen, try not to jizz in your pants," he said, introducing Fairbanks. Then, making his way to the center of the circle, he picked up where he'd left off, recounting an interview he'd just given to a Japanese news crew.

"They go, 'How do you feel—Mr. Trump?'" McInnes said, in a cartoonish Japanese accent. "I go, 'Yep, Trump, love him, great.' They go, 'And how do you feel— white power?' I go, 'White power? What the fuck? Fuck off!' And I kicked them out. Seriously, where do people even get this shit from? There's, like, five guys in the country who are actual white supremacists, and you can tell who they are 'cause they wear robes and clip-clop around on horseback!" The young men chuckled. It wasn't clear what they were supposed to say in response, if anything.

"It's too cold out here," McInnes said. "My dick is shriveling up." In case his meaning wasn't plain enough, he put his hand down his pants and stuck one finger through the fly. "I'm leaving before I get AIDS," he declared, and went inside.

I turned to chat with the Proud Boy standing next to me. A contractor from North Carolina, he was barrel chested and at least a head taller than everyone else. Beneath his blazer, he wore a black T-shirt emblazoned with the words "Proud Boys," in the style of the Jack Daniels logo. I asked him why he'd joined the group. "'Cause I'm proud to be white!" he said. "These days, suddenly, everyone is so divided, you can't say anything. Being a white cis male is the worst thing you can be. Like Gavin always says, why should I apologize for being who I am?"

He tried to swig from his beer and realized it was empty. "It's OK to be a nationalist, and it's OK to have pride in yourself," he went on. "But you put either of those concepts together with being white, and suddenly you're an insane Nazi bigot. No. Fuck that." He shook my hand firmly, looked me in the eye, and grinned politely. "Pleasure meeting you," he said, and went inside to get another beer.

———

Zach, a skinny Proud Boy wearing a baggy blazer, was twenty-three and looked even younger. He had dimples, and a few seraphic curls protruded from beneath his red MAGA hat. When someone else on the roof deck made a particularly derogatory joke, Zach would smile, pull his cap low, and cast his eyes downward, looking both embarrassed and invigorated. Some of the Proud Boys had tickets to the DeploraBall; others, including Zach, were hoping to bluff their way past security. "I'll walk over and see what happens," he said. "I'm just happy to be here, honestly."

He lived a few miles away, in the middle-class Maryland suburb where he'd grown up. "Everyone I know has exactly the same opinions," he said. "'Trump' is synonymous with 'deranged moron.' It's an article of faith, and I guess I'm just not a follow-the-leader kind of guy." This was what had piqued his interest in *The Gavin McInnes Show*: a desire to see sacred cows led to the slaughter.

I understood where he was coming from, almost literally. I, too, grew up in anodyne liberal suburbia. When I was a teenager, I longed, like teenagers everywhere, for something that might help me stand out, or at least help my personality cohere. The best I could come up with was a safe simulacrum of punk-rock rebellion. I tried to grow my hair out like Kurt Cobain, but instead I ended up with a lamentably bouffant ginger butt cut. I chain-smoked, which gave me heartburn. No one was particularly impressed with my insufferable shtick; girls certainly weren't. But I convinced myself that I was on the side of righteousness. I was standing up to the Man.

The worst kind of person, I decided, was a conformist, an institutionalist, an establishment shill. I invented principles, retroactively, to justify my convictions, but my only truly consistent principle was contrarianism. Fatuous bourgeois bullshit was all around me, and I was the only one with enough integrity to see through it. If everyone else trusted the line they were being fed in the history textbooks, or in *The New York Times*, then I would be an iconoclast, questioning the dominant narrative.

It seemed at the time like a matter of ethics, but ultimately it was reducible to aesthetics. All things being equal, it's always cooler to be a rebel than an institutionalist. *Defy convention. Blow up the system. Question everything.* I never saw a

Kurt Cobain poster that said "Some Norms Might Actually Be Worth Preserving" or "Question Some Things, But Don't Go Crazy."

Politics didn't come up much, because no one around me was all that political. When I did take an interest in politics, it was in college, through books. By then, questioning the dominant narrative no longer made me special; questioning the dominant narrative was homework. I wonder now what might have happened to the eighth-grade version of myself if I'd felt coerced into accepting some mandatory political orthodoxy, and if I'd been able to dig up succinct and seductive counterpoints to that orthodoxy, whenever I wanted, simply by glancing at the internet on a computer I kept in my pocket.

Much later, when I found myself working in the inner sanctum of contemporary journalism, I started to let go of my knee-jerk contrarianism. Gradually, reluctantly, I admitted to myself that institutions can also have significant upsides. I never deluded myself into believing that the norms of traditional journalism were infallible, or worthy of exaltation, or intrinsically cool. (Nobody thinks gatekeeping is cool, not even the gatekeepers.) And yet, as it turns out, it's possible for a thing to be uncool and also necessary. Let's say you're hosting a dance party in a dark warehouse. You decide not to put up any illuminated exit signs—they don't fit with your aesthetic. You're above maximum capacity, but you don't want to be a buzzkill and start kicking people out. Someone pulls a fire alarm; it's a prank, and everyone ignores it. In the unlikely (but not impossible) event that you smell a gas leak or see billowing smoke, you're going to need a contingency plan, and a functional PA system.

"Gavin is so free, so no-fucks-given, the way he talks," Zach said. "It's a dopamine rush, listening to him—like, how can he get away with *saying* this shit? It could be some insane drinking story, or sex story, or whatever, and then the next minute he's actually making an evidence-based argument about how traditional gender roles make women happier, or about how cultural Marxism infected the media. You start listening with an open mind, and you go, Actually, I've never heard anyone make that case before."

McInnes often asserted that conservatism was "the new punk rock," and there was something to this, at least on the level of pure energy. He had made himself into a kind of renegade. His style was certainly edgier and more bracing than that of any CNN pundit. And his Janus-faced jester routine afforded him a lot of flexibility: when he made a cogent argument, he was a political commentator; as soon as he crossed a line, he was only joking.

All things being equal, it's cooler to be a rebel than an establishment shill. But all things aren't equal. Some norms—such as welcoming the stranger, or respecting the dignity of women, or resisting the urge to punch random pedestrians in the face—really are worth preserving. It's definitionally non-edgy to affirm this sort of thing. It feels obvious, sentimental, conformist. Sooner or later, though, most people grow up and stop trying to prove how edgy they are. Sometimes, when everyone in the world is angry at you, it's because you're a singularly perceptive iconoclast assailing the hypocrisy of the system. Other times, when everyone is angry at you, it's because you're just being an asshole.

• • •

Our hosts on the roof deck were Mary Clare Reim and Yonathan Amselem, a couple in their late twenties who were engaged to be married. They lived in one of the condos downstairs. "Call me Yoni," he said. "I'm Sephardic, mixed with a bunch of other stuff, but I just let all the protesters think I'm an evil Christian cis white man 'cause it's better for their narrative." A corporate lawyer, he had heard about the Proud Boys on *The Gavin McInnes Show*. "The left is no fucking fun anymore!" he said.

A few weeks before the inauguration, Mary Clare said, McInnes "mentioned on Facebook, or somewhere, that he needed a place to crash in D.C."

"I offered our place immediately," Yoni said. "I met him for the first time, like, two hours ago." He was clearly starstruck. "He walks in, drops his suitcase, and starts changing into his tuxedo, right in the living room, drinking a beer. He's just, like, *himself*—the guy from the show—except in my friggin' apartment."

"He listens to Gavin every day," Mary Clare told me. "I can hear him cracking up from the other room."

"I like Gavin more than a friend," Yoni said, giggling.*

"Gavin has funny moments, and sometimes he makes actual good points," Mary Clare said. "But then he'll talk about diarrhea for twenty minutes and totally lose me."

---

*I'd heard enough of McInnes's show to know that the Proud Boys considered any version of this joke—the insinuation that their homosocial fraternal organization was actually a homoerotic fraternal organization—to be the soul of wit.

"She's a nice Catholic girl," Yoni explained.

They resembled a sitcom archetype—the unkempt, heavyset man who, through a combination of haplessness and low-key charisma, ends up with the slender, beautiful blonde. In a departure from the archetype, though, Mary Clare was not a mouthy, long-suffering housewife but a policy wonk.

"I'm an analyst at a think tank," she said.

"The Heritage Foundation," he said. "She's a big shot."

"To be honest, I had a lot of problems with Trump at first," she said. "I write about education policy, and a lot of the higher-ed proposals his campaign put out didn't really add up." She started to explain, beginning with a few statistics about federal subsidies to universities.

"Aaaand, this is where I start to check out," Yoni said.

McInnes returned to the roof deck and, with a flourish, introduced two women, one in her midfifties and the other in her early twenties. The older woman handed me her business card, which identified her as an "author and cultural activist" with the Twitter handle @SpankCityHall. "I started the Indiana Tea Party," she said. "Before that, I was a dominatrix with a dungeon in my basement, and guys paid me to paddle 'em on the ass. Life's a trip, huh?" She wore a fur vest and a fur cossack hat. "My wardrobe tonight is Russia themed," she said, "in honor of my hunky alpha-male crush, Vlad Putin."

One of the Proud Boys, staring at the younger woman, whispered, "Wait, I think I know who that is." As she approached, he asked her, "Aren't you Lauren Southern?"

She gave him a long, withering stare. "No," she said, and walked away.

"Well, shit," the Proud Boy said. "Someone told me Lauren Southern was gonna be here."

It was an understandable mistake. Both Lauren Southern and the woman on the roof deck, Laura Loomer, were rising social media stars with peroxide-blonde hair. Southern was perhaps best known for crashing a feminist rally in Vancouver while holding up an antifeminist sign (THERE IS NO RAPE CULTURE IN THE WEST); her YouTube video of the confrontation was viewed more than two million times. Loomer, a strident Islamophobe and conspiracy theorist, kept a lower profile, in part because she had, until recently, worked undercover. She was an employee of Project Veritas, a New York–based nonprofit that tried to undermine liberal institutions through journalistic stings. A few of these were inarguable successes;

others backfired humiliatingly; most often, the results were overhyped and under-whelming.*

Fairbanks had settled on a couch, chain-smoking and gazing at the green-glass towers of downtown D.C. Mary Clare sat down next to her and asked, "You have the most Twitter followers of anyone here, probably, right?"

"I guess, except for Gavin," Fairbanks said. "I have about eighty."†

"*Thousand*?" Mary Clare said. "Gosh, that's awesome. I have, like, none. But all I ever tweet about is student-loan interest rates, so I guess it's not that surprising."

Sitting on the other side of Fairbanks was her boss, Mindia Gavasheli, the Washington bureau chief of Sputnik News. He'd worked as a TV producer in Russia—first at two regional networks in his hometown of Krasnodar, then at two national networks with a pro-Kremlin slant—before moving to the United States. Tonight, he seemed thrilled to be among the Deplorables.

"We should have an after-party at the Trump," he said, referring to the Trump International Hotel, on Pennsylvania Avenue, which had opened four months earlier.

"I don't think they're technically open tonight, but I'll text the manager," Fair-banks said. "I'm there, like, every other night, and I tip, so he definitely owes me one."

Luke Rudkowski sat nearby, watching Facebook Live on his phone. "Alex Jones is streaming from a mile down the road," he said, chuckling. "Looks like he's wasted."

"Amazing, let me see," Fairbanks said. Rudkowski tilted his phone to let her watch.

Jones was standing in front of the Capitol, swaying gently, speaking with even more ardor and less coherence than usual. In person, he was addressing about a dozen stray tourists; on Facebook, he had a live audience of nearly four thousand. "The arrogant globalists who believe the power of humanity is theirs, because they hijack control of it . . ." He trailed off.

---

*Throughout the 2016 race, Loomer posed as a Clinton volunteer in several states, wearing a concealed camera and trying to entice campaign employees into saying or doing something nefarious. In almost a year and a half, she documented just one possible violation of campaign rules—a Canadian woman buying a hat and a T-shirt from a merchandise table, which could be classified, technically, as a foreign campaign contribution. When Project Veritas scheduled a press conference to debut this footage—at the National Press Club, incidentally—the big reveal was so anticlimactic that several of the reporters in attendance wondered whether it was a joke. (Not long afterward, Donald Trump signed a letter of intent to develop a Trump World Tower in Moscow.)

†A demicelebrity's number of Twitter followers was a common proxy for internet fame, albeit a crude one. Many of the DeploraBall VIPs had six-figure follower counts—fewer than the official account of, say, *Newsweek*, but far more than the average *Newsweek* reporter. In the months following the DeploraBall, the VIPs' followings would continue to grow apace. By 2018, many of them—Gavin McInnes, Laura Loomer, Alex Jones—would be banned from Twitter and several other platforms, stifling both their income and their influence.

"Oh, shit, is he crying?" Rudkowski said. He and Fairbanks cracked up, but I couldn't tell whether they were laughing with Jones or at him.

"The rediscovery of our destiny is at hand!" Jones shouted, his face streaked with tears.

"I don't blame him for crying," the woman in the fur hat said. "The intelligence agencies are all trying to kill him, you know."

"We gotta go to the DeploraBall now," Jones said. "I'm gonna sneak off and piss on some tree or something and we're gonna get there."

Loomer sidled up to Rudkowski and perched on the arm of his chair.

"Hey," she said, in a tone that suggested an intimate rapport.

"Hey," he said, in a tone that did not.

She sat for a few seconds, trying and failing to meet Rudkowski's eyes. After a while, she stormed off.

"What's with her?" Fairbanks asked. Rudkowski didn't answer.

In a blog post about the Proud Boys, McInnes had written that "the meetings usually consist of drinking, fighting, and reading aloud from Pat Buchanan's *The Death of the West*," a book arguing that declining white birth rates and "uncontrolled immigration" would soon result in a "Third World America." That night, I'd already seen plenty of drinking, and a good amount of vaping. As for fighting, the Proud Boys anticipated it eagerly—McInnes, in particular, kept cracking his knuckles and stretching his neck, like a boxer on the way to the ring. But the part about public reading may have been aspirational; for one thing, McInnes had forgotten to pack a copy of *The Death of the West* in his suitcase.

"I've got one, actually," Zach said, digging into his backpack. He'd read McInnes's blog post and planned ahead.

"Nice!" McInnes said. "We'll do a little toast."

The Proud Boys gathered inside, most of them holding a beer in one hand and a phone in the other, capturing each other capturing the moment. McInnes gave a brief, rousing speech. "We are here celebrating the inauguration," he said. "We will be accosted by social-justice warriors that are mad that private citizens are going to enjoy ourselves. But, before we go, I would like to read a brief passage that the Proud Boys thoroughly enjoy." He cleared his throat, adjusted his glasses, and opened the paperback to the designated page.

"In the story of slavery and the slave trade," he read, "Western Man was among the many villains, but Western Man was also the only hero. For the West did not invent slavery, but it alone abolished slavery." For someone who claimed to have a postracial outlook, McInnes spent a lot of time talking about race. He finished reading—"The time for apologies is past"—and started a brief round of applause for himself.

Lee Atwater, a Republican consultant and the Paganini of the modern political dog whistle, once explained the Southern Strategy, a ploy by which his party used coded racism to appeal to white voters. "You start out in 1954 by saying, 'Nigger, nigger, nigger,'" Atwater said. "By 1968, you can't say 'nigger'—that hurts you, it backfires—so you say stuff like 'forced busing,' 'states' rights,' and all that stuff, and you're getting so abstract." Ronald Reagan, running for president in 1980, delivered a campaign speech in Neshoba County, Mississippi, where three civil rights workers had been murdered sixteen years prior. "I believe in states' rights," Reagan said. When he became president, he hired Atwater as a White House aide, then as the deputy director of his reelection campaign. The day after the 1984 election, which Reagan won in the biggest landslide in American history, Atwater left the government to join a D.C. lobbying firm cofounded by Paul Manafort and Roger Stone.

Atwater didn't invent the Southern Strategy. Barry Goldwater used it, unsuccessfully, in 1964; then Richard Nixon won with it, pitching himself as a law-and-order candidate who spoke for what he would later call a "silent majority." He was channeling the language of Pat Buchanan, one of his top strategists and speechwriters. Buchanan, who referred to himself as a paleoconservative, was a racist by most definitions of the word. "Heredity, rather than environment, determines intelligence," he wrote, erroneously, in a private White House memo to President Nixon. "And every study we have shows blacks 15 IQ points below whites on the average." The memo argued that promoting racial integration in public schools was a waste of government money. Buchanan, who went on to become President Reagan's communications director, was too shrewd to use such frank rhetoric in public, but he often came close. In *The Death of the West*, he wrote, "In their hearts, who truly believes in the equality of all civilizations, cultures, faiths?"

Before "America First" was Donald Trump's motto, it was the motto of postwar jingoists such as Buchanan (and, before that, of Nazi sympathizers such as Charles Lindbergh). Before "Make America Great Again" was Trump's campaign slogan, it was Ronald Reagan's campaign slogan.* Even Trump's central policy theme, severe immigration restrictionism, seemed to be borrowed largely from Ann Coulter, a fire-and-brimstone nativist who advocated mass deportations and the revocation of birthright citizenship. In her 2015 book, ¡Adios, America!, Coulter called the construction of a physical barrier along the southern border "the only sane, logical thing to do." A prepublication copy of the book was delivered to Trump Tower in May. The next month, in Trump's speech announcing his candidacy for president, he said, "I would build a great wall—and nobody builds walls better than me, believe me, and I'll build them very inexpensively—I will build a great, great wall on our southern border." Later, when Trump referred to black-majority countries as "shitholes," and to African American politicians as "low-I.Q. individuals," he was just restating plainly what other American nativists had been insinuating, in slightly subtler registers, for decades.

William F. Buckley Jr., the founding editor of *National Review* and the foremost gatekeeper of postwar conservative opinion, spent most of his career trying to enforce the bounds of acceptable right-wing discourse. His "great achievement," *The Dallas Morning News* wrote in 2004, "was to purge the American right of its kooks"—the extremists, paranoid conspiracists, and unusually virulent racists. It was a testament to Buckley's stature, and to his magazine's power as a vector for popular ideas, that these purges were so effective.

Then again, extremism is a relative term. Buckley let a lot of bigotry slip past him. He also produced a good amount of it himself. When he was eleven, four of his older siblings burned a cross on the lawn of a Jewish resort in Connecticut; young Billy cried because he wasn't allowed to tag along. In 1957, when he was thirty-one, Buckley wrote "Why the South Must Prevail," a column arguing in favor of legal segregation "for whatever period it takes to effect a genuine cultural equality between the races." This was, shamefully, not considered an extreme position at the time.

In 1991, Buckley wrote a book-length essay about Buchanan, who was a merciless critic of Israel. Buckley set out to investigate whether Buchanan's anti-Zionism

---

*Reagan's version began with "Let's"—a distinction without a difference, like the eighth note that separates the bassline in "Under Pressure" from the bassline in "Ice, Ice Baby."

was tinged with anti-Semitism. The ultimate verdict was a qualified yes: "I find it impossible to defend Pat Buchanan against the charge that what he did and said during the period under examination amounted to anti-Semitism." Buchanan never wrote for *National Review* after that.

By the standards of a Buckleyan purge, this one was only semieffective. The charge of anti-Semitism clung to Buchanan for years, yet it hardly ended his career. "The greatest vacuum in American politics is to the right of Ronald Reagan," Buchanan said in 1987, and he set out to fill that vacuum, hosting a nationally syndicated radio show and a talk show on CNN. In 2002 he cofounded a magazine called *The American Conservative*. His goal, he told an interviewer at the time, was "to recapture the flag of the conservative movement." *The American Conservative* was willing to publish opinions that were too edgy, or too racist, for the editors of *National Review*. By then, no single outlet held a monopoly on acceptable right-wing thought."

Buchanan ran for president as a Republican in 1992 and 1996. Both times, he campaigned on a platform of immigration restrictionism and "Western values." The nativist faction of the GOP bayed at his dog whistles, but that faction had not yet taken over the party. In 2000, Buchanan ran again, this time pursuing the nomination of the Reform Party. As it happened, one of Buchanan's potential opponents was an ideologically pliable tabloid celebrity named Donald Trump. "He's a Hitler-lover," Trump said of Buchanan. "He doesn't like the blacks, he doesn't like the gays. It's just incredible that anybody could embrace this guy." He mused about challenging Buchanan for the nomination of the Reform Party, possibly with Oprah Winfrey as his running mate, but then dropped out of the race without officially entering it.

Was Trump lying in 2000, when he called the Republican Party "just too crazy right"? Or was he lying in 2016, when he ran only slightly to the left of Viktor Orban? It's impossible to know. Trump has an unusual capacity for self-contradiction, but the trait is hardly unique to him. In the middle of his gimlet-eyed description of the Southern Strategy, Lee Atwater began to wonder whether covert racism was actually a form of social progress. "I'm saying that if it's getting that abstract, and that coded, that we are doing away with the racial problem one way or the other," he said. Atwater had just admitted that an innocuous-sounding policy proposal, such as a tax cut, could be both intended and understood as a stand-in for bigotry; in the next breath, he started to convince himself that sometimes a tax cut is just a tax cut. That's the strange thing about dog whistles. Sometimes, when it's convenient, both the hounds and the hunter can forget what all the barking and snarling was about in the first place.

* * *

It was time to go. The Proud Boys tilted back their heads, draining what was left of their beers, and left the roof deck, half the group squeezing into a single elevator car. "I hope I get to whoop some Antifa commie's ass," one Proud Boy said, before adding, "in self-defense, of course." Another Proud Boy paraphrased one of McInnes's oft-repeated maxims: "You're not a real man until you've had your heart broken, broken a heart, had the shit beaten out of you, and beaten the shit out of someone."

Halfway down to the lobby, the elevator stopped and a resident of the building got on—a middle-aged African American man, in gym clothes, taking his dog out for a walk. The doors closed, and there were a few seconds of tense silence. The woman in the fur hat spoke first, to no one in particular. "You know," she said, "Putin's cock is so big you can see it from space." Everyone, even the guy in gym clothes, had to laugh at that.

Just before the elevator reached the lobby, Yoni said, "Guys, I gotta fart."

"Don't," Mary Clare said sternly.

He did.

"Dude!" Mary Clare said. "Seriously? In a packed elevator?"

"It's my country now," Yoni said, with an impish smile. "I can do what I want."

The group set off for the Press Club, a twenty-minute walk away. McInnes led the pack, looking wired. He slapped himself on both cheeks, forced a yawn, and bugged his eyes wide. "If no one fights me tonight I'm gonna be so *bored*," he said. Turning to walk backward like a tour guide, he gave instructions to the group. "Where's that tall guy?" he said, summoning the contractor from North Carolina to the front.

The Proud Boys walked in the shape of an upside-down V, taking up the width of the sidewalk; the women huddled behind them, shielded from view. "Remember, guys, the whole point is to protect the ladies," McInnes said. His chivalry, however, did not extend to slackening his pace. The women had to remove their high heels and trot to keep up.

While the Proud Boys were stuck at a corner waiting for a WALK sign, a guy on a bicycle stopped and shouted, "Fuck Trump!"

"What'd you say?" Zach snapped. "Say that again, pussy!" Trembling with adrenaline, he glanced toward McInnes to see how his show of bravery was going over. But McInnes, who was busy chatting with Fairbanks, hadn't noticed.

The man threw his bicycle to the ground and started to approach, looking a bit bigger with every step. "Sure, I'll say it again," he said. "Fuck. Trump."

The light changed. Zach put his head down and kept walking.

A block away from the Press Club, we began to hear the roar of the crowd. Fairbanks put on her poncho. Rudkowski started filming on his phone. "Bravest men in front!" McInnes shouted. "Tight and close! Women in the middle!"

We rounded the corner. The street, closed to car traffic, was filled with hundreds of protesters. Masked figures darted through the crowd, waving the red-and-black Antifa flag; flames leapt out of metal trash cans; a boom box was playing a slow rap beat, and rim shots reverberated between buildings. A row of police officers, wearing neon-green vests and holding plastic shields, stood shoulder to shoulder, creating a buffer between the protesters and the partygoers. "Have a nice time, Nazi scum!" one protester shouted at a silver-haired couple as they walked inside. Other protesters confronted the police officers, singing an old union song with a haunting pentatonic melody: "Which side are you on? Which side are you on?"

A few of the protesters found a way around the police line and stood between the Proud Boys and the entrance. McInnes, trying to lure one of them into a fight, licked the man's face; he recoiled, shouting, but didn't fight back. Another protester, wearing a black ski mask and carrying an Antifa flag, passed by McInnes without incident, but McInnes shoved him anyway, then punched him in the face. "What the fuck?" the man shouted. Two police officers rushed to arrest the protester, while several other officers escorted McInnes into the Press Club.

In the lobby, unscathed, Fairbanks took off her poncho and straightened her dress. "We made it!" she said. "Thank you for protecting me."

"Don't mention it, m'lady," McInnes said.

Zach tried to sneak in with the group, but the guards stopped him. The rest of the Proud Boys disappeared inside, the doors clicking locked behind them. Zach, alone now, turned to face the roaring crowd. Until that instant, he'd been borne along by triumphal, unthinking energy; now, suddenly, he wondered why he was there in the first place, how much any of this mattered. He wished he could dematerialize and reappear at home, in his family's warm, brightly lit living room, watching a baseball game with his dad, or reading on his phone—thinking about anything other than politics. He took off his red MAGA hat and stuffed it inside his blazer, the better to blend in with the crowd. Then he speedwalked to the end of the block, turned a corner, and disappeared into the night.

CHAPTER THREE

The Contrarian Question

Roger Stone stood in the lobby of the Press Club, wearing a tuxedo and radiating indignation. The organizers of the DeploraBall hadn't set aside enough tickets under Stone's name, so he and his entourage—a few friends and family members, and a camera crew from Vice News—had decided to leave. "This is an insulting absurdity," Stone said on his way out.

It was hardly his most pressing problem. Earlier that day, he'd received a call from a *New York Times* reporter. The paper was about to break the news that the FBI, NSA, and CIA were all investigating whether Stone had colluded with Russian operatives on behalf of the Trump campaign. "Here's my on-the-record quote," Stone had told the reporter. "Bullshit. Nonsense. Totally false."

After Stone left the party, I followed Fairbanks and the Proud Boys inside the Press Club and up to the thirteenth floor, where they walked down a plushly carpeted hallway, past the Bloomberg Center for Electronic Journalism, looking for the open bar in the First Amendment Lounge. A news crew stopped McInnes for an interview, and he regaled them with the story of his scuffles outside. He didn't claim self-defense. "I saw this Antifa guy carrying a cardboard flagpole, as required by law, and I got so mad that a so-called anarchist was following the cardboard regulations," he said. "So I punched him." He repeated the tale throughout the night, on and off camera, keeping the main plot points consistent but heightening the incidental details a little more each time. "I think that when I punched him, my fist went into his mouth and his teeth scraped me on the way out," he told one reporter. "Now I might get loser AIDS."

We kept moving toward the bar. In my peripheral vision, I saw a hunched, spectral figure who looked like a desiccated Matthew Broderick. "OMG, it's

Martin Shkreli," Fairbanks whispered. Shkreli, a sinister pharmaceutical entre-preneur, was then under federal indictment for securities fraud.* I tried to intro-duce myself, but he emitted a guttural, nonsyllabic noise and slipped away into the crowd. At some point, Rudkowski drifted from the group; the next time I saw him, he was in a corner chatting with a perky blonde in a baby-blue taffeta dress. "Oh, *that's* Lauren Southern," the Proud Boy who had confused her with Laura Loomer said. "Yeah, she is way hotter."

Fairbanks, walking in front of me, rummaged through her purse, found her Comet Ping Pong and Pepe the Frog pins, and affixed them to her dress. There were about a thousand guests at the DeploraBall, many of whom had paid be-tween one hundred dollars and twenty-five hundred dollars to get in. Almost ev-eryone wore at least one piece of flair: a Legal Immigrant T-shirt; an Adorable Deplorable sash; a Germans for Trump button; MAGA hats in red, white, blue, black, pink, camo, silver, and gold.

Just before Fairbanks reached the bar, a partygoer tapped her on the shoulder. She gave him the one-way-mirror stare of the famous and semifamous: he knew her, but she didn't know him. "I follow you!" he said. "I love all your stuff! Lemme get a selfie with you?" He and a friend flanked Fairbanks, ready to pose. She shot me a look of gratified resignation—*duty calls*—and I left her behind to minister to her fans.

I walked past an easel, prominently placed and brightly lit. It held an oil por-trait: George Washington, in three-quarter profile, wearing a MAGA hat. Under normal circumstances, a cheeky depiction of a Founding Father wouldn't bother me. All things being equal, why not stick it to the Man? Similarly, if forced to choose between placing my trust in either a swaggering, rebellious citizen or the CIA, I'd usually be inclined to side with the rebel. And yet. And yet when the CIA says that an allegation of election interference is worth investigating, and a dis-sembling dirty trickster says that it's not, I'm afraid I have to trust the CIA. *Ques-tion some things, but don't go crazy.* Of all that I resented about the Deplorables,

---

*Best known for acquiring the license of a rare drug and then raising the price by 5000 percent, Shkreli was often called "the most hated man in America." In addition to his day job as a swindler, he was a prolific Twitter troll. His trolling technique was one of the oldest and simplest in the world: misbehaving constantly, daring people to hate-watch him. He was the unruly kid in the back of the classroom, the one with a bottomless desire for all forms of attention, negative and positive. With the advent of social media, Shkreli had access to hundreds of millions of new ears to flick.

one of the things I found most irksome was that they forced me to think like an establishment shill.

All night, in every room of the Press Club, I heard partygoers using the acronym MAGA. They used it as a verb ("I can't wait to MAGA!"), as an adjective ("Ain't no party like a MAGA party"), and as a stand-alone interjection ("MAGA!!!"). For a year and a half, on every social media platform, the Deplorables had waxed breathless about the extent to which they and their MAGA brethren were about to MAGA until every last shitlib had been pwned and rekt and BTFO'd. To hear them talk, though, it seemed clear that few of them had ever said the words out loud. For one thing, they couldn't even agree on whether the first A in MAGA should be rounded or unrounded.*

I ran into Mike Flynn Jr., whose father, General Mike Flynn, was the incoming national security adviser. "Follow Mike @Cernovich," General Flynn had tweeted a month before the election. "He has a terrific book, Gorilla Mindset." The recommendation likely came from Flynn Jr., a Cernovich superfan and a fervent Twitter conspiracy theorist.[†] I asked Flynn Jr. why his name hadn't appeared on the DeploraBall's VIP list. "I'm keeping it low-key tonight," he said. "I'm just a fan of these guys."

In my left hand was a small white reporter's notebook, spiral bound at the top. I carried it for most of the night, even when I wasn't taking notes, as a form of ID. (The only thing worse than a reporter was a sneaky reporter.) Several of the Deplorables, eyeing the notebook, made sure to tell me exactly how they felt about the media. I heard many variations on the same icebreakers: "Are you gonna write

---

*I found the acronym uniquely galling, for personal reasons. When I was two years old, before anyone had coined the word "MAGA," I coined the word "Magah," with two rounded As. It was a substitute for "grandma," which I couldn't yet pronounce. It stuck. From then on, according to me, my siblings, my close friends, and my caller ID, my grandmothers were named Magah Dorothy and Magah Clare. "I don't know how anyone listens to his drek," Magah Clare said, in the spring of 2016, when I visited her one-room apartment on West End Avenue. We were talking, as everyone was at the time, about Trump. "You know what he is? A gonif. You know that word?" Magah Clare was one of my favorite people in the world—sharp tongued, clear eyed, fiercely intelligent. She grew up in Bensonhurst; her father was a socialist garment worker who spoke almost no English; she read everything, including *The New Yorker*, but she didn't have enough money to finish college. Her religions were atheism, workers' rights, Beethoven's Seventh, and a keen aversion to bullshit. Throughout 2016, every time we had lunch, she would ask me, rhetorically, what was *wrong* with people, how anyone could even *consider* trusting that man. I didn't have a pithy answer, and she didn't really expect one. She died in the spring of 2017. The only consolation was that no one ever told her how the gonifs had stolen her nickname, along with everything else.
†After the election, both Flynns were hired by Trump's transition team. In December, hours after the gunman at Comet Ping Pong was arrested, Flynn Jr. tweeted, "Until #Pizzagate proven to be false, it'll remain a story." He was fired from the transition team, but his father stayed on.

something nice about us, or are you gonna write fake news?" "You're not planning to call us white supremacists, are you?" A few people asked about my motives—sometimes in an inquisitive spirit, sometimes in an inquisitorial one.

I had a simple rule for this sort of situation: no matter what I was asked, I would never lie. I answered most questions forthrightly and thoroughly, but sometimes, when I thought that a fully candid answer might get me ejected or assaulted, I mumbled something true but evasive, then changed the subject.

"So what's your angle, partner?" a man shaped like a professional wrestler asked me. He was wearing sunglasses despite the ballroom's darkened interior.

"Oh, you know," I said. "Trying to meet people and ask them questions."

He perched his sunglasses on his forehead and rested a thick hand on my shoulder. "You know what I mean," he said, with a smile that did not seem designed to put me at ease. "Where're you coming from? Politically."

I paused for a moment, considering several possible answers, and then chose one. "Look at me," I said. I swiveled my head owlishly, letting him take in the view from all angles: pallid, angular face; red beard; dorky horn-rimmed glasses. "I live in Brooklyn," I continued. "I write for *The New Yorker*. I have a single-speed bike. Take a guess, and your guess is probably close enough."

The wrestler was tickled by this. "Get a load of my dude over here!" he said, beckoning to his date. Then, to me: "You stand here and you tell her exactly what you just told me. I'm gonna go get us all beers."

One woman, without a word of introduction, grabbed me by the wrist and led me out of the ballroom to a small, windowless hallway near the Fourth Estate Restaurant, where her date was sitting by himself and vaping. He looked up at us impassively while she jabbed a finger in the general direction of his face. "He's Spanish!" she said. "Sheriff Clarke is here, an African American gentleman, and everyone is treating him with nothing but respect! Do we look like Nazis to you?" I wrote down what she was saying, then handed her my notebook and asked her to share her name and email address. Instead, she tore out the page with her words on it, ripped the page to shreds, and scattered them like confetti on the carpet.

· · ·

The prevailing mood inside the ballroom was mirth with a base note of rage. Any familiar three-syllable chant—"Drain the swamp!" or "Build the wall!" or "Lock

her up!"—could be initiated by anyone at any time, with no more effort than dropping a match in a dry forest. Yoni, carrying a bourbon cocktail in each hand, tried
to invent a chant of his own: "We like fun!" It didn't take.

Cernovich, the emcee for the evening, walked onstage, stood behind a lectern,
and called for the crowd's attention. He wore a suit with no tie, fashionably mussed
hair, and a week's worth of stubble. (From a distance, he could pass as vaguely
Schwarzeneggerian.) Behind him was a blue Trump banner and a flagpole flying a
limp American flag. "It's good to see everyone from Twitter here in real life," he
said. "We *ran* Twitter during the election."

"We still run it!" a partygoer shouted.

Cernovich had an adenoidal tenor and a lisp, and he spoke in a clipped, fitful
cadence, wheeling his wrists in tight circles whenever he got nervous. Still, he
could be an effective orator when he was indignant. "The fake-news media didn't
want to talk about real stuff," he said. "But we talk to the people, and that's why I
knew Trump would win." The editorial "we" referred to Cernovich Media, a name
he had invented for a media brand consisting of himself.

He mentioned Paul Ryan, the Speaker of the House, and the crowd booed on
cue. Ryan was a rock-ribbed conservative, not a transgressive culture warrior, and
the Deplorables considered him yet another Deep State snake. "Some people call
him Cuck Ryan," Cernovich mused. "But this is family friendly, so I'm not going
to call him Cuck Ryan. You won't hear me say that tonight."*

Cernovich invited a few other VIPs to the stage, one by one. James O'Keefe of
Project Veritas said, "I'll make it public: I'm going after the media next." Laura
Loomer, his former employee, sat at the bar texting. No female speakers were
summoned to the stage. "We love President Trump, and it's not a political thing,"
Jack Posobiec said. "We found that we were living in a situation where truth was
fake and fake was truth and news was lies and we all knew about it but nobody was

---

*"Cuck," short for "cuckold," was the Deplorables' preferred insult of the moment. Only Deplorables and their
fellow travelers used the word in earnest; most people found it either jarring or baffling, which was part of the
point. A cuckold is a man whose wife is unfaithful or pregnant with someone else's child. The term has a long
history of racist connotations—for centuries, from *Othello* to *The Birth of a Nation* to internet porn, white men
have expressed their racial anxieties through fiction about black men "taking our women." But the white nationalists of the alt-right expanded and sharpened the metaphor, conjuring the image of the United States as a damsel
with an exposed southern border, her purity at risk of defilement by brown hordes. Whenever a congressperson,
especially a white Republican congressman, suggested a bipartisan approach to immigration reform, the alt-right
hordes on Twitter were quick to denigrate him as a "cuckservative." To the alt-right, such congressmen were not
merely moderates, or self-interested politicians; they were race traitors.

talking about it and there were some problems in our country and we said, 'We're gonna do something about it and you can't shut us up.'"

Between speeches, Cernovich curated a feeble variety show. A speed painter from Staten Island unveiled a caricature of a muscle-bound Trump. A folk singer strummed "The Times They Are A-Changin'" on an acoustic guitar festooned with a QR code. An aspiring pop star, who looked like a member of One Direction crossed with an apricot pug, performed his one viral hit, an Auto-Tune-heavy whine-rap anthem called "Trumpified." ("In debt to our ears, but please have no fears / The Trump is here / Oh, hell yeah.")

Shortly before Gavin McInnes was called to the stage, I asked him what he planned to talk about. "Oh, the usual—race and IQ," he said. "And the JQ, of course." By "race and IQ," he meant an idea that had been repeatedly debunked but had never fully gone out of style: that white people were genetically smarter than black people. The JQ stood for the "Jewish Question," which came in familiar flavors ("Why are Jews overrepresented in media, academia, and banking?") and more ominous ones ("What should we do about the Jews?"). McInnes was joking— whether he was tempted to talk about those topics onstage or not, he knew better than to try it. In theory, he and the other DeploraBall VIPs were free-speech absolutists who believed that any idea ought to be permissible in any venue. In practice, they knew that certain subjects should only be broached in private, or via dog whistle.

Glancing at the notebook in my hand, McInnes sighed and clarified. "Look, I'm not alt-right, dude," he said. "They care about the white race. We care about Western values." Some of his allies had taken to calling their ideology "civic nationalism," as opposed to white nationalism. Until recently, the white nationalists and the civic nationalists had sustained a shaky alliance, both groups affiliating themselves with the big-tent faction known as the alt-right. Now a branding war was starting to tear the movement apart.

During the long 2016 presidential campaign, Donald Trump seemed to draw on pools of dark energy not previously observed within the universe of the American electorate. The mainstream media, eager to name this newly visible category of voter, used a catchall term: alternative right, or alt-right. The word fit nicely in headlines and chyrons, and it appealed to newspaper editors and TV-news producers who hoped to connote frisson and novelty without passing explicit judgment. Instead of denouncing the alt-right, reporters often described it as "divisive," or "racially charged." They tried to present both sides neutrally, as journalistic convention seemed to require.

The definition of alt-right continued to expand. By the summer of 2016, it was such a big tent that it included any conservative or reactionary who was active online and too belligerently antiestablishment to feel at home in the Republican Party—a category that included the Republican nominee for president. This was an oddly broad definition for what was supposed to be a fringe movement, and yet no one seemed eager to clear up the semantic confusion. The Clinton campaign played up the alt-right's size and influence, while the alt-right was all too glad to be perceived as vast and menacing. There was no way to measure precisely how many Americans were alt-right, and there never would be. Estimates ranged from a few hundred to a few million. Still, what mattered was not the movement's head count but its collective impact on the national vocabulary.*

Throughout the campaign, the tent stayed big. "We're the platform for the alt-right," Steve Bannon said in July 2016, when he was running the pro-Trump web tabloid *Breitbart*. Later that year, after leading the Trump campaign to victory and being tapped to serve as chief White House strategist, Bannon claimed that he'd only meant to align himself with an insurgent brand of civic nationalism, not with ethnonationalism. Yet a core within the movement still insisted on a narrower definition of alt-right, one based on explicit anti-Semitism and white supremacy. This core had always existed; no one who was versed in the far-right blogosphere could have missed it.

Mainstream journalists, or at least the ones who were paying attention, were daunted by the fiscal precarity of their industry, the plummeting cultural authority of their institutions, and the unpredictable dynamics of social media outrage. The more these threats loomed, the more journalists clung to one of the

---

*There was no party, PAC, or other official organization called the alt-right. There were no membership rolls. The definition of alt-right changed constantly, even within the movement; people who were leaders one week were cast out the next. Most of the alt-right's adherents were anonymous, and their devotion was inconsistent at best; many would have disavowed their beliefs in an instant if asked by a pollster (or a parent). The movement's primary home was not in corporeal space but on the internet. The number of people who would be willing to show up at an alt-right rally, or to put up a yard sign for an alt-right candidate, was dwarfed by the number of people who would download an alt-right podcast or post anonymously to an alt-right hashtag. So it's hardly surprising that, when it came to estimating the size of the movement, there were no solid numbers. Besides, even numbers that were supposed to be solid—e.g., Hillary Clinton's poll numbers—turned out to be not very solid after all.

few professional axioms that still seemed beyond dispute: in all matters of political opinion, a reporter should strive to remain neutral. This is true enough, for certain kinds of journalists, when applied to certain prosaic debates about tariffs and treaties. When it comes to core matters of principle, though, it's not always possible to be both evenhanded and honest. The plain fact was that the alt-right was a racist movement full of creeps and liars. If a newspaper's house style didn't allow its reporters to say so, at least by implication, then the house style was preventing its reporters from telling the truth.

Neutrality has never been a universal good, even in the simplest of times. In unusual times—say, when the press has been drafted, without its consent or comprehension, into a dirty culture war—neutrality might not always be possible. Some questions aren't really questions at all. Should Muslim Americans be treated as real Americans? Should women be welcome in the workplace? Are there children locked in the basement of Comet Ping Pong? To treat these as legitimate topics of debate is to be not neutral but complicit. Sometimes, even for a journalist, there is no such thing as not picking a side.

By all accounts, Richard Spencer coined the term "alt-right" in 2008. In 2010, he founded AlternativeRight.com, "an online magazine of radical traditionalism." He was not coy about the kind of traditionalism he had in mind: one that would reverse many of the civil rights and social norms established during the twentieth century, especially those promoting racial integration. Spencer knew that advancing his agenda would be a formidable task, beyond the scope of what most gatekeepers considered acceptable. Still, he dared to dream.

Having dropped out of a Duke PhD program in European intellectual history to "pursue a life of thought-crime," Spencer split his time between the Virginia suburbs and his parents' ski chalet in Montana, subsisting largely on inherited wealth and writing turgid blog posts about Nietzsche, Wagner, and eugenics.* After a while, he took control of a meager D.C. think tank and began to give interviews to the mainstream press, affecting the persona of a tweedy public intellectual. In his own niche publications and podcasts and conferences, when he assumed that

---

*The first few times people told me the source of Spencer's family fortune, I assumed that they were being facetious. It was too on the nose. Later, I looked it up and saw that it was true: thousands of acres of Louisiana cotton fields, which Spencer's forebears had owned for generations.

the normies weren't listening, he expressed his views more bluntly. The "ideal," he said, was "the creation of a white ethnostate on the North American continent." (He claimed that this might be achieved through "peaceful ethnic cleansing," though he was vague about how the "peaceful" part would work.) The white ethnostate would not include Jews, who were innately conniving and who would undermine any society they were allowed to infest.*

A few pro-Trump activists, anticipating a future reckoning, tried to erect barriers within the big tent, albeit flimsy ones. "Mike Cernovich is not part of the alt-right," Mike Cernovich, who often referred to himself in the third person, wrote on his blog in the summer of 2016. This sentence was clear enough, but the rest of the blog post was tortuous and cagey. He didn't decry the alt-right's bigotry; in fact, he went out of his way to do the opposite. "No ideas are off limits with me," he wrote. "Who cares if someone is racist?" He added, "Until the right wins for once, I have no interest in arguing with the alt-right or disavowing anyone. Once the right has some actual power, then it will be time to have an ideological civil war."

That November, Republicans won the presidency, both houses of Congress, and two thirds of state legislatures. The ideological civil war emerged into the open. Richard Spencer's think tank hosted a conference in a government building in Washington, D.C., and Spencer gave a self-congratulatory keynote address, sipping occasionally from a glass of whiskey. "The alt-right always took President-elect Donald Trump and his chances seriously," he said. He contrasted this attitude with that of "the mainstream media—or perhaps we should refer to them in the original German: Lügenpresse." The epithet, for "lying press," was one of Joseph Goebbels's favorites.

Spencer's speech grew more emphatic, rousing the audience to its feet. "For us, as Europeans, it is only normal again when we are great again," Spencer, who is from Texas, said. "Hail Trump! Hail our people! Hail victory!" The last phrase was a translation from the original German: "Sieg Heil." Spencer raised his glass, holding his arm high in the air. Several members of the audience raised a single arm in response, their fingers extended stiffly in full Nazi salutes.

---

*This was perhaps the starkest iteration of the "Jewish Question": "Are Jews white?" The civic nationalists didn't give the question much thought; the white nationalists were obsessed with it, and insistent that the answer was no. When I informed my normie friends that Richard Spencer and his ilk did not consider Jews to be white, my friends tended to react with disbelief, or with a concise rebuttal: "But Jews *are* white." These were people who maintained that race was a social construct; and yet they often acted as if the racial categories they'd grown used to were not only meaningful but indestructible.

Ironically, but also predictably, Spencer had permitted a Jewish videographer from *The Atlantic* to capture all this, and the resulting footage went viral. On cable news and across social media, Spencer became the indelible face of the alt-right, and the alt-right became indelibly linked to neo-Nazism. Spencer claimed half-heartedly that his supporters had raised a "Roman salute," not a Nazi salute, but even he didn't seem to take the excuse seriously. The whole spectacle—Hailgate, as it came to be known—forced everyone associated with the alt-right to make a choice: stand with Richard Spencer, or disavow him and the term he'd invented.*

"Alt-right" had proved a durable and potent label, and it had no obvious replacement. On Twitter, civic nationalists floated potential monikers for their half of the movement: the New Right, the MAGA Movement, the Deplorables. The out-and-proud white supremacists continued calling themselves the alt-right; they referred to the splinter group condescendingly as the "alt-light."

"I knew something like this would happen eventually," Cernovich said a few days after Hailgate. "We'll figure out a new name. The first order of business is getting that Nazi shit way the fuck away from me. Too toxic, from a branding perspective."

Another co-organizer of the DeploraBall was a young man who went by the handle Baked Alaska, an indefatigable troll with impressive followings on Twitter and YouTube. About a month before the party, he tweeted, "Jewish people run 95% of American media that is very interesting."

Cernovich reprimanded him privately, by text. "Stupid, man, you are listed as a featured guest," he wrote. "No more fuck-ups. No Nazi salutes, no JQ bullshit."

Baked Alaska did not appreciate being told what to do. "I'm about having fun Mike, this isn't fun anymore," he texted back. "Too many rules." He was banned from the DeploraBall, and his name was stricken from the invitation. "I have a lot of tolerance for goofing off online," Cernovich wrote on his blog. "I don't freak out or get triggered. But we all have lines." When Cernovich found out that Richard Spencer had bought a ticket to the DeploraBall, Spencer was also banned.

This infuriated some of Cernovich's followers, who were constitutionally averse to gatekeeping of any kind, and who had taken him both seriously and

---

*"So now the alt-right brand is damaged, it's associated with Nazism, and normal Americans aren't gonna support that," Paul Ramsey, a white nationalist who had formerly identified as alt-right, said on YouTube. "Which is a shame, but it's really OK. . . . We have our man in office now. We don't need to call ourselves alt-right."

literally when he'd said that no ideas should be beyond the pale. "If free speech is so important to you why ban @bakedalaska from the #deploraball?" a young woman with the handle @urwrong1mright tweeted at Cernovich. "Seems fugged up."

In a hallway of the Press Club, after all the VIP speeches were over, I ran into Cernovich and asked him whether he was having fun. "Packed house, people seem to be enjoying themselves," he said. "But ask me tomorrow, after I know there was no violence and nobody posted any selfies with Roman salutes. Then I'll be happy."

We were standing near a photo booth. Cassandra Fairbanks, who happened to be passing by, hugged Cernovich from behind and pulled him into the booth, where they took a few sets of photos—one wearing Trump masks, one wearing Hillary masks, one posing as themselves. "Are you convinced we're not Nazis yet?" Fairbanks asked me, slurring a bit, as she emerged from the booth. "It's a bullshit, ridiculous accusation, honestly, I don't even know where it comes from." She reminded me, for the third time, that her mother was Puerto Rican. "You should just relax," she told me. "Put down that notebook and go get drunk."

• • •

I chatted with another of the DeploraBall's VIPs, a slim twenty-eight-year-old named Lucian Wintrich, who wore a tailored black suit, a black MAGA hat, and tortoiseshell glasses. He had the bone structure of a cologne model and the flighty, unctuous demeanor of a novice cardsharp. He started many sentences—a setup to a racist joke, a vaguely conspiratorial premise about George Soros—but finished few of them. Standing next to him was Jim Hoft, a man in his fifties wearing a burgundy velvet smoking jacket. "Lucian works for me," Hoft shouted, more loudly than necessary. "I run *The Gateway Pundit*, one of the biggest sites in the Midwest. A million pageviews a day. A *day*. And that's because we deliver the *real fucking news*."

Sheriff David Clarke took the stage a few minutes later, wearing his trademark black cowboy hat and a tuxedo with a wide orange cummerbund. He faced the audience and gave a rigid military salute, his facial expression somewhere between stony determination and smoldering fury. He turned upstage to salute the American flag, inducing rapt applause from the crowd. Then he walked to the flag, pulled it toward him, and kissed it tenderly on the seam where the stars met the stripes. The crowd, at this point, was approaching Beatles-at-Shea-Stadium levels of euphoria.

"Pretty sure that's against Flag Code," a man behind me said.

"Go fuck yourself, bro," another man responded.

"Hot *damn!*" Clarke shouted from the lectern. "Donald Trump is not the president of the United States as of noon tomorrow without *you*. He knows that, and I know that."

I leaned against a wall, taking notes. Even with the crowd's euphoria at its peak, I could sense a distinct locus of attention somewhere behind me. I turned around. A few feet away, in the semidarkness, stood Peter Thiel. I'd heard rumors that he was a secret donor to the DeploraBall, but none of the party's organizers had expected him to show up—why would a capitalist grandee, the cofounder of PayPal and one of the most revered investors in the country, risk tarnishing his reputation by mixing publicly with pariahs? Yet here he was, looking slightly overwhelmed. The protesters outside had their picket signs; the Deplorables inside had their flair; I had my notebook; but Thiel stood alone and empty-handed, not holding so much as a drink or a smartphone.

Thiel had a long history of espousing contrarian views, ranging from offensive to merely provocative. In 2016, he added another heterodox position to his list, becoming the most prominent Trump supporter in Silicon Valley. A throng of young men in MAGA hats now hovered around him, pitching business ideas and angling for selfies. "It's so awesome how you took out *Gawker*," one of them said.* "Who're you gunning for next?"

Thiel ignored the question and waited for someone else to speak, but no one did. "There seems to be some genuine enthusiasm in this room," he said, unenthusiastically.

The young man repeated his question: "I was asking if you're gonna go after any other media outlets or whatever."

"I understood what you were asking," Thiel said. "I was introducing a new topic." He had a delicate, froggy voice and a tendency to overenunciate. Shouting small talk in a noisy room almost seemed to cause him physical pain.

I waited out the throng, introduced myself to Thiel as a journalist, and told him that I wanted to interview him at some point—or now, if he wasn't too busy. He turned to glance at me, then turned back toward the stage, saying nothing. I

---

*In 2007, *Gawker*, an irreverent metamedia web tabloid, published a piece alleging that Thiel was gay. A few years later, apparently as retribution, Thiel covertly bankrolled an unrelated invasion-of-privacy suit, brought by the professional wrestler Hulk Hogan, which caused Gawker Media to go bankrupt. Thiel later told *The New York Times* that he saw no contradiction between his plot to exterminate a journalistic outlet and his devotion, as a libertarian, to a free press: "I refuse to believe that journalism means massive privacy violations."

rambled to fill the silence. When I mentioned that I worked at *The New Yorker*, he turned to face me. "All right, I have a question," he said. "Were your colleagues genuinely excited about Hillary? I mean, not preferring her to the alternative, but real, Obama-like levels of excitement?"

"Good question," I said. "Some were, most weren't."

"Ah," he said. I waited for him to continue, but apparently this was all he had to say.

I asked him why he'd decided to attend the DeploraBall.

"I know some people here," he said, his eyes darting from side to side. "I think I might be leaving soon."

Before he could walk away, I mentioned that I'd recently read his 2014 book, *Zero to One*. Several times in the book, Thiel poses what he calls "the contrarian question": "What important truth do very few people agree with you on?" (Thiel's answer: "Most people think the future of the world will be defined by globalization, but the truth is that technology matters more.")*

I told him that since reading his book I'd been mulling my own answer to the contrarian question.

"Oh," he said. He didn't encourage me to continue, but he didn't turn away, either. So I told him my answer.

"Most people assume that there's an innate, reliable correlation between how good something is and how popular it will be," I began. "I think the correlation is unreliable at best." Thiel held one of eight seats on the board of directors at Facebook, a company whose public-facing dogma took for granted that "good" and "popular" were interchangeable concepts. Interviewed by *Time* in 2010, Facebook's founder, Mark Zuckerberg, said, "The best stuff spreads, whether it's the best news article, or the best song, or the best product, or the best movie." Zuckerberg's entire company—indeed, the entire social web—flowed from this premise. The idea seemed to be that the most momentous human decisions—questions of taste, of policy, even of morality—would best be settled by the open marketplace of ideas, or by the literal marketplace. If this premise was correct, then getting rid of informational gatekeepers seemed like a no-brainer, a textbook example

---

*In addition to the contrarian question, Thiel offers a more worldly corollary: "What valuable company is no one building?" He argues that coming up with "good answers" to this pair of questions is a prerequisite to "creating value" and "building the future," two phrases that turn out to be synonyms, essentially, for becoming a rich tech entrepreneur like Peter Thiel.

of what businesspeople like Thiel called disintermediation. But what if the premise was wrong?

I finished my rant. Thiel was silent for several seconds. To be polite, I turned
away and let him gather his thoughts. In addition to serving on Facebook's board,
Thiel was the company's first outside investor; he had since sold most of his shares
in the company, but he still held Facebook stock worth more than $35 million.
Given this conflict of interest, it seemed unlikely that he would fully endorse my
view. Still, I was curious to see which points he would concede and which he
would refute. Even Thiel's enemies acknowledged his fierce intellect and his flair
for extemporaneous debate. As I waited for him to speak, I felt a flash of premon-
itory embarrassment: surely he was about to dismantle my argument.

Onstage, David Clarke was nearing the climax of his speech: "When I hear
people say that we need to reach across the aisle and work with people, with the
Democrats, you know what I say? 'The only reason I'll be reaching across the aisle
is to grab one of them by the *throat!*'"

When I turned back toward Thiel, he was gone.

●   ●   ●

In 1961, three years before the historian Richard Hofstadter identified a paranoid
style in American politics, President Kennedy remained confident that "the basic
good sense and stability of the great American consensus" would ultimately prevail. If there was a great American consensus in 1961, it was both reflected and
shaped by the core institutions of the Fourth Estate, which were then at the height
of their power. Walter Cronkite was on his way to becoming the most trusted man
in America. Edward R. Murrow, Cronkite's boss and predecessor, had just left
CBS News to join the Kennedy administration, where he would write propaganda
to be disseminated by the State Department. The nation's most prominent journalists, from celebrity newscasters to unheralded assignment editors, were, by
and large, upper-middle-class white men in gray suits. Many were blinkered
coastal elites, either too circumspect or too myopic to risk departing meaning-
fully from the socially acceptable narrative, even when elements of that narrative
(the Gulf of Tonkin, the death of Fred Hampton) were misleading or flat-out false.
Too often, what seemed like stability and consensus was actually achieved by stifling dissent, muting marginal voices, or writing off productive conflict as trivial
noise. In the 1988 book *Manufacturing Consent*, Edward Herman and Noam

Chomsky warned that the symbiosis between government power and corporate journalism, if left unchecked, could allow media gatekeepers to mislead a credulous public in any number of ways. This was true. And yet Herman and Chomsky couldn't have known that they were writing at the beginning of the end of an era—that, just two decades hence, the Fourth Estate would no longer command widespread attention and respect, and reasonable observers would no longer be able to use the phrase "good sense and stability" to describe American discourse, at least not with a straight face.

When it was founded in 2004, Facebook billed itself as "an online directory that connects people through social networks at colleges." Within a few years, this self-description had morphed into a far more grandiose mission statement: "Facebook gives people the power to share and make the world more open and connected." Mark Zuckerberg was careful not to call himself a gatekeeper. On the contrary, he portrayed himself as a Robin Hood figure, snatching power from the gatekeepers and redistributing it to the people, who could presumably be trusted to do the right thing.

Traditional media gatekeeping was, inarguably, a deeply flawed system. But what if it turned out to be, like democracy, the worst system except for all the others? If history was an arc bending inexorably toward justice, then there was no need to worry about any of this—technological disruption could only lead the world more efficiently in the right direction. If history was contingent, however, then removing the gatekeepers, without any clear notion of what might replace them, could throw the whole information ecosystem into chaos.

CHAPTER FOUR

To Change How We Talk Is to Change Who We Are

The DeploraBall ended around midnight, at which point everyone spilled onto the sidewalk, chatting and smoking cigarettes. It was an unseasonably warm night. The protesters and police were gone. As I left the building, the first person I saw, standing directly in front of the exit, was Richard Spencer. He wore a khaki corduroy jacket, black leather gloves, and his signature high-and-tight haircut—what his supporters called a fashy haircut.

Gavin McInnes sneered at Spencer. "Have you been waiting for us all night?" he said. "Pathetic. Why don't you just leave us alone, you fucking Nazi?"

"You're a cuck, Gavin," Spencer said.

Then, breaking character, they smiled and embraced.*

An Infowars reporter pulled McInnes aside for an on-camera interview. Once again, he repeated the tall tale of his brawl with the Antifa protester: "My fist went into his mouth, and I felt his tongue—it was like holding a boa constrictor's clit."

Two drunk partygoers, watching the interview, dared each other to walk into the frame:

"Jump in front of the camera and say 'Bill Clinton is a rapist.'"

"Bill Clinton is a racist?"

"Dude, no. 'Rapist.'"

"I can't troll Infowars with that meme. Infowars *invented* that meme."

Cernovich saw Spencer and walked halfway down the block to avoid him. A

---

*"Gavin's had Richard on his show," a Proud Boy standing next to me explained. "They don't agree about the J.Q. stuff, necessarily, but they agree on other stuff, and they've always had good debates." After Hailgate, however, "Gavin started saying we shouldn't be seen with them"—meaning the alt-right. "But then he also always talks about how we should never punch right and should only punch left instead. So I don't know what the fuck to think."

few of the other VIPs, however, inched closer to Spencer—he was notorious, but notoriety was a kind of currency. Fairbanks kissed him on the cheek and they started talking without preamble, as if continuing an ongoing discussion. Earlier, when I'd texted her to ask when I should arrive at her house, she'd replied, "One person wants to leave before you get here. . . . He's a pretty controversial figure." It now seemed clear, although she would neither confirm nor deny it, that the controversial figure had been Spencer.

He posed for a photo with Laura Loomer, who draped a hand on his shoulder. "I'm Jewish, you know," she said as they smiled for the camera.

"Yeah, no shit," Spencer said, between clenched teeth.

"How do you know, from my Twitter?" Loomer said.

"Yeah, and from your nose," Spencer said.

Loomer was having a rough night. She had come to D.C. under the impression that she and Rudkowski were dating, only to realize, after watching him flirt with Lauren Southern all night, that her impression was mistaken. "I talked to him last month, and he said, 'If I end up going to the DeploraBall, I'll definitely go with you,'" Loomer told me. "I guess he's full of shit, like everyone else."

Yoni shook Spencer's hand and asked for a photo. "I don't mean to bother you," he said. "I'm just some random guy."

"Not at all," Spencer said. "That's why I'm here." They chatted for a minute, bonding over their mutual distaste for Angela Merkel.

After Mary Clare took their photo, Yoni turned to Spencer and said, "You're a lot nicer than the internet makes it seem."

"I'm a nice guy!" Spencer responded. "I'm just misunderstood." He looked Mary Clare up and down, then turned back to Yoni. "Dude, she is *way* better looking than you," he said. "Does she have blackmail material on you or something?" Yoni's smile faded. Spencer's did not. It seemed that he was earnestly trying to deliver a compliment, but that he didn't quite know how to pull it off.

While most people gravitated toward Spencer, Spencer gravitated toward me, the only mainstream journalist within his line of sight. Having been prohibited from entering the DeploraBall, he had instead spent the evening "having dinner and drinks with some friends nearby." One of those friends was Mike Enoch, from New York City. Enoch was a pseudonymous alt-right podcaster and one of the cofounders of *The Right Stuff*. A week earlier, Enoch's real name and address had been revealed against his will—a form of retribution known online as doxing—putting his job and his marriage in jeopardy. He and the others were still out drinking, but Spencer had left them, he said, "to come here and maybe inspire some people to join us, if they want a real dissident movement."

I brought up Hailgate. "I admit, I was being naughty and provocative," he said. "Sometimes you have to shock the bourgeoisie. And look, I got a lot of negative blowback from it, but I also got thousands of new followers." I asked whether he'd always disliked Cernovich and the other DeploraBall organizers. "Oh, we all played nice during the election, and some of them are still nice behind the scenes," Spencer said. "But now they're trying to pull off a kind of Goldilocks strategy— edgy but not too edgy. It's not going to work. The alt-right without racial realism? It's just Trump cheerleading."

"What are the key texts of the alt-right movement?" I asked. "Who is its intellectual leader?"

He gave me a withering look, implying that this was a stupid question. "I am," he said.

On the ground was a picket sign that a protester had left behind: POVERTY IS A CRIME AGAINST HUMANITY. A Proud Boy picked it up and handed it to Spencer. He held the sign with one hand and balled the other hand into a fist, raising it in a gloved power salute.

Fairbanks, laughing, took a photo. "Can I tweet this?" she asked.

"Go right ahead," Spencer said. "I'm not even sure I disagree with this sign's sentiment, honestly."

"God, I'm gonna get so much shit for posting this," she said. The prospect seemed to delight her. "Maybe I'll put it on Instagram, too."

Spencer left for the DeploraBall's unofficial after-party at Shelly's Back Room, a cigar bar across the street. Fairbanks stayed behind and finished her cigarette. "He's not so scary, right?" she asked me. "I'm still a hippie at heart, I guess. I just want everyone to get along."

Spencer spent more than an hour at the after-party, antagonizing everyone he could find. Several of the DeploraBall's guests took the bait, apparently eager for a fight. "How exactly are you gonna make America whites only?" a tall, bearded alt-light blogger named Jack Murphy asked Spencer, shoving him in the chest. "Cattle cars? What's the plan, dude?"

Mike Cernovich pulled them apart and talked Murphy down. "Handle your shit later if you want," Cernovich said. "But this place is full of journalists. You throw a punch, that becomes the story."

Before I left the cigar bar for the night, I checked in with Cernovich one last time. The DeploraBall had ended with no Sieg Heils, no vandalism, no serious rule breaking. "I think we pulled it off," he said. "High energy, low drama. We're setting a template for what the new right wing looks like." He invoked the Overton window, a metaphor invented in the 1990s by a libertarian think tank to explain how cultural vocabularies fluctuate over time. Ideas in the center of the Overton window are universally acceptable, so mainstream that they are taken for granted. The outer panes of the window represent more controversial opinions; radical opinions are close to the window's edge; outside the window are ideas that are not just unpopular but unthinkable.

The point of the metaphor is that unthinkability is a temporary condition. The window can always shift. "Right now I'm seen as this fringe lunatic, and all the people you met tonight are seen that way," Cernovich said. "But there are more of us than people realize, and we've tapped into something more powerful than they understand. The window is not static, bro. They can't keep calling us fringe forever. Wait two years, five years, ten years. You'll see."

• • •

The day after the DeploraBall, Richard Spencer attended the inauguration wearing a tie, a red MAGA hat, and a rain poncho. "Crime and gangs and drugs . . . have stolen too many lives," Trump said. "This American carnage stops right here and stops right now." When the speech was over, Spencer stood just outside the security gates and opened Periscope, the video-livestreaming app owned by Twitter. With his phone's camera on selfie mode, Spencer ad-libbed for an online audience of more than twenty thousand people. On the street behind him, strangers passed by without glancing in his direction. "I was afraid that Trump was going to—maybe not cuck out, but kinda try to evoke Kennedy," Spencer said. "He didn't . . . and I think that's a great thing. It was a populist speech. He was talking about identity."

"Hail the chief," a commenter wrote.

"Hail victory," another wrote.

"He did not address the JQ," someone complained.

"Richard," another commenter wrote, "Cassandra Fairbanks thinks you're cute."

As the crowd filed out behind him, Spencer continued his exegesis of Trump's first inaugural. "Stephen Miller probably wrote it," he said. "I like Stephen Miller in terms of his hard-hitting stuff; in terms of poetry, it wasn't that great." Miller, Trump's thirty-one-year-old chief policy adviser, was an undergraduate at Duke when Spencer was a graduate student there, and they were both members of a small club called the Duke Conservative Union. "We knew each other quite well," Spencer had told me the previous night. "I'm surprised more people haven't picked up on that connection."

The morning after the election, an alt-right blogger called Vox Day published a blog post celebrating all that the movement had achieved. "This is your victory, all of you who voted for Trump, who memed for Trump, who donated to Trump," he wrote. But he exhorted his readers to keep up the pressure. Trump's election was only one step toward the larger goal of establishing a white ethnostate. "Donald Trump has a lot to do," he continued. "It is the Alt-Right's job to move the Overton Window and give him conceptual room to work."

●　●　●

A few hours after the inauguration, on a street corner in downtown D.C., Richard Spencer gave an interview to an Australian news crew. A protester hovered in the background of the shot, holding a sign that read WHITE LIVES MATTER TOO MUCH. Other protesters interrupted the interview, peppering Spencer with questions:

"Are you a neo-Nazi?"

"No, I'm not a neo-Nazi."

"Do you like black people?"

"Yeah, sure."

"Would you marry a black woman?"

No response.

Spencer was asked about a green lapel pin he was wearing.

"It's Pepe," he explained. "It's become kind of a symbol—"

Before he could finish the sentence, an Antifa protestor in a black ski mask swooped into the frame and punched Spencer in the side of the head. Spencer staggered sideways, his fashy haircut askew.

I was a few blocks away, walking to the Airbnb where Lucian Wintrich was staying for the weekend. "Holy shit, you're gonna love this," he said as I opened the door. He had a dozen tabs open on his laptop, each displaying a different Spencer getting punched. It had taken only a few minutes for the incident to be transformed into a meme—for a flesh-and-blood street clash to become just another thing on the internet. (Soon, the footage would be remixed with hundreds of backing scores: Bruce Springsteen, Chance the Rapper, Celine Dion, the *Curb Your Enthusiasm* theme song.)

Wintrich, smoking a cigarette, kept opening new iterations of the meme, guffawing at each one.

I suggested that sucker punching anyone, even one's enemies, might not be a good idea, morally or tactically.

"Whatever, fuck that asshole," Wintrich reasoned.

He said that he resented Spencer for making the rest of the Deplorables look bad by association. I also suspected, although of course Wintrich wouldn't admit it, that he was envious of Spencer's newfound viral fame. "He's reaping what he sowed," Wintrich said. "I don't even think he's a real white supremacist, anyway. I think he's a leftist CIA plant sent to discredit our movement."

"How much of what you say do you actually believe?" I asked.

Instead of answering, he looked up at me and grinned. There would be more inauguration balls that night, both official and unofficial, and Wintrich had an ambitious party hopping itinerary ahead of him. "Hold this," he said, handing me his burning cigarette. "I have to finish painting my toenails before I put on my tux."

* * *

For much of 2015 and 2016, while everyone I knew was incredulous at the notion that Donald Trump thought he could be president, I was in my office, on the thirty-eighth floor of the World Trade Center, reading such blog posts as "Global Elite's Secret Plan Revealed" and "The Rational Racist" and "Misogyny Gets You Laid." Whenever a colleague walked in and saw what was on my screen, I scrambled to say several things that should have gone without saying. I was not reading up on the merits of bigotry because I was open to being convinced. I was not scouring the internet rumor mill for titillation, or to scratch a contrarian itch. Something was happening, and I was trying to figure out what it was.

My colleagues and friends urged me to move on. Don't feed the trolls, they said, not even with your attention. Just ignore them and eventually they'll slink away. They have to. Their ideas are simply too odious, their affect too intolerable. In the long run, there's no way they can win. As Hillary Clinton often said, referring to the most unsavory elements of Trumpism: "This is not who we are."

Who were we? The campaign went on and on. Every week, the Sunday talk shows were given over to the same set of questions. These sounded like the usual noises of political punditry—predictions about district maps and ground games—but they were proxies for more foundational questions about human nature and the long arc of history. At a dinner party, someone might mention a bit of news about voter ID laws in Wisconsin; two beers later, everyone would be enmeshed in a deeper, more desperate conversation about the intrinsic goodness* or badness† of the American people.

At first, I accepted the Brooklyn dinner-party consensus: it was inconceivable that Trump could win. Shortly after he descended on a gold-colored escalator, referred to Mexicans as "rapists," and announced that he was running for president, my wife heard from an Ecuadorian friend who had seen the news and was distraught: if this is how he talks now, what if he actually takes office? We informed her, with confident forbearance, that a Trump presidency was not within the realm of possibility. I was keen to keep believing this, and so, for a little while, I did. And yet a part of me couldn't help remembering a sentence I'd read on *The Right Stuff*: "The culture war is being fought daily from your smartphone." Would a bumbling demagogue actually win the presidency? I had a hard time imagining it. *Could* he win? That was a different question.

Pretty soon, whenever the topic came up, I started appointing myself devil's advocate. If someone argued that our national character was fundamentally munificent and enlightened, that we couldn't possibly fall for raw bigotry and chintzy propaganda, I would reply: Yes, we can. A small part of me was just trolling. A bigger part of me was stating the obvious, or what would have been obvious if we weren't so invested in thinking it unthinkable. Anything *can* happen. America was having a kind of national conversation, but too often it was reduced to a binary debate: optimistic determinism or pessimistic fatalism. What if that debate was a dead end? What if fate had nothing to do with it?

---

*Those looking for evidence that our national character was inherently noble didn't have to look much further than Thomas Jefferson, author of the rhapsody of pluralism that is the Declaration of Independence.

†Those looking for evidence that our national character was inherently barbaric didn't have to look much further than Thomas Jefferson, author of a classified ad in *The Virginia Gazette* demanding that a runaway slave, a "knavish" young man "inclining to corpulence," be returned to his plantation at once.

On a relatively slow day in the early weeks of 2016, I went out for lunch with a journalist I admired, a gatekeeper within our industry. Ribs, corn bread, iced tea, chocolate-chip brownies: the Atkins-era equivalent of three-martini decadence. By then, I was worried. "He really might win," I said.

The journalist didn't do a spit take, but that was the gist. He definitely laughed. "Come on," he said. "You don't mean that."

"What's stopping him?" I insisted. Trump was intolerable in a hundred different ways; but tolerance is a social norm, not a law of nature, and social norms can and do change.

I continued tracking the luridly ugly edges of the internet. The stuff kept proliferating, and it seemed to me that it could have a greater impact than most of us wanted to admit. I was in eighth grade in 1998, when a disreputable blogger named Matt Drudge helped break the story that would lead to the president's impeachment. After 9/11, the internet swelled with alternative facts to explain the inexplicable, and "truth" came into wide use as an Orwellian synonym for its opposite. Then, during college, came social media, and with it the swift flattening of all information and opinion. In the open marketplace of ideas, what was to stop a lie from outcompeting a fact? Why couldn't nihilist trolls and misogynist snake-oil salesmen accumulate real power?*

Part of me felt that it was alarmist, almost demeaning, to spend too much time panicking about the rising tide of ugliness online. Another part of me felt that it would have been irresponsible to ignore it. The task of journalism—or *a* task of a certain kind of journalism—is to look squarely and honestly at the world while also projecting a calm air of decency and dispassion. With each passing week, those two ideals were coming to seem more and more irreconcilable.

"Look, we happen to live in a free country," one of my colleagues said. "People can click on terrible links if that's how they want to spend their time."

This was true, of course. And yet I made counterarguments, trying to con-

---

*Nearly a quarter century after he wrote the Declaration of Independence, Thomas Jefferson became a candidate for president. He may have been an idealist, but he also wanted to win. He paid a pamphleteer, in secret, and the pamphleteer spread some scurrilous rumors about Jefferson's opponent, John Adams—calling him, for instance, "a hideous hermaphroditical character which has neither the force and firmness of a man, nor the gentleness and sensibility of a woman." Jefferson's opponents, in turn, accused him of being "the son of a half-breed Indian squaw," which was false. Later, Jefferson's pamphleteer turned against him and accused him of having impregnated his slave Sally Hemings, which was probably true. In the twenty-first century, the only surprising thing about noxious political propaganda is that anyone still finds it surprising.

vince both my colleague and myself. "Those terrible links influence what people think, how people behave, who people vote for," I said.

"Is anyone surprised that there's awful stuff on the internet?" my colleague said.

"Everything is the internet now," I said, "and the awful stuff might be winning." I couldn't guarantee that the ugliness would prevail, of course. On the other hand, I couldn't guarantee that it would not, and neither could anyone else.

• • •

After Trump won, the late professor Richard Rorty enjoyed a posthumous moment of mini-virality. My Facebook feed was full of people posting an eerily prescient excerpt from Rorty's *Achieving Our Country*, a collection of political lectures published in 1998. With the left wing of the Democratic Party in decline, Rorty argued, the only politicians "channeling the mounting rage of the newly dispossessed" were right-wing populists. If this continued, he wrote, then, sooner or later,

> something will crack. The nonsuburban electorate will decide that the system has failed and start looking around for a strongman to vote for. . . . One thing that is very likely to happen is that the gains made in the past forty years by black and brown Americans, and by homosexuals, will be wiped out. Jocular contempt for women will come back into fashion. . . . All the sadism which the academic Left has tried to make unacceptable to its students will come flooding back.

What was unacceptable can become acceptable. Acceptability is just a norm, and norms can change for the better or for the worse.

Whenever this passage was posted on Facebook, commenters tended to treat Rorty's words like a prophecy, a revelation of the fact that the American experiment had always been doomed to fail. But Rorty put no stock in revelation. "We should face up to unpleasant truths about ourselves," he continued, "but we should not take those truths to be the last word about our chances for happiness, or about our national character. Our national character is still in the making." As the title of his book suggests, he did not believe that we are doomed or that we are saved. He did not believe that We Are Good or that We Are Bad. He believed something more liberating and also more terrifying: that history is contingent, that the arc bends the way people bend it.* The American attitude toward fascism has long been an article of faith: it can't happen here. But if history is contingent—if anything *can* happen—then our worst fears are not impossible but improbable, which is not at all the same thing.

Electoral prognostication was only Rorty's hobby. He was mainly a philosopher. Just as Darwin had shown that biology proceeds not by design but by evolution, Rorty held, so might contemporary philosophy show that history is the result of countless human actions, not the fulfillment of an eternal plan.

In his 1989 book, *Contingency, Irony, and Solidarity,* Rorty invoked the concept of "vocabularies," by which he meant broad systems of thought—"the moral vocabulary of Saint Paul versus Freud's, the jargon of Newton versus that of Aristotle." According to Rorty, the way a society talks to itself—through books, through popular films, through schools and universities, through mass media—determines that society's beliefs, its politics, its very culture. Why, after almost a century of legalized apartheid, did the United States start to pass antisegregation laws? It was not the result of the inevitable arc of history, or of white Americans finally living up to their inherently noble character. Rather, it was made possible by decades of political and intellectual work—by organizers and preachers and artists and all sorts of other people, many of them perceived as fringe, who gradually pointed the way toward a better moral vocabulary. And yet the arc could also bend in the other direction. How did Weimar Germany, one of the most progressive societies in modern Europe, descend into barbaric madness? It was possible, in part, because Germans spent a long time treating barbaric madness as inconceivable, and then their sense of what was conceivable began to change.

Rorty argued that a transition from one moral vocabulary to another happens roughly the way a paradigm shift happens in science. Premodern people believed that the sun revolved around the Earth; now everyone, except for a few internet conspiracy theorists, believes the opposite. This shift didn't occur because the sun decided to

---

*Rorty took the title of his book from a sentence by James Baldwin in *The Fire Next Time*: "If we—and now I mean the relatively conscious whites and the relatively conscious blacks, who must, like lovers, insist on, or create, the consciousness of the others—do not falter in our duty now, we may be able, handful that we are, to end the racial nightmare, and achieve our country, and change the history of the world." Baldwin did not overlook the cruelty of bigoted white people; in fact, he wrote, "neither I nor time nor history will ever forgive them." Still, he devoted much of his career to examining the grievances of white bigots—not because he wanted to acquiesce to them, but because he wanted to understand them, if only to anticipate the damage that aggrieved white people could cause. Baldwin did not delude himself that changing the world would be simple, or even likely. But, history being contingent, he believed that it was possible.

intervene in human life, revealing its true nature. Rather, a few scientists learned to speak differently about the world, and then a few more learned to speak that way, and then, eventually, everyone else learned to speak that way, too. "The world does not speak," Rorty wrote. "Only we do." To change how we talk is to change who we are.

• • •

In January 2009, in the days leading up to Obama's first inauguration, an innocent, ecumenical mood came over downtown D.C. Teenagers hastened to help old ladies cross the street. A guy on a crowded Metro played a disco remix of a Stevie Wonder song, loud and distorted, on his phone; instead of glaring at him, people started dancing. No one seriously believed that one black president would make the United States a postracial country. We knew that we were playacting, that the moment would pass. Both despite and because of this, everyone seemed determined to make the most of it.

The moment passed. In January 2017, people in D.C. wept openly—sitting on benches on the National Mall, standing in line at the Sbarro in Union Station—and the weeping didn't even seem out of place, as if the whole city had been transformed into a hospital waiting room. I was walking down Eighteenth Street, in Adams Morgan, when a motorcade of black town cars approached, blaring their sirens to part the traffic in front of them. "Pence," someone near me averred, citing some insignia on a license plate. We all stopped on the sidewalk to watch. One driver, while pulling his SUV to the side of the road, lowered his windows and played "My President," an unofficial Obama-campaign anthem by Young Jeezy, at full volume, until the last town car was out of sight.

It was a Friday night, the first night of the Trump administration. I stopped by a loft apartment where some friends were gathered for a loosely Shabbat-themed potluck dinner. The notion of a dance party was raised a few times, in a hypothetical way, and then dropped. No one felt up to it. At dinner, we piled our plates with salad and lentils and rice and passed around twelve-dollar bottles of red wine and did our best to avoid talking about Trump. This, too, was part of the hospital etiquette. We all knew that the prognosis was daunting at best, catastrophic at worst. Why dwell on it? People made plans to meet up the next morning, at various landmarks at various precise times, for the Women's March. Someone told a joke. Someone else burst into tears. The last thing anyone wanted to talk about was the intrinsic goodness of the American people.

After an hour, I stood up and found my coat. I had to get back to the same cigar bar to meet up with some of the Deplorables.

"Guess we're just not as much fun as the Nazis, huh?" a friend said.

"They're not all Nazis," I said, attempting a feeble, apologetic grin. I understood that we were each operating on some level of irony, but I couldn't tell which level, exactly, or whether mine was the appropriate one. In the cab on the way to the cigar bar, I tried to reassure myself that the work of a journalist was to go out into the world, even into its most uncomfortable and morally squalid corners, and try to disinter a few shards of truth. I thought I believed my own pep talk, but I couldn't be sure. The pentatonic protest melody kept thrumming in my head: *Which side are you on?*

I'd been covering the bad-guys-on-the-internet beat for a few months, and in that time I'd experienced several such encounters with relatives, colleagues, strangers at weddings. Sometimes these encounters verged on subtle interrogations, as if I were a spy suspected of having been turned into a double agent. With friends, it was usually more like a gut check: just making sure that, all jokes aside, we still agreed that these guys were beyond the pale. Not every Trump supporter, but certainly the social media demicelebrities at the forefront of the alt-right and alt-light movements, the ones who sold this swill for a living.

Every time I reassessed how I truly felt about the demicelebrities, I discovered that, in my heart of hearts, I was not at all confused. I found them deplorable. This wasn't a personal assessment—some of them were worse company than others, but I have a relatively high tolerance for intolerable people. Nor was it a political assessment, really; like Trump, the Deplorables were not fundamentally political figures. They were metamedia insurgents. Some were web-savvy bigots; some were soft-brained conspiracists; some were mere grifters or opportunists. Their opinions about specific matters of policy were almost beside the point. Of course, reasonable people can and should disagree in good faith, both about mundane issues (tort reform) and incendiary ones (immigration, abortion). But anybody who was paying attention could see that the leaders of the Deplorable movement were not good-faith interlocutors. They didn't care to be.*

---

*Many of their opinions were ephemeral and weakly held, subject to change based on rhetorical expediency. When they did make a consistent policy demand (e.g., "Build the wall"), it was often in service of such a reprehensible ulterior motive (e.g., white nationalism, or "Western chauvinism") that it couldn't be taken at face value. Even more strangely, many of them claimed to support such policies as student debt relief and universal health care—proposals that were more aligned with democratic socialism than with any recognizable form of conservatism.

Throughout the 2016 election, the mainstream media continued to lavish attention on the group they insisted on calling the alt-right, but they never found a way to cover the group with real nuance and moral clarity. They tended to describe it as a political movement, albeit one situated on the outer edge of the Overton window. *Picture the most conservative American voting bloc you can think of; then keep going, a step even further to the right. That's where you'll find the alt-right.*

This was a category error.* The metaphor of the window is a metaphor of connection: to be anywhere within it, even near its far-right edge, is to be granted a kind of legitimacy, to be in dialogue with everyone else. The Deplorables weren't interested in dialogue. They were fine with being described as controversial, even dangerous, so long as they were placed somewhere within the bounds of recognized political opinion. Their long-term goal was to shift the Overton window, or to smash it and rebuild it in their image.

•　•　•

After another long night at the cigar bar, around the time my eyes started to sting and the Deplorables grew too intoxicated to be useful, I took a Lyft back to Shaw, a D.C. neighborhood named for a Civil War colonel from an abolitionist family. Two of my closest friends, married lawyers who were expecting their first child, had opened their small rowhouse to a dozen visitors. I expected everyone to be asleep, but I'd forgotten to account for the hospital vibe, which had warped time into an irrelevant abstraction. The kitchen was warm and brightly lit; a Spotify algorithm was DJing via Sonos; almost every inch of floor space was occupied by an air mattress or a human body. "You smell like hipster fascism," one of the hosts said, handing me a whiskey and a slice of babka.

Everyone was making picket signs for the next day's march—squinting over glossy expanses of posterboard, sliding permanent markers across the floor to one another, trying to decide which tone their slogans should strike. Snide? Hortatory? What was the point of a protest again? RESIST BIGLY, one sign read. DONALD, YOU ARE IN WAY OVER YOUR HEAD! read another. I couldn't stay for the march—

---

*Journalism has both descriptive and normative functions, and they sometimes conflict. Descriptively, it wasn't always wrong to refer to a particular Deplorable as, say, a "far-right provocateur." Normatively, it often would have been better to put the term in more context, or to talk about the Deplorables as dangerously, untenably racist, or to avoid talking about them at all.

I had to leave town for more reporting, and it was almost time to check in for my early-morning flight—but I made a suggestion. Three letters, followed by an exclamation point: "Sad!"

Some on the left still found it comforting to assume that every Trump supporter was a shiftless rube under a demagogue's spell. The reality I'd seen so far was more unnerving in its complexity. The leaders of the Deplorable movement were deeply wrong on many fundamental questions, both empirical and ethical, but they weren't guileless or stupid. They were deft propagandists who, having recognized that social media was creating an unprecedented power vacuum, had set out to exploit it. As Hillary Clinton often said of the rancor that fueled Trump's campaign, "This is not who we are." The sentiment was nice to hear, but it was wishful thinking. We are not Good. We are not Bad. Our behavior is a product of many contingent factors, not least our cultural vocabulary, and our cultural vocabulary can change.

Movable Type

I n 1476, about two decades after the publication of the Gutenberg Bible, a mer-chant named William Caxton built Britain's first printing press in a house near Westminster Abbey. The following year, he used it to publish a book, one of the first ever mass-printed in English, called *The Dictes and Sayings of the Philoso-phers*. The title was redundant: "dictes" and sayings were the same thing. More-over, "dictes" was a made-up word, part of a clumsily literal rendering of the title *Les Dits Moraux des Philosophes*, the popular French anthology from which Cax-ton's book had been translated. The French anthology was a translation of a Latin anthology, which was a translation of a Spanish anthology, which was a transla-tion of an Arabic anthology, which had been collected from oral tradition and written down in eleventh-century Egypt.

The book was what classicists call a doxography—a list of ancient thinkers and what they said, or what they were said to have said. There were twenty-two chap-ters. Each one opened with a thumbnail biography of a philosopher; this was fol-lowed by a greatest-hits compilation of that philosopher's dictes, presented in no discernible order and without segues or punctuation. The chapter on Socrates in-cluded a brief summary of his life and death, a few descriptive details ("when he spake he wagged his little finger"), and a recitation of his various opinions, including his opinion that philosophy should only be transmitted orally, not through books.

Almost none of the dictes were philosophical in the sense that we now under-stand the term. Rather, they were anecdotes, unjustified opinions, mystical apho-risms ("Thought is the mirror of man, wherein he may behold his beauty and his filth"), alarmist diet tips ("Wine is enemy to the soul, and is like setting fire to fire"), and paeans to a deity who was made to sound blandly, anachronistically Christian. The chapter on Pythagoras began: "Pythagoras said that it is a right blessed and noble thing to serve God." Omitted was the fact that Pythagoras was a pagan who believed in reincarnation and occult numerology. Still, at least

Pythagoras was a real person. Some of the other philosophers memorialized in the *Dictes*, such as Zalquinus and Gac, probably never existed at all.

As it turns out, the book was shot through with fake news. Caxton did not introduce these errors; they were there all along. According to the *Encyclopedia of Arabic Literature*, the original Egyptian anthology, on which all subsequent translations were based, was "highly influential as a source of both information and style" despite the fact that it was "almost entirely inaccurate, and the sayings themselves highly dubious."

Because human beings are vain and prone to self-flattery, the story we often tell about the printing press is a story not of contingency but of linear, teleological progress. It goes like this: before Johannes Gutenberg invented movable type, books were precious objects, handwritten by scribes and available only in Latin. Common people, who couldn't afford books and wouldn't have been able to read them anyway, were left vulnerable to exploitation by powerful gatekeepers—landed elites, oligarchs of both church and state—who could use their monopoly on knowledge to repress the masses. After Gutenberg, books became widely available, setting off a cascade of innovations, including but not limited to the Reformation, the Enlightenment, the steam engine, journalism, modern literature, modern medicine, and modern democracy.

This story isn't entirely wrong, but it leaves out a lot. For one thing, Gutenberg didn't invent movable type—a Chinese artisan named Bi Sheng did, using clay and ash, three and a half centuries before Gutenberg was born. For another, information wants to be free, but so does misinformation. The printing press empowered such religious progressives as Erasmus and John Calvin; it also empowered hucksters, war profiteers, terrorists, and bigots.* Nor did the printing press eliminate the problem of gatekeepers. It merely shifted the problem. The old gatekeepers were princes and priests interposing themselves between the commoners and their God. The new gatekeepers were entrepreneurs like William Caxton, or anyone else who had enough money to gain access to Caxton's technology.

---

*In the fifteenth and sixteenth centuries, as mass printing spread through Germany, so did waves of anti-Semitic violence. Some historians have argued that the former caused, or at least contributed to, the latter. The printing press enabled Martin Luther to distribute his Ninety-five Theses in 1517; it also enabled him, in 1543, to distribute one of his lesser-known works, a pamphlet called *On the Jews and Their Lies*. "I shall give you my sincere advice," Luther wrote. "First, to set fire to their synagogues or schools and to bury and cover with dirt whatever will not burn, so that no man will ever again see a stone or cinder of them." In 1572, Luther's followers sacked the synagogue of Berlin. According to *Antisemitism: An Annotated Bibliography*, "The printing press played an indispensable role in disseminating Luther's antisemitism."

From the beginning, Caxton was ambivalent about his status as a gatekeeper. He seemed uneasy even acknowledging this power, much less deciding what to do with it. In an epilogue to *The Dictes and Sayings of the Philosophers*, Caxton wrote a behind-the-scenes account of how his edition of the book had come into existence. First, he hired a translator to render the French anthology into English. When the translation was done, Caxton read the manuscript and "found nothing discordant therein"—well, except for one thing. "In the dictes and sayings of Socrates," he wrote, the translator "hath left out certain and divers conclusions touching women." In the French version, and in all previous versions, the chapter on Socrates had included a sudden digression into petty misogyny—not a philosophical argument or a witty allegory, just a vituperative jag, apropos of nothing. ("Socrates saw a woman sick, of whom he said that the evil dwelleth within the evil. And he saw a young woman that learned to write, of whom he said that men multiplied evil upon evil.") In the English translation, as the translator had delivered it to Caxton, the digression was gone.

Did Socrates actually utter the words in question? Like most classical-era Greeks, he probably was a misogynist—he was also, by most accounts, fine with pederasty and slavery—and yet one would assume that if Socrates did walk around dispensing non-sequitur denunciations of women, he at least found a way to be more eloquent about it. In any case, William Caxton, nearly two thousand years after Socrates' death, had a decision to make. The translator had excised the troublesome passage, but Caxton, as the publisher, had the final say. Should he overrule his translator and restore the original text? Or should he let the censorship stand, implying that even if such insults were acceptable in ancient Athens or medieval Cairo, they were now beyond the pale?

After many sentences of ornate hand-wringing, Caxton tried to have it both ways. He decided to translate the misogynist passage into English and reproduce it in full; but instead of restoring it to its original context, in the Socrates chapter, he put it in the middle of his epilogue, as if to quarantine it from the main text.

Then, as soon as he'd announced his decision, he attempted to rationalize it. In the rest of his epilogue, he tried to imply that he wasn't a gatekeeper after all. The choice wasn't really his, he argued. He was merely serving his customers, who deserved to hear all perspectives and make up their own minds. Besides, anyone who was offended should blame Socrates, not Caxton; better yet, a reader who disliked the passage could "with a pen race it out, or else rend the leaf out of the book."

About five centuries later, in the 1960s, the U.S. Department of Defense built the computer network that would evolve into the internet. At first, this technology was so unprecedented that it could only be understood by metaphor: web, page, link, node, matrix. A generation of futurists and TED Talkers emerged, explaining the vast new system to the laity in a spirit of wide-eyed techno-utopianism. They compared the World Wide Web to a superhighway, to a public square, to a marketplace of ideas, to a printing press. Anyone who was spending a lot of time on the internet surely knew that many parts of it felt more like a dingy flea market, or like a parking lot outside a bar the moment before a fight breaks out. The techno-utopians must have been aware of those parts, too, but they didn't mention them very often.*

A few nerdy young men, most of whom accepted the basic tenets of techno-utopianism by default, created early versions of blogging software: LiveJournal, WordPress, Blogger, Movable Type. Soon afterward, another cohort of nerdy young men founded a few fast-growing social networks: MySpace, Reddit, Twitter, Facebook. They didn't pretend to know exactly how social media would be used, and they gave even less thought to how it might be misused. They wanted to "change the world," but they didn't bother specifying that they wanted to change it for the better—that part was implied, and besides, it was supposed to happen more or less automatically.

Even after they started to accrue vast wealth, they kept referring to themselves as disrupters, or hackers. They wielded unprecedented power, but they seemed uneasy acknowledging it, much less deciding what to do with it. They often implied that their amplification of all voices, even the most corrosive, was an inevitable by-product of technological progress. In fact, it was a choice.

———

*There were a few skeptics, too, but they were largely ignored. In 1994, Alan Kay, a renowned forefather of computer programming, spoke at a national conference "about the Information Superhighway and its implications." Most of the attendees—including the keynote speaker, Vice President Al Gore—were techno-utopians. Kay was not. "The new dynamic media we are discussing today will have an immense transforming impact on society similar to that of the printing press," he said. "But much care has to be taken with design and education in order for the change to be positive. We don't have natural defenses against fat, sugar, salt, alcohol, alkaloids—or media." Kay wasn't dismissed as a Luddite or an ignoramus—he couldn't be, given his estimable career as a programmer—but he was treated as a crank, or as a cynic, when in fact he was merely acknowledging contingency. In an email, Kay told me that his only retrospective regret was that he wasn't skeptical enough. "None of us were so pessimistic about humanity as to imagine just how blind 20th-century citizens in a so-called civilization could be," Kay wrote. "The last 25 years have revealed much more about the problems of being human."

In early 2012, Facebook announced its intention to become a public company. On page 67 of an SEC filing, right after sections about inflation risk and interest-rate sensitivity, was an open letter signed by Zuckerberg, Facebook's twenty-seven-year-old CEO, soon to become its majority stockholder. "At Facebook, we're inspired by technologies that have revolutionized how people spread and consume information," he wrote. The letter claimed that Zuckerberg and his employees were wont to stand around their open-plan office, chatting about their eagerness to democratize global discourse. "We often talk about inventions like the printing press and the television—by simply making communication more efficient, they led to a complete transformation of many important parts of society," he wrote. "They encouraged progress. They changed the way society was organized. They brought us closer together." This story wasn't entirely wrong, but it left out a lot.

On the day Facebook went public, Zuckerberg's personal fortune increased by more than $8 billion. Still, he kept up a strict semiotic regimen that downplayed his power. He worked at a bullpen desk, alongside a few of his two thousand employees, in the company's headquarters in Menlo Park (vanity address: 1 Hacker Way). He wore a daily uniform of a gray T-shirt and jeans. (The T-shirts cost about three hundred dollars each, but he didn't publicize that fact.)

It was a boom time for techno-libertarianism. Barack Obama, whose political ascent had been facilitated by an online groundswell, often spoke in a tone of optimism, even utopianism, about the salubrious effects of social media. "In the twenty-first century, information is power," he said in a 2011 speech on Middle East policy. "The truth cannot be hidden." Social media entrepreneurs, eager to be perceived as dispassionate and democratic, pledged to keep their platforms "content neutral." If they thought of themselves as gatekeepers at all, they seemed to take for granted that the gates ought to be thrown wide open. Twitter's executives often referred to their company as "the free-speech wing of the free-speech party." This all seemed, at first glance, like an unambiguous victory for freedom, and who didn't love freedom?

And yet, the more closely you looked, the less obvious it all seemed. The First Amendment applied only to the government, not to private businesses. Instead of citing the First Amendment itself, then, social media companies invoked fealty to analogous "free-speech principles." Which principles, exactly? For centuries, the meaning of free speech had been refined and reinterpreted in universities, in legislatures, in the courts, in the press.* In Silicon Valley, however, weighty decisions about free speech might be made in the course of an afternoon, in a cramped conference room full of complimentary bottles of seltzer and kombucha, by a small team of harried computer engineers. Often, they had no long-term plan other than hacking together a "minimum viable product," "shipping" their code as quickly as possible, and then "iterating"—all start-up euphemisms, essentially, for trial and error.

The disrupters had gleaned, through cultural osmosis, that free speech was a value worth protecting. Beyond that, they weren't expected to spend much time thinking through the underlying principles. Instead, they released their products into the world and then waited to see what would happen. In their most optimistic moments, they could convince themselves, and sometimes everyone else, that the internet had finally eliminated the problem of gatekeepers. But it had only shifted the problem.

At a public event in Rome in 2016, a few hours after a private audience with the pope, Zuckerberg was asked whether he saw himself as an editor. "No," he said, tittering uncomfortably. "We're a technology company, not a media company. . . . We build tools. We do not produce content." In other public settings, he tested out slight variations on this argument. Sometimes he tried to absolve himself of decision-making power; sometimes he acknowledged his power, but framed his actions as compulsory, or inherently noble, implying that the freedom to share opinions online was akin to a human right. Sometimes he deployed several dodges, one after another, in the tradition of William Caxton: information wants to be free; besides, people who take offense at what they've read should blame the author, not the messenger; anyway, the ultimate responsibility lies with each individual reader.

Zuckerberg repeatedly insisted that Facebook was a platform, not a publisher. If some disgruntled teenager wanted to quote Socrates' vituperative opinions about women—or if, for that matter, a teenager wanted to share his own vituperative opinions—then who was Zuckerberg to stand in the way? He might not personally endorse every view expressed on his platform, but he believed in giving power to the people.

---

*James Mill, a so-called philosophical radical writing in early-nineteenth-century England, argued that the first priority should be universal suffrage; once society became more truly democratic, he hoped, freedom of speech would take care of itself. His son, John Stuart Mill, dissented sharply from this view, arguing that freedom of speech was of paramount importance, and that it required protection from the tyranny of the majority. Subsequent generations of political theorists found flaws in both Mills' arguments, or discarded them in search of a new set of free-speech principles. And still, after all that debate, to call the question unsettled would be an understatement.

Each individual social media feed became a unique and unpredictable blend of fact, satire, rumor, propaganda, alarmist diet tips, and advertainment. There were not enough Caxtons to go around. For every vile or propagandistic post that got weeded out, a hundred others bloomed. In the United States, the disruptive effects of social media coincided with a period of stark economic inequality, cultural unrest, and rapid demographic change. In 2013, for the first time in American history, a majority of infants in the country were nonwhite, a fact that many white Americans perceived, consciously or unconsciously, as a threat. This was the kind of topic that was difficult to discuss productively even under ideal conversational conditions. The conditions on social media, to put it mildly, were far from ideal.

Still, the new internet platforms continued to flourish, empowering both pro-social and antisocial voices. One essay on *Return of Kings*, a well-known "neomasculinist" blog, cited Plato, Aquinas, and Aristotle. The headline was "Mate, Hate is Great! A Philosophical Defense of Misogyny."* Another blogger, writing under the pseudonym Quintus Curtius, envisaged "a future where classical knowledge will be driven underground . . . as not being in tune with modern feminism and political correctness." He warned his readers that "the commissars of modern culture don't want you to know too much about history, or about how things were like in previous eras." When he wrote these words, in 2014, the most powerful informational gatekeepers in the country included some of its biggest tech companies: Amazon, Twitter, Facebook, and Google. And yet Quintus's dystopian reverie was published on a proudly misogynist blog that enjoyed a verified Twitter account, a popular YouTube channel, a podcast on iTunes, and a prominent position in Google's search ranking. His self-published book of "essays on life, wisdom, and masculinity" was selling briskly on Amazon. The "commissars of modern culture" were not censoring Quintus's noxious brand of male supremacy. If anything, they were promoting it.

---

*I first learned about this essay in *Not All Dead White Men*, a lucid account of how internet misogynists use and misuse the Greek and Roman canon. The book is by Donna Zuckerberg, a classicist based in Silicon Valley. She told me, "As a scholar, you have a mixed reaction when you see people online saying things like, 'Ovid was the first pickup artist.' In one sense, you go, Sure, that seems accurate, narrowly speaking. In another sense, you feel like saying, 'Are you sure you are understanding the *Ars Amatoria* in its full context?'" She edits an online classics journal, *Eidolon*, which is published on the blogging platform Medium; the misogynist discourse she analyzes also takes place online, on message boards and subreddits devoted to "men's rights." "When a discussion in one of those places goes way off the rails," she continued, "I'm often left wondering: How much of this is a design problem? How much has to do with the way the discussion is structured, verbally and visually, on the platform? How might this conversation be more productive in a classroom or another real-life space?" She acknowledged that this concern was "ironic, I guess, or at least notable, given who my brother is." She trailed off, then asked to speak off the record. Her brother's first name is Mark, and he is the founder and CEO of Facebook.

PART TWO

A Human Superpower

The internet is almost the perfect distillation of the American capitalist ethos, a flood of seductive choices. . . . I can't think of a better summing up of what America's strengths and weaknesses are right now.

David Foster Wallace, 2000

CHAPTER FIVE

The Gleaming Vehicle

In April 2014, looking for new story ideas, I attended a tech conference in a stylish hotel in Lower Manhattan. The conference was called F.ounders, a word that no one, including the founders of F.ounders, could decide how to pronounce. Half of us stammered over the stray period. The other half ignored it. It stood for nothing, apparently, except for the general concept of innovation.

I arrived just in time for cocktail hour, which was being held in a well-appointed room with sweeping sunset views of the lower Hudson. An organizer handed me a complimentary tote bag, a laminated badge bearing my name and job title, and a little black book—one of the few paper facebooks I'd seen since the advent of Facebook—containing the headshot and bio of every entrepreneur, engineer, and venture capitalist in attendance. I flipped through it, looking for names I recognized.

One was Eli Pariser, an activist turned entrepreneur. Pariser was the former director of MoveOn.org, a left-wing nonprofit specializing in online organizing. More recently, he'd written *The Filter Bubble*, a book demonstrating that as huge tech companies grew huger, they were fracturing the Internet into millions of bespoke internets. The more personal data they had about you, Pariser warned, the better their algorithms would get at showing you links you'd feel compelled to click on. This was called microtargeting. To the tech companies—and to advertisers, propagandists, or anyone else with a message to spread—this seemed like a win-win. But for American democracy, Pariser argued, the consequences could be dire. "Most personalized filters have no way of prioritizing what really matters but gets fewer clicks," he wrote. "In the end, 'Give the people what they want' is a brittle and shallow civic philosophy."

At the time, Google owned almost 40 percent of the online advertising market, and Facebook owned another 10 percent. Some analysts were already warning that they might comprise a duopoly. Both companies' business models, especially Facebook's, were built around microtargeting. Filter bubbles, in other words, were not a temporary bug but a central feature of social media. It was hard to see how the latter could flourish without the former. If filter bubbles were bad for democracy, then, were Google and Facebook also bad for democracy?

It was a fair question, almost an obvious one, and yet the cultural vocabulary of the time did not allow most people to hold it in their heads for long. Pariser's book was published in 2011, the year of the Arab Spring—which was organized, in part, via social media, and which was often called the Twitter Revolution. Mark Zuckerberg had just been named *Time*'s Person of the Year; in the hagiographic cover photo, his eyes were oceanic and farseeing, dreaming up ingenious new ways to forge human bonds. If some movies and books portrayed him as shifty, even a bit ruthless, it was still possible to imagine that ruthlessness, in the tradition of Thomas Edison or Steve Jobs, was merely the cost of doing business.* Zuckerberg's motto, "Move Fast and Break Things," was generally treated as a sign of youthful insouciance, not of galling rapacity. Facebook's users—more than a billion of them—seemed happy. Its investors were delighted. If social media wasn't a good product, then why was it so successful?

At the time, it was still considered divisive (at swanky New York tech conferences, anyway) to wonder whether the behoodied young innovators of Silicon Valley might turn out to be robber barons. It was far more socially acceptable to extol the gleaming vehicle of technology—to gaze in amoral awe at its speed and vigor—than to ask precisely where it was headed, or whether it might one day hurtle off a cliff.† Such questions had come to seem fusty and antidemocratic; people who spent too much time worrying about them were often dismissed as

---

*"Understanding who you serve is always a very important problem, and it only gets harder the more people that you serve," Zuckerberg told *The New York Times* in 2014. Either this phrasing reminded nobody of "To Serve Man," the dystopian *Twilight Zone* episode, or nobody saw fit to mention it.
†There were some skeptics, of course. The heady utopianism of the Tahrir Square uprising in Cairo soon gave way to the despotic rule of the Muslim Brotherhood, and then to a military coup; Tunisia, the birthplace of the Arab Spring, became a breeding ground for ISIS; human-rights activists began to ask whether the Twitter Revolution had moved fast and broken the Middle East. "By allowing protesters to scale up quickly, without years of preparation, digital infrastructure acts as a scaffold to movements that mask other weaknesses," the sociologist Zeynep Tufekci argued in the *Journal of International Affairs* in 2014. The same year, in a report called "Reflections on the Arab Uprisings," Marc Lynch, a political scientist at George Washington University, wrote, "The new Arab media and social media proved to be just as capable of transmitting negative and divisive ideas and images as they had been at spreading revolutionary ones." These warnings were incisive, but they were not widely heeded.

cranks or Luddites. To a techno-optimist, there was only one way the vehicle could possibly be going: forward.

So, in Silicon Valley and in much of the national press, *The Filter Bubble* was taken as mild, constructive criticism.* Pariser was treated not as a lone protester staring down a phalanx of tanks but as a decorous bystander asking the tank commanders to turn their wheels a few degrees to the left. Some of the new gatekeepers denied the existence of filter bubbles; others acknowledged the problem, privately or even publicly, but seemed either unwilling or unable to do much about it. In the meantime, Pariser reasoned, if he couldn't change the way the content on social media was filtered, maybe he could change the content itself. So, the year after his book came out, Pariser went into the content-aggregation business. He cofounded *Upworthy*, a company whose posts were designed to go viral on Facebook.

It wasn't news to anyone at F.ounders that the traditional news industry was collapsing. Some of the fine points were debatable, but the contours of the recent history were clear enough. First, around the turn of the century, came the transition from print to web. Instead of buying a newspaper at a physical kiosk, now you could browse an infinite online kiosk for free. Instead of paying to run a classified ad, you could post one, in seconds, on Craigslist. The internet had released a cascade of information: countless international wire services, ancient scriptures, legal libraries, and anime message boards, all available instantaneously. For newspaper publishers, this was a devastating threat to their business models. But for many readers, although the web made their lives more convenient, it didn't change their reading habits very much. If you were used to scanning the front page of *The Denver Post* every morning, you could now scan the *Post*'s home page instead.

By 2014, the industry was in the midst of a more profound shift: the transition from the open web to the social web. You could still start your day by going straight to denverpost.com, but, statistically speaking, nobody did that anymore. Now you went to Facebook or Google or Reddit or Twitter, where all the world's information sources—*The Denver Post*, *The Denver Guardian*, your ex-pastor,

---

*"It was always positioned as an interesting intellectual question but not something that we're going to go focus on," a Facebook employee later told *The New York Times*.

your estranged aunt, Alex Jones, Van Jones, Geico, a twelve-year-old influencer from Norway—clamored for your attention within a single stream. In the TV era, gatekeepers had controlled the flow of information, but at least the consumer could always change the channel. In the Facebook era, the browsing experience felt so passive, so close to nonvolitional, that the standard metaphor was no longer consumption but viral infection.

Denver Post reporters knew how to cover a mayoral race or a Rockies game. Most of them didn't know, and didn't care to learn, how to promote their articles on social media. *Upworthy*, by contrast, was built around the dual goals of "click-ability" and "sharability." It was still true, as Pariser had pointed out in his book, that social media algorithms had "no way of prioritizing what really matters." But now, instead of advocating for the algorithms to be fixed, he hoped to adapt to them, manipulating Facebook's insentient censors into letting a few chosen links go viral.

At the time, *Upworthy* didn't create any content. Instead, it scoured the web for short videos about hope and human triumph, then repackaged those videos with catchier headlines, more tantalizing thumbnail images, and the like. Each change was intended to make a post slightly more clickable and sharable, the way each tweak to a race car's body made it a bit more aerodynamic. Old-school journalists were trained to spend most of their time thinking about reporting, writing, and fact-checking; the headline was generally an afterthought. *Upworthy*, responding rationally to the upside-down incentives of the social web, outsourced content production entirely and focused instead on headline writing. At least twenty-five headlines would be generated for each post; a few rival headlines would then be tested against one another, algorithmically, to determine which was best. (It went without saying that "best" was synonymous with "most popular.")*

By the spring of 2014, *Upworthy* and its many imitators had developed a formula for making headlines as clickable as possible. The headlines often conveyed just enough information to be enticing but not quite satisfying, leaving a "curios-

---

*In 2012, *Upworthy* employees were invited to a conference to deliver a talk about (what else?) how to achieve virality. One of their slides, labeled *"Upworthy*'s Editorial Process," featured a stock photo of a toilet, followed by an eight-step headline-writing process. Step 1: "You HAVE to crap out 25 headlines for every piece of content." Step 2: "You WILL write some really stinky headlines." Step 3: "Once you start getting desperate, you start thinking outside the box." Step 3 was confusing—according to the logic of the metaphor, it seemed like an entreaty not to shit on the floor—but, as it turned out, "thinking outside the box" was actually encouraged. "#24 will suck," the slide continued. "Then #25 will be a gift from the headline gods and will make you a legend."

ity gap." A Facebook user scrolling through her feed could only satisfy her curiosity by clicking on the link, giving *Upworthy* another pageview. (A Montana slam poet's video about self-love, which she'd posted to YouTube as "Self love poem," became, on *Upworthy*, "She Lied to Herself Every Night for a Year. Here's What Happened When She Was Honest.") This headline style came to be known as clickbait. It was easy to parrot, or to parody; mainstream outlets did both, winking at the phenomenon while profiting from it. *The Onion* launched a spinoff site, *ClickHole*, devoted to satirizing the new genre.* There were also "clickbait spoilers," such as the Twitter account @SavedYouAClick, whose only purpose was to spoil *Upworthy*-style headlines ("Julia Roberts Will Literally Never Have a Bigger Role") by providing the missing information ("The voice of Mother Nature in a commercial"). And yet, despite all this, clickbait worked astoundingly well. A year after it launched, *Upworthy* reported 87 million unique visits a month—more than *The New York Times*.

Curiosity is not the only way to get clicks, of course. Humor also works, as do lust, and nostalgia, and envy, and outrage. There are as many ways to attract a person's attention as there are to bait a mousetrap, and some baits work better than others. "Content that evokes high-arousal emotion is more likely to be shared," two Wharton professors wrote in 2012. "Positive and negative emotions characterized by high arousal (i.e., awe, anxiety, and anger) are positively linked to virality, while emotions characterized by low arousal (i.e., sadness) were negatively linked to virality."

High-arousal emotions are also called activating emotions. They are emotions that lead to measurable behaviors—in this case, clicking or liking or sharing a link—as opposed to deactivating emotions, which are more likely to induce torpor or paralysis. In real life, of course, both kinds of emotion have their place. When a well-adjusted person faces a setback—say, a death in the family—a deactivating emotion is often the only appropriate response. On the viral internet, however, deactivating emotions are merely market inefficiencies. From the standpoint of sheer entrepreneurial competition, what matters is not whether a piece of online

---

*One *ClickHole* post in particular served to illustrate just how thoroughly the science of clickable headline writing had been decoupled from the art of writing. The post ran under this headline: "The Time I Spent on a Commercial Whaling Ship Totally Changed My Perspective on the World." The body of the post was the entire text of *Moby-Dick*.

content is true or false, responsible or reckless, prosocial or antisocial. All that matters is how many activating emotions it can provoke.*

As the prevailing style of social media clickbait mutated, Facebook would occasionally announce new tweaks to its News Feed algorithm, promising to disseminate "more high-quality content," or to show its users "stories that are important to them." But Facebook's larger goal, which always went unstated, was not to spread high-quality content; it was to entice more users into spending more time on Facebook.

•   •   •

Continuing to scan my conference facebook alphabetically, the next name I recognized was Jonah Peretti. As an undergraduate, Peretti had written a paper called "Capitalism and Schizophrenia: Contemporary Visual Culture and the Acceleration of Identity Formation/Dissolution." Using the clotted jargon of "Lacanian and post-Lacanian psychoanalytic theory," the paper decried the advertising industry for exacerbating "the accelerating rhythm of late capitalism."

Ten years later, Peretti further accelerated the rhythm of late capitalism by founding *BuzzFeed*, a media company that combined advertising, entertainment, and journalism in novel and sometimes unscrupulous ways. *BuzzFeed* went on to earn billions of dollars in revenue, mostly by producing branded content targeted to millennials. Peretti, like Pariser, designed his site with virality centrally in mind. At the top of each *BuzzFeed* post were one or more "badges" (Cute, Ew, LOL, OMG), each corresponding to a different activating emotion. The goal of the content was to elicit a response—a share, a like, a hate-read, an indignant comment. Any response was a form of engagement, and engagement was the lifeblood of the viral internet.

BuzzFeed's headline style, like *Upworthy*'s, was both mockable and highly effective. *BuzzFeed* did produce its own material, although much of it was native advertising—ads disguised as editorial content. The site's signature form was the listicle ("10 Jokes That Prove Bathroom Humor Never Gets Old," sponsored by Charmin). *BuzzFeed*'s headline writers, hoping to make their content ever more

---

*Three MIT computer scientists, writing in *Science* in 2018, found that false rumors on Facebook evoked more high-arousal emotions than the actual news, which was more likely to inspire such deactivating emotions as malaise and confusion. This was one of the explanations for the paper's main finding: that fake news is consistently more likely to go viral than the truth.

"sticky" and "infectious," pioneered several ingenious audience-targeting strategies, including a kind of promiscuous narrowcasting. "24 Problems Anyone Can Relate To" would have had no natural constituency, but "24 Problems You'll Only Understand If You're Welsh" stood a good chance of going viral within Wales. And, publishing space on the internet being unlimited, there was no reason to stop at Wales; you could also publish "27 Devastating Problems Only People from Jersey Will Understand" and "29 Things Only People Who Work in Public Radio Will Understand" and "20 Things Only People with Glasses Will Understand."*

A month before F.ounders, Peretti wrote a memo to his staff, hailing *BuzzFeed*'s staggering rate of growth. He noted, correctly, that social media had made information delivery more democratic.† But now that he was writing from the perspective of a capitalist and a techno-optimist, he failed to mention that social media had also accelerated the rhythm of daily life, making it more chaotic and bewildering. Suddenly, every piece of content—every article, every listicle, every image, every ad—seemed like just another piece of flotsam in a congested stream, one more distraction to wade past before finally succumbing to exhaustion and clicking on the headline about what happened to the poet when she was honest. (Spoiler: she learned to love herself.)

I closed my facebook and dropped it back inside the tote bag. The most basic tasks of a traditional news editor—such as deciding which stories to feature prominently, which ones to downplay, and which ones to forgo entirely—rested on the assumption that not all news was fit to print. This assumption, in turn, rested on a usefully vague definition of fitness, one that could account for many factors: salability and sensationalism and greed, to be sure, but also some version of the public interest. Now that editors no longer had a monopoly on informational gatekeeping—now that this power was passing, more and more, from humans to algorithms—fitness was coming to mean something more stark and Darwinian.‡ High-arousal posts beat low-arousal posts; the fittest content proliferated, and everything else was driven toward extinction. I found the whole situation discomfiting,

---

*All real examples.
†"The *BuzzFeed* of today, thanks to these massive technological and demographic trends, reaches more people than the combined circulation of the 1950s versions of *Time*, *Life*, the New York *Times*, and the Washington *Post*. It is very hard to beat the scale of the social, mobile web!"
‡"I have called this principle, by which each slight variation, if useful, is preserved, by the term Natural Selection," Darwin wrote in the fifth edition of *On the Origin of Species*. "But the expression often used by Mr. Herbert Spencer of the Survival of the Fittest is more accurate, and is sometimes equally convenient."

but I couldn't even fully articulate the problem, much less think of a solution. Maybe one of the f.ounders could help.

I wedged into the crowd shoulderfirst, accepted a glass of sparkling water and a small plate of shrimp dumplings, and looked for someone to talk to. I scanned the laminated badges on various clavicles, doing my best to parse the refrigerator-magnet start-up names (Struq, SHFT, PubNub) and predictably wacky job titles (iOS Ninja, Hacker-in-Residence). Each conversation began with a gentle Socratic inquiry by which I tried to arrive, after a few wrong turns, at an understanding of what a futurist or a hacker-in-residence did all day. In most cases, the answer amounted to buying or selling ads on Google or Facebook.

It soon became clear that this crowd did not contain the likes of Peretti and Pariser. They might have been taking preprandial power meetings or power naps; possibly they were on an even higher floor of the hotel, drinking higher-grade sparkling water. Here in the free-dumpling room, most of us seemed to be journalists, PR flacks, or midlevel office stiffs.

I networked. I don't remember the details of each start-up's burn rate or mobile onboarding flow; what I remember, above all, is the prevailing absence of self-deprecation. At other industry events I'd covered—a record-label party, a gala for a nonprofit—the midlevel Bartleby types exuded a whiff of humility, even if it was false humility. At F.ounders, everyone seemed to have internalized the promises that kept the young and avaricious flocking to Silicon Valley: *You can do well by doing good. You are building the tools of human connection and social progress. All incentives are aligned.* Two months later, when the satirical sitcom *Silicon Valley* included a montage of start-up founders pledging to "make the world a better place through Paxos algorithms for consensus protocols," I felt a twinge of déjà vu.

For the first few years of his career, Philip Roth's books were wild yawps of rebellion—against his Jewishness, against the puritanical norms of northern New Jersey, against various forms of fatuous bullshit. But Roth also wrote, in 1986, "I'm never more of a Jew than I am in a church when the organ begins." This was what it felt like to be a reluctant institutionalist. I was not so loyal to traditional media institutions that I failed to see their faults; but then the choir of digital evangelists would start to sing their hosannas, and I would get my back up. I didn't know what a "more open and connected" internet would mean for the world. Neither did the disrupters, or anyone else. If I'd had faith in the predestined arc of history—if I'd trusted that the gleaming vehicle of technology would naturally self-correct, like a driverless car, even with the rest of us asleep at the wheel—then I might have been more content to watch as the car rushed forth, crashing through every gate in its path. But what I believed was both more liberating and more terrifying: technology, like the arc of history, can carry us in any direction.

CHAPTER SIX

Viral Guy

At dinner, the seating algorithm placed me next to Emerson Spartz, a twenty-seven-year-old with the saucer eyes and cuspidate chin of a cartoon fawn. According to the little black facebook, he was a "middle-school dropout," a "*New York Times* bestselling author," and the founder and CEO of Spartz Inc. based in Chicago.

I asked what his company made, or did, or was. "I'm passionate about virality," he responded. I must have looked confused, because he said, "Let me bring that down from the thirty-thousand-foot level." The appetizer course had not yet arrived. He checked the time on his cell phone, then cleared his throat.

"Every day, when I was a kid, my parents made me read four short biographies of very successful people," he said. "I decided that I wanted to change the world, and I wanted to do it on a massive scale." This was the beginning of what I would come to recognize as his standard pitch for Spartz, both the person and the company. Although he had an audience of one, he spoke in a distant and deliberate tone, using studied pauses and facial expressions, as if I were a conference hall or a camera lens.

"I looked at patterns," he said. "I realized that if you could make ideas go viral, you could tip elections, start movements, revolutionize industries." He told me that Spartz Inc. specialized in "fun stuff—entertainment, not hard news." He called it a media company, but it sounded more like an aggregator and distributor of preexisting content. "The ability to spread a meme to millions of people," he continued, was "the closest you can come to a human superpower."

The concept of the meme was invented in 1976 by Richard Dawkins, an evolutionary biologist at Oxford. In his book *The Selfish Gene*, Dawkins argued that genes are "the fundamental unit" of natural selection, and that they exist to per-petuate themselves, not to perpetuate any organism or species. In one chapter, he wondered whether something analogous to natural selection might also occur in human culture—whether "tunes, ideas, catch-phrases, clothes fashions," might evolve the way plants and animals do. If so, this evolution would take place by means of a "unit of cultural transmission," which Dawkins called the meme. "Just as genes propagate themselves in the gene pool by leaping from body to body via sperms or eggs," he wrote, "so memes propagate themselves in the meme pool by leaping from brain to brain."* The survival of a meme, like the survival of a spe-cies, was not assured by some predetermined plan; it depended, quite simply, on the meme's ability to self-replicate.

As the decades passed, the "leaping from brain to brain" became exponen-tially more scalable. In an endnote to the 1989 edition of *The Selfish Gene*, Dawkins wrote, "Computers are increasingly tied together. Many of them are literally wired up together in electronic mail exchange.... It is a perfect milieu for self-replicating programs to flourish." He was talking about computer viruses. He couldn't have predicted *BuzzFeed*, or *ClickHole*, or Pepe, or Pizzagate.

As far as I could tell, Emerson Spartz wasn't using his memetic superpower either for good or for evil, exactly. He was using it mainly to monetize cat GIFs. He told me that his company oversaw about thirty active sites, each serving up procrasti-nation fodder for adolescents of all ages: Memestache ("All the Funny Memes"), OMGFacts ("The World's #1 Fact Source"),† GivesMeHope (*Chicken Soup for the Soul*—the twenty-first-century, Twitter-style version").‡ The content was mostly user generated and unvetted, and it just kept rolling in.

Spartz's self-pitch normally lasted about fifteen minutes, but this took much longer, because I kept interrupting. I wasn't trying to berate the guy; I was trying

---

*N. K. Humphrey, an evolutionary psychologist at the University of Cambridge, took the idea a step further: "When you plant a fertile meme in my mind, you literally parasitize my brain, turning it into a vehicle for the meme's propagation in just the way that a virus may parasitize the genetic mechanism of a host cell."

†When I visited OMGFacts.com the next day, one of the most popular "facts" on the site was "Nicholas Cage natural odor is similar to the sweat of a homeless man!" [sic]. The source for this was a tabloid article, then ten years old, about a porn star who'd once dated Cage.

‡Some of these user-generated aphorisms were later compiled in a small book called *Gives Me Hope: The 127 Most Inspiring Bite-Sized Stories*. This was what Spartz was referring to when he called himself a bestselling author.

to understand his thinking, which seemed emblematic of the style of thinking that pervaded the rest of the room, if not the entire social media industry.

"Viral memes can certainly be powerful," I said. "But what about the ones that don't have much of an effect? Or the ones that change the world for the worse, not for the better?"

Spartz's face went blank. "Can you rephrase your question in a more concrete way?" he said.

I brought up *Kony 2012*, a half-hour documentary about the Ugandan warlord Joseph Kony. "An amazing viral campaign," Spartz said. "That's exactly what I mean, about how sharing memes can lead to real-world positive change." Within a few days of its release on YouTube, *Kony 2012* had been viewed more than 100 million times—an enviable level of popularity even for a Taylor Swift video, much less for a morbid documentary about child soldiers. Its stated goal was to "make Kony famous," and it achieved this goal, at least for a time. And yet the director of the film, Jason Russell, was not an expert on the Gordian geopolitics of East Africa.* His one simplistic demand—that the U.S. military capture or kill Kony— was controversial, to say the least. Moreover, it was never fulfilled. Despite the film's popularity, Kony and his soldiers remained at large—possibly in the remote forests of the Central African Republic, though no one knew for sure. Should all this, I asked Spartz, be considered a success?

He shrugged. "To be honest, I didn't follow too closely after the whole thing died down," he said. "Even though I'm one of the most avid readers I know, I don't usually read straight news. It's conveyed in a very boring way, and you tend to see the same patterns repeated again and again."

Still, he was happy to offer advice. "If I were running a more hard-news-oriented company and I wanted to inform people about Uganda," he said, "first, I would look it up and find out exactly what's going on there. Then I would find a few really poignant images or storylines, ones that create a lot of resonant emotion, and I would make those into a short video—under three minutes—with clear, simple words and statistics. Short, declarative sentences. And at the end I'd give people something they can do. Something to feel hopeful about."

---

*Russell was a former Christian missionary turned anti–child soldier activist. As *Kony 2012* rocketed to popularity, Russell's nonprofit received millions of dollars in donations, most of which he spent on salaries, overhead, and further promotion of the film. At the peak of the campaign's viral success, Russell suffered a mental breakdown, and TMZ released footage of him pacing through downtown San Diego, nude, ranting incoherently. This footage, too, went viral.

I asked Spartz if there was anyone he was hoping to meet while he was in town.

"I'm mostly here to meet potential investors," he said. "I know I'm not supposed to just come out and say that, but it's the truth."

"Anyone you look up to, or want to get advice from?" I asked.

"The only people here who do what I do better than I do it are Eli and Jonah," he said, referring to Pariser and Peretti. "I'd kill to be as good at virality as those guys."

I wasn't sure whether to interpret this as a statement of modesty or of raw ambition. Spartz had recently raised $8 million of venture-capital funding. As new-media companies like *Upworthy* and *BuzzFeed* evolved into established brands, he hoped to disrupt the disrupters. He didn't see the old-media dinosaurs as his competitors—not because he felt unequal to the challenge, but because he assumed that the dinosaurs would soon collapse under their own weight.

The entree was served: conference chicken, a notch above wedding chicken and below gala chicken. Glancing down at my laminated badge for the first time, Spartz noticed that I worked at *The New Yorker*. "For instance, here's how I would improve your product," he said. "Way more images. That's number one. Who has ever looked at a big long block of text and gone, 'Ooh, exciting?' I tell my employees all the time: Every paragraph they write should be super-short, no more than three sentences. And I mean *short* sentences. Periods are better than commas. Boredom is the enemy."

I couldn't deny that this sounded like an effective recipe for a certain kind of success. And yet, I sputtered, if maximizing clicks was the only goal, why would any magazine or newspaper need to employ fact-checkers—or reporters, for that matter? Why not simply recycle press releases, rewriting the boring quotes to make them snappier? Why not replace all Syria coverage with Kardashian coverage? Why not forget about words altogether and go into something more remunerative, like video, or mobile gaming, or strip mining?

Spartz cocked his head and waited for me to finish my rant. Clearly, in his eyes, I was revealing myself to be a Luddite. "It's always possible to make a slippery-slope argument," he said. "Those arguments don't interest me. I'm interested in impact." Art without an audience was mere solipsism, he said. "The ultimate barometer of quality is: if it gets shared, it's quality. If someone wants to toil in obscurity, if that makes them happy, that's fine. Not everybody has to change the world."

Spartz left before dessert, which he called "a low return on investment, calorically." On his way out, in lieu of a business card, he sent me an email. "Hi. Stay in touch!" the subject line read. The entire text of the email was "Viral guy."

• • •

The Tuesday after F.ounders, at *The New Yorker*'s editorial meeting, I told my colleagues about Emerson Spartz. I knew that the internet had a way of making even the most innocuous enterprises seem novel or nefarious, so I did my best to check my biases. There was nothing surprising about an entrepreneur peddling frivolous entertainment. This was, after all, an older and more lucrative business than the one we were in, the artisanal bundling of literary journalism with wry single-panel cartoons. What interested me was not Spartz's content per se but his method of spreading it, which did seem genuinely new.

In the second half of the twentieth century, when the bulk of popular information was spread through TV, a knack for persuasion in one domain (Roger Ailes, Nixon campaign adviser) could be transferred with insidious ease to another (Roger Ailes, CEO of Fox News). In the Facebook era, the boundaries between domains were being blurred out of existence. Facebook is not only one of the world's biggest video platforms; it's also a gaming company, a dating service, a classified section, a photo vault, a newsstand, and a virtual-reality film studio. Content is content is content, all commingling in a single stream.

A quote on the front page of *The Washington Post* is more likely to be accurate than a quote on Page Six of the *New York Post*, or a quote in your ex-pastor's Facebook post. A fact in the *Harper's* Index is more likely to be true than a fact on OMGFacts. Moreover, some journalism aims to transcend mere trustworthiness, taking on the rarefied status of art. Traditional journalists noticed these distinctions, but the data showed that many consumers did not. Social networks weren't helping; on the contrary, their designers downplayed such distinctions, in the interest of content neutrality.*

Many writers and filmmakers and photographers felt that their work had nothing to do with the content churned out by sites like Spartz's. In some meta-

---

*When your friend posted a link on Facebook, the interface made it look like all other links, no matter whether it came from nytimes.com or ntyimes.com or thenewyorktimessucks.wordpress.com. To see where the content originated, you had to squint until you found a line of text at the bottom of the post—tiny, light gray, and easily ignorable.

physical sense, they were right. In terms of pure memetic Darwinism, though, the Facebook era had thrust *The New Yorker* and Spartz Inc. into the same ecosystem, if not into direct interspecific competition. The content on Facebook was as varied as the human imagination, yet all of it was propagated in the same way: by getting people to click and share links. Spartz's pitch was that he could make users feel enough activating emotion that they would be likely to share the links he wanted them to share. In other words, his line about virality being a superpower was cheesy self-promotion, but it was also basically true. He was using this super-power to sell mildly amusing memes, but he could just as easily use it, in the future, to sell pasta or porn or populism. It wasn't even a transferable skill; it was the same skill.

"The guy who started this company—how old is he again?" a story editor asked.

"Twenty-seven."

"Jesus. I can't tell whether I want to smack him or hire him."

David Remnick, the editor of the magazine, sighed theatrically. "I love the Youngs, I really do," he said. "But you guys are going to destroy everything, aren't you?"

•   •   •

I flew to Chicago in late May, met Spartz outside his downtown office, and walked across the Loop with him to another tech conference. He'd been invited to give a speech. "A lot of it is going to be redundant for you," he said. The event, at the Museum of Contemporary Art, was called the Millennial Impact Conference, and participants had been asked to discuss how young people could "build move-ments to create change." This was not Spartz's specialty. "I basically have only one speech," he told me. "It's about how to make things go viral. I have personal pref-erences about how I would want those principles to be applied,* but in practice they can be used for pretty much anything."

We ran into Jimmy Odom, a thirty-three-year-old businessman with shoulder-length dreadlocks. In the relatively small pond of Chicago's start-up scene, Spartz was a big fish, and Odom took the opportunity to ask him a few specific questions

---

*His personal preferences seemed to be those of the average twentysomething Chicagoan—socially tolerant, fond of sports and beer and burgers, and so on—but he was vague about his politics.

about business strategy. Then, turning to me, he described Spartz as "inspiring" and "legitimately awesome."

"Why won't you accept my friend request?" Odom asked him.

"I literally can't even see it," Spartz said, grinning apologetically. "Facebook puts a cap on how many friends you can have"—five thousand—"and I'm at the limit."

Spartz was young, but he'd already been in the virality business for more than half his life. In 1999, when he was twelve, he built MuggleNet, which became the most popular Harry Potter fan site in the world. He appeared on CNN and Fox News, and J. K. Rowling invited him to her palatial estate in Scotland. He eventually outgrew Rowling—when I asked whether he'd read *The Casual Vacancy*, Rowling's post-Potter adult novel, he rolled his eyes—but he remained fixated on the increasingly competitive goal of commanding young people's attention online. "As I became less motivated by my passion for the books, I got obsessed with the entrepreneurial side of it, the game of maximizing patterns and seeing how big my reach could get," he said.

Web development is a low-overhead enterprise, especially when you live with your parents. MuggleNet made hundreds of thousands of dollars, and Spartz funneled his earnings into Spartz Inc. building a new site every few weeks. When internet culture became fascinated with "fails"—news bloopers, embarrassing autocorrects—he built sites like As Failed on TV and SmartphOWNED. When the data showed that heartwarming stories were starting to draw more visitors, he let his old sites languish and built GivesMeHope, a repository for uplifting anecdotes (all anonymous and unverified). Eventually, most of these sites stopped attracting many new visitors. The sites stayed online, but dormant—crammed with dead links and still-active ads—like junk satellites orbiting the Earth.

Spartz took the stage, wearing a cordless microphone in addition to his daily uniform (heathered T-shirt, dark jeans, tidy mop top). A screen behind him displayed his first slide, in jaunty type: "Hi! I'm Emerson Spartz. I want to change the world."

When he was growing up, Spartz said, his parents made him read "four short biographies of successful people every single day. Imagine for a second what happens to your brain when you're twelve and this is how you're spending your time." He used his hands to pantomime his mind being blown. "The ability to make things go viral felt like the closest that we could get to having a human super-power."

He offered practical tips: "Use lists whenever possible. Lists just hijack the brain's neural circuitry"; "Facebook is the viral home of the internet. Facebook should be eighty percent of your effort, if you're focused on social media."* Behind me, two women in their fifties took notes on legal pads. In summary, Spartz said, "The more awesome you are, the more emotion you create, the more viral it is." One of the women whispered, "Really impressive."

I met Spartz in the greenroom. "I'm giving advice that works, but it's no prob-lem for me to give it away," he said. "This stuff is so basic, if you don't already know it, you're way too far behind to catch up." He took off the cordless mic and left without stopping to see the exhibition upstairs, a retrospective by the contempo-rary "post-medium" artist Isa Genzken. "People have hoity-toity reasons for pre-ferring one kind of entertainment to another," he said later. "To me, it doesn't matter whether you're looking at cat photos that inspire you or so-called 'high art' that inspires you."

I made plans to meet Spartz back at his office, then walked upstairs. The exhi-bition space was beautiful, brightly lit, and intentionally disorienting, full of room-size installations that warped my sense of scale and proportion. I spent sev-eral minutes staring at a huge sculpture made of baby dolls wearing helmets, translucent plastic chairs suspended at odd angles, and two beach umbrellas em-blazoned with the Coca-Cola logo. "These works," a curator's statement read, "in-corporate photographs, kitschy souvenirs, pop culture cast-offs, cheap household products, and high-end design objects, obliterating any hierarchy of value be-tween them."

---

*Eighty percent wasn't a random figure; it was a reference to the Pareto principle, also known as the 80/20 rule, which was such a core tenet of Spartz's thinking that he often used it as a transitive verb ("How can we 80/20 that?"). In the early twentieth century, an economist named Vilfredo Pareto observed that 20 percent of Italians owned 80 percent of Italy's land. In the twenty-first century, management consultants stretched this observation about inequality into a universal law about productivity. "80/20 APPLIES TO EVERYTHING!" blared one of Spartz's favorite books, *80/20 Sales and Marketing: The Definitive Guide to Working Less and Making More*. "You can read 20 percent of this book and get 80 percent of the benefit."

CHAPTER SEVEN

Basically My Nightmare

The Spartz Inc. headquarters looked like the set of a reality show about an effortfully chill start-up: bright-red walls, a hammock, a refrigerator full of free snacks, an aquarium full of sea monkeys. There were games everywhere—Xbox, Blokus, Ping-Pong—but I never saw anyone playing them. Emerson Spartz and his three dozen employees sat at undivided workstations; the layout was ostensibly nonhierarchical, but in practice the desks closest to Spartz were occupied by the most highly valued employees. Next to Spartz was his chief financial officer, who had an MBA and described himself as the company's oldest employee "by a hundred years." (He was thirty-six.) Other workstations were for data scientists and developers; in a distant corner of the office sat the "content producers," five recent college grads who put together the company's blog posts.

There were no office phones, and nobody talked much. Instead, they chatted constantly on an IM platform called HipChat. For hours at a time, the only sounds were the chugging of the building's ventilation system, Top 40 hits played at low volume, and the occasional chortle in response to a GIF. When something had to be discussed face-to-face, staffers arranged to meet in one of several glass-walled conference rooms, each of which was named for a region of Westeros, the fictional land depicted in *Game of Thrones*. Because I wasn't on their HipChat, I had no advance notice before a meeting was about to happen; I simply saw people in various parts of the room stand up in unison, unplug their laptops, and carry them silently toward King's Landing or Casterly Rock.

On my first full day in the office, the company was in the process of revamping its flagship site. In the morning, it was called Brainwreck.com ("The #2 Most Addicting Site"). By the afternoon, it had been relaunched as Dose.com ("Your Daily

Dose of Amazing"). The new design, Spartz explained, had a more "premium" feel, with cleaner lines and more muted colors. The name Brainwreck sounded destructive, but Dose was more ambiguous—either a dose of Vicodin or a dose of vitamins—which allowed for more flexibility. Readers might not trust a site called Brainwreck Travel or Brainwreck Politics, but Dose could, in theory, expand in almost any direction.

For now, it was a simple aggregation site devoted to funny or interesting photos. Around the office, posts on Dose were called "lists"—as in, "The list about albino animals is crushing it right now." They were collections of images arranged to tell a story ("This Dad Decided to Embarrass His Son in the Most Elaborate Way Possible. LOL"), make an argument ("Bacon-Wrapped Onion Rings Are Perfect for Appetizers, Burgers, and Life"), or present variations on a theme ("The 21 Most Unusual Horses That Make Even Unicorns Seem Basic"). A teenager absentmindedly clicking links on Reddit or Facebook would probably, at some point, end up on a site like Dose; Spartz's goal was to make the site sticky enough to hold visitors' attention for a few minutes before they wandered away to look at something else.*

Spartz, in his speeches, sometimes referred to himself as a "growth hacker." In practice, though, he was more like a day trader, investing in memes that appeared to have momentum. "Exactly where we find our source material took a lot of experimentation to get right," he said. "But the core of it is simple: taking stuff that's already going viral and repackaging it." His proprietary algorithm scoured the internet for images and stories that seemed to be generating a lot of activating emotion (at least, according to the relevant metrics).† The content producers then acted as arbitrageurs, adapting those images and stories into lists on Dose. Sometimes this required a bit of reassembly; other times, it was as simple as copying the source material in full, without bothering to rearrange any images or correct any typos, and then reposting it on Dose under a catchier headline.

One of Spartz's mantras was "Originality is overrated." "If you want to build a successful virus, you can start by trying to engineer the DNA from scratch," he told me. "Or, much more efficient: you take a virus that you already know is

---

*At the time, Brainwreck/Dose was getting about 30 million pageviews a month. This was, I couldn't help but notice, roughly the same as the monthly traffic to newyorker.com.
†Such content could be anywhere: a big viral site like *BuzzFeed* or *Upworthy*; a competitor closer to Dose's size, like ViralNova or TwistedSifter; a niche corner of Twitter or Reddit or Pinterest.

potent, mutate it a tiny bit, and expose it to a new cluster of people." Long before *Kony 2012*, Joseph Kony was old news to the few Americans who followed African politics closely. Only by exposing Kony's outrageous crimes to the rest of the American population was the meme able to grow into an epidemic.*

• • •

Spartz's headline-testing algorithm worked much like Upworthy's. "People call it A/B testing," he said. "But it's more like A/B/C/D/E testing. Why test only two variants when you could test five, or twenty-five?" At first, a Dose post appeared under as many as two dozen different headlines, distributed at random. One person's Facebook feed might include a link to "You Won't Believe What This Guy Did with an Abandoned Factory"; another person, looking at her own Facebook feed from the other side of the room, might see "At First It Looks Like an Old Empty Factory. But Go Inside and . . . WHOA." Spartz's algorithm measured which headline was attracting clicks most quickly; after a statistically significant threshold was reached, the "winning" headline automatically replaced all the others. "I'm really, really good at writing headlines," Spartz told me. "But any human's intuition can only be so good. If you can build a machine that can solve the problem better than you can, then you really understand the problem."

Almost every time I glanced at his screen, he was studying one of several data-analytics programs, which broke down his sites' traffic into dozens of metrics. He commissioned more detailed reports from his in-house data scientists, segmenting his visitors according to as many metrics as possible—age, sex, location, income.† The more he came to know about who was visiting his site, the more effectively he would be able to market to them through Facebook's microtargeting tools. In the meantime, he could always fall back on what might be called macro-targeting: packaging links in ways that were likely to induce a spike of activating emotion in almost everyone who saw them. All publishers, even those without

---

*If Mary Mallon had been a housewife, Spartz pointed out, she would have infected only her family. It was because she worked as a cook that she is remembered by history as Typhoid Mary. Typhoid is a bacterial infection, not a virus; also, although I was hardly a marketing expert, it seemed unwise to associate one's business model with fever, exhaustion, delirium, and death. Still, his point was well taken.

†When he wasn't getting enough data from his own sites, he bought user data from third-party sources. The harvesting and selling of user data was a common practice at the time; it didn't attract much notice, but those who did notice it found it quite unnerving. In 2014, David Lazarus, a *Los Angeles Times* business columnist, called a Verizon data-harvesting program "one of the more outrageous examples of how businesses loudly proclaim their commitment to safeguarding consumers' privacy while quietly selling us out to the highest bidder."

much money or technological sophistication, could learn how to macrotarget. It was a sledgehammer, not a scalpel, but it seemed to work remarkably well.

When I asked Spartz how many of his editorial decisions were based on maximizing traffic, he gave me an impatient look. What else would they be based on? "Analytics is so baked into everything we do that I can't even imagine having a separate discussion about it," he said.

Once more, I tried to check my biases. Spartz was not a Ugandan warlord or an ocean-polluting tycoon or a neofascist. He was just an awkward young man trying to make a buck on the internet. Facebook had laid out clear incentives, and Spartz was doing his best to follow them. And he was merely a midlevel amplifier; hundreds of other businesses, both smaller and larger than his, were engaged in more or less the same hustle.

Then again, wasn't this precisely the problem? For now, Spartz was A/B testing headlines about abandoned factories, siphoning market share from other procrastination sites. But if he ever felt like diversifying, it was easy to see how he might be able to disrupt, say, a legacy travel magazine. Instead of paying to send a world-class photographer to a far-flung locale, Dose Travel could send a drone, or use screenshots from Google Earth. Instead of hiring a travel journalist to write an original narrative, Spartz could write an automated script to paraphrase Wikipedia, or he could hire a contractor on Mechanical Turk to make something up. The Dose Travel piece would be less good, in some metaphysical sense, but that didn't necessarily mean that it would get less traffic.

Or Spartz could launch Dose Politics, using a similar approach. Instead of the antiquated journalistic model, wherein the content of a publication represented the thoughts and feelings of the individuals who made it, Spartz could crowdsource questions of newsworthiness and taste and decency, allowing them to be settled by the open internet. Would the audience be more likely to click on "We Are a Nation of Immigrants, Instagram's Snuggliest Labradoodle Reminds Us" or "17 Patriotic Americans Whose Lives Were Destroyed by Open Borders. #9 is Basically My Nightmare"? The only way to know for sure would be to run an A/B test and find out.

In 2014, there were governmental regulations, imperfect though they may have been, preventing pharmaceutical companies from filling their gelcaps with sawdust, or public-school teachers from filling their lesson plans with Holocaust denialism. Media was different. For many good reasons, starting with the First Amendment, the information market was relatively unregulated. And yet everyone knew the bromides, no less true for being trite, about how a democracy can't function without a well-informed electorate.* In the near future, what was to prevent large swaths of the internet—including the parts of the internet that used to be called newspapers and magazines—from looking more and more like Dose? What was insulating the American press from a full-speed race to the bottom? Nothing, as far as I could tell, other than tradition and inertia and the capricious whims of the market.†

The techno-utopians of Silicon Valley assumed that all would be for the best in a postgatekeeper world. This was possible, of course, but there was no way to be certain. Already, social-media-optimized content mills were outcompeting sober policy journals and threadbare alt-weeklies. Pulitzer Prize–winning reporters, unable to earn a living wage, kept fleeing journalism for jobs in PR or social media marketing. Even an alarmist like myself didn't presume that the Spartzification of the entire media ecosystem would happen overnight. Could it happen within five years? Fifteen? I tried telling myself that I was indulging in slippery-slope thinking, but this did nothing to allay my fear that we were already slipping.

• • •

When Emerson Spartz was a child in La Porte, Indiana, he had the highest batting average on his Little League team. "I quickly started seeing patterns," he told me. He wasn't very fast, but he noticed that Little League catchers were so bad at throwing to second base that almost any runner could advance. "I started stealing pretty much every time," he said. "It worked extremely well, but that wasn't what the coach cared about, apparently." The coach told him to stop; when Spartz kept stealing, the coach punished him by batting him eighth. "I gave him a statistical

---

*"A popular government without popular information, or the means of acquiring it, is but a Prologue to a Farce or a Tragedy," James Madison wrote in 1822. In the twenty-first century, with a looming climate crisis and a glut of nuclear warheads, the potential for human tragedy is orders of magnitude more grave than Madison could have anticipated.

†None of this implies, by any stretch, that the First Amendment should be ignored or diluted. It does imply, however, that the First Amendment, no less than the Second, raises dilemmas that are not easily resolved by glib, one-size-fits-all absolutism. First Amendment law is contingent, like everything else. In 1969, when the Fairness Doctrine was challenged on First Amendment grounds, the Supreme Court upheld the law unanimously. In the past few decades, however, the court has been on a more civil-libertarian kick. This has both costs and benefits.

explanation of why it made no sense to put your best hitter at the bottom of the order," Spartz said. "You can imagine how that went over."

He was a precocious student who chafed at classroom structure. A few weeks into seventh grade, he asked his parents if he could be homeschooled. His mother, Maggi, was the breadwinner, working at a local philanthropic foundation. His father, Tom, became Emerson's teacher.

One Sunday, I rented a car and drove Emerson and his wife, Gaby, from Chicago to La Porte, where his parents still live. We headed east on Interstate 90 for just over an hour, passed a few cornfields, and then pulled into a driveway. Tom Spartz, a voluble man with a double chin, spoke in passionate bursts that sounded like fortune-cookie aphorisms spliced together. As he welcomed us into the house, I asked about his role in his son's intellectual growth. He said, "I don't care what expectations you have, all of the great—we'll call them 'developers'—were just continually shaking with energy. You want to keep 'em moving, keep 'em loose, keep 'em testing. I saw this stuff coming long ago. When you see the momentum, you'll be laughing at how obvious it all was."

After Emerson started being homeschooled, his brother Dylan joined him. Tom showed me the den, which he had used as the boys' classroom, filling it with whiteboards and inspirational posters. Now that the boys were grown, the den was just a den. On a weight-lifting bench, Tom had arranged a two-foot stack of the "short biographies of successful people" that Emerson often mentioned. They turned out to be extremely short: a single-sided page each, photocopied from a small right-leaning newspaper called *Investor's Business Daily*. Each page distilled a life of setbacks and accomplishments into a pull-quote moral. (Karl Malone: "Practice makes perfect." Mel Blanc: "Never give up.") Apart from the mini-biographies and enough algebra to satisfy state requirements, Tom's pedagogy was flexible and self-directed. The boys listened to motivational audiobooks by Tony Robbins and watched documentaries by Ken Burns. They learned arithmetic in part through "Kroger math"—on trips to the supermarket, as Tom added items to the cart, Emerson and Dylan kept a running tally of the total price.

Tom shuffled through the pile of biographies, picked out a page about the novelist Pearl S. Buck, and skimmed it. "It shows that she was away from her normal world, and all of a sudden she's writing about the East," he said. "It's like, wow, can you imagine?" I asked Tom if he had encouraged the boys to read Buck's novels.

He shook his head and said, "You lay out a hook, but you don't put it in the fish's mouth."

On the drive back to Chicago, Emerson delivered a rapt soliloquy about artificial intelligence. "We'll soon get to a point where AI fully surpasses us," he said. "Self-driving cars will take over from humans, who suck at driving, relatively speaking. Drones will take pictures in war zones instead of endangering human photographers. The benefits will be enormous. When you think about what asymptotic growth looks like, there's no way humans are going to be able to keep up." I interrupted him to ask whether I should stay on the highway or merge into the exit lane. He hesitated briefly.

"We could just google it," his wife said from the backseat.

"No, Gaby, I know exactly where we are," he said curtly, and told me not to turn.

A Katy Perry song was playing on the radio. "Art is that which science has not yet explained," he said. "Imagine that the vocals are mediocre in an otherwise amazing song. What if you could have forty people record different vocals, and then test it by asking thousands of people, 'Which one is best?' To me, that's a trickle in an ocean of possible ways you could improve every song on the radio."

CHAPTER EIGHT

Eating the World

Tech-world dogma holds that a start-up is only as smart as its founder. Thus it's incumbent on all founders—as a matter of job security, not just ego boosting—to convince the world, or at least their board of directors, of their brilliance. Spartz was constantly dispensing life hacks, business aphorisms, and statistics he'd memorized from pop-psychology paperbacks. Walking with him through downtown Chicago, he shared tips on how to become a more efficient pedestrian. As we sat for lunch at a restaurant, he started quoting from *Never Eat Alone*, a book about "the power of relationships" by "master networker" Keith Ferrazzi. (A minute later, a man took a seat at our table, and I realized that this had been Spartz's oblique way of telling me that he'd invited someone to join us.)

Tech is a big industry dominated by a small and relatively stagnant social hierarchy. At the top are a few men—Peter, Reid, Mark, Marc, Elon—whose quirks are easy enough to emulate. Spartz was not in that top tier, but he was desperate to join it one day. He took an interest in the handful of iconoclastic ideas—Moore's Law, Metcalfe's Law, the singularity, the simulation hypothesis—that preoccupied nearly every member of Silicon Valley's A-list and almost no one else. He read the books and blogs that the A-listers recommended. Like them, he adopted a signature daily uniform. *Originality is overrated.*

"I keep hearing people around town talking about this young man as a Steve Jobs kind of guy," Gary Holdren, a Chicago venture capitalist and one of Spartz's chief funders, told me. "I think his stuff is indicative of where digital media is headed." Equally indicative was Spartz's sales patter. Just as Lee Atwater said explicitly what other political strategists were canny enough to conceal, Spartz talked in public the way other tech CEOs talked in private.

In *Liar's Poker*, his 1989 Wall Street memoir, Michael Lewis described a newly ascendant, egregiously conceited type of alpha-male bond broker. This type had a name: they called each other Big Swinging Dicks. "Everyone wanted to be a Big Swinging Dick," Lewis wrote, "even the women."

A quarter century later, the A-list entrepreneurs of Silicon Valley occupied an analogous place in the American power structure, but their self-presentation was less aggressive. Instead of "Greed is good," their aspirational bromides were "Think different" and "Don't be evil." Instead of Dionysian feats of consumption—Porsches and cocaine binges and morning cheeseburgers—they drove electric cars and subsisted on seaweed and Soylent. They didn't deny themselves the pleasures of good old-fashioned capital, but they were equally covetous of social and intellectual capital. Their fondest wish was to be considered luminaries, Renaissance men,* the smartest guys in the room. They were Big Swinging Brains.

They spoke with alacrity and unbridled confidence, making brash assertions that were contrarian in familiar ways, each offering expert opinions on more topics than it was possible for one person to be an expert in. Were they luminaries? To be a truly original thinker, it seemed to me, one had to be comfortable plumbing the outer bounds of one's knowledge, even pondering the unknowable. But Big Swinging Brains were often loath to admit that their knowledge had limits; they would sooner pivot to a topic they knew about, or at least knew how to talk about. "The test of a first-rate intelligence," according to F. Scott Fitzgerald, "is the ability to hold two opposed ideas in the mind at the same time, and still retain the ability to function." A BSB was more likely to summarize two opposing sides of a debate and then, without pausing for breath, explain which side was right, or, even better, why both sides were wrong.

Like any powerful group with a well-defined set of interests, the Silicon Valley overlords tended to be receptive to ideas that aligned with those interests and hostile to ideas that challenged them. Ideas that were fundamentally incompatible with their life choices—for example, the notion that the whole enterprise of technocratic capitalism might turn out to be at best a lark and at worst a catastrophe—they considered laughable, unthinkable, far outside the Overton window.†

---

*In this one respect, at least, they were just like the Big Swinging Dicks: almost all of them were men.
†All social groups have prevailing biases, of course. Traditional media gatekeepers are no exception. (The press is uniformly in favor of press freedom, for example.) But journalists are, by and large, a neurotic and embattled bunch; self-critique comes naturally to them. This means that, as a group, they tend to exhibit what Richard Rorty called "ironism," a quality that, crucially, allows a vocabulary to remain supple and open to self-correction. An

According to the prevailing vocabulary of the techno-utopians, everything could be quantified, A/B tested, refined in the crucible of the market. "Take political campaigns," Spartz told me. "Compared to growth hackers, the people running political messaging are in the Stone Age. If the smartest people decided to take over politics and start winning elections, it'd be child's play." For one thing, he said, hackers had the advantage of objectivity. "If I were running a political campaign, I wouldn't be sitting around in my office—'Well, if we framed the debate in this way, I bet it would resonate,'" he said. "You don't have to guess. You put a hundred slogans out there, then look at the data. Which ones are people sharing? Then, once you find the best one, you just"—he made a fist and pounded it against his flat palm—"ram it into people's skulls."

The film industry was also ripe for disruption. "The way they do testing now is they get a few people in a room and give them a questionnaire: 'Did you like the ending?'" he said. "That's about one millionth of the amount of testing they should be doing. Literally."

"But what if the director is an artist?" I asked. "What if the audience wants Ending A, but the director says, 'I still want Ending B'?"

Spartz scoffed. "Hollywood is *filled* with those people," he said. "That's why they're so far behind."

I asked him to name the most beautiful book he'd ever read.

"Can you rephrase that question more clearly?" he asked.

I couldn't.

"A beautiful book?" he said. "I don't even know what that means. Impactful, sure."

He was proud to make a living on the internet, he said, because it was the closest humanity had yet come to creating a pure meritocracy. "At the thirty-thousand-foot level, the internet is a giant machine that gives people what they want," Spartz said. "How can you do better than that? It exposes people to the best stuff in the world."

---

ironist, Rorty wrote, "has radical and continuing doubts about the final vocabulary she currently uses, because she has been impressed by other vocabularies." The same could not be said of the new gatekeepers in Silicon Valley. Their prevailing vocabulary had much to recommend it—it was socially tolerant, evidence-based, open to experimentation—but the BSBs were hardly ironists. They took their own dogma quite seriously, and they were rarely impressed by anyone but themselves.

I made the obvious rejoinder: it also exposes people to the worst stuff in the world.

"Well, that would be your subjective judgment," he said, pique rising in his voice. "That's you paternalistically deciding what's bad for people. Besides, businesses exist to serve the market. You can have whatever personal values you want, but businesses that don't provide what the customers want don't remain businesses. Literally, never."

Once, in Casterly Rock, Spartz told me, "The future of media is an ever-increasing degree of personalization. My CNN won't look like your CNN. So we want Dose eventually to be tailored to each user." On a whiteboard behind him were the phrases "old media," "Tribune," and "$100 M." He continued, "You shouldn't have to choose what you want, because we will be able to get enough data to know what you want better than you do."

I was reminded of Chris Cox, who grew up a few miles away from where we were sitting, in a prosperous Chicago suburb called Winnetka. Cox, one of the top product managers at Facebook, was often described as Mark Zuckerberg's heir apparent. In 2006, he'd helped lead Facebook away from its original product—static personal profiles—and toward its dynamic News Feed, which would be algorithmically personalized for each user. In 2010, *The Wall Street Journal* ran an adulatory profile of Cox, who "envisions a world where social design can improve many more aspects of life online." The reporter quoted Cox spinning out the details of his hypothetical utopia. "You turn on the TV, and you see what your mom and friends are watching, and they can record stuff for you," Cox said. "Instead of 999 channels, you will see 999 recommendations from your friends. The music store will look like that, as will the newspaper. It would just be good if we could all be connected through these currently anonymous devices."*

In the accompanying photo, Cox sat in a yellow armchair in Facebook's headquarters. Behind him was a poster that said in bold red type, DONE IS BETTER THAN PERFECT.

---

*In March 2019, Mark Zuckerberg indicated that Facebook would retreat from this expansive vision, focusing instead on "private, encrypted services." A few days later, Chris Cox announced via Facebook post that he was leaving the company. "As Mark has outlined, we are turning a new page in our product direction," Cox wrote. "This will be a big project and we will need leaders who are excited to see the new direction through." The tech press parsed the post carefully enough to pick up the subtext: apparently, the category of people who were excited about Facebook's new direction did not include Cox.

———

"There is much to discover on the Facebook, the online community for college students," a *Washington Post* reporter wrote in the paper's Style section in late 2004. She did warn, however, that "it's all a little fake—the 'friends'; the profiles that can be tailored to what others find appealing; the 'groups' that exist only in cyberspace." A few weeks later, Mark Zuckerberg, looking for investors, visited the office of *The Washington Post* and met with Donald Graham, the paper's publisher and CEO. They agreed on a verbal deal: the *Post* would pay $6 million for 10 percent of the company. Zuckerberg later called Graham in tears—a Silicon Valley venture-capital firm had offered a more generous investment, and he was tempted to take it. Graham, impressed by the young man's display of rectitude, gave him his blessing to renege on the deal. Three years later, Graham joined Facebook's board of directors. "Facebook has completely transformed how people interact," he said in a press release. "Mark's sense of what Facebook can do is quite remarkable."

In 2007, a *Washington Post* columnist lamented the rapid ascent of "Amazon .com," which was "so smart in the way they cater to human weakness, bad judgment, poor taste." In 2008, another *Washington Post* columnist wrote, "I loathe Amazon even though I know it is the future and will prevail." In 2013, with revenue in decline, Donald Graham sold *The Washington Post*, which his family had owned and overseen for eighty years, to Jeff Bezos, the founder and CEO of Amazon, soon to be the richest person in the world.

By that time, it no longer made sense to think of business and tech and media as separate entities. Business was tech, and tech was taking over everything: movies, TV, travel, journalism.* Whether the nerd princelings of Silicon Valley understood themselves to be gatekeepers or not, it was becoming increasingly clear that their smallest impromptu decisions were having enormous downstream effects on how billions of people spoke and thought and, ultimately, acted in the world. To change how we talk is to change who we are.

---

*In 2011, the venture capitalist Marc Andreessen argued that "software is eating the world." He gave example after example. "The world's largest bookseller, Amazon, is a software company," he wrote. "Today's dominant music companies are software companies, too: Apple's iTunes, Spotify and Pandora." He continued listing industries that were being disrupted: photography, telecom, cars, even agriculture. His argument was divisive at the time, but it ended up being so prescient that several of the ascendant start-ups Andreessen wrote about—Netflix, Pixar, Square—would soon be thought of simply as dominant companies in their fields, not as software companies per se.

I wondered whether they found this power burdensome, and if so, whether they found the burden humbling, or overwhelming—the way I would feel overwhelmed if I woke up to discover that I had somehow been put in charge of the energy grid, or some other key piece of infrastructure that I didn't fully understand. Maybe BSBs were constitutionally incapable of feeling overwhelmed. In any case, there was no law that said you had to understand a piece of social infrastructure in order to own it, or to break it.

Business was tech and tech was media. Content was content was content, and coders controlled the sluices through which all content flowed. The luminaries of Silicon Valley didn't hesitate to offer their bold opinions on almost every subject; and yet, when it came to basic questions about the future of media, their rhetoric turned fuzzy. *Businesses should give customers what they want. Media companies should meet audiences where they are. Journalism should be objective and thorough.* These truisms seemed unobjectionable enough until they came into conflict with one another, which happened all the time. What if your customers claimed to want rigorous, dispassionate journalism, but their browsing habits revealed that they actually wanted hot takes and salacious hate-reads? What if, in order to meet customers where they were, you had to bowdlerize your writing, or give up on writing altogether and pivot to video? What if quality and popularity were sometimes correlated negatively, or not at all?

In early 2016, I was invited to a lunch discussion in an executive boardroom. At the head of the table, a Big Swinging Brain—one of the Biggest—talked for more than an hour without touching his sandwich. He dilated on a wide array of topics (state health-care exchanges, the future of the trucking industry, the panic of 1873), displaying uncanny recall and mental acuity. He acknowledged dilemmas and contradictions in his thinking; he even pointed out awkward conflicts between what he found preferable economically and what might be preferable civically, even morally. I began to wonder whether I'd underestimated the BSBs. Maybe I should learn to stop worrying and love my overlords.

Then I asked him a question about the importance of good journalism and good art, the corrosive effects of bad journalism and bad art, and the best way to forestall the Spartzification of the internet. It seemed clear—not just to me, but to anyone who was paying attention—that things were drifting in an unnerving direction. How would humanity avoid a clickbait death spiral?

"I don't think there's an answer to that," he said, his tone suddenly turning flinty. Apparently I had revealed myself to be a Luddite. "If I were in the media business, I would focus on making a product that people actually want. Because that's how business works."

I couldn't imagine him being so flippantly fatalistic about any other civilizational hazard that the free market had failed to address. The Renaissance men of Silicon Valley were known for spending an unusual amount of time and money addressing thorny existential problems, such as the achievement gap in American public schools and the excess of carbon in the atmosphere. They even invested millions of dollars in problems that hadn't come into existence yet, such as hostile AI.* In 2016, the Chan Zuckerberg Initiative, the nonprofit founded by Mark Zuckerberg and his wife, Dr. Priscilla Chan, announced its intention to "help cure, prevent, and manage all disease in our children's lifetime"; several well-capitalized bioengineering start-ups, including a $1.5 billion initiative at Google, went even further, resolving to cure death. But somehow the BSBs balked at the problem of addictive, low-quality clickbait. They had taken control of the media industry, then moved fast and broken it; now they claimed no responsibility for fixing it. When the prospect of a clickbait death spiral came up, they tended to affect an odd sanguinity. They didn't quite deny the existence of the problem— they just did their best to ignore it, or to reframe it as either trivial or inevitable.†

In the eighteenth century, the philosopher David Hume identified a common slippage that came to be called the is-ought fallacy. An interlocutor starts by

---

*Many BSBs feared that the wrong kind of artificial intelligence would destroy humanity, or the planet—a nearly literal interpretation of software eating the world. The prospect was a remote one, and purely hypothetical, but within certain Silicon Valley circles it was a constant obsession. "It's hard to fathom how much human-level AI could benefit society, and it's equally hard to imagine how much it could damage society if built or used incorrectly," read one sentence from the mission statement of OpenAI, a "non-profit research company" founded in 2015. It wasn't clear whether or how OpenAI would be financially solvent. Still, its nine financial backers— including Peter Thiel, Elon Musk, and the president of Y Combinator—pledged, collectively, a billion dollars.

†At our lunch, the BSB characterized my critique by way of a food analogy. "So you're saying that people like milkshakes and onion rings, and you want them to eat kale," he said. "Well, good luck with that." I found this strange, given that an ambitious initiative to prevent obesity—to alter various incentives, both governmental and nongovernmental, with the goal of helping people resist the natural self-destructive urge to binge on sugar and fat—seemed like precisely the sort of initiative that a civic-minded Silicon Valley philanthropist like himself might support (unless he happened to own stock in McDonald's). Our conversation took place in the spring of 2016. Donald Trump, the consummate milkshake-and-onion-rings candidate, was the front-runner in every Republican poll.

observing the way something *is*, then gradually transitions to an argument about the way it ought to be, as if one followed from the other. Techno-libertarians often explained how the media economy worked (*The market doesn't support what the market doesn't support*), as if this also accounted for how the media economy *ought* to work (*If Facebook isn't good, then why is it so successful?*). Old-school media gatekeepers sometimes made the opposite argument, a kind of ought-is fallacy: *What we publish is good enough that it ought to be popular; therefore it is destined to become popular.* Sadly, even when the premises were true, the conclusion was often wishful thinking.

• • •

Several times, in Chicago, I asked Spartz if I could talk to his content producers. He discouraged me, first subtly and then explicitly. "They don't have as much personal discretion as you might think," he said. "What we do is pretty algorithmic."

Finally, he relented and let me speak to Chelsea DeBaise. Her name rang a bell. Earlier, in a meeting with his chief data scientist, I'd watched Spartz as he squinted over a spreadsheet. It ranked all five content producers by how well their posts were doing—open rates, share rates, and on and on. DeBaise was at the bottom of the list.

"Chelsea's clearly underperforming, but I can't figure out why," the data scientist said.

"Weird," Spartz said. "It's not like she's a worse writer. Is she deviating from the sourcing criteria?"

"I'll keep an eye on it," the data scientist said.

DeBaise met me in Casterly Rock, wearing a baseball cap advertising Van Gogh Vodka. She'd only been working at Spartz Inc. for a few weeks; before that she'd been a student at Syracuse University, where she majored in writing and contributed to the school newspaper. Her best story, she said, was a feature about local poverty, for which she spent several days reporting in homeless shelters around Syracuse. "Stories like that—heavily reported, with one-on-one interviews—there is a lot of value in that," she said. "But then you have to think about impact. A Dose story I did in an hour would shatter that one, in terms of reach."

After college, DeBaise wanted to write. But she needed a stable job with a decent salary, so she ended up applying to a lot of tech start-ups. "I was willing to sort of put my journalism practice on the back burner," she said. "But since I've come here I've found that a lot of those skills—attention to detail, an affinity for research—have actually come into play. I was surprised, in a pleasant way." That morning, she had posted half a dozen lists to Dose, including "33 Photos of People Taken Seconds Before They Die. #10 Is from My Nightmares" and "No Matter How Much You Stare, You Won't Be Able to Guess What These Photos Really Are Of." While writing Dose headlines, she admitted, "there is a part of Syracuse University Chelsea that's, like, 'I don't know if this is the way I should write it.' But then another part of me is, like, 'Actually, there's pretty definitive evidence that this version will get a better response.' So is the goal for people to look at it and be, like, 'Wow, that girl wrote a really articulate headline'? At some point, you have to check your ego."

When we spoke, DeBaise was reading *In Persuasion Nation*, a book of dystopian short stories by George Saunders, in which the oppressive force is not a totalitarian government but the all-seeing eye of targeted advertising. One story, "My Flamboyant Grandson," takes place in Midtown Manhattan in the not-so-distant future. As the narrator and his grandson walk up Broadway, devices implanted in the sidewalk mine digital information from strips in their shoes. Eye-level screens show them "images reflective of the Personal Preferences we'd stated," imploring them to visit a nearby Burger King. DeBaise only opened the book outside the office, she told me, because she sometimes burst into tears while reading it.

"You know the quote from *Spider-Man*—'With great power comes great responsibility'?" she said. "Well, a tremendous amount of media attention means a lot of power. We're lucky that Emerson is inherently a good person, because if you had someone that smart who wasn't? Lord knows what would happen."*

---

*A few years later, I reached DeBaise by phone. She told me that when we'd first met, she'd been in the middle of "what I guess you could call an existential crisis," which soon resulted in her quitting Dose to work for an education-related nonprofit. "In hindsight, we were just recycling content with no regard to what it actually was, solely paying attention to the metrics," she said. "It's not like we were the only clickbait factory doing that, but we were part of this wave of businesses exploiting the implicit trust that readers have—that if they see something online that looks like it's coming from a real source, that there's probably some thought and reliability behind it. These days, I don't know how many people have that trust anymore."

CHAPTER NINE

Brainwreck Politics

On the plane back to New York, I started to write my piece about Emerson Spartz. I tried not to be too harsh. He was still young. Maybe he'd change one day. Besides, I was well aware that my cautionary tale about new media would be published in a bastion of old media, and I didn't want it to seem more vindictive than necessary.

Writers generally don't pick their own headlines, but they're allowed to make suggestions. I proposed calling my piece "TL;DR," an internet initialism for "too long; didn't read." Some people around the office didn't know what it meant, which indicated that some of our readers wouldn't, either. Instead, we settled on "The Virologist."

Above a *New Yorker* headline is a word or phrase, in small type, called the rubric. A piece reported in São Paolo might use the rubric Letter from Brazil; if the piece was reported in various points throughout the Amazon, the rubric might be Our Far-flung Correspondents. A lot of rubrics are Annals of Something-or-other—Annals of Science, Annals of Crime, Annals of the Former World, Annals of Annals. Pieces about journalism often run under the rubric The Wayward Press; The Publishing World is for pieces about publishing. But Emerson Spartz wasn't a pressman or a publisher. What was he? We considered Annals of Entertainment, or Annals of Technology, or Annals of Marketing. None seemed quite right. Annals of Virality? Too cute. We ended up with Annals of Media, which, it turned out, had never been used before.

During the editing process, I spent several hours in the fact-checking department, corroborating statistics and tweaking phrases to avoid potential ambiguity. Was it really fair to say that Dose's algorithmic model "leaves almost no room for curatorial discretion"? We removed the sentence, just to be safe. Behind us as we worked was a parody poster that one of the fact-checkers had mocked up in Photo-Shop and tacked to the wall. In bold red type, it proclaimed, TRUE IS BETTER THAN DONE.

For the first few decades of its existence, *The New Yorker* contained no photographs and no table of contents. Many pieces of writing had no headline or byline at the top—just a rubric followed by an opening sentence. The writer's name appeared at the end of the piece if it appeared at all. Sometimes, you didn't know whether you were starting to read a piece of fiction, reportage, criticism, or humor; you just had to figure it out as you went. These austere design choices could be interpreted as signs of the editors' respect for their readers, or their disdain, or both. A consumer product has to be user friendly; an art object reserves the right to be inexplicable or stubbornly useless. *The New Yorker* aspired to be both a consumer product and an art object. (This was much easier to pull off, solvency-wise, in the 1960s and '70s, when magazines were flush with advertising revenue.)

The design, both in print and online, remains relatively minimalist—staid typefaces, no pull quotes—but, in the era of the Google-Facebook duopoly, aloofness is no longer a viable growth strategy. *The New Yorker* has a social media team, which has succeeded at drawing in many new subscribers. Still, the team can only do so much with the material they're given. In the virality industry, pieces may vary in length, style, and quality, so long as they deliver a sharp and immediate dose of activating emotion. But a nuanced *New Yorker* piece—a good one, in other words—doesn't always evoke a discrete emotion right away. Some *New Yorker* pieces are hard to finish. Some pieces, after you finish them, lodge quietly in your brain and unfurl there over a period of hours, or days, or weeks. Some pieces inspire more questions than answers; some leave you reeling at the vast and specific strangeness of the world; some make you feel indignant and impotent and ambivalent all at once. These mental states may be conducive to human flourishing, but most of them are deactivating emotions, and deactivating emotions don't tend toward virality.

In the early days of newyorker.com, print headlines and web headlines were one and the same. By the time my piece about Spartz came out, *The New Yorker* had started to experiment with its own relatively simple form of A/B testing. Now print pieces had one title in the magazine and another title on the internet.* When the Spartz piece appeared online, it was called "King of Clickbait." This was slightly harsher than the tone I was hoping to strike, but it worked. For about a day, it was the most popular piece on the site, until it was displaced by a slideshow of the most-read *New Yorker* pieces of the past year. The whole situation was ironic in five or six distinct ways, and yet I tried to see it through a lens of techno-optimism. At least people were reading my piece! Or clicking on it, anyway.

• • •

The day I left Chicago, Spartz was scheduled to have lunch with Bernie Marcus, the cofounder of Home Depot and one of the two hundred richest people in the country. "He wants advice about virality," Spartz told me. "Like everyone, he's got messages he wants to spread. You're starting to see how the superpower can be applied to anything, right?"

Marcus was a budget hawk, a die-hard Zionist, and a right-wing megadonor. Once, on a conference call with conservative activists, he said that retailers who do not promote Republican candidates "should be shot." "I assume he wants to push an agenda that I'm personally not super excited about," Spartz said. Still, he never considered turning down the meeting. His job was to make effective tools. How people used those tools was none of his concern. "You don't just network with people who share your beliefs," he told me. "That's a good way to end up with a small mind."†

In 2016, Bernie Marcus donated $7 million to pro-Trump Super PACs. One of them, a PAC called Make America Number 1, paid more than $5 million to Cambridge Analytica, a British consulting firm that used online microtargeting to boost voter turnout for Trump, inhibit voter turnout for Clinton, and help

---

*At each step, the headlines became a bit more explicit (at least, by *New Yorker* standards). The web editors explained the logic: *New Yorker* subscribers, thumbing through paper copies of the magazine at their leisure, might not be put off by a droll headline, or even by a headline so elliptical as to be incomprehensible. Maybe they'd be enticed by something else on the page—the photo, the first few sentences, the byline—or maybe they'd need no enticement, relying instead on their faith in *The New Yorker*'s editorial sensibility. But most browsers on Facebook or Twitter weren't like readers with the magazine spread before them; they were more like commuters hurrying past a bookstore on a wide public street. They might not even notice that they were passing a bookstore at all, much less feel the urge to wander inside. To capture their attention, the thinking went, you had to be a bit more aggressive.
†In *Never Eat Alone*, Keith Ferrazzi brags about his ideological flexibility, giving public-speaking tips to Howard Dean in one chapter and sucking up to William F. Buckley in another. Chapter 28, "Getting Close to Power," starts with this epigraph: "As long as you're going to think anyway, think big." It's from *The Art of the Deal*, a book ghostwritten by Tony Schwartz on behalf of Donald Trump.

nationalist memes go viral on Facebook. "The traditional model where fifty million people receive the same blanket advert is being replaced by extremely individualistic targeting," Alexander Nix, then the CEO of Cambridge Analytica, said a couple of weeks before the election. Nix was not the only entrepreneur trying to enhance the old art of political propaganda with the new tools of social media. As long as these entrepreneurs stayed within the bounds of campaign-finance law, nothing about their work was illegal, or even particularly surprising.

After the election, Brad Parscale, the digital director of the Trump campaign, sat for an interview with *60 Minutes*. "I understood early that Facebook was how Donald Trump was going to win," Parscale said. He explained to the reporter, Lesley Stahl, how his digital team had helped Trump achieve this goal. A simple campaign ad might be spun out into thousands of variations, which could then be tested against each other. On a laptop, Parscale showed Stahl an ad in which Clinton's "basket of deplorables" quote was superimposed over a photo: a few of the upstanding Americans Clinton was ostensibly defaming. In one iteration of the ad, the upstanding Americans were older white women; in another, they were uniformed police officers; in yet another, they were a diverse group of millennials. Facebook users would see whichever version they were most likely to find persuasive, based on the personal preferences they'd stated (and some they hadn't stated). In another TV interview, with *Frontline*, Parscale sounded even more overtly Spartzian. As opposed to traditional campaign advisers, who still market tested their slogans "anecdotally," Parscale said, "We used data and machine learning to learn which ads worked better." *You don't have to guess. You put a hundred slogans out there, then look at the data.*

While the main campaign operated out of Trump Tower in New York, Parscale assembled a digital team of more than a hundred in San Antonio. They worked in a rented office next to a ten-lane highway. Cambridge Analytica sent Parscale advice and analysis. He also got help directly from the source. "Facebook employees would show up for work every day in our offices," he said on *60 Minutes*. "I asked each one of them, by email, 'I wanna know every single secret button, click, technology you have.'"* On the day of his inauguration, Donald Trump filed the paper-

---

*Facebook later confirmed to *60 Minutes* that it had sent employees to embed with the Trump campaign. ("We encourage all candidates, groups, and voters to use our platform to engage in elections," the company's statement read, in part.) Facebook had offered similar help to the Clinton campaign, but the offer was rebuffed.

work for his 2020 reelection campaign. The following year, he announced who would run it: Brad Parscale.

Obviously, Emerson Spartz did not cause Donald Trump to rise to power. But the conditions that made Spartz's success possible—the attention market's slide into raw Darwinism, the widespread conflation of quality with popularity, the coarsening of the national vocabulary—were among the main conditions that made a Trump presidency possible. In 2017, on YouTube, I watched Spartz deliver a new version of his self-pitch, in the form of a TEDx Talk. It started out the same as the old version. "If you could make things go viral, that was like having a superpower," he said. "You could tip elections, overthrow dictators, start movements, revolutionize industries. And it worked. And this happened." On a screen behind him, he displayed a collage of images, none of which mentioned the tipped American election of 2016. Rather, they were screenshots representing Emerson Spartz's achievements in business: his face on CNBC, his photo in *Forbes*, an article about him in *The New Yorker*. He'd chosen to highlight the print headline, "The Virologist," which was ambiguous enough to seem laudatory. And he'd cropped the image so that the article's subtitle—"How a young entrepreneur built an empire by repackaging memes"—ended with the word "empire."*

---

*"These issues are definitely more complex than I thought back then," Spartz told me by email in 2019. "I'm still optimistic but definitely less techno-utopian because of how much *Black Mirror*-y stuff has happened, and as I grow up I've learned to see previously invisible complexities." When we'd first met, Spartz had described artificial intelligence as "an amazing gift." He now described it as "likely the single biggest existential risk to humanity."

CHAPTER TEN

The Sailer Strategy

For a long time—for a period, to be precise, that began in the 1960s and ended abruptly on November 8, 2016—Washington insiders from both parties tacitly agreed on a set of commonsense assumptions. For example: it's impossible for an openly racist candidate to win a national election. Presidential candidates could make appeals to white racists—indeed, all of them did so—but only delicately, using dog whistles. Ronald Reagan denied that his "states' rights" speech had anything to do with race. By the time of the 1980 general election, he was all sunny, inclusive optimism. Bill Clinton, speaking before Jesse Jackson's Rainbow Coalition in 1992, denounced the rapper Sister Souljah, comparing her to David Duke. And yet, seconds later, Clinton said, "We can't get anywhere in this country pointing the finger at one another across racial lines." During the primary election in 2000, campaign operatives who seemed to be working on behalf of George W. Bush spread rumors that Bush's opponent, John McCain, had "fathered an illegitimate black child." In the general election, though, Bush campaigned as a compassionate conservative with a centrist approach to immigration. "*El sueño americano es para todos,*" he said at a campaign rally in Philadelphia. *The American dream is for everyone. We are a country of immigrants. We are at war with terrorism, not with Islam.* This, too, was part of the bipartisan consensus: all candidates must speak in magnanimous platitudes about melting pots and universal goodwill. To do otherwise, everyone assumed, would be unpresidential, un-American, unthinkable—would be, more to the point, a self-defeating electoral strategy.

In the 2012 election, Mitt Romney flirted with the angry nativist fringe of his party before tacking back to the center. He snuck into Trump Tower through a back entrance to seek the endorsement of Donald Trump, who was by then a full-blown Twitter conspiracist. After winning his party's nomination, Romney ran, more plausibly, as a bland moderate. It didn't work.

When the election was over, Reince Priebus, the head of the Republican National Committee, convened a panel of GOP strategists to explain Romney's loss and to chart a way forward. In a hundred-page report, the strategists emphasized that the party had no choice but to tack toward the center, especially on issues of race and pluralism. "Many minorities wrongly think that Republicans do not like them or want them in the country," the report said. The GOP needed to cast out the hard-liners and "champion comprehensive immigration reform. If we do not, our Party's appeal will continue to shrink to its core constituencies only."*

A dozen years earlier, Steve Sailer, a prolific opinion columnist with a small but passionate online audience, had reached the opposite conclusion. Sailer, then a forty-one-year-old living in Southern California, had retired early from a successful career in marketing in order to write full time. When the venerable conservative magazines would publish his work, he wrote for them; when they wouldn't, which was more often the case, he posted his columns on his own blog. On November 28, 2000, while the Bush and Gore campaigns were still arguing over hanging chads in Florida, Sailer wrote a blog post. Citing exit-poll data, he demonstrated that if Bush had increased his share of the white vote by just 3 percent—if 57 percent of white Americans had voted for him, rather than 54 percent—he would have won in a landslide. Sailer then expanded his hypothetical: what if, in order to win those additional white votes, Bush had embraced a platform so caustic, so openly hostile to racial minorities, that he lost every nonwhite vote? "Incredibly," Sailer found, "he *still* would have won."

By Sailer's lights, this meant that Republicans should drop their disingenuous platitudes and campaign openly as a white-identity party. Then, once they were in power, they could enact prowhite policies—deporting undocumented immigrants, reducing immigration quotas, retracting birthright citizenship—thus maintaining a white majority that could deliver future elections to the GOP. He knew the mainstream counterarguments, which all seemed to boil down to the same thing: *White people shouldn't organize in their own interest, because that would be racist, and*

---

*In 2017, Reince Priebus would go to work for Donald Trump, the least pluralistic American president in recent memory, only to be fired six months later.

racism is bad. That argument didn't matter to Sailer. He maintained that a prowhite campaign strategy would work, and that it was the best way to save the country from ruin. By 2012, he had been making this argument so vociferously for so long that, in ultra-right-wing circles, it was called the Sailer Strategy.

The American dream is for everyone. This was the sort of gauzy logic that Sailer loved to tear apart. On the contrary, he argued, the American dream is only for Americans; moreover, politicians should enforce strict rules about who was allowed to become an American, revising those rules, if necessary, to privilege immigrants from certain regions over others. "An immigration policy, by its very nature, is about discriminating, about selecting whom we should admit and whom we should keep out," he wrote. Without such policies, he strongly believed, the United States would cease to be an Anglo-Christian nation, which would lead to poverty, crime, and internecine struggle. "But intelligence is discrimination, so intelligence is racist," he continued sarcastically. "In contrast, suicidal stupidity isn't racist. So it's better." This was a worldview he called "citizenism," distinguishing himself from the paleoconservatives, radical traditionalists, white nationalists, and white separatists with whom he had subtle doctrinal differences.

Many minorities wrongly think that Republicans do not want them in the country. Well, Sailer felt no particular animus toward any individual, unless the individual had done something to earn it, and yet some minority groups—say, undocumented gang members—would be right to think that he didn't want them in his country. Nor, frankly, did Sailer take for granted that all men were created equal, that European Americans and African Americans were born, on average, with identical levels of intelligence and work ethic and proclivity to violence. He didn't take it on faith that racial groups differed intrinsically in these ways; he was just posing the question, following the facts wherever they happened to lead.

After the 2012 election, Sailer showed, again using exit-poll data, that Romney could have won without making any overtures to Hispanic voters, or to any other minority voting blocs. All he needed, again, was more white votes—specifically, more support among working-class white men in the Rust Belt. "The hidden story of the 2012 election just might come down to Romney not appealing to blue-collar white guys in this swing region," Sailer wrote. How could Romney have appealed to them? Sailer suggested one way: a hard-line stance on border security. In states like Michigan and Wisconsin, he wrote, "Immigration should be the perfect issue for the GOP to use to split the rank and file from their Democratic bosses."

Sailer still considered himself a conservative, although the arbiters of palatable conservative opinion, such as the editors of *National Review* and *The Weekly Standard*, had long ago stopped commissioning his work. Many of his peers in dissident right-wing punditry—John Derbyshire, Peter Brimelow, Ann Coulter, Jared Taylor—had been cast out of the conservative establishment for similar intellectual heresies. A few of them embraced their outcast status, gaining attention through confrontational acts of televised sophistry. (Ann Coulter was especially adept at this tactic, tiptoeing just close enough to the you-can't-say-that-on-television line to ensure that she would always be invited back on television.) The others kept blogging, biding their time.

Sailer felt confident that no part of the Sailer Strategy was unconstitutional or illegal. In more than a decade, no one had been able to point out any serious mistakes in his arithmetic or his logic. The real problem, as far as he could tell, was that his ideas made powerful people uncomfortable.

Conservatives often referred to the Overton window, or to political correctness. Sailer went a step further. Of all the malign forces that he perceived in the world, perhaps the most pernicious was what he called "the Narrative"—a nonnegotiable vocabulary that every member of polite society was required to learn. Political correctness was just a small part of it. Americans absorbed the Narrative every day—in their schools, in the media, through mass entertainment, through thousands of tiny social cues. The brainwashing was so total as to become invisible; people internalized the axioms so deeply that, after a while, they couldn't think without them. Simply to point out the existence of the axioms, much less to call their truth into question, was to become a dangerous brute, a pariah.*

According to the Narrative, Islam is a religion of peace; therefore, the mullahs calling for bloodshed had to be ignored or explained away. According to the Narrative, race and gender are social constructs; therefore, newspaper articles and car commercials had to avoid depicting any meaningful difference between European Americans and African Americans, or between men and women. According to

---

*Sailer borrowed the term from *I, Sniper*, a thriller by the novelist Stephen Hunter. In the book, one character, a newspaper reporter, explains the concept: "The narrative is the set of assumptions the press believes in, possibly without even knowing that it believes in them. It's so powerful because it's unconscious. It's not like they get together every morning and decide 'These are the lies we tell today.' No, that would be too crude and honest. . . . They don't even know they're true believers, because in theory they despise the true believer in anything."

the Narrative, American citizenship is a civil right that is owed to every one of the world's seven billion inhabitants—Sailer called this the Zeroth Amendment, because "it's not in the Constitution, but it's treated as if it were"—so anyone seeking high office had to speak about immigration in magnanimous platitudes. This, Sailer believed, was why the Sailer Strategy was never invoked in *The Economist* or *The Wall Street Journal*, or on CNN or Fox News, or in official GOP reports. It defied the Narrative.*

On his blog, he referred to his ideas as "crimethink"—the word George Orwell used, in *1984*, for any thought that Big Brother didn't want you to have. By that analogy, of course, Sailer was Winston Smith, a vigilante hero struggling against tyranny. He understood that the analogy was melodramatic. He had no reason to assume that anyone at the NSA was even aware of his blog, much less conspiring to censor it or arrest him for its contents. The tyrannical force in the twenty-first-century United States was not a Ministry of Truth but the pervasive reach of the Narrative. "It's naive to imagine that a government would have to pay people to do this kind of thing," Sailer wrote. "In the current year, we now know that plenty of people would join the Volunteer Auxiliary Thought Police for free."

It seemed obvious that the marketplace of ideas was rigged against him. He was free to write what he wanted, but a small contrarian blog was no way to spark a national movement. Many normal American voters, Sailer thought, might consider his views quite unobjectionable, even obvious. But first normal Americans would have to be exposed to his ideas, and the guardians of the Narrative—the gatekeepers who controlled the movie studios, the ad firms, and the mainstream press—would never allow that to happen.

•   •   •

The system of Narrative control that Sailer had in mind was an old-fashioned one, with firm boundaries patrolled by human gatekeepers. But, whether Sailer noticed it or not, those boundaries were eroding quickly. In 2008, the marketing agency Universal McCann published a report declaring that the "age of mass

---

*"The immigration debate happens on a high level of abstraction and sentimentality," Sailer told me in one of our interviews. "It explains some otherwise inexplicable events—for instance, Angela Merkel, this cautious and middle-of-the-road politician, deciding to let in a million refugees. Where does that come from? Well, it kind of comes from the Zeitgeist, from this Narrative that has taken shape over time, in which it's increasingly seen as morally unacceptable that some people live in nice countries and other people live in not-nice countries. To me, it just seems nuts to make policy this way."

media" was giving way to the "age of social media." Anyone with web access, any-where in the world, was now not only a receiver of news but also a transmitter. Facebook, valued at $15 billion and rising, had recently gained its hundred-millionth subscriber. Meanwhile, American newspaper circulation was declining for the sixth consecutive year. Informational power was being democratized, or at least entrepreneurialized: you could spread almost any message you wanted, as long as you could get a crowd to listen. On the cover page of the Universal Mc-Cann report were a group of stylized cartoon characters with cyberpunk outfits, asymmetrical haircuts, and featureless faces. They stood on a grassy knoll over-looking a hypermodern skyline, raising their fists and 3G-enabled devices in the air. The tagline was "How the internet turned us all into influencers."

William F. Buckley, the last singular arbiter of conservative opinion, died in 2008, a few months before the report came out. He had no comparable successor, no conservative panjandrum who could dictate which ideas deserved to flourish and which did not. Several individuals and institutions tried to fill this role, but it seemed that this old kind of gatekeeping was becoming less feasible with every passing year. Many decisions about the spread of information were now made algorithmically. The algorithms were not designed to gauge whether an idea was true or false, prosocial or antisocial; they were designed to measure whether a meme was causing a spike of activating emotion in a large number of people. And Sailer's citizenism—more colloquially known as intellectualized white nationalism—was just such a meme.

Sailer and other far-right heretics, many of whom Buckley had banished to the fringes of the movement years earlier, now reconvened online. They built their own publications (*The American Conservative*, *Taki's Magazine*, *VDARE*), and promoted them using new tools such as WordPress and Twitter and Reddit. These were more powerful distribution mechanisms than fifty-year-old print maga-zines, anyway, and they had the added benefit of being content neutral. Through social media, the heretics lured visitors to their own sites, where they spoke even more freely, arguing from first principles. No thought was beyond the pale. Un-sayable opinions were repeated, again and again, until they became sayable. In the comments sections, the writers and their burgeoning audience debated what they should call themselves. The New Right? The American Renaissance? The Dissi-dent Right?

In November 2008, about sixty ex-academics, autodidacts, and freelance opinion writers gathered in a hotel ballroom outside Baltimore. They were there for the inaugural meeting of the H. L. Mencken Club, which described itself as a "society for the independent right." Earlier that month, Barack Obama had defeated John McCain to win the presidency, but the heretics in the hotel ballroom would have been equally dismayed by either result.* "There are things that everybody knows are true but can't be said," Peter Brimelow, the editor of *VDARE*, asserted in his keynote speech. One such thing, he continued, was the Sailer Strategy—"the need for Republicans to mobilize their white base."†

Paul Gottfried, a cantankerous former professor in his sixties, gave a speech that amounted to a generational baton-passing. The paleoconservatives, among whom he counted himself, had "spent their lives butting their heads against the American conservative movement," with little to show for it. But now, suddenly, "we have youth and exuberance on our side." He mentioned "a growing communion" of "websites that are willing to engage sensitive, timely subjects"; fans of these sites, Gottfried hoped, would form an energetic new cohort of dissident right-wingers, which he dubbed "the post-paleos."

Gottfried's remarks were later published on takimag.com, the website of *Taki's Magazine*. Writers don't pick their own headlines. Instead, the site's managing editor, Richard Spencer, coined a phrase for the new cohort of dissidents, a phrase that he thought would be catchier than "post-paleos." He titled Gottfried's speech "The Decline and Rise of the Alternative Right."‡

• • •

Sites like *Taki's* and *VDARE* inspired more alt-right sites, animated by an even more flippant, feral energy: *The Right Stuff, Danger & Play, Radix Journal*, the tech section of *Breitbart*. These sites were often laden with gleefully racist jokes, images of Greco-Roman statuary, and high-flown encomiums to "Western civilization."

---

*From the group's mission statement, as revised in 2016: "The HLMC is in no way allied to either of the two national political parties, and it should not be confused with the 'conservative movement.' We were in fact founded precisely because that movement has suppressed open discussion and seems entirely beholden to corporate donors and Republican Party bosses. From the standpoint of Conservatism, Inc., our group belongs to the 'basket of deplorables' that Hillary Clinton denounced in her presidential campaign."

†Brimelow had been purged from *National Review*, and from conservative respectability, in the late 1990s, after repeatedly insisting that nonwhite immigration would cause the imminent downfall of the United States. After he was purged, his xenophobia grew only more frantic and more explicit. He founded *VDARE* in 1999. The site was named for Virginia Dare, the first white child born on American soil.

‡In mid-2016, Gottfried, who is Jewish, insisted that he and Spencer be given credit for "co-creating" the term "alt-right." After Hailgate, he reconsidered, saying, "Any suggestion that I might be associated with what is depicted as a neo-Nazi movement is especially offensive."

The authors implied, or sometimes stated outright, that diversity was not an asset but a Trojan horse, or that authoritarianism was preferable to democracy, or that white male dominance was what had made antiquity great. These were ideas that polite society found abhorrent, of course, but the alt-right bloggers only treated this as further evidence of their own intellectual potency. After all, true crime-think is supposed to shock the bourgeoisie.

For a certain kind of reader, discovering these alt-right sites felt like stumbling onto a countercultural intellectual vanguard. These enthusiastic readers then took to Reddit and 4chan and Twitter and Facebook, spreading the heretical gospel. On social media, from behind an anonymous avatar, you could share more or less whatever you wanted—a Holocaust joke, an absurdist meme, a thought-provoking lie. You could post something because you believed it, or because you didn't believe it and you wanted to see who would. You could post something because you valued freedom of thought for its own sake; you could post something solely to get a reaction; you could post something without even knowing why, just because you felt like it.

Some parts of Reddit, and most of 4chan and 8chan,* were dominated by a culture of "shitposting," or posting whatever shit happened to pop into your head. There were endless subgenres of shitposting, with new ones invented practically every day. If you were expressing nostalgia for Pearl Jam and *Boy Meets World*, you were '90s posting. If you acted technologically illiterate or scandalized by raunchy humor, the way a clueless baby boomer might, you were boomer posting. Bane posting was when people treated Bane, the homicidally nihilistic villain from the *Dark Knight* trilogy of Batman movies, as a hero.† Trying too hard—letting yourself be swept away by earnestness or urgency, in defiance of the casual vibe of the internet—was called effort posting.‡

Amid all the arcane and sarcastic memes were glimmers of sincerity: statistics, rhetorical questions, and other breadcrumbs that were supposed to lead normies

---

*To most normies, the differences between 4chan and 8chan would have been tough to spot, a matter of splitting hairs. The sites were similar in many ways—internet ethnographers often spoke interchangeably of "chan culture," or "channers." The main difference was one of degree: 8chan was for people who felt that the hardcore rhetoric on 4chan wasn't hardcore *enough*.

†This might have seemed like a sign of sociopathy, if taken literally. But who took memes on the internet literally?

‡In 2019, a young white man, apparently radicalized on the alt-right internet, slaughtered fifty Muslims in Christchurch, New Zealand. Shortly before the massacre began, he wrote on 8chan, "It's time to stop shitposting and time to make a real life effort post."

down the path toward full alt-right radicalization. What kind of people followed the breadcrumbs? Some were hypercontrarians, addicted to the rush of asking forbidden questions and rejecting widely accepted answers. Some were alienated young men—restive, thwarted, full of depthless rage at women or at the world. Some had come to think of their lives as fictional simulations and were eager to experience a new timeline. And some, like a villain from the *Dark Knight* trilogy, just wanted to watch the world burn.

The new alt-right converts, more and more of them every month, continued to form communities on social media, where their voices continued to be amplified. The mood felt increasingly volatile, electric, like a parking lot outside a bar before a fight breaks out. In 2014, the alt-right hordes started coalescing around a more overt set of talking points: that racism was realism, that diversity was code for white genocide, that nonwhite immigration posed an imminent threat to Euro-American sovereignty. Then, in the summer of 2015, the hordes came to a sudden and unexpected consensus. They would use social media shitposting to help Donald Trump—a doddering pop-culture punch line whom they had rebranded, with web-savvy irony, as a triumphant "God-Emperor"—in his implausible quest to become the next president of the United States.

●　　●　　●

At the H. L. Mencken Club's annual meeting in 2010, one of the keynote speakers was Steve Sailer. "Richard Spencer has asked me to speak," he began, "on the topic 'Can HBD Trump PC?'"

"PC" stood for political correctness. "Trump" was a common verb, not a proper noun. "HBD" stood for human biodiversity—a phrase that had gone viral within the alt-right blogosphere, largely owing to Sailer's repeated use of it. Human biodiversity: the hypothesis that people are different, that they differ in predictable ways, and that some groups of people—some races, for example—have drawn stronger cards in the genetic lottery. On Sailer's blog, most discussions of human biodiversity ended up returning to one specific, enduring idea: that white people are inherently smarter than black people.

"In an intellectually healthy world, of course, the study of human biodiversity wouldn't be imperiled by the reign of political correctness," Sailer said. The problem, as usual, was the Narrative: "You watch your TV and learn from it what kind of thoughts raise your status and what kind lower your status." As long as mass-media gatekeepers kept portraying citizenism as low status, Sailer believed, the commoners would fall in line. Maybe one day, someone would subvert this status game, "shatter political correctness," and rebuild the Overton window, but he couldn't imagine who that person might be.

On June 16, 2015, Donald Trump stood, stiff and red faced, as an escalator carried him down to the lobby of one of his eponymous skyscrapers. A group of onlookers—many of them background actors who would be paid fifty dollars, in cash, upon leaving the building—held up signs and snapped photos with their phones. In the background, a PA system blasted "Rockin' in the Free World," an antijingoist anthem by a Canadian pacifist. When Trump got to the lobby, he gripped a lectern with both hands, looking both cocky and profoundly uncomfortable. He lied about the size of the crowd in front of him, mocked his political opponents ("They sweated like dogs"), and claimed that Muslim terrorists had "just built a hotel in Syria," which was so far from being true that journalists would later struggle to figure out which false rumor he might have been referring to. He said, of Mexican immigrants, "They're rapists." He was five minutes into his presidential campaign.

A few minutes later, he said, "We need somebody that can take the brand of the United States and make it great again. It's not great again." He announced that he was running for president, and the background actors cheered. The sound operator cued up "Rockin' in the Free World" again, to serve as Trump's exit music, but Trump didn't exit. Instead, he gestured for the volume to be turned down, then went on talking for another thirty minutes.

The whole spectacle was so discordant with the Narrative that most mainstream pundits discounted it, albeit for conflicting reasons. Trump was a huckster; his campaign was a publicity stunt; he would soon drop out of the race; he had no ideology; his ideology was sophomoric and inconsistent; his ideology was seductive and dangerous. Besides, he had no path to electoral victory.

Steve Sailer, meanwhile, kept blogging about the Sailer Strategy.

• • •

In 1989, David Duke, the founder of the Knights of the Ku Klux Klan, was elected to the Louisiana House of Representatives. The following year, he came close to winning a Republican primary for the U.S. Senate, capturing 43 percent of the vote. He was able to do all this, in part, because of his name recognition, which he maintained by constantly appearing on television. He seemed to assume that all press was good press. He was fine with being described as controversial, even dangerous, as long as he was placed somewhere within the bounds of recognized political opinion.

Blatant racists like Duke were a staple of the tabloid talk shows of the 1980s and '90s, the ones hosted by Geraldo Rivera and Sally Jessy Raphael and Oprah Winfrey. "It is definitely not a secret that hatred and racism is alive and well in the United States," Ricki Lake said on her daytime talk show in 1993. "But why? And where does this hatred come from? Today, we will talk to young women who are proud to be members of the Ku Klux Klan." The next hour of television did little to illuminate where American racism came from. "I think you're all screwed up," one audience member shouted, pointing at the women onstage. The rest of the audience erupted in applause.

Such ritual humiliations were good for ratings (everyone loves a good fight); they were good for social cohesion (nothing brings people together like a common enemy); they were also good for catharsis, in the original sense.* What is racism? Racism is a bad humor that dwells only in bad people. Where are the bad people? They are there, on the stage, under the bright lights, wearing shoulder pads and tacky teased hair and defiant sneers. Racism does not reside among us, the audience. You can tell because they are the ones being pointed at and we are the ones doing the pointing.

I was nine years old when that *Ricki Lake* episode aired. When I was home sick from school, I would often watch the daytime talk shows—I was especially fond of Sally Jessy Raphael, because of her bright-red glasses—and I always had precisely the reaction I was supposed to have. I remember thinking, in words, *Who could possibly hate other people because of the way they look?* Racism seemed like an exotic affliction—one of nature's cruel and inexplicable mistakes, almost like a rare birth defect. At school, I was taught to associate late November with the Pilgrims and late December with Jesus and mid-January with Martin Luther King, who preached love and tolerance and envisaged a day when Americans would be judged not by the color of their skin but by the content of their character.

Was I being indoctrinated? Yes, I suppose I was being indoctrinated. I was also

---

*One of the purposes of staged drama, Aristotle wrote, is to "excite pity and fear," thus "effecting the proper purgation of these emotions." Catharsis, in Greek, means purging, or cleansing: you call forth the bile in order to rid yourself of it.

being indoctrinated to believe that puppies are cute, and that gravity is a force that causes objects to fall to Earth, and that it's rude to interrupt people while they're talking. Another word for the indoctrination of children is education. There is no such thing as a society without a Narrative; there are only better Narratives and worse ones.

In retrospect, my main complaint about my indoctrination is that it didn't grow more sophisticated more quickly. Gravity does cause objects to fall to Earth, but it's not a force; it's a result of the curvature of space-time, which isn't quite the same thing. The version of Martin Luther King that I learned about in elementary school (and then, with minor variations, in middle school and high school) was a storybook version of King: a stoic who had faith that our nation would eventually live up to its founding principles. This was true enough, but it left out a lot. The real Martin Luther King also believed that the United States was a fundamentally "sick" country, and that "justice for black people cannot be achieved without radical changes in the structure of our society."

In 1991, Duke ran for governor of Louisiana. Translating his ideology into the vocabulary of the moment, he positioned himself as a chastened mainstream Republican. "I'm a Christian person, and I think we all evolve in our lives," he told Phil Donahue, on Donahue's daytime talk show. Duke didn't disavow his former ideology, but he tried to make it sound abstract, in the style of the Southern Strategy: "People are now talking about the reverse discrimination going on, they're talking about the need to reform the welfare system, they're talking about the fact that forced busing is damaging education."

Donahue, playing the role of the sober, objective newsman, neither agreed nor disagreed with Duke's talking points. He let Duke go on for a few minutes before cutting to commercial: "We'll be back with Mr. Duke, the candidate, in just a moment." In the first round of voting, Duke came within two percentage points of first place, triggering a runoff. He lost the runoff election, but he won a majority of the white vote.

CHAPTER ELEVEN

The Invisible Primary

I n the fall of 2015, I had breakfast with an anchor at a major TV network. For months, Donald Trump had been the front-runner in every Republican primary poll. The anchor and I talked about what most of the country was talking about, and would continue talking about for the foreseeable future: the astonishing rise of Trumpism, how unstoppable it seemed to be. The anchor and I were supposed to be members of the Fourth Estate, yet we felt powerless to do anything but watch the phenomenon unfold.

"How about a voluntary media blackout?" I suggested. "No more covering his tweets. No more covering every rally. Why take the bait?"

"Even if I agreed with your premise, which I'm not sure I do," the anchor said, "it wouldn't matter. First, there's no way Fox News would participate in any blackout. Second, everyone knows that Trump is the story that gets ratings right now. Nothing else even comes close. Which means that the moment I tell my boss 'I'm not covering Trump' is the moment my boss tells me, 'OK, it was fun working with you, we've got someone on their way right now to replace you.' And then, even if all of TV could somehow be turned into a Trump-free zone, there's still the internet."

Right: the internet. I must have been reading too many think pieces* about how Trump's lead would vanish as soon as the mainstream media stopped "giving him oxygen." This metaphor made sense only if one imagined a scenario with a single oxygen source: Trump as deep-sea diver, say, with cable news as his scuba tank. But Trump was more like a wizened, ageless tortoise in an aquarium full of

---

*Where did I find these think pieces? On the internet, of course.

decentralized air pumps. TV and national newspapers were major oxygen sources, to be sure, but there were many others: shock-humor podcasts, celebrity-gossip blogs, foreign wire services, viral clickbait start-ups. And then there were the social networks, perhaps the biggest oxygen pumps of all, which were powered by millions of regular people who loved Trump or hated Trump enough to keep talking perpetually about Trump. Everything he did or said—everything he *was*— incited a sharp spike of activating emotion, positive or negative, in almost everyone. He was a ready-made viral meme.

TV executives are obsessed with ratings, but they're also motivated, at least to some degree, by other factors: news judgment, time constraints, a sense of fairness, a capacity to feel shame. Social networks, on the other hand, were supposed to transcend such messy human subjectivity in pursuit of pure neutrality. They were designed to be feedback machines, giving users not what they needed but whatever they were likely to want, based on their stated and unstated preferences. Broadcasters could have decided to stop giving attention to Trump, and once in a while they did. But that wasn't really possible on social media, where the content consisted of whatever people felt like talking about.

• • •

Andrew Breitbart, the John the Baptist of the Deplorables, is often credited with the maxim "Politics is downstream from culture." Like all maxims, it's reductive— the stream flows in both directions—and yet it was a shrewd, simple insight that led him to other shrewd, simple insights. In 2011, on Fox News, Breitbart was asked whether Donald Trump was a conservative. "Of course he's not a conservative," he said. However, a few seconds later, he added that someone like Trump could be a formidable presidential candidate: "Celebrity is everything in this country."

To most pundits at the time, this seemed paradoxical. How could a nonconservative be the standard-bearer of the conservative movement? Why would the Republican Party let that happen? But Breitbart understood that the Republican Party doesn't decide who its nominee will be. Voters do. Voters are just people, and people like who they like.

The chattering classes might assume that the factors that matter to them—the candidates' policy agendas, their performances in TV debates, the endorsements they receive in local newspapers—will be the main factors that determine how people vote. But there is no rule requiring voters to pay attention to newspapers, or to cogent articulations of policy, or to anything else. If politics is downstream from culture, then political information spreads the way all information spreads. People base their behavior, including their voting behavior, on whatever scraps of information they happen to notice and remember: tabloid headlines, unclicked Google ads, specious rumors, reruns of *The Apprentice*.

Breitbart wasn't blinded by political orthodoxy because he didn't know much about it. Rather, he was a new-media savant, an early employee at both the *Drudge Report* and *The Huffington Post*—a disrupter. "My goal is to destroy *The New York Times* and CNN," he said, in 2010. "The media class is the wall that we have to climb over in order for our voices to be heard." Much of what Breitbart knew about politics he'd learned from a slim book called *Rules for Radicals*, published in 1971 by the community organizer Saul Alinsky. Alinsky was a leftist, and both Barack Obama and Hillary Clinton cited *Rules for Radicals* as a formative influence. Yet the tactics in the book are nonpartisan—"Power and fear are the fountainheads of faith," Alinsky wrote—and a good number of twenty-first-century Alinskyans, if not a majority, are right-wing radicals.

Breitbart died in 2012. By then, it was starting to become clear that the best way to promote a radical message—one that institutional gatekeepers might find threatening or subversive—was to exploit the amoral openness of the social web. In addition to his maxim about politics and culture, Breitbart left behind an even simpler slogan, one that consisted of a single word: "War." Or, as it was inevitably rendered by the social media foot soldiers who picked up the mantle of their fallen general: "#WAR."

In a 2008 book called *The Party Decides*, four political scientists argued that every presidential nominating process begins with an "invisible primary." Before the first vote is cast, "party insiders" narrow the electorate's choices, making preferred candidates seem inevitable and dark-horse candidates seem implausible. The relevant factors in an invisible primary were said to include endorsements, donations, and "the media."

This last term was not defined anywhere in the book, presumably because its authors, like most educated people, assumed that they knew what "the media" was. (As a proxy for media coverage, they measured how often a candidate appeared in *Time* and *Newsweek*, which they called "a representative source, but not a perfect one.") If they had tried to define the media, they might have invoked such criteria as the power to shape public discourse, or to spread information quickly to large swaths of the American populace. Applying those criteria in the age of social media, it was no longer clear why, apart from cliquishness or nostalgia, the label should apply to professional journalists but not to amateur podcasters, or to Twitch streamers, or to any bug-eyed doomsayer with a popular YouTube channel.

In 1972, a poll suggested that Walter Cronkite was the most trusted man in America. In 2013, according to a *Reader's Digest* poll, the most trusted person in America was Tom Hanks. Michelle Obama, the highest-ranking political figure on the list, came in at No. 19, below Dr. Oz; Judge Judy was eight spots above Justice Ruth Bader Ginsburg. "The extent to which celebrity is prized in our society and has infiltrated politics is shocking to me," one of the authors of *The Party Decides*, Marty Cohen, said in a 2016 interview on NPR. He was trying to explain, in retrospect, what his theory had failed to predict. "Things that are very easy to debunk are gaining currency in politics," he added. "We've lost the gatekeeper."

• • •

Richard Dawkins coined the word "meme" in 1976, when he was in his thirties. For the next four decades, he continued teaching and writing bestselling books, and the meme of the meme kept evolving. By 2016, the memification of political discourse had become impossible to ignore. After Brexit and before the American election, I arranged to interview Dawkins by phone.

First, I told him about a wedding I'd recently attended in Vermont. The father of the bride, in his toast, had spoken first about the family's ancestry and then about a set of ethical teachings that had been passed down through generations—categories that he referred to, respectively, as "the genes" and "the memes." I happened to be standing next to the bride's younger sister, so I heard her when she turned to a friend and whispered, with affectionate forbearance, "Dad is such a dork. He has no idea what a meme is."

Dawkins laughed. "I hope you put her right!" he said. "The word seems to mean, to her generation, a picture with capital letters on it." This definition, he continued, was "curiously narrow—a bit like deciding to use the word 'animals' to mean only rabbits."

We talked about the virality industry, which he saw as a potential threat to liberal democracy. "We may be at a threshold," he said. "In the past, I would've been tempted to say, about the internet, that although everybody has a megaphone, in many cases it's a quiet one. You can put up a YouTube video, but who's going to watch it? Now, however ridiculous what you're saying is, if you make it memetically successful, something really bad can spread through the culture."

When books were first published in late medieval Europe, Dawkins said, many novice readers were too dazzled by the medium to be appropriately skeptical: if it was printed on vellum, it was probably true. Perhaps, he speculated, something similar was happening now. "If a drunken yob yells abuse at you on the street, you just ignore it," he said. "But if you see someone yelling some bit of nonsense on Twitter, right next to a link to a *New York Times* editorial or an official statement by the queen, you don't quite tune out the nonsense in the same way."

He sighed. "It's a pessimistic thought," he said, "but remember: from the replicator's point of view, whethe'r the replicator is a gene or a meme, success just means spreading itself. The survival of the species is not a factor."

$$\bullet \quad \bullet \quad \bullet$$

Every week, Trump said something so outrageous that it was deemed a campaign-ending gaffe. Every week, Trump remained the Republican front-runner. Most pundits continued to assure their audiences, and themselves, that his lead was a passing fluke. Nevertheless, it persisted. "I could stand in the middle of Fifth Avenue and shoot somebody and I wouldn't lose any voters," Trump said in January 2016. "It's, like, incredible."

I logged on to Facebook and scrolled through my personalized News Feed: Trump outrage, outrage about Trump outrage, baby photo, joke about Trump outrage. By default, Facebook is a well-sealed filter bubble—you share with the people in your bubble, and they share with you. But if you ever want to see outside your bubble, all you have to do is look.

At the top of my screen was a tool I used so seldom that I sometimes forgot it was there: Facebook's search bar. I typed in a few phrases ("International Jewish cabal," "Huma Abedin Muslim Brotherhood spy," "Only men can be president"). No idea was too outlandish. Whatever I looked for, I found it. The search results didn't include much nudity or profanity, both of which Facebook's moderators were quick to remove; but I did find plenty of invented crime statistics, misleadingly doctored photographs, and all manner of covert and overt bigotry.

These were a few of the oxygen bubbles keeping the Trump campaign alive. There were hundreds of them, more every minute, pumped out by sensationalist outfits with forgettable names: Liberty Writers, Being Patriotic, Expensive Designer Memes.* There was a good amount of left-wing garbage, and there was a lot more right-wing garbage. Some of it was standard xenophobic scaremongering based on thin sourcing or no sourcing at all. ("Burger King Just Announced THEY WILL FOLLOW ISLAMIC SHARIA LAW! Stop them!") Some headlines named the activating emotion they aimed to produce and then ended abruptly, leaving a curiosity gap. ("You Won't Believe What Hillary Just Did! OUTRAGE.") There was a Facebook page called Fashy Memes, with stick-figure comics of shit-libs confessing to their status-signaling hypocrisy. Other viral posts contained no words at all—just an image of Trump looking heroic, or of Clinton looking ghoulish and frail, or of a black person caricatured as a monkey.

I wasn't shocked to find racism and sexism on the internet. If anything, many of the memes, at least on Facebook, were surprisingly tame. (Reddit and 4chan were another story.) Nor was I baffled by the existence of rudimentary political propaganda, which has existed since the dawn of democracy.[†] What surprised me was how rapidly the stuff was spreading.

My time with Emerson Spartz had trained me to look, whenever I saw a new meme on Facebook, at a small set of numbers at the bottom of each post. These were tallies of the post's engagement—how many comments it had received, how many times it had been liked or shared—which were harbingers of its present and future virality.[‡] I scrolled through dozens of posts ranging from banal to bizarre to casually violent. Many of them had engagement tallies in the thousands, or in the tens of thousands. For a moment, I took solace in the fact that most of the memes I was seeing were so outré that they would be unprintable in any reputable

---

*Most of these pages were operated by real red-blooded Americans; but it later became clear that a few of them, including Being Patriotic, were the work of the Internet Research Agency, a St. Petersburg–based company generating pro-Putin propaganda. In early 2018, an American grand jury indicted the Internet Research Agency, along with several other Russian individuals and entities, for meddling in the 2016 U.S. presidential election.

†Every human society has included an unruly fringe, and the fringe has always found a way to speak. On the day Mount Vesuvius erupted, in the year 79, the walls of Pompeii bore graffiti as salacious as any Reddit thread. On the Vicolo del Panettiere: ATIMETUS GOT ME PREGNANT. Inside the Inn of the Muledrivers, next to a doorpost: WE HAVE WET THE BED, HOST. I CONFESS WE HAVE DONE WRONG. On a wall of the Eumachia Building: SECUNDUS LIKES TO SCREW BOYS. Inside the basilica: A SMALL PROBLEM GROWS LARGER IF YOU IGNORE IT.

‡The way Spartz put it was that every time a post was shared, its content was "exposed to a new cluster of people," who could then share it further. Moreover, engagement statistics were signals to Facebook's algorithm that a meme was picking up momentum. The algorithm was designed to reward success with more success: if a meme was being shared quickly, it would show up more prominently in other people's feeds, causing it to spread even faster.

newspaper. Maybe that would limit their reach. Then I reconsidered: more than fifty percent of American adults looked at Facebook daily, but less than fifteen percent subscribed to a newspaper. With nearly unfettered access to Facebook's immense audience, why would a propagandist need anything else?

One morning in 2016, David Remnick walked into my office and glanced at my computer screen. I was wearing headphones and I hadn't heard him come in. I must have been exploring a particularly foul patch of social media undergrowth, because he grabbed my shoulder, nodded toward the screen, and said, "OK, what the hell is that?"

"Have a seat," I said.

I repeated a few of my Facebook searches, bringing up toxic memes and propaganda posts and reading out the engagement stats below each one: five thousand shares here, fifteen thousand likes there. By way of contrast, I opened the official Facebook pages of *Reason, Foreign Affairs, The Nation, The Weekly Standard*—any outlet I could think of, so long as it contributed more substantively to the pursuit of human knowledge than the Fashy Memes Facebook page. In some cases, the old gatekeepers seemed to be doing just fine. A few of the newer, more social-media-oriented companies (such as *BuzzFeed* and *Vox*, both of which produced a good deal of high-quality journalism) were doing better than fine. But, in many side-by-side comparisons, the bigots and propagandists were winning.

Then came the gut punch: *The New Yorker*'s Facebook page. A recent landmark piece of investigative journalism, conclusively linking Bashar al-Assad to international war crimes: eighty-seven shares. A lively and authoritative assessment of Aretha Franklin's career, written by Remnick himself and including lengthy quotes from President Obama: seventy-eight shares. An intricate and poignant story about immigration and child care, one of the finest pieces of writing I'd ever read: fifteen shares. I kept scrolling until I found a post or two—a brash opinion column, a crowd-pleasing piece of satire—with share tallies in the triple digits. Nothing in the thousands.

"I get it, I get it," Remnick said. "It's not auspicious. But where's the story in it?"

Most people, myself included, had grown accustomed to thinking of social media as an emergent property of the popular will, or of the open market, or of dumb luck. Teens posted their dance videos on Snapchat, and maybe, if the viral gods were smiling, a few of them got booked on *Ellen* and enjoyed fifteen minutes of mainstream fame. But the virality industry was not actually an unknowable mystery. It was, rather, the product of a large number of small human choices. At every step, there were people behind the curtain: consumers making and sharing the content, engineers designing the algorithms that distributed the content, moderators culling the content or failing to cull it.*

Something was happening online: a new kind of invisible primary, an attempt, either coordinated or spontaneous, to stretch the Overton window so radically as to drag the notion of a Trump presidency into the realm of the imaginable. Who was doing it? Trump was a ready-made meme, but the virus wasn't propagating itself. There were already credible rumors that some of the pro-Trump activity was being generated by Russian troll farms; still, even if many of those rumors turned out to be true, the Russians couldn't possibly account for all of the activity, or even most of it. Whatever was happening, it was comforting to assume that it was happening *to* us—that the American electorate was being manipulated by ratings-obsessed executives at CNN, or by rapacious Wall Street bankers angling for corporate handouts, or by Putin. But the truth was that a lot of what was happening to the American people was being done by the American people. I just didn't know who was doing it, exactly, or how.

"What if I could find the people who are peddling this stuff?" I said. "What if I could find the Emerson Spartz of fringe politics?"

Remnick's eyebrows shot up. He saw it right away. "That could be a story," he said.

---

*A more Rortyan way of putting this: social media, the whole churning mess of it, seemed as if it were animated by little more than chance and the momentum of history, but it was better understood as a product of human contingency.

PART THREE

Too Big to Ignore

The desire . . . to make a face or say a dirty word. Was this the face they all wanted to make? To show somebody, to show everybody? They wouldn't do it, though; they wouldn't get the chance. Special circumstances were required. A lurid, unreal place, the middle of the night, a staggering unhinging weariness, the sudden, hallucinatory appearance of your true enemy.

Alice Munro, 1977

CHAPTER TWELVE

Beyond Good and Evil

Mike Cernovich grew up in Kewanee, a small hog-farming town in central Illinois. His mother, a homemaker, hadn't finished high school; his father worked at a local factory. On Sundays, the family worshipped in home churches, where the preachers spoke in tongues and taught the inerrant truth of the Bible. Mike's mother heard voices, and some days she was too depressed to get out of bed. The congregation formed a prayer circle around her, trying to cast out her demons, but it didn't work. Eventually, she got desperate and went to the hospital. They diagnosed her as bipolar and gave her medication, and she started to feel better after that.

Mike had two younger brothers and an older half sister. They didn't starve, but there were holes in the carpet that their parents couldn't afford to fix, and the grocery budget was too tight to allow for any snacks between meals. Once, Mike dropped a glass jar of peanut butter and it shattered on the kitchen floor. He looked at it for a long time—the sticky mound coated in glittering dust, a sail of glass jutting into the air—before accepting that he would have to throw it all away.

Cernovich was a Croatian name, but nobody in the family cooked any traditional dishes or expressed any nostalgia for the Old Country. They were Americans. Mike's paternal grandfather came to Kewanee at the age of five. As a young man during World War II, he joined the navy and fought in the Pacific; then he came back to Kewanee and worked as an Illinois state policeman for three decades before retiring and collecting his pension. He was a party-line Democrat, but some of his children, including Mike's father, ended up voting for Reagan and thinking of themselves as Republicans. They ribbed each other about it sometimes, the way a Cubs fan might tease a White Sox fan, but nobody took politics all that seriously.

Mike was a shy kid, pudgy and brooding, with an angry streak that often turned inward. He had asthma and eczema—not debilitating, but enough to make him feel uncomfortable almost all the time. Intelligent and contrarian, he could debate anything with anyone. Sometimes, though, he'd argue with the wrong person—challenging a teacher's unearned authority, or asking a preacher how a benevolent God could send non-Christian babies to Hell—and this would land him in trouble. For the most part, he kept to himself.

He was eager to finish high school, but he didn't give much thought to what would come afterward. A lot of guys in Kewanee joined the military; the ones who didn't tended to stay in town, get married, and look for work at a restaurant or a gas station or a big-box store. A few made it as far as the University of Illinois, either the main campus in Urbana-Champaign or the one in the state capital, Springfield; but even if they graduated, they usually just ended up back home. When Mike was a junior in high school, the top student in the class above him got into the University of Chicago. Only years later did Mike learn that this was a rare achievement—at the time, he figured that a city was smaller than a state, so the University of Chicago had to be a less selective school than the University of Illinois.

When he was seventeen, Mike enlisted in the National Guard. Two weekends a month, and for two weeks over the summer, he trained at the National Guard Armory in Kewanee. He liked it well enough—he practiced marksmanship, got in shape, even learned how to box and won a few amateur fights. It still sounded corny when adults moralized about the value of hard work, but Mike also started to see the truth in it. He remembered when he couldn't do five push-ups in a row; now he could do fifty, no problem.

After he graduated from high school, he thought about signing up for active duty. It was the late 1990s; the U.S. wasn't fighting any ground wars, but still, maybe he'd get assigned to an army base somewhere exotic. His father, who wasn't usually much of a talker, sat him down and tried to change his mind. "You're smart enough for college," his father said. "Just try it and see. If you don't do it now, you'll end up working dead-end jobs like me." There was a community college in the neighboring town, a few miles south on Route 78. Mike didn't always get along with his father, but he respected him enough to sign up for a semester.

The professors let him criticize any text, including the Bible and the Constitution. You were allowed, even encouraged, to make extreme arguments: that logic or truth or beauty were meaningless concepts, or that studying the words of dead white slaveholders was a waste of time. The professors claimed that they wanted their students to be as open minded as possible, but of course that wasn't really true. There were limits, and you learned pretty quickly what they were. When you discussed the *Republic*, for example, you weren't supposed to wonder whether Plato may have been right that, when it came to most tasks outside the home, "a woman is inferior to a man." It struck Mike as a bit hypocritical to place constraints, even informal ones, on intellectual discourse. Wouldn't Plato, of all people, have wanted his ideas to be debated openly?

Still, Mike loved college. He transferred to the Springfield campus of the University of Illinois, and the Illinois Veteran Grant Program paid his tuition. Learning to write a twenty-page paper was like training to do fifty push-ups—it seemed like you couldn't do it, and at first you couldn't, but you just did one push-up, and then a week later you could do five, and then eventually you could do fifty. You were the same person all along, but at first you had a mental image of yourself as someone who couldn't achieve your goal, and that mental image was the first thing you needed to overcome. Although he didn't say it out loud to anyone, he had decided that he didn't want to be a Christian, he didn't want to be poor, and he didn't want to spend his whole life stuck in Kewanee. Those had always seemed like things that were bound to happen to him, but he wasn't just going to let the expected things happen to him anymore.

He was drawn to modern Continental philosophy, especially Friedrich Nietzsche, whom he considered a visionary. Not only was Christianity incorrect, Nietzsche wrote; it was absurd, "unbelievable," and everything that rested on it—"for example, the whole of European morality"—was overdue for "a sequence of breakdown, destruction, ruin, and cataclysm." This would be painful, Nietzsche argued, but also necessary, because traditional morality was a form of spiritual enslavement, a way for the ruling classes to keep the rest of society fearful and weak. A more natural state of affairs would be for "the higher man" to seek power and self-fulfillment, not through Christian meekness but through bold force of will. "A human being who strives for something great considers everyone he meets on his way either as a means or as a delay and obstacle," Nietzsche wrote in *Beyond Good and Evil*. Such a striver would need great reserves of confidence and perseverance, because truly independent thinkers were often scorned and marginalized, at least during their lifetimes.*

Whenever Mike considered what his own version of self-fulfillment might look like, he thought more about the pursuit—the hero's journey, as Carl Jung called it—than about the end result. The goal was almost irrelevant. It probably wouldn't be money. As far as Mike could tell, most rich people didn't seem all that happy. Maybe it would be something more like influence, or a legacy that would outlive him. The only way he could describe it, when he tried putting it into words, was that he wanted to become too big to ignore.

His survey courses in philosophy also covered postmodernists like Foucault and Lacan and Derrida. A lot of what they wrote struck him as faux-intellectual bullshit, but he boiled it down until it made sense to him. The postmodernists seemed to be arguing that there was no single, absolute truth—that everything was just a narrative, a socially contingent power struggle, which implied that even history and current events were subject to personal interpretation, the way novels and movies were. Mike didn't know whether this was objectively true, but it was an interesting way to look at the world. Outside of class, at a Barnes & Noble, he bought copies of *Adbusters*, the radical left magazine that would one day inspire the Occupy protests. As the name implied, *Adbusters* carried no ads; it railed against late capitalism and all forms of corporate media, promoting such initiatives as Buy Nothing Day and TV Turnoff Week. Convinced that TV had done nothing to improve his life, and generally indisposed to half measures, Mike got rid of his TV and ended up abstaining for five years.

During summer break, he went back to Kewanee and worked at Menards, a chain home-goods store. One of his coworkers, a middle-aged guy named Greg, recognized Mike's intelligence and drive, calling him "a budding Tony Robbins." Greg recommended Ayn Rand's *Atlas Shrugged*. Mike drove to Peoria to buy it, and he was persuaded by Rand's endorsement of radical selfishness. Why should great men—the "prime movers" who made society flourish—be held back by mediocrity and red tape? Until someone convinced him otherwise, he decided, he would be a libertarian.

---

*"Mike was not just clever but actually smart, which is rare," Peter Boltuc, a philosophy professor at the University of Illinois, said. "One of the most teachable students I've ever had. My main worry was that he would take the Nietzsche stuff too literally—the will to power, 'male virtues,' the transvaluation of values—that he would maybe even follow it all the way to the Heidegger stuff, the Nazi stuff. I did worry about that. I tried to give him other things to read, and other people to connect with, so that he wouldn't get too lost."

His closest friend in Springfield was Melvin Armstrong, a political-science student and a committed leftist. A few times a week, they went powerlifting together; every Friday night, after leaving the gym, they'd go to Ryan's, a restaurant with an all-you-can-eat dinner buffet.* Armstrong, who is black, had grown up in the foster-care system of Bloomington, Illinois, and then earned a GED. He and Cernovich ragged on their classmates from Lake Forest and Winnetka, the soft, entitled rich kids who had no idea what it was like to apply for a loan or to hold down a shitty job. Cernovich made Armstrong watch *Good Will Hunting* with him again and again, especially the scene where Matt Damon tells the smug Harvard student, "You dropped a hundred and fifty grand on a fuckin' education you coulda got for a dollar fifty in late charges at the public library."

"You'll be serving my kids fries at a drive-through on our way to a skiing trip," the Harvard guy retorts.

"Yeah, maybe," Will says. "But at least I won't be unoriginal." Then Will challenges the Harvard guy to a fight, the guy backs down, and Will ends up getting the girl.

Once, Cernovich was hanging out with a bunch of Armstrong's friends, all of whom were black. One of them needed to get to his girlfriend's house. "Borrow my car," Mike said, handing the guy his keys.

Everyone burst out laughing. "Cerno, are you stupid?" Armstrong said.

"It's an old junker," Cernovich said. "Trust me, no one will steal it."

"That's not the point," Armstrong's friend explained. "If I get pulled over, what am I supposed to say? 'You see, officer, some white guy *gave* me his car, that's why my name doesn't match the registration'?"

"If that happens, have the cop call me," Cernovich said. "I'll vouch for you."

They laughed even harder at this. "You really are something else, man," Armstrong said.

Cernovich tried to look at things rationally. "Blacks are treated differently by police, and this is such a duh point that it's not even worth arguing," he wrote later. "Yet I don't toe the party line. . . . I don't hate myself for being white. I don't 'check my privilege.' I rather like myself, actually."

---

*"We set records for the amount of protein consumed," Armstrong said later. "They certainly lost money on us."

He graduated and applied to law school. He was good at arguing, and a law degree seemed like a way to gain cultural capital, although he still wasn't sure what he would do with it. He chose Pepperdine—not because it was a Christian school, although that was what he told his parents, but because it was in Malibu, overlooking a ruggedly beautiful stretch of the Pacific. No one had been able to talk him out of libertarianism, so when he got to Pepperdine he joined the Federalist Society. A few weeks into school, he asked one of his classmates, a good-looking woman from a well-educated family, for a ride to an off-campus bar. They had such a good conversation on the way that they forgot all about the bar; instead, they spent the whole night driving around and talking. They didn't have much in common, at least superficially—she was neither white nor working class, and she wasn't particularly interested in philosophy or politics—but they fell for each other, and before they finished law school they were married.

In 2004, a few weeks before graduation, Cernovich made his first website. It was a legal blog called *Crime & Federalism*; its mission was "to expose prosecutorial, police, and other governmental misconduct." Writing under a pseudonym, Cernovich posted straightforward Supreme Court news ("Cert. Granted in *Raich*") and occasional digressions into online solipsism ("Woo hoo! I just made it to Page 1 of Google for the search term federalism"). He was still indisposed to half measures, and he started pushing his contrarian ideas to their most radical conclusions. Part of him, the part that craved social acceptance, was tempted to cling to his old, safe beliefs; but true intellectual courage would mean rethinking everything from first principles, pursuing the truth wherever it led. "No shepherd, and one herd!" Nietzsche wrote in *Thus Spoke Zarathustra*. "Everyone is the same: he who feels differently goes voluntarily into a madhouse." In college, those words had seemed like a cryptic fable. The older Cernovich got, the more they seemed like a prophesy, even a personal challenge. How would he live if he were truly unafraid? Where would he go if he could leave the herd behind?

He had trouble finding work after law school, largely due to an unresolved rape charge. A few summers earlier, back home in Illinois, he'd had sex with a woman he knew from college. He claimed that, although they'd both been drinking, the sex was consensual. The woman claimed that it wasn't, and she went to the police. Five years later, in 2009, Cernovich was cleared of the charge and his record was expunged.

The experience seemed to break something open inside of him. "When you are falsely accused of rape," he said on a podcast later, "you realize that everything you had been told about the legal system was a lie. What other lies have we been told, and what are the source of those lies?" He blogged about his case on *Crime & Federalism*, referring to it as *State v. Anonymous*. Near the end of the post, without identifying himself as Anonymous, he slipped into the first person. "That case completely changed my view on how the criminal justice system treats date-rape cases," he wrote. "I reject feminism as the enslavement philosophy that it is."

After law school, his wife got a job as an in-house lawyer for a tech company. They moved to San Francisco, renting an apartment a couple of blocks away from an elliptical urban garden called South Park.* The California Bar Association wouldn't accept him—his rape charge was still pending—so he couldn't join a law firm or start a solo practice. Instead, he picked up whatever freelance work he could, doing legal research or writing unsigned briefs. The rest of the time, he read widely across the open internet. In college, he'd been exposed to new ideas in his classes, or in magazines, or through friends. On social media, bouncing from tab to tab, he might encounter a dozen mind-blowing ideas before lunch. It was as if he'd been becalmed in a sailboat for years and now, suddenly, gale-force winds were blowing him in all directions.

He started blogging about much more than crime and federalism. Whenever the mood struck, he would open his laptop, take a series of sharp, deep breaths, work himself into a flow state, and start typing. The words that came out were often a surprise even to him. Every time he pressed "Publish," he could feel his pulse quicken. "Soon enough, adrenaline becomes your trusted friend," he wrote. "You inhale deeply through your nostrils, and feel the life-affirming drug lift your soul."

He floated outlandish theories about gender relations ("Men are the new black"), nutrition ("If you're not already taking 3–6 grams of fish oil and 2,000 IUs of Vitamin D a day, you're literally killing yourself"), endocrinology ("Steroids are not just effective, they are healthy and life enhancing"), and politics ("America is a powder keg that is about to erupt"). By now he was blogging under his real name.

---

*Two years later, in 2006, a small podcasting company called Odeo pivoted to become a small "microtexting" company called Twitter. Its first headquarters was a nearly windowless space at 164 South Park, around the corner from where the Cernoviches lived.

This was risky—in theory, his innermost thoughts could be read by almost anyone in the world—and yet blogging still felt almost private. It seemed to occupy a middle space: less vulnerable than exposing your inner psyche on national TV, less pathetic than ranting alone in your kitchen.

As a libertarian, Cernovich believed in taking cues from the free market. He kept expecting to express an idea so strange or depraved that his readers would recoil; but the more extreme his views became, the more traffic he seemed to get. When the Supreme Court heard a case about whether the New Haven Fire Department's hiring policies were racially discriminatory against white people, his response was not a dry legal analysis of affirmative action, but a heated first-person essay about what it was like to grow up poor: "Fuck you and your Harvard-attending ass lecturing me about white privilege." The comments section of his blog lit up. A few readers were offended, but most were gratified. "Those Harvard types that make the laws don't know the real America," one commenter wrote.

Cernovich took a jaundiced view of politics, high finance, academia, and celebrity culture. "Never trust a man who combs his hair so as to cover his shiny dome, and then flaunts a wife young enough to be his daughter," he wrote in 2006, in a post called "Donald Chump?" He recommended a documentary version of *Manufacturing Consent* and an hour-long lecture by Elizabeth Warren on the collapse of the middle class. In other posts, lest his liberal readers get too comfortable, he'd express deep skepticism about gun control or climate change.* A slave took moral instruction from his superiors; a free man thought for himself.

• • •

In 2010, Cernovich was six years out of law school, still living with his wife in San Francisco, still not admitted to the bar. In addition to his freelance legal work, he bought the URL Fit-Juice.com, where he blogged about health cleanses and hawked a series of self-published recipe books.† This brought in a modest amount of income, but the truth was that his wife, who was now a high-ranking employee at Facebook,

---

*"Is global warming man-made? I don't know, and I don't have an opinion," he wrote. "Everything I had ever been told about steroids was a lie. Why then should I take anything climatologists say on faith?"

†*Juicing for Athletes, Juicing for Men, Juice Power*. Although he occasionally alluded to his use of exogenous testosterone, these books were mostly about the licit kind of juicing.

earned more than enough to provide for them both. (In addition to her salary, she was paid in Facebook stock—nearly three hundred thousand shares, all told.)

Later, in a blog post, Cernovich bragged about having dined at Sheryl Sandberg's house: "Mark Zuckerberg and his flunkie (forget his name—Chris Cox?) were insecure around me. That's when I learned that money can't buy what I have." The post didn't mention that he'd attended the dinner as his wife's date. He seldom wrote about his domestic situation; when he did, he mentioned it obliquely, spinning it as a form of postfeminist empowerment. "How much money does a man need to make?" he wrote later. "Not much, actually, if you reject the social pressures associated with being what the slave masters call a 'real man.'" In reality, though, he couldn't ignore the gulf between the scale of his online bluster and the modesty of his real-life achievements.

The tone of his blog grew blunt and caustic. He explained obvious things in a condescending tone ("Almond milk is not cow's milk"; "Most people misunderstand cocoa"). Because there was no absolute morality, he started arguing, any man who wanted power should simply take it. "In society, there are two sets of rules," he wrote. "One for alphas and one for betas." If readers were delicate enough to be offended by his words, or too stupid to understand them, then they were free to leave. And yet, the harsher his tone got, the more his readership grew. This no longer surprised him. People were drawn to brute displays of simian dominance, whether they admitted it or not. Maybe others wanted to live in a fantasy world where everything was cushy and altruistic and nice guys finished first, but Cernovich preferred to see reality for what it was. This didn't come naturally to him. After all, he had been raised to turn the other cheek. But he still thought of his life as a hero's journey—he hadn't forgotten his aspiration to become too big to ignore—so he set about reconditioning himself.

Whenever he had a forbidden thought, the old half of him was tempted to suppress it, but the newer, more aggressive part of him chomped at the bit. He referred to women as "cuntnags" and "spinster-sluts." One of his blog posts consisted of a single sentence—"What happens when you mount a hidden video camera to a hot chick's ass?"—and a link to a YouTube video. This was crowd-pleasing content, but he hadn't yet mastered the art of the curiosity gap. The post's headline—"Everyone Stares at a Nice Ass"—served as its own inadvertent clickbait spoiler.

All of this was smutty by the standards of a criminal-jurisprudence blog, but it was tame compared to other blogs Cernovich had been reading. *Return of Kings* was a blog by Roosh V (short for Daryush Valizadeh), an Iranian-Armenian-American in his thirties. Valizadeh traveled the world writing self-published sexual-exploitation baedekers (*Bang Colombia, Bang Estonia*), but appeared to live in his mother's basement in Maryland. *Roissy in D.C.* was a pseudonymous blog that seemed to be written by a forty-three-year-old white guy living in the Adams Morgan neighborhood of D.C. These blogs, and a small nexus of related discussion forums and message boards, comprised what was coming to be known as the manosphere, where disgruntled straight males shared their frustrations and desires—including, most commonly, their desire to meet women and have sex with them. Blogs giving advice on how to do this were called PUA sites, or "game" sites. PUA stood for "pickup artistry"; "running game on" women meant seducing them by capturing and manipulating their attention.

In the manosphere's nascent ideology, feminism was considered not only an unjustified form of affirmative action but a perverse, destructive delusion. Cernovich linked to a 17,000-word blog post, written in a lordly tone and rife with charts and statistics, which claimed that "misandry is the new Jim Crow." The most effective way to gain "immense personal power," according to another influential manosphere post, was to exhibit the "dark triad" of personality traits: Machiavellianism, narcissism, and psychopathy.*

Cernovich was reading a lot of this stuff, and it was beginning to infect his thinking. He found it off-putting at first. Some ideas he didn't dare discuss with casual acquaintances, or even with his wife. And yet, when he considered the underlying arguments with an open mind, he had to admit that he couldn't always think of a way to refute them.

To the extent that mainstream journalists covered the manosphere at all, they tended to reduce it to the pursuit of sex. (A long piece in *The Weekly Standard*, in 2010, ran under the headline "The New Dating Game.") Cernovich thought that sex was important, but he also thought the manosphere was also getting at something deeper. On his blog, he'd been lambasting "feminism's war against men"; now even that descriptor was coming to seem pale, almost polite. He started to wonder whether the problem was actually more elemental than that—a brain-

---

*Other parts of the manosphere were not about how to attract women but about how to avoid them. Several forums were devoted to "men going their own way," or MGTOW. Some of these men were voluntarily celibate ("volcel"), aspiring to a kind of postmodern asceticism. Other men were involuntary celibates ("incels") who seemed inconsolably angry at women who wouldn't sleep with them, or at women in general. Their forums were full of what they called rape jokes, although most of them weren't very funny, and some didn't seem like jokes at all.

washing so pervasive that even to notice it was to become a pariah, to go voluntarily into a madhouse.

In the sci-fi movie *The Matrix*, a gnomic figure called Morpheus sits across from Neo, a computer hacker. "You're here because you know something," Morpheus says. "You've felt it your entire life. That there's something wrong with the world." This is because the world Neo perceives is not the real world; he actually lives inside the Matrix, a simulation designed "to blind you from the truth."

"What truth?" Neo asks.

"That you are a slave," Morpheus says. He leans forward and holds out a capsule in each palm. "You take the blue pill, the story ends, you wake up in your bed and believe whatever you want to believe," he says. "You take the red pill, you stay in Wonderland, and I show you how deep the rabbit hole goes."

Neo takes the red pill, and the hero's journey begins.

In 2011, Mike wrote a *Crime & Federalism* post called "The Rise of the New Independent Male." "Men are natural information seekers, but for most of our lives, we were denied access to information," he wrote. "Then came the Internet." Something was stirring, some kind of "political-culture movement"; he was a part of it, but even he couldn't yet name it or fully understand it. "We know that both *The Wall Street Journal* and *New York Times* are scam publications," he continued. "We know that Democrats and Republicans are scoundrels and thieves, and do not speak for us. What are the implications of this new reality?"

Below the post, a commenter wrote, "I don't know that nihilism itself can actually build anything."

"It's not that we know nothing," Cernovich responded in the comments. "It's that everything we know is a lie. Now what?"

CHAPTER THIRTEEN

A Filter for Quality

The internet was full of red pills if you knew where to look for them, or even if you didn't. It wasn't just gender—it could be race, or GMOs, or the history of the Federal Reserve. You never knew when you might bump into Morpheus. Sometimes, it seemed, you could be minding your own business and Morpheus would find you.

Obama ran for president, and the pundits on cable news often praised his campaign for its sophisticated social-networking tools. But much of what the campaign did with those tools—canvassing, phone-banking, fund-raising—was just the normal business of electoral politics, made more efficient by computers. There was a deeper technological shift happening, but it was still inchoate and hard to describe. In 2008, at a rally in Lakeville, Minnesota, Obama's opponent, John McCain, took unvetted questions from the audience. "I can't trust Obama," one woman said. "I have read about him, and he's not—he's not—he's an Arab." McCain took the cordless microphone out of the woman's hand and corrected her while backing away. The moment was recapped on cable news, where it was treated as proof of McCain's Buckleyan willingness to rebuke the fringes of his party, and on *Saturday Night Live*, where it was treated as a joke. Few people thought to wonder exactly what the woman had been reading, or which content-distribution algorithm had served it to her.

Obama won the election. "We gather because we have chosen hope over fear, unity of purpose over conflict and discord," he said in his inaugural address. This seemed true, or at least plausible, to those Americans who were still getting their information from *USA Today* and the CBS Evening News. But in the backwaters of the internet, the conspiratorial hum continued to grow louder.

Two days after the 2008 election, at the Palace Hotel in San Francisco, there was a tech conference called the Web 2.0 Summit. It featured keynote speeches by several BSBs, including Mark Zuckerberg. "I would expect that, next year, people will share twice as much information as they are this year, and then the year after that they'll share twice as much," he said. This became known as Zuckerberg's Law, and it turned out to be basically correct. More and more people were contributing news to, and getting news from, their social feeds; meanwhile, the very definition of "news" was being transformed. A few years earlier, Zuckerberg had said, "A squirrel dying in your front yard may be more relevant to your interests right now than people dying in Africa." This wasn't meant to be a public-facing adage like Zuckerberg's Law. Rather, it was an internal directive to the engineers who would build Facebook's News Feed algorithm, instructing them to show whatever a particular user was likely to find most relevant—i.e., most clickable—at any given moment.

In the age of social media, anyone could be an influencer. Money, credentials, cleverness, personal connections—all were helpful, of course, but you could make do without them. You didn't have to know how to code, or even how to write; you didn't have to show your face or use your name. All you needed was a meme with momentum.*

The conference in San Francisco was called Web 2.0 because its organizers believed that the internet was in the midst of a momentous transition: the shift from the open web to the social web. Web 1.0 was dominated by big institutions, but Web 2.0 would give the power to the people. The paradigmatic Web 2.0 innovation was the social network. If the open web was a vast landscape dotted with isolated viruses, then social networks would be like the advent of air travel, enabling a virus to conquer the world in a day.

Paul Graham, a renowned computer engineer and venture capitalist, wrote a post on his personal blog about what Web 2.0 meant to him. One of the things it meant was online "democracy," in the form of freedom from informational gatekeepers. "Amateurs can surpass professionals, when they have the right kind of

---

*"Best time in history to be alive," Mike Cernovich wrote. "You don't need permission or the right family to succeed. If you want it, take it."

system to channel their efforts," Graham wrote. The social web, he hoped, would be this kind of system.

In 1998, before the tech bubble burst, Graham sold his first software company to Yahoo for $49 million. After that, he often showed up at tech conferences around the Valley, looking the part of the semiretired Mountain View millionaire (polo shirt, khaki shorts, Birkenstocks). "Like a lot of guys who got rich from technology, I've been meaning to give seed money to new start-ups," he wrote. In 2005, he finally got around to it: he cofounded Y Combinator, a boot camp for aspiring entrepreneurs.

Within a few years, thousands of young coders, some of them still in college, had applied to Y Combinator. The three percent who were accepted moved to the Bay Area, where, for three months, Graham and his team provided mentorship, technical advice, and access to their personal network of rich investors. Graham did all this, he wrote, because "start-ups are on balance a good thing. . . . Focus on helping founders, and everything else will follow." More tangibly, Y Combinator took a 7 percent stake in every company that completed its program, an investment portfolio that would soon be worth tens of billions of dollars.

Graham wasn't a household name in the rest of the country, but within Silicon Valley he was widely revered—a BSB's BSB.* Aspiring entrepreneurs read Graham's blog religiously; they quoted it, from memory, in casual conversation. He wrote essays about Lisp programming and Bayesian filtering, but he also took on more far-ranging subjects: "Why Nerds are Unpopular," "Why Smart People Have Bad Ideas," "How to Make Wealth."

Graham's essayistic voice exemplified the BSB attitude—blithely dismissive of received wisdom, self-assured to the point of hubris.† He approached most topics with the pragmatic swagger of an engineer. When you're writing code, or getting a business off the ground, you can solve problems by applying time-tested axioms, or you can solve them by flouting convention and reinventing the wheel. All that matters is whether your solution works, or seems to work.

Graham instructed the young entrepreneurs in Y Combinator to take business advice from people who had successful track records in business. Yet he encour-

---

*The New York Times, over the years, has called him "a well-known investor and esteemed figure in Silicon Valley," "the closest thing the start-up world has to a pre-eminent guru," and "the closest thing the technology community has to either a Bertrand Russell or a P. T. Barnum."
†From "Keep Your Identity Small": "I finally realized today why politics and religion yield such uniquely useless discussions." From "How to Do Philosophy": "Most philosophers up to the present have been wasting their time."

aged everyone to take his advice on a wide range of topics, far more than it was possible for one person to be an expert in. What gave him this confidence? The democratic spirit of the internet. "Anyone can publish an essay on the Web," Graham noted. "Who are you to write about x? You are whatever you wrote." He put his trust in quantifiable metrics. In his official bio, he mentioned how many pageviews his essays had received. It was a large number. What better credential could anyone ask for?

In March 2005, Graham gave a talk at Harvard called "How to Start a Start-up." In the audience were Steve Huffman and Alexis Ohanian, two undergrads from the University of Virginia. It was spring break of their senior year. Huffman, a computer science major with chipmunk teeth, a thatch of blond hair, and an alpha-nerd blend of introversion and self-assurance, had been coding since he was eight years old. His favorite programming language was Lisp, and, as he put it later, "If you're a fan of Lisp, you inevitably become a fan of Paul Graham." They approached Graham after the lecture, and Huffman asked for his autograph.

A week later, when Graham started accepting applications for the inaugural class of Y Combinator, he encouraged Huffman and Ohanian to apply. Ohanian—dark-haired and tall, with a goofy kind of charisma—was not a coder, but he was a techno-optimist who believed that start-ups could "make the world suck less." He and Huffman proposed a company that would let people order food on their cell phones.

Graham rejected the food-ordering idea, but he liked Huffman and Ohanian, so he accepted them on the condition that they think of something else. What they came up with was a simple link aggregator—a site for sorting and surfacing the best stuff on the web. Anyone could post a link to anything. Next to each link would be two voting buttons, an up arrow and a down arrow. That was pretty much it. The site was called Reddit. They referred to it, aspirationally, as "the front page of the internet."

The text was small blue Verdana on a white background. People posted links to funny news stories ("Public Schools Begin to Offer Gym Classes Online"), baubles from the far corners of the web (a grad student blogging his way through Wittgenstein's *On Certainty*), and midnight dorm-style conjecture ("Why the Probability That You Are Living in a Matrix Is Quite High"). Ohanian—using his Reddit handle, kn0thing—posted a news story called "Researchers Map the Sexual Network of an Entire High School." Huffman—using his handle, spez—posted "The 86 Rules of Boozing," from *Modern Drunkard Magazine*. Both links were big hits on Reddit, which wasn't a surprise. The cofounders understood the site's vibe implicitly, because the vibe was being formed, in real time, around their personalities.

Reddit's sorting algorithm was purely democratic, which is to say anarchic. The links with the most "upvotes" rose to the top of the page. There was no economic incentive for people to click or share; Huffman and Ohanian hoped that other basic human motives, such as curiosity and vanity, would be enough of a draw. They turned out to be right.

Every time a link was upvoted, the user who'd submitted it would get one "karma" point added to his or her profile; a downvote would take a point away. Business consultants would soon start referring to such online design tactics as "gamification"—but Huffman, coding Reddit alone in his bedroom, was proceeding less by strategy than by instinct, trying to build the kind of site that someone like him would find irresistible. The site's frequent users—redditors—started visiting multiple times a day, or multiple times an hour, or multiple times a minute. They mocked the site's built-in enticements, referring to the karma system as "meaningless internet points." This was basically true. Still, there was no evidence that those who noticed the futility of the game were any less likely to play it.

Six months after Reddit went live, Huffman added a new function: comments. Now, in addition to links, users could type their thoughts, and other users could thread their thoughts below those thoughts, enabling a post to turn into a discussion. Each comment, like each link, could be upvoted or downvoted. This system allowed the cream to rise to the top. It also allowed redditors to gang up on people or ideas they disliked, downvoting them into oblivion. If the latter was an abuse of the system, then it was a form of abuse that existed from the start. On the day Reddit launched, Ohanian posted the site's first link. Huffman, sitting at his computer a few feet away, immediately downvoted it. He didn't have any particular objection to the link Ohanian had posted; he hadn't even clicked on it yet. He was just being a jerk. "I consider myself a troll at heart," he said later. "We now think of trolls as these racist, vile creatures, and obviously I don't consider myself that. But making people bristle, being a little outrageous in order to add some spice to life— I get that. I've done that. That was kind of how I grew up on the internet."

Redditors went by pseudonyms, so it wasn't always possible to know exactly who was saying what. Still, many of the site's early adopters, if not most, seemed to be sharp-tongued, contrarian young men like Huffman and Ohanian, interested in video games, computer programming, and crass, recursive humor. The Reddit community developed a bent for irreverence and an antipathy to pious groupthink. Reason was preferable to emotion. Irony was prized above ingenuousness. The site's design, its tone, its meaningless internet points—all served to make it a petri dish for inside jokes and pet theories and hermetic, self-reinforcing worldviews.

In the early days, Reddit had few official policies about what should or shouldn't be posted. Huffman and Ohanian were too busy keeping the site from crashing. Besides, even if they'd had the time to write down rules, they would have been loath to restrict the free flow of information. "Like most programmers at the time, we were pretty libertarian," Huffman said later. "Not in the political, Ayn Rand sense—more in the 'Fuck you, don't tell me what to think,' outlaw-hacker sense."

In late 2005, Paul Graham posted his essay about Web 2.0. "Another place democracy seems to win is in deciding what counts as news," he wrote. "I never look at any news site now except Reddit. I know if something major happens, or someone writes a particularly interesting article, it will show up there. Why bother checking the front page of any specific paper or magazine?" Sites like Reddit functioned as "a filter for quality," he added. The gatekeepers had only been getting in the way. The news could be improved the way everything else could be improved: disrupt, disintermediate, democratize, give the power to the people.

•   •   •

In 2017, the Supreme Court heard a case about a North Carolina law that prevented registered sex offenders from using social media. Did the law violate the First Amendment? Before answering that question, the Court had to consider another question: what is social media? In sixty minutes of oral argument, Facebook was compared to a park, a playground, an airport terminal, a polling booth, and a town square. Justice Sotomayor asked a question about high schoolers looking for jobs on LinkedIn. Justice Alito tried to compare Google+ to BettyCrocker.com. "Everybody uses Twitter," Justice Kagan said. "This has become a crucially important channel of political communication."

Of all possible metaphors, it might be best to compare founding a social network to hosting a party. It starts out small, with just the hosts and a few of their friends. Then word gets out, and strangers start to show up. People take cues from the environment. Mimosas in a sun-dappled atrium suggests one kind of mood; grain alcohol in a moldy basement suggests another. Sometimes, a pattern emerges on its own: Pinterest, a photo-sharing site founded by three men, happened to catch on among women. In other cases, the pattern seems more premeditated—more like a result of implicit gatekeeping. If you're fourteen, TikTok's user interface is intuitive; if you're twenty-two, it's intriguing; if you're forty-five, it's impenetrable. This encourages older people to self-deport.

Suppose you throw a party. Early on, you're busy greeting people, fetching drinks, making sure the sound system works. Everyone seems to be having a good time. You could stand outside the front door with a flashlight, interviewing each potential guest, but instead you decide to leave the gates open. You don't think about what might go wrong. On the whole, people are basically trustworthy. Why would someone want to ruin the party?

Inevitably, things go wrong. You play an obscene song. Someone complains. You play an unobjectionable song. Everyone stops dancing. One person sneaks into the bathroom for a cigarette, and you decide to look the other way—you sort of like the idea of hosting a raucous party, the kind with a trace of illicit smoke in the air. But then people start smoking in the hallway, and on the dance floor, and someone has an asthma attack. Sleazy men start making aggressive passes at women; word gets around, and many women decide to leave. Someone spreads a rumor that the bartender is poisoning the drinks. Another person makes a racist joke, and several people laugh; before you can confront them, they scatter into the crowd.

What can you do? You don't want to let things get out of hand. You consider pausing the music, turning on all the lights, maybe identifying a few of the troublemakers and dragging them out by the collar. That would set an example, but it could also spoil the mood, and the party might never recover.

By far the easiest solution, and the only one that will set you up to be perfectly consistent in the future, is to do nothing, or almost nothing. You can't spend all your time policing everyone. Instead, you establish a clear, simple policy: as long as none of your guests do anything violent or illegal, they can say whatever they want. After all, you believe in free speech.

———

In 2005, Reddit was a sparsely attended party: a few sharp-tongued young men in a dank, cavernous warehouse. At the time, Facebook was only available to college students, and in order to join it you had to provide your real name, your birthday, and a valid school email address—the equivalent of being carded at the door. To join Reddit, all you needed was a username that hadn't been claimed yet. You could start as many accounts as you wanted, all without providing a profile photo or a name. This encouraged creativity, and also mischief.

A few months in, Huffman built the warehouse's first internal walls. People were posting links to vulgar and violent content—which was fine, except that Huffman wanted users to have some idea of what they were about to click on before they clicked on it. He labeled some content NSFW—not safe for work—and quarantined it from everything else. That was the end of pure democracy.

The NSFW content was shunted into a new room: reddit.com/r/NSFW. The separation of content proved useful, so Huffman made more rooms, called subreddits, each devoted to a specific topic: r/Programming; r/Science; r/FreeCulture, for techno-libertarians. He made a subreddit called r/Politics, not to amplify political news but to sequester it. "I don't like thinking about politics all the time," he said later; links to news stories were getting too popular, clogging up his feed. "So I went, 'OK, nerds, talk about politics all you want, but go do it over here.'" Yet the walls between rooms were always permeable. If a political link or a programming link got upvoted enough times, the algorithm would crosspost it to Reddit's home page.

Huffman and Ohanian believed in free speech, but they also believed in limits. "We always banned people," Huffman said later. "We just didn't talk about it very much." Reddit was so small that Huffman could do most of the banning himself, on an ad hoc basis, using his common sense. "It wasn't well thought out or even articulated, really. It was, 'That guy has the N-word in his username? Fuck that.' Delete account." Bans were carried out inconsistently, because there was no set of consistent principles underlying them.

In 2006, Huffman and Ohanian sold Reddit to Condé Nast, an old-media conglomerate that owned more than twenty magazines, including *Wired*, *Vanity Fair*, *Vogue*, and *The New Yorker*. The sale made them twenty-two-year-old millionaires, but they didn't fit in at a big corporation, and three years later they left.

Huffman spent a few months backpacking in Costa Rica, played a lot of Call of Duty, and then cofounded a travel-search company. Ohanian became an angel investor and a techno-optimist at large, sometimes referred to in the press as "the Mayor of the Internet." In their absence, the warehouse party that was Reddit grew bigger and wilder, and ominous cliques started to gather in the corners.

CHAPTER FOURTEEN

Attention Is Influence

While Mike Cernovich's wife worked long days at the office, he spent most of his time at home, scouring the internet. Sometimes, even after she got back from work, he ignored her and kept his eyes fixed on the screen. The marriage was falling apart. In January 2011, he wrote a *Crime & Federalism* post explaining how to make two days' worth of pork roast in a crockpot. The headline was "Bachelor Cooking/Muscle Meals."

He started a new blog, "an online magazine for alpha males," and called it *Danger & Play*, after a line from *Thus Spoke Zarathustra*.* The blog was full of pickup advice and lurid sex stories.† Any inhibition he'd displayed at *Crime & Federalism* was gone. If adrenaline was a drug, then he needed higher and higher doses to feel its effects. In one post, he would deny that he was a misogynist; a few weeks later, he'd write a post called "Misogyny Gets You Laid." He knew that he was pushing the envelope, but he was pleasantly surprised by his readers' tolerance for edginess. "As a woman, this post at first alarmed and disturbed me," a British commenter wrote. "Then I realised you had a point." She was commenting on a post called "How to Choke a Woman During Sex."

For years, Cernovich had considered his informational intake to be eclectic, but he now realized that he'd only been scratching the surface. He read interviews with Nick Bostrom, a philosopher who posited that what we perceive as reality might actually be a computer simulation. He read Steve Sailer, whose refusal to

---

*"The true man wants two things: danger and play. For that reason he wants woman, as the most dangerous plaything."
†"Pick-up follows a Pareto principle (the 80/20 rule)," he wrote. "If a club is open for four hours, your best chance of meeting women will be in a given one-hour block of time."

kowtow to the Narrative had apparently caused the Southern Poverty Law Center to label him an extremist.* He read a blog by an autodidact named Mencius Mold-bug, who argued that American democracy was a failed experiment that should be replaced by totalitarianism.† On his own blog, Cernovich started developing a more overt theory of white-male identity politics. His opponents were beta males, losers, or cucks; anyone who was too scared to debate controversial ideas, such as human biodiversity, had probably been cowed by the Narrative or indoctrinated by the globalist media.

One taboo opinion tended to beget another. Roissy, for example, was no longer just a pickup artist; he was now a full-blown anti-Semitic white nationalist whose slogan was "Diversity + Proximity = War." Cernovich didn't go that far—after all, his own wife wasn't white, a fact that the alt-right trolls on Reddit and 4chan would certainly

---

*In 2008, the SPLC announced this designation in a blog post. The comments below the post were unmoderated, and the following were quickly upvoted to the top:

> No, he's not politically correct, and his views on race are certainly not popular or pleasing to many. But he's not the strawman you're envisioning.
> Sailer is simply someone who approaches social questions WITHOUT assuming that all groups of people are the same. It's a valid assumption.
> Isn't it time the SPLC provided a complete list of acceptable things to think, say and do, so we poor benighted dupes of Evil won't go wrong any more?
> What Tribe owns the major Media outlets in the USA? There is the Problem.

†Moldbug's essayistic voice exemplified the BSB attitude—blithely dismissive of received wisdom, self-assured to the point of hubris. A dropout from a PhD program in computer science, he approached the entire corpus of philosophy, history, and political theory with the swagger of an engineer, setting out to flout convention and re-invent the wheel. "The other day I was tinkering around in my garage and I decided to build a new ideology," his first post began. "People have been talking about ideology since Jesus was a little boy. At least! And I'm supposedly going to improve on this? Some random person on the Internet, who flunked out of grad school, who doesn't know Greek *or* Latin?" He raised these hypothetical objections, of course, only to dismiss them. He went on to imply that his lack of formal qualification was actually one of his primary qualifications, because it enabled him to see through the tissue of lies that he called the Cathedral—a system of brainwashing so total, so self-erasing, that even to notice it was to become a pariah.

Beginning in 2007 and ending in 2014, Moldbug unfurled his bespoke ideology on his blog, *Unqualified Reservations*. He wrote in a prolix, purple style, a hybrid of Thomas Carlyle and Tom Robbins. His blog became a ca-nonical text in the alt-right, although he never self-identified with the movement—he usually called himself a formalist, while his followers usually called him a neoreactionary. Moldbug taught himself world history via Google Books, and his essays drew on a perversely eclectic array of primary sources, the more obscure the better—Gaetano Mosca, Francis Yeats-Brown, Wolfgang Schivelbusch. He had no truck with settled historical debates, points of academic consensus, or universal politico-ethical axioms along the lines of "Freedom is desir-able" or "People should be treated equally." In a post called "Why I am not an anti-Semite," he began by noting that his father was Jewish, then continued to hold forth dispassionately on the Jewish Question. Another post, called "Why I am not a white nationalist," was relatively ambivalent—"I'm not exactly allergic to the stuff"—and it linked approvingly to Steve Sailer, Jared Taylor, and other racist crimethinkers. Moldbug declared himself a full-throated defender of "human cognitive biodiversity," the idea that there are inherent racial differences in IQ—about which, he suggested, "white nationalists [are] right, and everyone else [is] wrong."

In 2017, Joe Bernstein, of *BuzzFeed*, published a piece exposing emails sent to and from Milo Yiannopoulos. The piece revealed, among other things, that Yiannopoulos was in close contact with Moldbug, whose real name was Curtis Yarvin, and that Yarvin had spent the night of the 2016 election at Peter Thiel's house. When Yiannopoulos suggested that Thiel "needs guidance on politics," Yarvin responded, "Less than you might think! . . . He's fully enlightened, just plays it very carefully."

decry as "degenerate" if they ever found out. Still, he could see where the white nation-alists were coming from, and he found their arguments provocative even when he didn't agree with them. To an intellectually liberated man, no idea was off-limits.

Mike's divorce was finalized in late 2011. His ex-wife kept the mattress; he kept the memory-foam mattress cover. She stayed in the apartment in San Francisco, and he bounced around—Las Vegas, Venice Beach. By the terms of the divorce, Mike was granted primary custody of the couple's dog, Amicus. He was also granted about a quarter of his ex-wife's Facebook stock. When the company went public the following year, his shares were suddenly worth $2.6 million. "I have had a seven figure payday," he wrote later. "I never have to work another day in my life."

Traffic to his blog was growing, but only incrementally. Most readers found *Danger & Play* by following a link from another manosphere blog. Links were a slow, one-to-one method of transmission; unless the mainstream showered the manosphere with attention, most normies would never know it existed. It wasn't as if Dr. Oz was going to invite Roosh to promote *Bang Estonia* on daytime TV, or Terry Gross was going to interview Cernovich about his choking techniques. He tried not to take it personally—deriving self-worth from the establishment media was just another form of slave mentality. Still, if he wanted to make himself too big to ignore, he'd have to find another way.

• • •

Roosh V had spent years consolidating a small but loyal following through his books and his blog. Around 2011, he began to use social media macrotargeting—in his case, a combination of rage-bait, trolling, and open bigotry—to propel his message into the mainstream. Exploiting content-sorting algorithms in this way was sometimes called a hack, but in fact macrotargeters were just using the social networks the way they were designed to be used.

Blogs were reverse chronological: the latest posts showed up first. But as so-cial networks grew bigger and more complex, it became impossible for most users to keep up with everything their friends posted, and feeds stopped being sorted by simple chronology. Instead, each social network developed its own set of content-sorting algorithms, many of which, despite the good intentions of the engineers who built them, would start to function as filter bubbles or radicali-zation engines. Facebook had its News Feed, which prioritized dying squirrels over famines in Africa, bringing microtargeting to the masses. YouTube had a recommendation algorithm that served up the videos you were most likely to watch next, based on your past behavior—an invitation down an endless series of rabbit holes.*

In 2011, Roosh V wrote a listicle called "15 Reasons Why Washington DC Sucks for Guys."† He promoted it using an old *BuzzFeed* trick: name-checking a specific locale in the headline, daring its denizens to stick up for themselves. It worked. A regional subreddit, r/WashingtonDC, linked to the post, calling Roosh "an unfunny, racist, misogynistic asshole." The Reddit thread amassed 242 comments ("I couldn't even finish it because this guy's head was so far up his ass"; "I can't believe I even gave that idiot a pageview"), including, eventually, a few comments from Roosh himself. "I got so much traffic from here and secondary links that I almost had to upgrade my hosting plan," he wrote. "Sure this reddit traffic is 98% anti-roosh, but I'll take the 2% who turn into regular readers." This comment was downvoted several times, but Roosh didn't mind the negative karma.

On *Danger & Play*, Cernovich wrote a post defending Roosh: the redditors who were calling him racist were only proving that "'racist' doesn't actually mean anything." Privately, Cernovich drew more specific lessons from this episode and others like it. He would later express them as his two primary laws of social media mechanics: "Conflict is attention" and "Attention is influence."

Cernovich joined Twitter, where he summarized his most outrageous ideas in fewer than 140 characters. ("There's no reason to ever hit a woman," he tweeted in 2013. "If you want to hurt her, destroy her soul.") Among a particular coterie of leftist Twitter superusers, Cernovich's online persona became a meme. Whenever he tweeted something egregious, the leftists would pass it around in a spirit of

---

*The most effective way for the video-recommendation algorithm to keep people glued to YouTube, it turned out, was for it to ramp up the intensity of its suggestions, sometimes at an alarming rate. You might search for nutrition advice and end up, three or four videos later, watching a Roosh V clip called "This Is Why You're Fat." You might start out listening to Adam Sandler's "Hanukkah Song" and end up learning shocking new information about the Jewish Question. The first video ever uploaded to YouTube, "Me at the zoo," was short and innocuous; after you were done watching that, however, the recommendation algorithm might show you a related piece of content that was more likely to cause an immediate spike of activating emotion, such as a clip of Harambe the gorilla dragging a three-year-old child through its enclosure at the Cincinnati Zoo.

†Like all of his writing, it contained plenty of offensive material. Reason No. 1: Women in D.C. are "sloppy, ugly, fat, and don't care about looking good for men." Reason No. 7: "There aren't enough cute white girls for white men who don't want to date minorities."

communal incredulity. One of them discovered Fit-Juice.com, and they started referring to Cernovich as JuiceBro; he adopted the nickname, hoping to neutralize its sting. He called his opponents social-justice warriors, or SJWs. He meant it as an insult, although some SJWs were happy to adopt the label—what was wrong with fighting for social justice?

On rare occasions, Cernovich made an argument and an SJW refuted it, or vice versa. More often, they communicated not through rebuttals but through repudiations—an OMG, a side-eye emoji, or a comment along the lines of "Wow. I can't even believe this kind of person still exists in 2013." This formulation was so familiar that, on 4chan and Reddit, it became another meme. "I can't even!" the anonymous trolls would write, mimicking the SJWs. "Wow, just wow. It is the Current Year!"

So it went, the name-calling and the meta-name-calling. "Being an SJW is just fragile narcissism and exclusion through virtue signalling," an anonymous Twitter user wrote. *To virtue-signal: to construct a self-righteous public persona advertising one's obeisance to the Narrative.* On manosphere blogs and alt-right subreddits, the prevailing assumption was that all human interaction was a cynical game; by this logic, every tweet about social justice had to be somehow self-serving. It didn't seem to occur to most manosphere disciples that some of what they saw as virtue-signaling might instead be sincere aspirations to virtue.

• • •

"After the tech early-adopters, journalists were next to take to Twitter," Jack Dorsey, the cofounder and CEO of the company, tweeted in 2015. "Journalists were a big part of why we grew so quickly." Journalists still love Twitter. They tweet to communicate, to procrastinate, and to self-promote; they also scan Twitter in order to arrive at an understanding of What's Happening in the World, which they then try to convert into story ideas.

No reporter can be everywhere, talking to everyone. Instead, reporters have traditionally used proxy techniques that range from more to less inadequate: anecdotal observations, interviews with experts, polling data. An opinion columnist turns a chat with her Uber driver into a parable about the gig economy. A TV talking head says, "Here's what I'm hearing," but what he really means is "Here's what a few well-placed acquaintances told me at dinner last night."

According to an old journalistic saw, "Two is a coincidence; three is a trend." It's a self-deprecating maxim, an admission that trend stories are rarely as meaningful as they are made out to be. Yet journalists continue to write trend stories, and editors continue to run them, if not out of laziness then out of low-grade ontological desperation. "Is this really a Thing?" an assignment editor may ask, fielding a pitch on an unfamiliar new subject—planking, or sexting, or Ron Paul's presidential run. "Oh, it's definitely a Thing," the reporter who pitched the story will say. "My kids and their friends can't stop talking about it." Hardly an objective measure of Thing-ness, but presumably better than nothing.

Understandably, given these circumstances, Twitter seemed like a godsend. Finally: a gold standard of Thing-ness. No longer would journalists have to rely on their personal judgment. Instead, Twitter's algorithm could tell them objectively, drawing on a sample size of millions, what was a trend and what was not.*

But Twitter was never meant to be a gold standard.† People talked about Twitter as if it were a real-time heat map of the national conversation; yet the platform was not an objective reflection of the thoughts and opinions of all Americans, or even of the less than 20 percent of Americans who had active Twitter accounts. What Twitter actually reflected was engagement: which memes were, at any given moment, generating the most activating emotion. This meant that the platform overrepresented controversy, which wasn't a novel problem. It also meant—and this part was new—that trolls and other macrotargeters could gin up pseudoscandals almost whenever they wanted. Both the techno-utopians who built the social networks and the gate-crashers who exploited them liked to assert that social media was a democratizing force. However, even when social media did give voice to the voiceless, the amplitude was never distributed equally. In a perfect democracy, each person gets one vote. In a world of trending topics and algorithmic feedback loops, equal representation isn't just impossible; it's not even the goal.

---

*Once journalists selected a topic to write about, they didn't even have to pick up the phone to get a quote. They could scan all relevant tweets, searchable by hashtag, and embed a few in the body of the story, before turning to the more lucrative task of writing a catchy headline.
† The list of trending topics looked authoritative at first glance, but in fact it was microtargeted to each user. Many people, including many journalists, didn't know this—they continued to refer to what was trending and what was not as if these were universal, stable categories. This created a new kind of filter bubble: the more you clicked on stories about soccer, the more you got the impression that the whole world couldn't stop talking about soccer; meanwhile, your roommate could be forgiven for thinking that everyone was live-tweeting tonight's episode of *The Bachelor*.

In addition to his blog, Roosh operated a members-only message board, Roosh VForum.com, where his hardcore fans could collaborate in semiprivate. Unlike Reddit, the forum had strict written rules ("No girls, homosexuals, or transsexuals"). Like Reddit, it employed the internet gamification tricks that were now so ubiquitous as to be almost imperceptible.

To join the forum, you had to choose a screen name (Tuthmosis, Handsome Creepy Eel) and a profile image (a flaming sword, a stock photo of Owen Wilson). If you posted a link or comment that your peers found useful, they could reward you with "reputation points"; the more points you accrued, the more medals and stars appeared on your profile. A user with just one star was labeled a "Recovering Beta"; three stars made you a "Wingman"; Roosh, with the maximum seven stars, was an "Innovative Casanova." (Cernovich, who posted frequently on the forum as MikeCF, was an "International Playboy.")

On October 7, 2013, Roosh instructed his followers to launch a new troll raid. Feminist bloggers often argued that women should not be stigmatized for their appearance. Roosh, on the contrary, felt that they should. "Find feminists/liberals who are pushing fat acceptance," he wrote on the forum, "and then shame them on twitter using the hashtag #FatShamingWeek." Dozens of Roosh's minions started tweeting all at once. "The greatest tragedy: a fat girl who actually would be a 8 or 9 if she just would lose weight," Quintus Curtius, a prolific manosphere blogger, tweeted, appending the hashtag. A nutritionist retweeted this a few seconds later. "I suspect if she knew what I represent, she wouldn't have retweeted it," Quintus gloated on the forum. "Too late now."

The goal of the Twitter campaign was to shock the SJWs into action. It worked. "I'm sorry but if the men who started #FatShamingWeek could stand up, I'm gonna have to ask you to sit the fuck down, and stop being pigs," one young woman tweeted. She disapproved of their behavior, and she was using social media to express that disapproval. She was also, whether she realized it or not, spreading their message by using their hashtag.

"You're the one who needs to stand up and sit down," Cernovich tweeted in response. "Those are called squats and you need to do some. #FatShamingWeek."

A few hours later, on the forum, Roosh posted again: "It's going viral on Twitter."

Prominently displayed on Twitter's landing page was a personalized, ever-changing list of "trending topics"—a few phrases and hashtags that were picking up a lot of momentum, according to a proprietary algorithm. The list was coveted real estate. If a meme was catching on with one or two clusters of people— misogynists and nutritionists, say—then an efficient way to expose it to the larger Twitter population was to get it trending. This increased the likelihood that it would be seen by millions of Twitter users, including journalists from every major publication, who could transmit the meme to the world.

Two days after Roosh V launched his troll raid, a headline appeared on *BuzzFeed*: "Some Terrible People on Twitter Have Decided That It's 'Fat Shaming Week.'" The badges at the top of the post (Trashy, Ew, Fail) made the writer's disdain clear, but her article included no narrative or analysis; she simply summarized Roosh's loathsome arguments, embedding fifteen tweets from his followers and linking to his blog. Other outlets ran similar pieces: "Fat Shaming Week Is Real, and It's Despicable"; "#FatShamingWeek Is Taking Over Twitter and Proves People Have No Souls." Roosh wrote a follow-up post on his blog, linking to each of the hit pieces and proudly citing the number of pageviews they'd brought in. "The exposure," he wrote, "has exceeded our expectations."

Trolls may be puerile, but they set an ingenious trap. By responding to their provocations, you risk amplifying their message. By ignoring them, you risk seeming complacent or complicit. The opposite of misinformation is correction, but corrections, for the most part, don't change people's minds. The opposite of normalization is outrage, but trolls use outrage as fuel. Trolls act in indescribably awful ways and then dare reporters to describe their actions dispassionately. But for reporters on the lurid ugliness beat, it's often impossible to be evenhanded and truthful at the same time.

Oddly enough, Dr. Oz did end up inviting Roosh onto his show. "There are monsters that lurk in the shadows of the internet, shaming and bullying people for the way they look," Oz said, as Roosh waited backstage. "It's time for them to come out from behind their computer screens." Roosh walked onstage and sat under the bright lights, and the studio audience had its moment of catharsis.

When the interview aired, Roosh wrote a blog post in which he sounded both plaintive and surprisingly naïve. "Of course I expected to be the 'bad guy' on the show, and knew they would ask me some pointed questions, but I could not anticipate how much of a massacre it would be," he wrote. By the end of the post, though, he had regained his alpha-male bluster. "I guess in the end I'm not that different from Dr. Oz," he wrote. "We have a different kind of jig we do in front of the camera, but in the end we're still doing a jig."

Within the manosphere, the consensus was that the Dr. Oz appearance had made Roosh look pathetic, but that it was a win for him nonetheless. "As much as I can't stand Roosh, he'll definitely grow in size for being on Dr. Oz," wrote a commenter on a small site called SlutHate.com. The next game blogger to pivot toward the mainstream, the commenter predicted, would be Mike Cernovich: "I expect him to try and write some shocker articles to give his 'gorilla alpha male' ass some attention."

• • •

"Twitter is my drug," Cernovich wrote—on Twitter, naturally—in 2014. "I can't kill people. That's illegal. I've had so much sex that beautiful women bore me. How can I get that rush? Twitter." Blogging had started to feel like a closed loop, a way to build rapport with old fans but not a way to bring in new ones. Twitter, on the other hand, was a party where the VIP section included everyone who was anyone: billionaires, agenda-setting journalists, A-list celebrities, heads of state. Cernovich didn't delude himself that the people behind the velvet rope were paying attention to him—not yet, anyway. But at least they were all in the same room.

One night, after a *Gawker* writer tweeted a joke that Cernovich misconstrued as an insult, Cernovich took to YouTube and challenged the writer to a boxing match. The writer didn't respond, and the boxing match never happened; still, the video went viral, drawing more online attention to Cernovich and more traffic to his site. The brilliance of the boxing challenge, he thought, was that it brought all subtext to the surface. He could engage in nitpicky intellectual debates, but that would only impress the brahmins in New York and D.C.; far better, from a branding perspective, to show that he was a big strong guy with a hot girlfriend who knew how to fight. That would impress everyone, on a gut level, whether they admitted it or not. "To beat a person, you lower his or her social status," he once wrote on *Danger & Play*. "Logic is pointless."

He continued thinking about his career in terms of boxing metaphors. To get bigger, he would have to punch above his weight. He had about ten thousand followers on Twitter. What if he could pick a fight with a heavyweight—an A-list celebrity with a few hundred thousand followers, or a few million? Most of them would be too smart to respond to his provocations. But, as the PUA blogosphere had taught him, you couldn't close if you didn't make approaches.

He offered a "cash reward" for damaging information about Nick Denton, the publisher of Gawker Media. Cernovich tagged Denton in the tweet, hoping to start a public row, but neither Denton nor anyone else took the bait.

The actor and writer Lena Dunham, tweeting in support of GMO labeling, wrote, "We deserve to know the truth about our food." Cernovich responded, "The truth about food is that you eat too much." She ignored him.

In September 2015, Seth Rogen, a movie star with three and a half million followers, tweeted, "If you think there's some conspiracy against white people, you are, I guarantee, a stupid white person."

Cernovich, tagging Rogen, tweeted, "If you think Seth Rogen is edgy, you are, I guarantee, a giant fucking pussy."

Two days later, Rogen responded. "I seem to have pissed you off," he wrote.

Emboldened, Cernovich delivered another jab. "Sucks @SethRogen is having marriage problems," he wrote. "Cuck life!"

"You seem so angry!" Rogen responded. "Do you need a nap?"

Cernovich jabbed again, in the same spot, in case his first insult had been too subtle. "Your wife won't fuck you," he wrote. "Hahahahahahahahahahahahahahaha."

Finally, Rogen retreated. "I'll stop now," he wrote. "Have a nice life."

A month later, out of nowhere, Rogen's wife entered the ring. "Well," she tweeted in response to Cernovich, "she definitely would fuck you!"

Her post was intended to be sarcastic, but tone is notoriously hard to convey over the internet. Cernovich archived and screengrabbed the tweets quickly, before they could be deleted. Then he wrote a blog post: "Seth Rogen Got Cucked on Twitter by His Wife (Here's How)." In the ensuing days, he gained thousands of new followers.

"You gotta think of your life as a story arc," Cernovich said in a podcast interview around this time. He'd decided to embrace the role of the antihero. "Antiheroes are flawed human beings, but we're doing the right thing," he explained.

"So when people try to attack us, the blows don't land the way they do on most people."

• • •

Cernovich had met a woman named Shauna, and they'd moved in together in Santa Monica. She worked in ad sales at CraveOnline, a "male lifestyle publisher" based in L.A. In late 2014, she quit her job, and she and Cernovich spent 2015 traveling through Europe, Asia, and the Middle East. (He could do his job from anywhere with internet access.) He posted pictures of himself sipping espresso in a Paris café and floating in the Dead Sea.

Once, as he walked through a train station in Budapest, he noticed hundreds of Syrian émigrés pitching tents, waiting to be resettled elsewhere in Hungary. Based on the media coverage of the Syrian crisis, he thought he knew what to expect: squalor, amputees, wailing children. Instead, he saw men playing soccer and flirting with girls. "It hit me: these people aren't refugees," he said later. "It's a hoax."

He posted his photos from the train station on Facebook, where they were viewed hundreds of thousands of times—another viral success. "On assignment from Cernovich Media, I traveled to Budapest-Keleti Railway Terminal," he wrote. "My original reporting blew the lid open on the media lies." He estimated that "over 70%" of Syrian refugees were "able-bodied young men," citing no evidence for the assertion and putting the word refugees in scare quotes.

Previously, he'd had a mental image of himself as a person who couldn't do what professional journalists did. But that mental image was the first thing he needed to overcome. Why couldn't he travel somewhere, take pictures, and write up what he saw? He could do it better than the traditional journalists, in fact, because he wasn't afraid to tell the truth, even if it contradicted the Narrative. The mainstream outlets had big budgets, dozens of employees, and decades of brand equity, but their size was also a liability. Cernovich, acting as the owner and sole employee of Cernovich Media, could be more nimble, more authentic, more disruptive. By honing his viral marketing skills, he could get his stories directly to the people. In the age of social media, a one-man operation and a billion-dollar enterprise were both part of the same Media Matrix. Ultimately, everyone was spreading content the same way: posting links online and trying to get people to share them.

———

In the United States, everyone was already preoccupied with a presidential election that was a year and a half away. Cernovich was dismissive at first. "No thinking man buys into this two-party political system," he once wrote. Then Trump entered the race. "I said if a Republican acted like me and ran for office, it'd be a movement," Cernovich tweeted in July 2015. "Donald Trump has proven me right. People are tired of pussies."

He kept blogging about nutrition and self-help, but he also started tweeting about politics, as a test. Why limit yourself to a niche audience when you could diversify? He developed a style of political punditry that fit his online persona—less Fox News contributor than mixed-martial-arts commentator. "Ted Cruz is brilliant but his look is off," Cernovich tweeted in 2015. "It's the neck fat. Career killer." Hillary Clinton was out of the question. Even before she entered the race, Cernovich tarred her with the worst insult he could imagine: "Hillary Clinton is an SJW."

To Cernovich's surprise, his audience loved his political content. So he followed their cues, tweeting and blogging more about politics. "Trump is winning," he wrote in September 2015, linking to a Wikipedia article about Nietzsche's theory of the transvaluation of values. In Trump, Cernovich recognized a fellow antihero. He wasn't perfect, but he'd never claimed to be perfect. Politics was a blood sport, but Jeb Bush and the rest of the cuckservatives preferred to be polite and play by the old rules. Only Trump was willing to smash the Overton window. "What are Trump's policies? I don't particularly care," Cernovich wrote on *Danger & Play*. "If Trump offends you," he wrote in another post, "it's because you live in a cucked world where no one speaks their minds."

He and Shauna moved back to California. He was an American, and if his country was going to war over its political future then he wanted to be a part of it. The liberals and neocons on cable news kept talking about how the next president had to be Clinton or Bush or Rubio—anyone who wouldn't challenge the Narrative on immigration or Islam or gender or race. "The media is against Donald Trump," Cernovich tweeted. "Well guess who hates the media." His implied answer was "almost everyone," which turned out to be correct.

He started reading up on the mainstream pundits and columnists, and he couldn't believe how many of them had similar backstories: Ivy League, nepotism, inherited wealth. No wonder they felt comfortable shilling for the establishment. "Look, if the experts decide tomorrow that we're going to war with Russia, who's gonna fight that war?" Cernovich said. "Jonah Goldberg and Ross Douthat? Fuck no. It'll be guys I know from Kewanee."*

The more boldly he spoke out against the media, the more his own brand as an alternative-media personality grew. "Why can't I start a competitor to Vice?" he mused on Twitter. "Maybe I'll start thinking about funding." In the end, the red pill might not have been quite the right metaphor. His eyes were now open to the existence of the Media Matrix; and yet, even as he condemned it, he could feel himself getting sucked into it.

Finally he understood: this would be his legacy. This was how he would make himself too big to ignore. "Twitter/YouTube/Google really give people the power," he tweeted. If he'd been born in another century, he might have been consigned to a life of valiant obscurity—a freethinking serf, never a leader. But he was alive in an era when anyone with the right set of skills could bend the arc of history. "I wake up every day full of passion and enthusiasm," he wrote. "Conflict inspires me, and I am only getting started."

---

*In *Good Will Hunting*, Will interviews for a job at the NSA, but he has no real intention of working for the military-industrial complex. Politicians and deep-state operatives have no compunction about starting costly foreign wars, Will explains to his interviewer, because "it won't be their kid over there getting' shot. . . . It'll be some kid from Southie over there takin' shrapnel in the ass."

CHAPTER FIFTEEN

Reductio

For much of 2016, I searched for an extremist meme peddler to write about. I wasn't after just any old extremist; I wanted to find an epitome of the social media age, someone with an alarming amount of unmerited influence and a clear plan for helping the lunatic fringe become the lunatic mainstream. The specific flavor of lunacy was of secondary importance. After all, I never asked Emerson Spartz to convince me that his listicles were accurate—that bacon-wrapped onion rings really were perfect for appetizers, burgers, and life. We hardly talked about his content at all. Instead, he showed me how he made his memes go viral.

I spent one uncomfortable summer afternoon with Colin Flaherty, a sixty-year-old white guy from Delaware. He wanted to see *The New Yorker*'s office—"I've always been curious what the belly of the beast looks like"—but that seemed like a bad idea for several reasons, so instead I took him to the Condé Nast cafeteria for a quick coffee and then whisked him outside, to City Hall Park, for an interview. We sat on a bench and Flaherty grumbled about the sorry state of the world. At the time, he had some twenty-five thousand subscribers on YouTube, but his account kept getting suspended for violating YouTube's rules. He told me that his goal was to expose the national epidemic of black-on-white crime, and the mainstream media's mysterious refusal to report on it. I made what I thought was a solid counterargument: that there was no epidemic of black-on-white crime, which explained the lack of media coverage.

Flaherty had no particular internet strategy. He seemed like a surly racist of the old-school variety—the kind of guy who, if he weren't ranting about black pathology on YouTube, would be ranting about black pathology on his front porch instead. In a pinned tweet, he tried to promote his most recent book, *Don't Make the Black Kids Angry,* by turning the title into a hashtag. But he hadn't noticed that hashtags could only consist of letters and numbers—that the Twitter algorithm understood any punctuation to be the end of a word—so his hashtag ended up being #Don, followed by a vestigial tail of unhighlighted letters.

Clearly, Flaherty would not be of much use to me. Next I tried Ben Goldman and Paris Wade, two twenty-six-year-olds who'd met when they were undergraduate business students at the University of Tennessee. Now they were living and working together in a studio apartment in the outer suburbs of San Francisco, sleeping on air mattresses and eating a lot of takeout burritos. Every twenty minutes or so, on a Facebook page called Liberty Writers, they would post another "news" bulletin based on little or no evidence ("IMPEACH HIM NOW! Obama's ISIS Tape Just Leaked & It's Even Worse Than You Can Imagine"). Each post was calibrated to incite a quick burst of activating emotion, usually fear or rage. The Facebook posts drove traffic to a site, LibertyWritersNews.com, which was laden with ads recommending herbal virility pills or one weird trick to bust belly fat.

They used pen names: Ben Goldman was Danny Gold, "America's #1 Writer," and Paris Wade was Paris Swade, "the best writer on the Internet." On the phone, Goldman was more modest. "Paris and I were busboys in a Mexican restaurant in Knoxville," he said. "Nobody else was really hiring. Then we put up a Facebook page, and suddenly we're making forty thousand bucks a month." He could hardly believe his good luck. I asked a few questions about yellow journalism and the fragility of the American democratic experiment, but neither topic seemed to hold his interest. "I approach what we do as a business, basically," he said. "Having strong beliefs can get in the way of building up a business sometimes."

He and Wade came from liberal families, and Goldman told me that each of them had "voted for Obama both times. But you can spend five minutes looking at the analytics and see what your audience wants. 'Hillary is a corrupt witch.' 'Comment below if you love our flag.'" He had his own personal beliefs, "but, regardless, when you know which narratives work, you feel pressure to drive those narratives. I'm sure you guys deal with similar pressures at the *New York Post.*"

"*The New Yorker,*" I said.

"Right," he responded. "What did I say?"

Pro-Trump clickbait was an easy way to make money, but I assumed that if that particular hustle ever became less lucrative, Goldman and Wade would be just as happy to hawk stock tips or real estate.

After the 2016 election, LibertyWritersNews.com and the Liberty Writers Facebook page both vanished. In 2018, I checked in on Goldman and Wade again. They were now living in the Las Vegas area, where Wade was running for Nevada State Assembly as a Republican.*

I called Mark Dice, a frequent guest on Infowars and a YouTuber with half a million subscribers. Dice's primary beat was exposing the Illuminati cult that controlled Hollywood. He did not seem to mean this figuratively. "I've shown, by pointing out secret messages in Lady Gaga's videos, that she's a Devil-worshipper," he told me. "I've called Kim Kardashian 'the big-butted anti-Christ.' That sort of thing. I'm not afraid to be politically incorrect." I asked Dice if I could spend a few days with him, observing how he made and promoted his videos. He declined.†

Next I approached the founder of Infowars, Alex Jones, who seemed willing to participate in a profile. I'd listened to his show for years, on and off, out of morbid curiosity. Jones treats facts the way cats treat small rodents, batting them around for a few minutes before butchering them for sport; still, when I paid more attention to the cadence than to the words, I sometimes found his millenarian rants oddly transporting. His opinion about global warming, to take an example more or less at random, was that the coastal elites had it exactly wrong—that the atmosphere actually needed *more* carbon dioxide, "a planet-saving nutrient." This wasn't a bad metaphor for Jones's whole broadcasting style: finding an informational environment already rich in toxins, he tried to help by disgorging as much poisonous gas as possible.

I had finalized my plans with the Infowars staff and was in the process of booking a trip to Texas when Jones changed his mind and rescinded the invitation. A few months later, he let a Vice camera crew film inside his studio. On a whiteboard in a conference room was a chart that some Infowars staffers had been working on:

---

*"Facebook shut down Liberty Writers News and its other related brands for relaying news to the public from an independent perspective," Wade's campaign website read. "Seeing first-hand what happens when constitutional protections are taken away reignited a long-standing desire within Wade to fight for ordinary Americans." There is, of course, no provision in the Constitution entitling anyone to a Facebook page; if anything, many First Amendment scholars have argued, the Constitution protects Facebook's right to ban pages such as Wade's. In the 2018 election, Wade lost to the incumbent, a Democrat, by 9 percentage points.
†"I'm very busy with the election approaching since it's a full time job debunking the mainstream media's lies about Trump and exposing the manipulation of the trending topics on social media which try to cast him in a false light," he emailed me. "I really wouldn't care if *The New Yorker* wanted to put me on the cover. I'm too busy producing my own content that gets seen by way more people than your magazine."

a two-dimensional map of the Media Matrix. A few dozen major outlets were ar-
rayed along a Y axis, from the most "state-run" to the most "independent," and
along an X axis, from "tyranny" to "freedom." Infowars was the freest and most
independent; ABC and CNN were the most state-run and tyrannical. In the middle of the chart were Vice News, the *Financial Times*, and *The New Yorker*.

•   •   •

I kept scouting for internet villains, and I found plenty, but none of them fit my
needs. What I was looking for, I started to realize, was a person whose undeserved
influence could demonstrate the brokenness of the entire system—in other words,
a reductio ad absurdum.

It's a rhetorical move at least as old as the Socratic dialogues. Someone articu-
lates a principle that seems to make sense on its face—*Justice means obeying the
law*, for example—and Socrates dismantles it, showing how it can lead to paradoxes. *What if your government makes an unjust law? Would justice then require
that you both obey it and disobey it?* Any principle that ends up producing such
absurdities was surely flawed to begin with.

In the early days of social media, the new gatekeepers didn't spend much time
delineating their abstract principles. For the most part, they proceeded according
to instinct, or aesthetic preference, or trial and error. (*We always banned people. It
wasn't well thought out or even articulated, really.*) When they did talk of freedom,
democracy, and giving power to the people, their lofty rhetoric was rarely subjected to Socratic scrutiny. Which people? How much freedom?

In early 2016, William Powers, an employee at the MIT Media Lab, wrote an
article about the 150 top "election influencers" of the moment, according to a quan-
titative analysis of Twitter data. "Thanks to the digital revolution," he wrote, "the old
behemoths of political influence, the two major parties and the traditional media,
have lost their former dominance." The most influential influencer on the list, to no
one's surprise, was Donald Trump. The next ten slots all went to individual politicians; the highest-ranked media organization, at number 12, was Fox News. At
number 32 was a site called Viral Buzz News, which billed itself as "a trendy take on
today's news, entertainment, social media trends and fresh talk"—not quite Dose
Politics, but not far off. Lower on the list were *Politico*, CNN Politics, and *The New
York Times*. Cher was sandwiched between Bill O'Reilly and the Associated Press.

Any media system that could lead to such absurd outcomes was surely flawed.

If this was how millions of Americans were getting the information that would shape their voting behavior, then something had gone terribly wrong.

I showed the list to a few people who knew the social media landscape well. More than once, their reaction was that the most surprising thing about the list was that Mike Cernovich wasn't on it.

• • •

That August, Hillary Clinton announced that she would give a speech linking Donald Trump to the alt-right. The afternoon before her speech, Cernovich sat on a veranda in Orange County, California, opened Periscope on his iPad, and started filming a video called "How to fight back against Sick Hillary and the #ClintonNewsNetwork." By "Clinton News Network," he meant CNN and the corporate media as a whole. "Sick" was supposed to describe Clinton both morally and physically. By "fight back," he meant using Twitter to gain ground in a larger informational war.

He slipped into his standard Periscope persona—part pundit, part life coach, part nativist demagogue. "Tomorrow, everybody's going to be googling the alt-right," he told his followers. "And you know what shows up? Jeff Bezos's blog, *The Washington Post*. Hoax articles, hoax sites are gonna come up." A torrent of heart logos, each generated by a viewer tapping the like button, surged up the right side of the screen. On the left side of the screen, also floating upward, were their comments (@beelman_matt: "PC is for PUSSIES"; @ciswhitemale: "Mike is a bosss"). Cernovich wore a plaid shirt, partially unbuttoned to display his chest hair. Behind him were a large, bright-blue swimming pool, a row of trimmed boxwoods, and a mountain glowing in the late-afternoon sun. (A comment from @CanadaUncuck: "nice pool.")

Cernovich insisted that he was not alt-right, but he kept slipping into first-person pronouns when he mentioned the movement. "We can control the narrative on Twitter," he said. "On Google, we've lost. Mainstream media we've lost." Already, in anticipation of Clinton's speech, the hashtag #AltRightMeans was trending on Twitter, with the alt-right's supporters and its opponents competing to define the movement in real time.*

---

*Any neutral online space—a trending hashtag, a Wikipedia article, a news site's comments section—could inspire this sort of spin battle, a free-for-all in which all sides scrambled to persuade onlookers through a combination of cleverness and brute force. Watching this sort of situation play out, I was always reminded of the moment

Cernovich talked for another seventy minutes as the sun set behind him, growing increasingly excited about Clinton's speech. By the end of his livestream, more than twenty thousand people were watching. "I want a full-scale media attack on me," he said. "I want this to become an international trending topic."

The next day, Cernovich watched Clinton's speech, livestreaming his reaction on Periscope. "Is she gonna fall?" he said, as Clinton approached the stage. "She's grabbing the handrail!" For months, Cernovich had been insisting that Clinton suffered from a grave neurological condition, and that the media was covering it up. Speaking and typing at the same time, he tweeted, "Sick Hillary grabs handrail as walking up steps. #AltRightMeans."

The hashtag continued to trend while Clinton spoke.

"#AltRightMeans I don't have to be ashamed of my heritage," Lauren Southern tweeted, with a stock photo of a blonde girl holding a Danish flag.

"#AltRightMeans tweeting about how Hitler might have been on to something from behind a Pepe the Frog avatar," Matthew Chapman, a Democratic activist, tweeted.

"I don't know what #AltRightMeans," a comedian named Maura Quint tweeted. "are those the ones who hate me b/c I'm a Jew, b/c I'm a woman or b/c I believe a hot dog is a sandwich?"*

In her speech, Clinton used the term as it was then commonly understood: a loose online affiliation of conspiracists, bigots, and social media trolls, with no single ideology unifying them all. Richard Spencer tried to reassert the term's intrinsic connection to white nationalism, telling a *Guardian* reporter, "Someone who is really alt-right recognizes the reality of race." But even the inventor of a meme can't always control how it evolves.

Clinton, behind a lectern, read out a few headlines from recent *Breitbart* articles by Milo Yiannopoulos. "Birth Control Makes Women Unattractive and Crazy," Clinton said. "Would You Rather Your Child Had Feminism or Cancer?"

---

in a basketball game when the ball goes out of bounds and the ref can't see who touched it last. Half the players point in one direction and the other half point just as insistently in the other, as if, with the right amount of pantomimed indignation, an unfavorable fact can lead to a favorable outcome. And sometimes it can.

*On Twitter, she spelled her name (((Maura Quint)))—an allusion to the Echo, a meme that was coined on Mike Enoch's blog, *The Right Stuff*. The Echo was meant to be a slur—a way for anti-Semites to identify and attack Jews—but some Jewish writers and activists had started trying to reclaim it by using it ironically.

She disapproved of these sentiments, and she was using her bully pulpit to express that disapproval. She was also, whether she realized it or not, amplifying Yiannopoulos's message. The troll's fondest wish is to trigger as many normies as possible, to hear his memes pass through the pursed lips of the powerful; yet even Yiannopoulos, a troll of unparalleled ambition, couldn't have anticipated that Hillary Clinton herself would repeat his words in front of a global audience.

Clinton didn't mention Cernovich, but she did denounce Alex Jones, who had suggested that the Sandy Hook shooting was staged and that its victims were child actors. When she reached this part of the speech, she went off script, her voice sinking into an unusually dire register: "I don't know what happens in somebody's mind, or how dark their heart must be, to say things like that."

When Clinton's speech was over, Yiannopoulos, writing on *Breitbart*, called it "a drive-by shooting with a water pistol fired from a mobility scooter." Cernovich, on Periscope, deemed it "boring," contending that it "contained way too many facts, didn't have a central theme." He was streaming from inside the living room. After a few minutes, though, Shauna asked him to go back outside. She was trying to watch the postspeech analysis on CNN, and she couldn't hear the TV.

Alex Jones responded to the speech a few hours after it ended, uploading a YouTube video of himself in his backyard. It was dusk, and cicadas were chirping in the background. "As I stand out here in the ninety-five-degree heat, as night falls, and I sweat, I guess I am figuratively in some type of fever swamp," he said. He scratched a mosquito bite on his forehead, then muttered about the Rockefellers and the Rothschilds. "People say, 'Oh my God, you've hit the big time—Hillary Clinton talked about you,'" he went on. "Give me a break. Hillary Clinton's average YouTubes, on her own channel, have, like, five thousand views. Our average one has hundreds of thousands."*

Clinton's speech "was the stupidest thing she could have done," Cernovich said. Clinton's social media advisers, he said, were "twenty-four-year-old basic bitches who feel triggered by us, and so they asked their boss to yell at us and make us go away. Well, we're not going away. They just made us stronger."

---

*Jones was exaggerating, but not by much. This rebuttal video got more views than Clinton's speech did on her official YouTube channel.

———

I emailed Cernovich and asked if I could spend a few days with him. Despite his antimedia bravado, it turned out, he talked to the media all the time. He wasn't naïve enough to imagine that *The New Yorker* would run a puff piece about him, he told me later. Still, however the article turned out, he felt confident that he'd be able to spin it as a victory. It might include a few snarky observations designed to lower his social status. Fine. Beyond that, what was the worst that could happen? Some understated insults in a fancy font? Every day, on Twitter, someone called him a rapist or a human-shaped shit stain, and it only seemed to make his brand stronger.

We talked on the phone, and I asked him quotidian questions. What did he do all day? How did he make money? And what *was* Cernovich Media, exactly—was he renting office space, hiring reporters, filling out W-2 forms?

Cernovich laughed. "I run a lean operation," he said. "Come out and you'll see it for yourself."

CHAPTER SIXTEEN

The Media Matrix

ernovich lived on a patch of coastline fifty miles south of Los Angeles, in a deep-red congressional district marked by temperate beaches and intemperate politics.* When he first told me his address over the phone, I asked him how I would recognize it. "You won't," he said. "It's one of those suburban tract-type deals where all the houses look exactly the fucking same."

Sure enough, every house on his cul-de-sac had a ceramic tile roof, beige stucco walls, a one-car garage, and a dash of pro-forma xeriscaping. He met me outside, barefoot, wearing a rumpled gingham shirt and jeans. I'd watched so many of his livestreams that I felt as if I knew him, but this was our first time meeting in person. He looked shorter and fleshier in person, and his eye contact was less steady than it was on camera.

A day-old *Orange County Register* lay at his feet, still wrapped in plastic. Cernovich Media was a lean operation indeed. Cernovich didn't even own a car, much less a satellite truck or a video-editing suite. Next door, a sticker on a garbage bin advertised a seamy web tabloid called *WorldNetDaily*, known for promoting the false rumor that Barack Obama had been born in Kenya. Cernovich hadn't met the neighbors. "They'd probably geek out if I told them my name," he said. "Then I'd have to say hi every time I see them, and maybe they'd want to be friends—nah, not worth it."

---

*At the time, the congressman representing Cernovich's district was Dana Rohrabacher, an ultraconservative Republican and by far the most Russia-friendly member of Congress. In June 2016, in a secret recording that was later leaked to reporters, Kevin McCarthy, the Republican House majority leader, said, "There's two people I think Putin pays: Rohrabacher and Trump."

He led me inside. "Shauna, d'you have pants on?" he shouted. "Not trying to get lucky, just letting you know there's a reporter here."

Shauna was in the kitchen, wearing yoga pants and a fluorescent-pink wicking tank top. (I already knew, from Periscope, that the house dress code was athleisure.) She was twenty-nine, six months pregnant, and as personable as her husband was taciturn. "I'm so embarrassed!" she said, apologizing for an imaginary mess. "We just moved in, like, two weeks ago."

The house was clean and compact, with still-empty picture frames and a couch covered in patterned throw pillows. There was a small, paved backyard, with a single lawn chair and a few dog toys scattered on the ground. The house I'd seen on Periscope—the one with the lush veranda and the swimming pool—belonged to Shauna's parents, who lived a few blocks away.

Shauna made espresso. "I'll take coconut cream in mine, if we have it," Mike said. He sat at the kitchen table and placed his laptop next to a scented candle and a teapot full of flowers. "Shauna's in charge of decorating," he explained. I sat next to him, opened my laptop, and made my font size as small as possible, so that I could type my unprocessed impressions without worrying that he'd read them over my shoulder.

He responded to a few emails, then scanned the recent Amazon sales figures for *Gorilla Mindset*, his men's rights self-help book. There were hundreds of reviews, most of which gave the book five out of five stars. In the Kindle store, *Gorilla Mindset* was filed under "gender studies." It was the top seller in that category, just above *We Should All Be Feminists*, by Chimamanda Ngozi Adichie.

Cernovich's book sales were both a point of pride and a rhetorical cudgel. "When a cuckservative or an SJW gets into a Twitter battle with me, and they're an author, one of my favorite moves is to go, 'How're your book sales doin', buddy?'" he said. "They back down after that, 'cause it's quantifiable. I sell books. The only SJW who really sells more than I do is Ta-Nehisi Coates—that guy's a whole tier or two above me. He's selling indulgences to white liberals, absolving them of their white guilt, which, I've gotta hand it to him, is a great niche market."

He checked his WordPress dashboard: "Right now one hundred twenty-eight people are reading *Danger & Play*. What's fun is when you get a hot story and watch the number tick up into the thousands, like a video game."

In another tab, he opened his Twitter analytics.* He asked me to open my own Twitter account, on my laptop, so that he could give me a free coaching session. "How many followers do you have?" he asked. The way he said it, he might have been asking me how much I could bench press. He continued, "There are a few easy things you can do right away to get your stats up."

"I'm good," I said. I didn't doubt that Cernovich's tips would work; I did wonder whether they would allow me to keep my job, or my self-respect.

He got a text from a friend. Rush Limbaugh had just mentioned the hashtag #ZombieHillary on the radio. "I would like to claim credit for it, but I can't," Limbaugh said. "Somebody on Twitter did it." That somebody was Cernovich, enlisting his followers to get the hashtag trending. "He'll never mention me by name," Cernovich said. "But he's at least listening to the periphery."

Shauna brought mugs of coffee to the kitchen table. She told the story of how she'd met Mike, in 2011, at a bar in Santa Monica. "He was pretty aggressive," she said. "He grabbed my arm, pulled me into him, and said, 'You fit nicely.'"

"It sounds creepy, but it looked less creepy in context," Mike said.

"It worked," Shauna said. "We were making out, like, five minutes later."

When they started dating, Mike said, "She was just, like, a little puppy dog.† I didn't take it seriously. But she just refused to go away, and now—"

"I'm married and pregnant!" Shauna said, smiling.

"And my life is over," Mike said, half smiling.

Shauna sat next to Mike, stroking his arm. "We're having a girl!" she said. "I think it'll be good for him, soften him up a bit."

They planned to name her Cyra, after Cyrus the Great. "I'll be nice to her, as long as she's not a basic bitch," Mike said.

Early in their relationship, Shauna read the archives of *Danger & Play*, including such posts as "How to Cheat on Your Girlfriend." "I would come home from work crying," Shauna said. "'How can you write these terrible things?' He'd go, 'You don't understand, babe, this is just how guys talk.'" (Advice from *Danger &*

---

*At the time, he had 109,000 followers. By summer 2019, he had 467,000. By the end of the year, he may have 50,000 more, or he may be banned from the platform.

†From a 2012 post on *Danger & Play*: "Be honest with yourselves. Women are not interesting. Like my dog, women are cute and adorable and funny when they lash out. (Unlike my dog, women are disloyal.)"

Play: "Always call your girl 'babe,'" to avoid mixing up names.) Shauna continued, "I was still upset, though, and he eventually deleted some older posts."

"I rewrote some of the *wording*," Mike insisted. "I never disavow things I've said." His facial expression remained impassive, but under the table he started wheeling his wrists in tight circles.

Outside, the weather was perfect, the sort of halcyon day that happens maybe ten times a year in New York and two hundred times a year in Orange County. We stayed inside, to avoid screen glare. I brought up a few of his many verifiable lies—about Muslim migration, campus rape statistics, and several other topics. He didn't deny or disavow any of his previous claims. Instead, he reinterpreted my line of questioning more abstractly. "Am I fake news?" he said. "No, I believe what I write. I might get things wrong here and there, but the hoaxing mainstream media gets things wrong all the time." He rattled off a list of stories in *The Washington Post* and *The New York Times* that were later corrected.

I made counterarguments: How did the proportion of their erroneous stories compare to the proportion on *Danger & Play*? What methods did he have in place to fact-check his stories before he ran them, or to issue corrections? Did he even do reporting, properly speaking? Yet my objections weren't landing. I could feel myself getting pulled into his frame.

"I'm sufficiently complex that there's no one truth about me," he said. "Am I a ranting maniac on Twitter? Yeah, but I'm also a pretty mellow married guy who's into hiking and walking his dog. Is Sean Penn kind of a basic bitch? Sure, but he got the only interview with El Chapo.* This is why the hoaxing media is so triggered by me. They can only keep saying 'Don't listen to him; he's not legit' for so long. I'll keep saying the opposite, and I'll keep getting more views on Periscope."

He took a sip of coffee and sat back, resting his hands behind his head. He was giving me good copy, and he knew it. "Look, I read postmodernist theory in college," he said. "If everything is a narrative, then we need alternatives to the dominant narrative." He smiled. "I don't seem like a guy who reads Lacan, do I?"

---

*In 2015, on assignment for *Rolling Stone*, the actor Sean Penn scored an exceedingly rare interview with the drug kingpin Joaquín "El Chapo" Guzmán, who was in hiding in the mountains of Sinaloa.

• • •

I kept trying to pin down what he actually believed. Of all the ways he could be spending his time, why was he working so hard to prevent Clinton from becoming president? "There are a million things wrong with Hillary," he said. "She's the pro-war
candidate. She's massively corrupt. She wants to let in more so-called refugees"—
especially those from the Muslim world—"which is an existential threat."*

But he wasn't merely interested in raising principled objections; he wanted to
have an impact on the election, and that meant identifying memes that would
incite a sharp spike of emotion. Stories about corruption might cause a moment of
brow-furrowing concern, but they didn't produce much social media engagement.
"I was looking at the conversation online—what was getting through to people
and what wasn't—and none of that was sticking," he said. "It's too complex. I
thought that the health stuff would be more visceral, more resonant from a persuasion standpoint, and so I pushed that."

In March 2016, during a Democratic debate, he tweeted, "Hillary's face looks
like melting candle wax. Imagine what her brain looks like." Later that month, he
tweeted a photo of Clinton winking, which he interpreted as "a mild stroke." By
August, it was "obvious" to him that Clinton was suffering from both a seizure
disorder and Parkinson's disease. On Twitter, he promoted hashtag after hashtag:
#HillarysHealth, #CoughingHillary, #SickHillary. Coughing, of course, is neither
a high crime nor a misdemeanor; yet it's relatively easy to make large swaths of
Americans feel disgust, especially about an older woman, and disgust is an activating emotion.

The health rumors echoed through the far-right recesses of social media. In
early August, they started to dominate the front page of the *Drudge Report*, which
became the meme's bridge to the mainstream. "Go online and put down 'Hillary
Clinton illness,' take a look at the videos for yourself," Rudy Giuliani, the former
mayor of New York and pugnacious Trump surrogate, said on Fox News. In early
September, Donald Trump tweeted, "Mainstream media never covered Hillary's
massive 'hacking' or coughing attack, yet it is #1 trending. What's up?" Still no
fire, but an expanding circle of smoke machines.

---

*A few days later, Donald Trump Jr. tweeted a variation on an old alt-right meme: "If I had a bowl of skittles and
I told you that just three would kill you. Would you take a handful? That's our Syrian refugee problem." Cernovich
told me, "Don Jr. gets it more than anyone."

Mainstream journalists remained unpersuaded, but they now deemed the rumor worthy of a response. On September 6, Chris Cillizza, a centrist *Washington Post* columnist and an astoundingly frictionless weathervane representing the latest in Beltway groupthink, published a piece called "Can We Just Stop Talking About Hillary's Health Now?" In the column, he talked about Hillary's health. "Led by Drudge, there have been questions circulating in the conservative media," he wrote. "Here's the thing: This is a totally ridiculous issue."

Five days later, Clinton collapsed after attending a memorial service at Ground Zero. "She fainted!" Cernovich wrote on Facebook. "Yes it happened, Hillary Clinton fainted and collapsed on camera." Clinton's explanation, which she offered only after the fact, was that she'd come down with pneumonia. Without months of priming by Cernovich and others, her collapse may have been seen as an isolated event; without the scrutiny from her social media antagonists, Clinton may have been less secretive about her illness. But as it happened, the mainstream press started to convince itself that Hillary's health might actually be a Thing after all. The incident was discussed on ABC, CNN, MSNBC, and Fox News. About two hours after footage of Clinton's collapse went viral on social media, Chris Cillizza published another *Washington Post* column. This one was called "Hillary Clinton's Health Just Became a Real Issue in the Presidential Campaign."

Cernovich gained more than four thousand Twitter followers in a day. Scott Greer, the deputy editor of the conservative tabloid *The Daily Caller*, tweeted, "Cernovich memed #SickHillary into reality. Never doubt the power of memes." Cernovich retweeted him. "I decline the Pulitzer for my work on Hillary's health," he wrote. "I will not accept a scam award from a scam organization."

CHAPTER SEVENTEEN

Fitness and Unfitness

In November 1880, Chester Arthur, a Republican, was elected to serve as James Garfield's vice president. The following month, *The New York Times* reported from near Arthur's hometown, in Vermont: "A stranger arrived here a few days ago . . . to obtain evidence to show that Gen. Arthur is an unnaturalized foreigner." The stranger was A. P. Hinman, who appeared to be a Democratic Party operative. The following week, Hinman sent a letter to the *Times* and several other newspapers, alleging that Arthur had been born in either Scotland or Ireland and was therefore ineligible to be vice president. The *Brooklyn Daily Eagle* printed the letter, calling the issue of Arthur's birth "an important and curious question." But journalists could find no evidence to support the rumor, and for a few months the story lay dormant.

In July 1881, President Garfield was shot and gravely wounded. Throughout the summer, as his condition deteriorated, journalists reconsidered Hinman's claim that Vice President Arthur, now next in line for the presidency, had been born abroad. *The New York Sun*, a pro-Democrat newspaper, launched a thorough investigation. In September, Garfield died and Arthur was sworn in as president. The following day, the *Sun* ran a long article announcing its finding: the rumor about Arthur's foreign birth was without merit.

In 1884, Hinman, now alleging that Arthur had in fact been born in Canada, self-published a 90-page pamphlet called *How a British Subject Became President of the United States*, a strange mash-up of tedious bureaucratic correspondence and self-aggrandizing poetry. Arthur disregarded it, as did the press. Many Americans, if not most, never heard about Hinman's allegations, and they had no appreciable effect on Arthur's legacy. In the 1880s, or even the 1980s, journalists could hamper the spread of a meritless story by debunking it, or simply by ignoring it.

Yahoo Answers is an online forum that allows anyone to ask any question, no matter how inane. On May 23, 2007, three months after Barack Obama announced his presidential campaign, there were dozens of active threads on the forum, including "What coulour tie should I wear?" and "I am little bit fat, & have big stomatch?" and "Global warming?" An anonymous poster added a new question: "If Obama bin HUSSEIN al Barack was born in Kenya, how can he run for president in the US?" This received forty-four replies, ranging from "He shouldn't run, I certainly won't be voting for him or the lesbian" to "sigh. dont be such a racist."

For a few months, the rumor about Obama's birth persisted in chain emails and obscure blogs, but traditional newspapers and TV broadcasters ignored it. After all, one of the primary responsibilities of the media is to mediate—to distinguish spin from substance, fact from fabrication—and the rumor, being without merit, was deemed unfit to print. By the Darwinian definition of fitness that prevailed on the viral internet, however, the meme was perfectly poised for success.

In 2008, *WorldNetDaily* picked up the story. The site, also known as *WND*, featured a big-tent hybrid of Moral Majority conservatism (columns by Phyllis Schlafly and Alan Keyes), nativist paleoconservatism (columns by Ann Coulter and Pat Buchanan), and full-on battiness ("Islam's 20-point plan for conquering the United States by 2020"). Its stories were often featured on the *Drudge Report*, which brought in a lot of traffic. Shortly before Election Day, *WND* published an article called "Obama 'Admits' Kenyan Birth?" Two days later, Rush Limbaugh, the most popular radio broadcaster in the country, invoked the rumor during drive time. "This birth-certificate business—I'm just wondering if something's up," he said. "I'm telling you, this has not reached the threshold until now, and it's popping up all over the place."

Donald Trump first flirted with a presidential run in 1987. He flew to New Hampshire four months before the state's crucial primary election to deliver what he insisted was not a campaign speech. (His proposed economic policy, verbatim: "Whatever Japan wants, do the opposite.") The stunt garnered a bit of mainstream press coverage—"New Hampshire Speech Earns Praise for Trump" was the headline in *The New York Times*—but not enough, apparently, to justify a full campaign. The crowd thrilled to Trump's jingoist bravado. "If he doesn't do it in '88, I'm looking forward to '92," an audience member told a reporter from the *Detroit Free Press*. It was still the age of mass media, however, and most members of the audience—the ones who did not happen to find themselves standing next to professional journalists—were receivers, not yet transmitters.

In 1999, Trump tried again, musing about a presidential run on *Larry King Live*. Again, the press responded with fleeting curiosity and then moved on, starving the story of oxygen. By the end of 1999, the only poll that listed Trump as a serious contender was a hundred-person "unscientific survey" conducted by the *National Enquirer.**

In 2011, Trump floated the most bizarre trial balloon in American political history. This time, instead of going straight to the mainstream media, he started by trying to generate buzz on the internet. First, Trump instructed his loyal fixer, Michael Cohen, to set up a site called ShouldTrumpRun.com.† Then Trump took to Twitter. "THe people at shouldtrumprun.com have got it right!" he tweeted. "How are our factories supposed to compete with China and other countries when they have no environmental restrictions!" (The erratic capitalization indicated that the tweet was not the product of a sleek PR firm but the handiwork of the man himself.)

Trump tweeted links to ShouldTrumpRun.com a couple more times, but the response was modest. There was nothing to command people's attention—no news hook, no controversy, no meme with momentum. Trump seemed to move on, tweeting about nonpolitical pursuits. ("THe Westminster Dog Show asked if I'd be interested in meeting Hickory, a Scottish Deerhound, who won Best in

---

*"The 2000 presidential election is neck and neck," the paper claimed. "But sorry, Al Gore, the real battle is between George W. Bush and Donald Trump!" David Pecker, one of Trump's closest friends, had taken over the *Enquirer* earlier that year.
†From the landing page:

> Empty promises echo across the nation every four years; stringing us along as we wait for something good to finally happen. Well it is finally here, and it is real. It is DONALD J. TRUMP.

Below this was a photo of Trump squinting, Rushmore-like, into the middle distance, along with a paradigmatically Trumpian epigraph: "It's cold outside . . . so where's the global warming?"

Show. She came to visit today!") Behind the scenes, though, he was still working to stir up interest in his presidential bid, or at least in himself.

Trump talked to Joseph Farah, the editor of *WND*, and to Jerome Corsi, one of the site's lead writers. "He was looking for a smoking-gun kind of sound bite that would resonate with people," Farah later told *The New York Times*. The sound bite Trump chose was the meme about Obama's forged birth certificate. Trump knew instinctively that the attention marketplace was oversaturated, that the usual things (an interview with Larry King, a visit with a prize-winning deerhound) were growing easier for the public to ignore. But an outrageous conspiracy theory about Obama's foreign birth—birtherism, as it became known—would incite a sharp spike of activating emotion, either positive or negative, in everyone who heard it.

For six weeks, Trump talked incessantly about birtherism, combining traditional media and social media in a kind of feedback loop. Whenever a journalist gave him a microphone, he talked into it; when there were no microphones around, he kept the conversation going online. On March 23, appearing on ABC's *The View*, Trump said, "I want him to show his birth certificate. There's something on that birth certificate that he doesn't like." Barbara Walters, one of the show's cohosts and a living embodiment of a traditional media gatekeeper, tried to shut down the conversation: "That's a *terrible* thing to say." It didn't seem to make a bit of difference. "I like it because it upset those lightweights on The View," one fan tweeted. Another wrote, "An orange man in the white house?"

Most candidates are willing to pander, but only up to a point. Eventually, even the most shameless and mercenary of politicians will run up against a fact too plain to contradict, a principle too sacred to violate, a layer of dignity that would be too humiliating to shed. But Trump seemed to have no interest in dignity, no capacity for shame, and no discernible ethos beyond self-promotion. The mob could point in any direction, and he would trundle forth. He was no expert in social media algorithms—he didn't even use a computer—but he knew how to read a room. Besides, on Twitter, the built-in analytics tools did most of the room-reading for you. One pattern was obvious: the more incendiary your message, and the more loudly and forcefully you repeated it, the more attention you could get. For most of his life, Trump could get press coverage only by doing something notable in the world—building a casino, cheating on his wife, giving a speech in New Hampshire. In the age of social media, the bar was lower. The precipitating event for mainstream-media coverage could be nothing more than "starting a conversation" online.

On May 16, 2011, Trump made an announcement on his Facebook page: "After considerable deliberation and reflection, I have decided not to pursue the office of the presidency." However, in the future, he wrote, "I will not shy away from expressing the opinions that so many of you share yet don't have a medium through which to articulate."

CHAPTER EIGHTEEN

The Transplant

Y ou guys want a snack?" Shauna said.

"Not now, babe," Mike said, keeping his eyes on his computer screen. She put out a bowl of pita chips anyway. He ignored it. I tried to resist, applying the self-control techniques recommended in *Gorilla Mindset*, but after a few minutes I looked down and saw that I'd eaten every chip in the bowl except one.

"I don't want to disrupt your schedule," I told him. "Just try to go about your day as you normally would."

"My days aren't structured at all, dude," he said. "I'm gonna be on Bill Mitchell's show at some point and on Gavin's show at some point. Otherwise, I mostly just go with the flow."

Shauna put on sneakers and got ready to walk to her parents' house. "They don't fully understand what Michael does," she told me. "They get that he likes Trump and that he puts stuff on the internet—they just don't get how that's a job." Her parents, secular Persian Muslims, left Iran before it became a theocracy. "My dad hates when women cover their hair," she said.

"We sometimes joke that he's more Islamophobic than I am," Mike said.

"My dad actually created an anonymous Twitter account so he could troll Muslims," Shauna said. "At the same time, he hates Trump, because he's, like, 'If he's saying negative things about different groups, then how do we know he's not going to come after Persians one day?' Even if you believe certain things, you shouldn't necessarily say it openly."

Mike wasn't so sure. "I don't think any ideas are off-limits," he said. "Actions, yes. Words, no." He stood up and stretched briefly, thrusting his chest forward and his arms back. "Lowers your cortisol," he explained.

A Skype call came in: a producer at *The Gavin McInnes Show*. Cernovich sat and smoothed his hair, checking his reflection in his webcam.

"Thanks for joining us, bro," the producer said.

"Nice to see you again, cutie pie," Cernovich said. "How's the angle looking? How's my hair looking?"

The producer put Cernovich on air, and he and McInnes spent fifteen minutes agreeing that, if you ignored most of the available evidence, Trump seemed to be winning. McInnes mentioned a video that was making the rounds on Twitter: a Trump supporter crashing a poorly attended Clinton event, filming it on his phone. "Not to trivialize what you do," McInnes told Cernovich, "but it shows how easy it is to be a real journalist—just fucking go there!"

"That's what I tell people," Cernovich said. "All you need is a smartphone and balls, and you can do real journalism."

Gavin McInnes, in addition to his online talk show and his late-night appearances on Fox News, had started contributing YouTube segments to the Rebel Media, an alt-light outlet founded in Canada in 2015. At various times, Lauren Southern, Jack Posobiec, and Laura Loomer have all been employed by the Rebel; so have Sebastian Gorka, a British-Hungarian Islamophobe who served briefly in the Trump administration, and Faith Goldy, a Canadian in her twenties whose bio described her as "a fearless journalist and devout Catholic." Her straight-to-camera commentary for the Rebel included such segments as "BOMBSHELL: Canada's Border Invasion Intensifies!" and "Is Soy Feminizing the West?"

Goldy—like Lauren Southern, one of her closest friends—referred to her racial politics as "identitarian." Both women were attempting a tricky Solomonic split: they publicly denied being white nationalists, yet they kept dog-whistling loudly enough to hold the alt-right's interest. Goldy and Southern belonged to the first generation to grow up with social media, and they'd both been red-pilled by a combination of premodern philosophy books and post-postmodern message boards such as 4chan. They were well practiced at cloaking their ideological commitments beneath several layers of irony, allusions, and emojis.

Anyone who was paying attention, though, could have discerned a consistent message. On assignment for the Rebel, Goldy and McInnes had traveled to Israel and Palestine. "This place is Muslim now!" McInnes reported in one video, standing outside the Church of the Nativity in Bethlehem. "We had it for I don't know how many hundreds of years."

"The only way we're gonna get Bethlehem back is if we launch the next crusade," Goldy said, adding, *"Deus Vult!"* This was an eleventh-century battle cry that Christian holy warriors had shouted during the First Crusade while killing Muslims and pillaging their cities.

McInnes never quite crossed the line into open white nationalism, but he often came close. The alt-right had something akin to a Pledge of Allegiance, an old white-nationalist shibboleth known as the Fourteen Words: "We must secure the existence of our people and a future for white children."* Alt-right trolls liked to goad alt-light demicelebrities into uttering the words. On YouTube, it became something of a game.

"Say it, Gavin," one of McInnes's guests implored him on his show. "You will prove that you are really at the crux of this movement." The guest broke the sentence into its constituent parts, like a priest leading a parishioner through a sacrament. McInnes followed along, repeating thirteen of the words but replacing "white" with "Western."

The commenters were crestfallen:

He's not fully committed to the cause
Gavin McCuckis
Memes over genes, or genes over memes?

Faith Goldy, by contrast, had no problem crossing the line. In a separate YouTube video, while failing to suppress an impish grin, she recited all of the Fourteen Words. "Is that controversial, though?" she said. "I think it's controversial to say the opposite."

---

*David Lane, the founder of a white terror group whose members murdered a Jewish radio host named Alan Berg in 1984, coined the Fourteen Words while in prison. The phrase found a new fan base a generation later, not only on YouTube but in some corners of the federal government. In 2018, a web developer named Laurie Voss linked to a press release that the Department of Homeland Security had issued. The title of the document was "We Must Secure the Border and Build the Wall to Make America Safe Again." "This is an actual story on an official government website with a 14-word headline starting with 'we must secure,'" Voss tweeted. "This is not an accident." In 2019, Brenton Tarrant shot a hundred people at two mosques in Christchurch, New Zealand, killing fifty-one. He left behind a seventy-four-page manifesto explaining his motives in question-and-answer form. "What do you want?" one of the questions read. His answer was simple: the Fourteen Words.

———

The civic-nationalist alt-light kept trying to declare its independence from the white-nationalist alt-right, but the effort seemed futile. In casual conversation, on televised news, even in think-tank reports, the definition of "alt-right" kept warping and blurring. Most people used the term interchangeably with "fringe weirdo," a concept that meant something different to everyone. "They're on the wrong side of history," a friend told me. She meant all of them. The distinctions didn't interest her.

My colleagues and friends assumed that I was an expert on the entire phylum of far-right internet villains, but I was only one man, and the internet was teeming with villains. I had to set priorities. The unapologetic Nazis were so obviously repellent that, at the time, they seemed like a mere oddity. Instead, I focused on the alt-light, which struck me as a more instructive test case.

Our country was undergoing a painful and sudden shift. The old national vocabulary was being dismantled, and it was too early to tell what would take its place. I sometimes imagined the process as a barbaric form of surgery, an unauthorized organ transplant. The ribcage of the body politic had been pried open; the alt-light demicelebrities were trying to sneak into the operating theater, insert their thinly disguised demagoguery, and then sew up the wound before anyone noticed. They weren't actual doctors, but you couldn't necessarily see that at first glance; they wore convincing-looking uniforms and spoke with authority, and for some people that was enough. Nobody, not even the alt-light themselves, knew whether the transplanted organ would be assimilated or rejected. We would all have to wait to find out.

• • •

Cernovich stood up, poured himself another cup of coffee, and sat back down at his laptop. He checked his direct messages on Twitter, responding to about one in twenty. "People send tips all day long," he said. "I can't even look at them all, much less chase them all down."

He read a few articles about Ahmad Rahami, who was suspected of planting bombs in New Jersey and Manhattan the previous day. Most of the articles noted that Rahami, who was born in Afghanistan, was a naturalized American citizen. Nonetheless, Cernovich said, "It's important to keep building an association. Hillary wants open borders? OK, this is what happens."

Developments in the Rahami case were big news in the New York area, but not everywhere on the internet. "If there's a story that can hurt Hillary, I want it in the news cycle," Cernovich said. "When I first started, that meant figuring out how news cycles work. If it's on *Drudge*, then it's on *Hannity*. If it's on *Hannity*, then Brian Stelter's talking about it on CNN. No one teaches you this stuff. You just study it and figure it out."

When he couldn't get the *Drudge Report* to pick up a story, Cernovich simply promoted it himself on Twitter. "The amazing thing is, you can just do it whenever," he said. "Here, I'll show you." He propped his iPad upright on the kitchen table, with the camera lens facing a mirror in front of him. He emitted a few hacking outbreaths—"Gotta breathe into my stomach first, to get oxygenated," he said—and then started filming. "And we're back," he began. "Mike Cernovich, *Danger & Play, Gorilla Mindset.*"

Within minutes, thousands of viewers had joined the stream. "We've gotta get a hashtag trending," he said. "We definitely need to remind the world that Hillary Clinton is bringing in the terrorists." Viewers made suggestions in the comments, and Cernovich read them aloud. "HillarysMigrants is good," he said. "Hillarys Terrorists is good. Yeah, just keep throwing them out."

Someone suggested #TerroristsForHillary. "Eh, a little too cutesie," Cernovich said. "You wanna be catchy, but if you overstate it too much then it loses its persuasive power, like 'basket of deplorables.'" He overlooked #SkunkKillary, #hillarys hitmen, and #hillarysmigrantcuntlickers, as well as a commenter who wrote, "Nice tea kettle of flowers, cuck."

"HillarysMigrants seems to be a popular one," Cernovich said. It was settled. He clarified the spelling: one word, no apostrophe. "Remind people that Angela Merkel, George Soros, Hillary Clinton—they're all together," Cernovich said. "Post pictures of them together." A commenter wrote "Evil Jew Soros"; Cernovich either ignored it or didn't see it. He kept talking for twenty more minutes, reading passages from George Orwell's *Politics and the English Language*, plugging his book, and referring to George Soros's son six times as a "basic bitch."

When the video was over, he searched for #HillarysMigrants on Twitter. There were hundreds of tweets, many of which included images, as he'd requested: Clinton and Merkel laughing conspiratorially; a macabre illustration of Clinton as a ventriloquist's dummy, sitting on George Soros's lap. Cernovich added a few tweets of his own, saying the words aloud as he typed them: "'The media won't tell you the truth about #HillarysMigrants.'" He tried another variation a few seconds later; it got fewer retweets, so he deleted it. "This is my one-man version of A/B testing," he said.

He searched for the hashtag every few seconds, yielding about a dozen new tweets each time. "It's hard to tell yet whether this is a killer hashtag or just an OK one," he said. "It's picking up some steam, but maybe not enough." After a few minutes, he gave up. "Doesn't look like they're going to let this one trend, for whatever reason," he said. "Should we grab lunch?"

Shauna unlocked a BMW X-class using a clicker in her purse, and we headed to a nearby strip mall. "I make her do the driving," Mike told me, from the passenger seat. "The deal is, 'I pay the bills. Driving is your job.'" Shauna just smiled and turned up the radio.

We ordered at a counter-service kabob place.* The food arrived on a plastic tray, and Cernovich set it down on a table inside, where there was air-conditioning. He was explaining something about his salmon kabob—why fish fat is the good kind of fat, I think, although I was only half listening—when he got a news tip by text. "We gotta get home," he said, wrapping up his leftovers.

"Should I stop at the Starbucks drive-through?" Shauna said.

"No time, babe," he said.

At an elementary school in Eagle Valley, Utah, a bomb scare was in progress. No reporters were on the scene; the only public source of information was a woman who lived across the street from the school, peering out her window and

---

*I paid. According to the rules of journalistic ethics, at least as I understood them, I was allowed to pay for my interview subjects' meals, although they couldn't pay for any of mine; I was allowed to bring them gifts, but I couldn't accept gifts from them, or pay them for their time. These rules made sense on their face, but they led to some absurd outcomes. When Milo Yiannopoulos self-published a book on July 4, 2017, Cassandra Fairbanks and Laura Loomer drove to New York for the release party. I met them at Katz's Deli and bought Loomer an overpriced sandwich. (Fairbanks, a vegetarian, made do with pickles.) There was a cordon of protesters outside Yiannopoulos's party, and as I crossed it, the pentatonic protest melody lodged itself in my head yet again. Admission to the party cost twenty dollars, and it came with a copy of Yiannopoulos's book. I didn't feel great about being used to goose a crypto-fascist's opening-week sales figures; but I wanted to report on the party, and it didn't violate any traditional rules of journalistic ethics, so I paid. (The party ended up being too distasteful for me to write about—Yiannopoulos had hired three little people to walk through the crowd wearing yarmulkes, his attempt to mock a rival named Ben Shapiro—but I did meet some useful sources.) A few months later, I ended up in a sad hotel restaurant in Walnut Creek, California, eating dinner with Yiannopoulos and his entourage. When the bill came, he tried to pay it. My fleeting moral intuition was that I should let him—it was the Mercer family's money anyway—but in the end I insisted on getting separate checks. I was a reluctant institutionalist, and there were enough norms being desecrated everywhere else in the world.

posting footage to Facebook Live. Mike opened Twitter on his phone, then commandeered Shauna's phone and opened Facebook on hers.

A man in a green robe and a turban was pacing near the entrance to the school, which had apparently been evacuated. "Could be a hoax, could be a drill, could be the real thing," Cernovich said. He tweeted a link to the Utah woman's live video. At the time, only seventy-seven people were watching; after Cernovich and others passed it around, the number climbed into the hundreds, then into the thousands.

I opened the video on my phone so that I could follow along from the backseat. A few seconds later, a tank rolled into the frame. "Fuuuuck," Cernovich said. "Anyone else getting goosebumps?"

At home, he rushed into the living room, stood his iPad on end, and started another Periscope. "You're watching this as it happens, folks," he said. "If this is a drill, it's one hell of a drill."

"Islam is cancer," one Periscope commenter wrote.

"Robot Lives Matter," wrote another.

After a few minutes, the police in Utah ordered the woman to step away from her window, and her Facebook feed went dead. The man in the turban turned out to be a local white man who was suffering from delusions; he was arrested, and no bomb was found. "I'm gonna call this mental illness rather than Islam," Cernovich told his audience. "You make up your own mind."

He ended the video and shrugged. "A lot of these things end up being dead ends," he said. "I don't get as blue balled by that as I used to."

It was 3:30 in the afternoon. I was exhausted. Cernovich went upstairs and changed into track pants. "I think I'll power down for the day," he said. "Go to the gym, relax a bit—maybe keep an eye on Twitter, but not closely."

Before closing Twitter, he took one last look at his direct messages. One was from a fan who claimed to have found a Reddit thread started by one of Hillary Clinton's IT staffers. Apparently, the staffer had been asking for help as he tried to delete Clinton's name, illicitly, from a cache of old emails. "My confirmation bias would love for this to be real," Cernovich said. "But honestly it seems too good to be true." When he clicked the link, though, he saw that the Reddit thread had just been deleted. "That's fucking interesting," he said. After five minutes of digging, he found an archived version of the thread; it looked legitimate, and legitimately incriminating. "Son of a bitch," he said. "This might actually be true." He tweeted, "Did sick Hillary's IT guy really ask for help on Reddit? Investigating."

He started to breathe heavily, drifting back into his muckraking flow state. "We're going to make a whole new news cycle about her fucking emails again!" he said. "This poor fucking woman." He started a new Periscope, and commenters suggested possible hashtags. "I don't think RedditHillary is a good hashtag," Cernovich said. "What else? HillarysITGuy? We're having a hard time."

After a few minutes, he grew impatient and made an executive decision: the hashtag would be #HillarysHacker. "How big this is cannot be overstated," Cernovich said. "I say this not just as one of the ten most recognized journalists in the world, but I say this also as a lawyer." While he was livestreaming, I opened Twitter and saw that—on my feed, anyway—#HillarysHacker was the number 2 trending topic.

I left Cernovich's house and took a quick walk on the beach, trying to clear my head. Then I checked into my hotel, switched my phone to silent mode, and slept for a long time. Overnight, the #HillarysHacker meme leaped into the mainstream. A conservative site called *Red State* picked up the story; Wikileaks tweeted about it; Fox News started covering it early in the morning. By the time I woke up, the story had appeared in *Vice* and *New York* magazine, and the House Oversight Committee had promised to investigate it. I checked Cernovich's Twitter feed: since I'd left him, he had tweeted dozens of times, as late as 1:30 A.M.

When I returned to his house, he was wearing the gingham shirt he'd worn the day before. "I didn't go to the gym last night," he said sheepishly. "I didn't get much sleep. I've gained twenty pounds during this fucking election." He mentioned that he'd been reading Andrew Breitbart's 2011 autobiography, *Righteous Indignation*. "There's a part where he's on a plane for five hours, without wi-fi, and he has withdrawal symptoms," Cernovich said. "I relate to that. And, you know, Breitbart had a huge cultural impact, but he died of heart failure at forty-three."

Cernovich was almost forty, and he wanted his hero's journey to last far longer than Breitbart's. He had big plans: writing more books, directing feature films, maybe even running for Congress. "If I sense that that's what the people want, then I do think I would feel a duty to serve," he said. "It sounds crazy to you, I'm sure, but I've learned not to count anything out." He said that he had a "postmodern theory" of reputational impermanence—which seemed to be, essentially, that almost every moral boundary was permeable and almost every fact was negotiable. "Nazi stuff and pedophile stuff—those are permanently disqualifying," he said. "Anything else, you can probably spin your way out of it." He was betting that his misogyny, his xenophobia, and his long record of lies would all be forgiven eventually—that in the America of the near future, Cernovichian ultranationalism would become the new normal. "Once that Overton window starts moving," he said, "it can move pretty fast."

When I'd first landed in California, before visiting Cernovich's house, I'd driven straight from the airport to the Hermosa Beach boardwalk, where Cernovich was hosting an outdoor meetup for *Danger & Play* readers. A few dozen people showed up, including a few women and a few people of color. Shauna, wearing a tight dress with a plunging neckline, sat at a table eating a bacon cheeseburger. "My friends assume there will only be awkward internet people at these things," she said. "I'm always telling them, 'There are actually some cute guys!'"

Cernovich sipped iced tea from a pint glass while his admirers asked him questions. "What about Hillary's body count?" a young man said. He was alluding to rumors, ubiquitous on the fringe internet, that Clinton had caused the deaths of dozens of her enemies—Seth Rich, Vince Foster, John F. Kennedy Jr.—either by ordering them killed or by murdering them herself.

"The more high-powered you are, the more people you know," Cernovich said. "The more people you know, the more dead people you know. So how much of that is confirmation bias?"

The admirer looked deflated.

"Then again," Cernovich said, "Bill's brother was a drug dealer, and they do have ties to organized crime, so who knows?"

The admirer perked up. "She's fucking going to prison," he said.

I talked to a big bald white guy who looked like Mr. Clean. He called himself a racial identitarian. "The game changer for me was Steve Sailer," he said. "Once I looked into human biodiversity—really looked at it, without worrying about the thought police—I went, 'Wow, how brainwashed have I been?'" I asked if he would tell me his name, and he laughed. "Not a chance," he said. "I have a job. I'm not trying to get doxed."

Jeff Martinez, a cybersecurity consultant with a surfer-bro twang, read Cernovich's Twitter feed every day, as a counterweight to traditional journalism. "The corporate news is fucking fake, dude," he said. "You can just tell." An informal poll revealed that no one at the meetup believed in polls. Trump was going to be president, no matter what the hoaxing media said.

Most of the conversations centered on free speech (which everyone was for) and political correctness (which everyone was against). "I'm sick of the censorship, the words you can't say," Steven McHale, a marketing analyst with coiffed gray hair, told me. "Every conversation feels radioactive." Another woman, an oncologist, spoke with a Soviet-bloc accent but refused to say where she was from. "When I first came to America," she said, "I didn't have to think so hard before saying anything. Now I do. That's sad."

A few weeks earlier, on a Sunday in Brooklyn, I'd biked to Prospect Park to meet some friends for a picnic—iced coffees, berries in vented plastic containers, *New York Times* sections rotating to each according to need.

"I recently realized what this election is," one woman said. "It's the article versus the comments section."

"Did you just come up with that?" her boyfriend asked, impressed.

"I think I saw it on Twitter," she said.

On the boardwalk in Hermosa Beach, a woman wearing an Infowars T-shirt asked me about *The New Yorker*'s comments section. How aggressively was it moderated? According to what bias? Was the government involved?

"We don't have a comments section," I said.

Her surprise quickly curdled to scorn. "Right," she said. "Of course you don't."

I told her about an analogy I'd recently heard: that this election was like the article running against the comments section.

"It *is*!" she said, her face brightening. "It's so true. The globalist elites versus the real Americans."

CHAPTER NINETEEN

Poise Is a Club

The week I visited Cernovich's house, the most popular video on his YouTube channel was called "Un/Convention: Exposing Fake News at the RNC and DNC." "You can no longer trust the media," a title card read over a score of throbbing dubstep. "Mike Cernovich attended both conventions. Here's what really happened." The screen pulsed with urgent, glitchy effects: the revolution, televised. Cernovich wandered around the half-empty streets of downtown Cleveland, wearing aviator sunglasses and a bandanna, filming with his selfie stick. "I wanna bring back real journalism to the people," he said.

Cernovich didn't post any footage from inside the Quicken Loans Arena, where the Republican National Convention had taken place, because he hadn't been granted access to the building. He had, however, been invited to a party a mile away, where the guest list included Milo Yiannopoulos, Richard Spencer, Roosh V, the Islamophobic blogger Pamela Geller, and Peter Brimelow, the founder of *VDARE*. The party was organized by Jim Hoft, of *The Gateway Pundit*, who had recently come out as a "conservative gay activist." The walls were lined with large framed photos—half-nude young men in MAGA hats, some carrying semiautomatic rifles—made by Lucian Wintrich as part of a project he called Twinks4Trump. Yiannopoulos and Geller gave speeches, sticking to three main themes: homophilia, Islamophobia, and MAGA. The logic went like this: some Muslim-majority countries oppress gay people; therefore, vote Trump. It was hardly an airtight argument. Yet the spectacle achieved its primary goal, which was to pack the room with reporters. (Laurie Penny, a journalist who attended the gathering and wrote about it for *The Guardian*, described it as "a carpeted ballroom on the seventh floor of hell.")

Two nights later, Trump gave a speech formally accepting the Republican Party's nomination. He wanted to be perceived as the law-and-order candidate, and he did not use subtlety to convey his message. "I will restore law and order," he said. "I am the law-and-order candidate." He claimed that "illegal immigrants with criminal records, ordered deported from our country, are tonight roaming free to threaten peaceful citizens."

The next day, *The New York Times* ran a piece of news analysis. "With all the political orthodoxy that Donald J. Trump tore up in his convention speech," it began, "he set aside a core tenet of the American narrative on immigration: that the United States is a nation of nations, built on the sweat and initiative of people who came from other countries." Steve Sailer wrote a barbed and boastful response: "NYT Complains Trump Doesn't Submit to The Narrative." For years, Sailer had blogged about citizenism in obscurity. Now his fringe vocabulary was hurtling toward the center of American discourse.

In a YouTube video for the Rebel, Gavin McInnes chided the establishment, especially the Republican establishment, for perpetuating "the rhetoric of 'We're a nation of immigrants.' We're not, by the way. We're a nation of citizens." Even Ann Coulter, speaking at a Trump rally in Iowa, marveled at how quickly the unsayable had been made sayable. "Since Donald Trump has announced that he's running for president, I feel like I'm dreaming," she said. "I can't believe I turn on the TV, and on prime-time TV every night they're talking about anchor babies, they're talking about sanctuary cities, they're talking about Mexican rapists."

Shortly before the election, Cernovich self-published another book on Amazon. It was called *MAGA Mindset: Making YOU and America Great Again.* The cover—a cartoon of a resplendent Trump, thick rays of fulvous sunshine, and an ascending phoenix—looked like a freeze-frame image from a Pixar adaptation of *Triumph of the Will*. In the book, Cernovich didn't make any explicit sops to white nationalism, but his dog whistles were as clear as ever.*

Whenever I confronted Cernovich about his long record of open misogyny, he downplayed his old tweets and blog posts as mere "locker-room talk." After a tape was released in which Donald Trump bragged about grabbing women "by the pussy," Trump used precisely the same excuse. "I don't know if someone gave him

---

*"No less than the Democrats, the GOP is characterized by a desire to change the essential nature of the United States through unlimited immigration," he wrote. "In defying political correctness, Trump has made himself politically bulletproof."

a copy of *Gorilla Mindset* or if it's just great minds thinking alike," Cernovich said, "but I am more impressed with Trump every day."

●   ●   ●

In late September, Cernovich flew to New York to cover the first Trump-Clinton debate, at Hofstra University on Long Island. He planned to spend the evening on the perimeter of campus, outside the Secret Service checkpoint, livestreaming and tweeting. "I wanna be with the people," he explained. Also, again, he hadn't been granted press credentials to get inside. A few hours before the debate started, he sent me a text from the road: "Almost there. U?"

I was inside the gates, with the rest of the establishment media. "Is there any way Hillary can lose tonight?" I asked Jesse Jackson, who happened to be standing next to me as we waited to pass through a metal detector. "Long answers," he said. "Gotta go short on words, long on meaning." Appropriately enough, that was all he said.

I passed through a beer tent sponsored by Anheuser-Busch ("#BrewDemocracy") and wandered toward the center of campus, where Fox News, CNN, and MSNBC had all set up temporary stages. It was unseasonably muggy; whenever the on-air lights went dark, makeup artists rushed toward the talent to blot and powder. VIP golf carts rolled by, laden with Beltway demicelebrities outpacing the selfie-seeking throngs.

On the MSNBC stage, Chris Hayes was on air, arguing via earpiece with Omarosa Manigault. A former reality-show villain known for her not-here-to-make-friends persona on *The Apprentice*, Manigault was now one of Donald Trump's most prominent campaign surrogates.

"I want to start with the birther thing," Hayes said.

"He's put that to bed and he's ready to move on," Manigault said, changing the subject to the economy.

Hayes tried to butt in several times by repeating the word "respectfully," but Manigault kept filibustering about jobs.

Nearby was a long row of smaller media tents: BBC, AFP, Al Jazeera, Czech Public Radio. A Hofstra student, wearing a badge identifying her as a Social Media Debate Volunteer, held her phone aloft, in selfie mode, as a bevy of satellite trucks idled behind her. "*So* exciting, you guys," she said. "HofDebate2016 is the hashtag. Follow on Snapchat, Instagram, Twitter, Facebook Live. Stay with us to get the full experience of the Hofstra student experience."

On the quad, for every Clinton or Trump sign, there was one promoting a joke candidate: Vermin Supreme 2016, Giant Swarm of Bees 2016. "Sir!" a student shouted, pretending to hold a microphone at ankle height. "Just one question, sir, if I may!" Looking down, I noticed that he was addressing a squirrel.

Here and there, groups of four or five young men—boys, really—strode forward, taking up as much space as possible, all rolling shoulders and self-satisfied grins. Most of them wore MAGA hats, but even without any identifying flair, you could tell at a glance that they were Trump kids. They had a giddiness about them, as if they were getting away with something. A line floated into my mind—"The entering boys, identified by hats, / Wander in a maze of mannered brick"—but I couldn't remember where it was from. I whispered the words to Siri, and she told me the answer.*

Hofstra's gym had been filled with folding tables, thirty rows deep. The space was officially called the Media Filing Center, but most people referred to it as Spin Alley. Every credentialed journalist had a seat, reserved by name, which came prestocked with an outlet strip, an Ethernet cable, and a brochure printed by Facebook, one of the debate's sponsors. "Facebook is the new town hall," the brochure said. "Be creative and go Live often!"

The walls of the gym were partitioned into backdrops—Fox News, Fox Business, FoxNewsGo—with an anchor standing in front of each one, staring into the middle distance. Everyone in the room was talking, simultaneously, to a different

---

*It was from a Karl Shapiro poem, published in 1940, called "University." I sat on a concrete landing and read the poem on my phone, then read it twice more. It begins:

> To hurt the Negro and avoid the Jew
> Is the curriculum

and it ends:

> the true nobleman, once a democrat,
> Sleeps on his private mountain. He was one
> Whose thought was shapely and whose dream was broad;
> This school he held his art and epitaph.
> But now it takes from him his name,
> Falls open like a dishonest look,
> And shows us, rotted and endowed,
> Its senile pleasure.

Later, I read more about the poem and learned which university Shapiro was writing about: his alma mater, the University of Virginia, in the city of Charlottesville.

group of people who weren't in the room. Two guys wearing glasses and skinny ties sat next to each other on canvas chairs. "Trade," one of them said. "Trade's gonna be huge tonight." A woman filmed them with a phone, streaming their analysis to some platform or another, or to several platforms at once.

I ran into Lou Dobbs, who was wearing pancake makeup and sipping from a tiny bottle of water. Dobbs had been a star anchor on CNN for almost three decades. After 9/11, though, his rhetoric grew increasingly xenophobic, and CNN let him go in 2009. His current show, on Fox Business, was one of Donald Trump's favorites.

I asked Dobbs if he'd heard of Cernovich. "Absolutely!" he said. "I follow him on Twitter. Seems very smart."

We parted, then Dobbs chased me down. "Can I revise that?" he said. "I'm not sure I follow him." (He did; they'd interacted on Twitter several times.) "I've seen his stuff, and I think it's interesting," he added. "Interesting is a good thing, right?"

Cernovich texted me a screenshot of a map, showing me where he was, and I walked off campus to find him. He was marching with a few dozen Jill Stein supporters who were looking for a designated protest area. "Trying to get to the free speech zone," he texted. "Police keep sending us to different areas. Some real psyops, man." His theory was that the police, possibly following orders from the Democratic Party, were intentionally giving protesters the runaround, to sap their morale. As he walked, he filmed a Periscope video called "No free speech at #Debates2016."

"Mainstream media's not gonna talk about this," he said.

The comments floated up the left side of the screen:

The cops are Soros people!
This country is a joke!
Harambe!

I gave up on trying to find Cernovich and got back to Spin Alley just in time for the debate. Cernovich, standing in an off-campus parking lot, watched it on his phone. In ninety minutes, Trump told thirty-four lies, a level of dishonesty that was, at the time, still surprising. "I hope the fact-checkers are turning up the volume and really working hard," Clinton said.

"Sick Hillary is heavily medicated," Cernovich tweeted. "She is struggling. Too much Xanax?"

When the debate was over, I found Cernovich in the parking lot. He was leaning against the hood of a car, still tweeting. Next to him was a fellow Twitter activist, a preppy-looking navy vet who exuded a manic intensity. "Jack Posobiec, Citizens for Trump," he said, giving me a vigorous handshake.*

Posobiec had given Cernovich a ride to Long Island, and he now offered to take us both back to the city. As he drove, Posobiec said, "Objectively—or, as objective as I can be—I think it was a pretty even fight."

"They both landed a few blows," Cernovich said. "The most pathetic thing she did was keep whining about fact-checkers. Everyone hates the media, and she's calling on them to white-knight for her? Looks weak."

Trump had spent much of the debate sniffling audibly, and I asked Cernovich whether he worried about Trump's health. "I wouldn't focus on that," he said. "I wouldn't be surprised if they messed with his mic to make it sound like that." He mentioned that, on Twitter, some of Trump's critics were still harping on birtherism, "which is such a boring, basic-bitch story at this point."

"It's, like, guys, find a new narrative," Posobiec said.

"The mainstream media has lost so much legitimacy at this point," Cernovich said. "If they reported, 'We just saw Trump beat the shit out of a guy on the street,' skeptical people like my readers would go, 'Really? Is there video? Was the video doctored?'" Traditional journalists would spin the debate in Clinton's favor no matter what, he said; his counterspin was a necessary corrective. "The left likes to talk about power structures, right? Well, the media still thinks of itself as speaking truth to power. What they don't realize is that someone like me is perceived as the new Fourth Estate. Maybe they should check their structural privilege."

In 2010, when Andrew Breitbart started a blog called *Big Journalism*, the name was ironic. In 2016, *Breitbart* got more traffic than the *Los Angeles Times*, and Steve Bannon, *Breitbart*'s editor-in-chief, stepped down to run a successful presidential campaign. Cernovich said, "Going by the statistics, I'm less influential than some people"—Trump, say, or Kim Kardashian—"but way more influential

---

*As far as I could tell, looking it up later, Citizens for Trump wasn't a 501(c)(3), or any other kind of registered organization—it seemed to be just a website and a Facebook page.

than some punk blogger at *Politico* or *The Weekly Standard* who thinks of himself as part of the media elite. Objectively, I *am* the new media."*

We emerged from the Midtown Tunnel, and I asked Posobiec to drop me off at the nearest corner. "Bit of unsolicited advice?" Cernovich said before I got out of the car. "I saw your tweet earlier." On the edge of campus, in a crowd of protesters, I had come upon two men—one wearing a My Little Pony leotard, the other wearing a knee-length galosh on his head—fighting over a rubber chicken. I tweeted a photo of them, along with the caption, "This is what democracy looks like."

"That could have been a fire tweet," Cernovich said. "Didn't get a lot of pickup, though. Next time, maybe try a photo filter or a snappier caption."

"OK," I said, opening the car door.

"I see what you were going for, though," Cernovich said. "You'll get there."

---

*This line of argument gained even more force two years later, when *The Weekly Standard* went out of business.

CHAPTER TWENTY

"Meta Post Script"

On Election Day, I stood outside a small Methodist church in Greensboro, North Carolina, that was serving as a polling place. A man named Larry, an African American in his seventies, was passing out flyers promoting a candidate for district court judge. "I spent twenty-two years in the army," he told me. "I saw Hawaii, New Zealand, Australia. I remember staring up at the Sydney Opera House, going, 'If a country boy from Reidsville, North Carolina, can make it here, anything is possible.'"

He made amiable small talk with everyone who passed, including those wearing MAGA hats. "I know I don't want that crazy man to be president, but I don't have hate in my heart for anybody," he said. Just before nightfall, a white man with a gray beard left the church. On his way to the parking lot, he stopped in front of Larry and delivered an unsolicited monologue about why he had just cast his vote for Trump. "Bill Clinton has an illegitimate mulatto child—you know that, don't you?" the man said. "That's fine. I'm OK with mixed people. But I'm just saying—why doesn't he talk about it?" He alluded to George Wallace, and segregation, and the myriad pathologies he ascribed to "the inner city." Larry looked at the pavement and didn't say much. Eventually, the man got in his car and left.

"I've seen a lot in this state," Larry said, his eyes still cast downward. "I've known people whose kin got lynched. In the last twenty years, or thirty, you didn't hear people saying these things. These days, suddenly, they feel like they're allowed to say it."

———

Early the next morning, my wife and I stood in the security line at the Raleigh airport. She was three months pregnant, and, even though the CDC said it was an unnecessary precaution, she opted for a pat-down instead of an X-ray scan. "Congratulations," the TSA agent said. "First one?"

My wife nodded. It was obvious that she'd been crying. The agent—black, fortyish, long braids—was, by airport standards, improbably kind. "What's the matter, honey?" she asked.

"Oh, you know," my wife said. "Just the world falling apart."

"It's not your job to worry about that," she said, sweetly but firmly, her eyes locked on my wife's eyes. "That baby is your world now. You got it?"

At the gate, two married couples wearing MAGA hats carried on a jubilant conversation while the rest of us sat in silence. When it was time to board, an attendant—white, fiftyish, press-on nails—scanned my boarding pass and asked, without glancing up, "How're we doing today, sweetie?" I'm no good at pleasantries, but even I knew that this question had exactly one acceptable response: a brisk smile, a sunny word or two, then keep the line moving. I didn't feel up to it. "Not great," I said. "Not doing great today."

Her hand, still holding my boarding pass, hovered in midair. She glanced up at me for the first time, as if assessing a potential threat or a glitch in the Matrix. There are few rules, even in a place as tightly regulated as an airport, about how to have a conversation. Instead, there are norms, which can be quaint, or outmoded, or oppressive, or a thin layer of protection against the abyss.

The previous week, in the *New Yorker* office, one of the web editors had shown me a mockup of what the site's home page would look like as soon as the election result was announced. A bold, simple illustration—a smiling Hillary Clinton against a Stars and Stripes background—and two panegyric essays tracing the long arc from the nineteenth-century suffragists to the first female president.

I asked him to show me the other one.

"Which?" he said.

"The other version of the page," I said. "If . . . for . . . the other result." The contingency plan.

"Oh," he said. "Yeah, we don't have one."

The morning after Election Day, David Remnick sent an email calling for a staff-wide meeting. "I think we could all use a moment today to get together to talk about what to do next," he wrote. "No matter what your politics, I know we can agree that this thing of ours, *The New Yorker*, has enormous potential, every day and every week, for good, for telling the truth, for thought, for resilience."

We met in a thirty-eighth-floor conference room with plate-glass windows overlooking the rooftop gardens of Goldman Sachs, and the Hudson River, and the skyline of Jersey City. I took a seat with a view of the Colgate Clock, but my eyes weren't focused on the time, or on anything in particular. In the ensuing days it would become commonplace to compare this feeling to a bad dream, but to me it felt less like a dream than like a sudden bout of illness, a stomach bug or a high fever—one of those disorienting days when time distends, when no arrangement of limbs can bring comfort, when the bad humor that was once somewhere out in the world, spreading ambiently from other people to other people, finally spreads to you, and you no longer have the luxury of ignoring it.

"I don't presume to know where everyone in this room stands, but you all know where I stand," Remnick said, rousing a few rueful chuckles. The previous night, as the returns came in, he'd written a blistering essay, which had since been published under the headline "An American Tragedy." This turned out to be our contingency plan.

"However you feel right now, though," he continued, "I hope you agree that we all have urgent work to do, and soon." The job was the same as it had always been, he said: to think carefully and critically, to tell the truth, to hold the powerful to account. This seemed, in that moment, both entirely correct and entirely inadequate.

We left the conference room and lingered in the hallways, making desultory conversation or standing in awkward silence. These were the first hours of the hospital vibe; we were still learning the etiquette. "I can't believe I'm about to close a piece about a fucking sarcophagus," a colleague said. "It feels ridiculous now." He was putting the finishing touches on a deft and perceptive story, in a forthcoming issue, about a team of archaeologists working to save endangered antiquities through digital scanning.

"Archaeology is still important," I insisted. "Technology is still important. We can't just ignore everything else in the world." At that moment, I didn't believe a word I was saying.

A web editor stopped by my office. "Wanna call up some of your alt-right guys, let them gloat a bit?" he said. "If you can stand it." I realized that I had assumed, unconsciously, that I would never talk to any of them again. In the next moment, I understood that I was probably about to start talking to them quite a bit.

I called Cernovich. He didn't gloat. "Today must be strange for you, huh?" he said.

It was the first time we'd talked since my piece about him was published.* The day the piece came out, he had tweeted about it several times, disclosing, among other things, his grudging respect for *The New Yorker*'s fact-checking process. ("Was on the phone for over an hour, multiple e-mails. They got biases/agenda, but not a hoax.") He'd also written a piece about my piece. "There's some snark in the article, but that's the East Coast style," he wrote on *Danger & Play*. "I go hard and have no issue with others doing the same." Privately, he'd sent me an email with the subject heading "Meta post script," to show me how much traffic he was driving to my piece through Twitter and "all other channels."

We conducted our postmortem interview. "This election was a contest between PC culture and free-speech culture," he said. "Most people know what it's like for some smug, elite asshole to tell them, 'You can't say that, it's racist, it's bad.' Well, a vote for Trump meant, 'Fuck you, you don't get to tell me what to say.'"

When the interview was over, Cernovich addressed me personally: "How're you holding up, man?" It was a trivial gesture, maybe even an insulting one, given how much he'd done to bring us to this moment; to my surprise, though, I couldn't help but find it almost touching.

"I'm fine," I said. It was my first time as a reporter lying to a subject. I said a hurried good-bye and hung up the phone. I was willing to suffer any number of

---

*The rubric of that piece, appearing for the second time in the magazine's history, was Annals of Media.

indignities for the sake of my work, but there was no way I was going to cry in front of Mike Cernovich.

I wrote the web piece. What else was I supposed to do? "One of the political-science clichés that hasn't been rendered obsolete by this election is that of the Overton window," I wrote. The alt-right had bent the window beyond recognition; their social media activism had "made it possible—made it conceivable—for Trump to be elected."

I used Cernovich's "smug, elite asshole" quote in my piece. It shouldn't have mattered, in the scheme of things, but I cringed a bit when I clicked on the published version and saw that the copy desk, in accordance with *New Yorker* style, had changed "elite" to "élite."

Trust Nothing

For a long time—for a period that predated the tech boom of the 1990s and that ended, or started to end, on November 8, 2016—the Big Swinging Brains agreed on a set of commonsense assumptions. *The best stuff spreads. The cream rises to the top. New technologies will disrupt old hierarchies, and this disruption will ultimately redound to the good.* This dogma was passed on to the inventors of social media, who swiftly inherited the earth. Techno-utopianism was the lingua franca of Silicon Valley. Anyone who didn't learn it overtly learned it by osmosis. To defy it was to go voluntarily into a madhouse—was also, more practically, to alienate potential investors.

In June 2016, Andrew Bosworth, a longtime friend of Mark Zuckerberg's and one of the top engineers at Facebook, wrote an internal memo about the prime directive underlying Facebook's aggressive growth strategy. "We connect people," Bosworth wrote. "Period." He acknowledged that users could, and often did, exploit the platform's openness in calamitous ways. "Maybe it costs a life by exposing someone to bullies," Bosworth wrote. "Maybe someone dies in a terrorist attack coordinated on our tools. And still we connect people. The ugly truth is that we believe in connecting people so deeply that anything that allows us to connect more people more often is *de facto* good." This was close to a textbook definition of Machiavellian techno-utopianism. And yet, at the time, it was seen as concordant with Silicon Valley's dominant moral vocabulary—provocative, but not unthinkable.

Two days after Trump won, Mark Zuckerberg was interviewed onstage at a tech conference. "The idea that fake news on Facebook, of which it's a very small amount of the content, influenced the election in any way, I think, is a pretty crazy idea," he said. "Voters make decisions based on their lived experience." This was a pretty crazy idea, and Zuckerberg spent the next two years attempting to walk it back.

Obviously, what people see on social media affects their "lived experience." We know this, in part, because Facebook has done research on it. In 2012, without notice or permission, the company tweaked the feeds of nearly seven hundred thousand of its users, showing one group more "positive emotional content" and the other more "negative emotional content." Two years later, Facebook's researchers divulged the experiment and published the results in a scientific journal. The finding was clear: people with happier feeds seemed to become happier, and vice versa. The study's authors called the phenomenon "massive-scale emotional contagion." In the ensuing years, social media continued to grow in size and influence, putting ever more sophisticated tools in the hands of advertisers, spies, politicians, and propagandists. Most people went on acting as if none of this was a problem—as if users would soon build up an immunity to massive-scale contagion, or that benign beliefs would be contagious but malignant beliefs would not be. It was comforting to imagine this, but there was no good reason to believe it.

"We built Reddit around the principle of, 'No editors. The people are the editors,'" Steve Huffman said. "That was the Y Combinator ethos, and it became our ethos. It wasn't even remarkable at the time—just sort of assumed." In the early days, Huffman and Ohanian sold T-shirts bearing one of their company's slogans: "Freedom from the press." Like all disrupters, they believed in unfiltered speech, the more of it the better. They didn't give much thought to what might go wrong.

Over time, each subreddit became a community with its own distinct culture. By the end of 2014, there were more than half a million subreddits: r/Science, r/MaleFashionAdvice, r/Trees (for marijuana enthusiasts), r/MarijuanaEnthusiasts (for tree enthusiasts), r/MildlyInteresting ("for photos that are, you know, mildly interesting"). Each subreddit was run by volunteer moderators—frequent posters who understood the vibe that the community was trying to achieve, and who set guidelines to keep it from going too far astray. Reddit didn't have nearly enough employees to monitor every part of its site. (Investors surely appreciated the company's low-touch, decentralized model, which allowed it to rack up a huge amount of traffic with a relatively tiny payroll.) Unless they were inundated with reports of illegal activity, Reddit's staff usually let the volunteer moderators enforce their own rules, or fail to enforce them.

The moderators could set incentives to promote wholesomeness, or novelty, or perversity—whatever they wanted, pretty much. On r/Aww, "a place for really cute pictures and videos," there were rules to keep things cute ("No NSFW content," "No 'sad' content," "No harassment"). On r/ChangeMyView, one of the few corners of the internet where truly constructive debate flourished, moderators promised to take down every "rude/hostile comment" and "bad faith accusation." But there were thousands of subreddits where the rules were more lax, and many of those communities turned toxic. "All sorts of weird things can happen online," Huffman said. "Imagine I post a joke where the point is to be offensive—like, to imply, 'This is something that a racist person would say'—but you misread the context and think, 'Yeah, that racist guy has a good point.'" He thought that this dynamic could explain a lot of otherwise inexplicable internet behavior. Often, he said, "Someone keeps pushing a joke or a meme to see how far they can take it, and the answer turns out to be: pretty fucking far."

In 2011, one popular subreddit—not in the top hundred, but big enough that the site's administrators were well aware of it—was called r/Jailbait. It was devoted to sexually suggestive photos of young-looking women. This was profoundly creepy, but probably not illegal—its moderators swore that all the women in the photos were eighteen or older—and Reddit allowed the community to keep growing.

That September, Anderson Cooper described r/Jailbait on CNN. "It's pretty amazing that a big corporation would have something like this, which reflects badly on it," he said. Traffic to r/Jailbait quadrupled overnight. Later, after someone on the subreddit apparently shared a nude photo of a fourteen-year-old girl, the community was banned. And yet its founder, an infamous troll who went by Violentacrez, was allowed to stay on Reddit, as were some four hundred other subreddits he'd created—r/Jewmerica, r/ChokeABitch, and worse.

In 2012, a *Gawker* journalist revealed Violentacrez's identity. He was Michael Brutsch, a forty-nine-year-old computer programmer living with his wife in a suburb of Dallas. A CNN reporter, interviewing Brutsch in Texas, asked him why he'd wrought so much destruction online. "Well, honestly," Brutsch responded, "the biggest thrill I got was those meaningless internet points."

Reddit's CEO at the time was Yishan Wong, an engineer who had worked at PayPal and Facebook. In an internal memo to his staff, he implied that he'd banned r/Jailbait reluctantly, and only because it had violated U.S. law. "We stand for free speech," he wrote. "We will not ban legal content even if we find it odious or if we personally condemn it." Reddit's goal, he continued, was to "become a universal platform for human discourse"; therefore, "it would not do if, in our youth, we decided to censor things simply because they were distasteful." This implied a corollary question, although Wong didn't raise it, perhaps because it didn't occur to him: If a universal platform for human discourse were to be overrun with "jailbait," grotesque misogyny, and Nazi propaganda, how would this affect human discourse?

Free-speech absolutism had been so central to Reddit's ethos for so long that many redditors couldn't let it go. Wong's successor as CEO was Ellen Pao, a former venture capitalist. Early in her tenure, Reddit announced a crackdown on involuntary pornography: if you found a compromising photo of yourself circulating on the platform without your consent, you could report it and the company would remove it. This seemed like a straightforward business decision; but many redditors, constitutionally averse to gatekeeping of any kind, treated it as the first in an inevitable parade of horrors. "This rule is stupid and suppresses our rights," wrote a redditor with the handle penisfuckermcgee.

A few months later, Reddit banned five of its most egregious communities, including r/FatPeopleHate and r/ShitNiggersSay. Again, many redditors were apoplectic ("We may as well take a one way ticket to North Korea"). Almost every day, abusive redditors called Pao a tyrant, an "Asian slut," or worse. She resigned in July 2015. "The Internet started as a bastion for free expression," she wrote in *The Washington Post*. "But that balancing act is getting harder. The trolls are winning."*

In July 2015, six years after leaving Reddit, Steve Huffman returned as CEO. He'd started Reddit in the hope of disrupting the gatekeepers, or perhaps eliminating gatekeepers altogether. Now, reluctantly but inescapably, he'd become a gatekeeper himself. He still preferred a laissez-faire approach to content moderation, all things being equal, but his stance had grown less absolute over time. It's

---

*Throughout his presidency, Barack Obama remained a relentless optimist. He generally portrayed social media as a salutary force, despite mounting evidence to the contrary. "I continue to believe Mr. Trump will not be president," he said in 2016. "And the reason is because I have a lot of faith in the American people." A commenter on r/The_Donald, responding to Obama's remarks, wrote, "FUCK THAT LOW ENERGY CUCK!"

one thing to be a civil libertarian in theory; it's another thing to start a warehouse party, watch it devolve into feral anarchy, and do nothing to clean it up.

One of Huffman's first acts as CEO was to ban a half dozen viciously racist subreddits, such as r/Coontown. "There was pushback, as there is whenever we ban anything," he said later. "But I had the moral authority, as the founder, to take it in stride." He acknowledged that "it's really hard to define hate speech," and that "any way we define it has the potential to set a dangerous precedent." And yet, he added, "I know the internet. Some people are reasonable, and other people just want to watch the world burn. So, at a certain point, with the latter, I'm, like, All right, fuck you guys. This is my site. Go burn down something else."

•   •   •

Reddit's headquarters are in a former NBC radio tower in downtown San Francisco. There are high ceilings with industrial-chic light fixtures, and a large common area with kombucha on tap. Each desk is decorated aggressively with personal flair—a "Make Reddit Great Again" hat, a glossy print magazine called *Meme Insider*. Working at Reddit requires paying close anthropological attention to the motley tastes of redditors, and it's not uncommon to see groups of fit, well-dressed employees cheerfully discussing the most recent post on r/CatDimension or r/PeopleFuckingDying.

Like all successful social networks, Reddit was a party that had grown too big too fast, and it was now trying to figure out how to control the chaos while still respecting its guests' basic autonomy. I had asked every major social media company to let me watch as they navigated these nettlesome trade-offs, but none of them were eager to give me the full access I requested. Twitter's PR representatives mostly ignored my emails. Snapchat's reps met me for breakfast once, then mostly ignored my emails. Facebook's reps talked to me for weeks, asking precise, intelligent questions, before starting to ignore my emails.*

Reddit had more incentive to be transparent. Anderson Cooper's reporting was hardly the only vividly terrible press that the company has received over the

---

*At one point, in Menlo Park, I paid a visit to Chris Cox, Facebook's chief product officer, perhaps the person most directly responsible for determining what the platform's two billion users saw when they opened their personalized feeds. We spoke for an hour, and I found him to be an astute and generous conversationalist. And that's all I can say about our meeting, because it was off the record.

years. When I typed "Reddit is" into Google, three of the top suggested auto-completions were "toxic," "cancer," and "hot garbage."

The first morning I visited the office, in early 2017, I sat in a glass-walled conference room observing a meeting about sexual content. Porn is allowed on Reddit, as long as it's legal, but the administrators do their best to keep it walled off from everything else.

"What about GentlemanBoners?" an engineer asked, referring to a semierotic subreddit.

"That's an interesting use case," Melissa Tidwell, the general counsel, said. "It's pretty tame, actually, when you look at it. But the average person is going to see the name and assume it's porn, so maybe we don't want it showing up in a standard search." It wasn't the most elevated conversation—Tidwell, an accomplished lawyer with a decade of experience in the tech industry, chortled self-consciously more than once—but boundary setting is crucial work, if not always high-minded.

"I am so tired of people who repeat the mantra 'Free speech!' but then have nothing else to say," Tidwell told me after the meeting. "Look, free speech is obviously a great ideal to strive toward. Who doesn't love freedom? Who doesn't love speech? But then in practice, every day, gray areas come up. Does free speech mean literally anyone can say anything at any time? Or is it actually more conducive to the free exchange of ideas if we create a platform where women and people of color can say what they want without thousands of people screaming, 'Fuck you, light yourself on fire, I know where you live'?"

On my way out of the meeting, I ran into Huffman in the hallway. Burning Man tickets had just gone on sale, and he was trying to persuade one of his employees to buy one. I followed Huffman into a conference room, where he sat at the head of a long table and made a sales pitch to a group of advertising executives from New York. Reddit provides a bountiful daily lunch spread, and everyone had a plate of salmon and salad except for Huffman. "I've been trying intermittent fasting," he said. "People on r/Nutrition swear by it."

Despite its bare-bones design, Reddit received a staggering amount of traffic. At the time, it was the fourth-most-visited website in the United States (behind Facebook, YouTube, and Google; ahead of Amazon, Twitter, and everything else). More quickly than anyone had anticipated, Reddit had actually achieved its goal of becoming a universal platform for human discourse. Still, the site could be a strange and forbidding place, and many advertisers were wary of it. Huffman tried to reassure the ad executives: the cofounder was back, and he was starting to tame the pandemonium. "The snarky, libertarian, anything-goes vibe" of early Reddit, he explained, "mostly came from me as a twenty-one-year-old. I've since grown out of that, to the relief of everyone." The executives around the table nodded and chuckled. "We let the story get away from us," Huffman continued. "And now we're trying to get our shit together."

• • •

On November 23, 2016, Huffman was in his office in San Francisco, perusing Reddit—or, rather, continuing to peruse Reddit, which, unless he was off the grid, he rarely stopped doing. It was the day before Thanksgiving. The site's administrators had just deleted the subreddit r/Pizzagate; this news was starting to spread across other subreddits, and Huffman was monitoring the reaction. The reason for the ban, according to Reddit's administrators, was not what people on the subreddit believed, but how they'd behaved—specifically, their insistence on doxing their enemies, a clear violation of Reddit's rules. The Pizzagate conspiracy theorists, in turn, claimed that they'd been banned because the Reddit administrators were in on the conspiracy.

Some of the conspiracy theorists left Reddit and reunited on Voat, a site founded by and for the detritus that Reddit sloughs off.* Other Pizzagaters stayed and regrouped on r/The_Donald, a popular pro-Trump subreddit. Throughout the presidential campaign, The_Donald was a hive of Trump boosterism; by this time, it had become a hermetic subculture, full of antic inside jokes and defiant rhetoric. The community's most frequent commenters, like the man they'd helped propel to the presidency, were experts at testing boundaries, dog-whistling just subtly enough to avoid getting kicked off the platform.

"It has come to our attention that the subreddit r/Pizzagate was shut down today," someone wrote on r/The_Donald. "We are going to have to be extra vigilant."

Within seconds, the comments about Pizzagate piled up:

Hmm I wonder why they're trying to suppress this . . . ?

---

*Most social networks had similar bizarro networks—holding tanks for the banned. Twitter's bizarro network was Gab; people banned from Patreon ended up on Hatreon; for a while, there was an alt-right clone of Go-FundMe called GoyFundMe.

Blatant censorship.

Well, that's just going to bring suspicion to those who didn't believe before.

Nice going, Reddit!

Redditors' screen names are prefaced by "u," for username. Huffman's is u/Spez. As he scanned r/The_Donald, he noticed that hundreds of the most popular comments were about him:

fuck u/spez

u/spez is complicit in the coverup

Fuck u/Spez

u/spez supports child rape

FUCK u/SPEZ!

One commenter wrote "u/SPEZ IS A CUCK," in bold type, a hundred and ten times in a row.

Huffman, alone in his office, wondered whether to respond. Privately, he had started to imagine The_Donald as a deeply misguided teenager who wouldn't stop misbehaving. "If your little brother flicks your ear, maybe you ignore it," he said later. "If he flicks your ear a hundred times, or punches you, then maybe you give him a little smack to show you're paying attention."

Huffman was the author of Reddit's source code, and, although redditors didn't yet know it, he could edit any part of the site in any way he wanted. He wrote a script that would automatically replace his username with those of r/The_Donald's moderators, directing the insults back at the insulters in real time. In one comment, "Fuck u/Spez" became "Fuck u/Trumpshaker." In another, "Fuck u/Spez" became "Fuck u/MAGAdocious."

The_Donald's users saw what was happening, and they reacted by inventing a conspiracy theory that, in this case, turned out to be true.

The Admins are suffering from low energy—have resorted to editing YOUR posts.

Manipulating the words of your users is fucked.

Even Facebook and Twitter haven't stooped this low.

Trust nothing.

———

After the incident came to light, it became a paradigmatic example of overreach. Tech gatekeepers had to do something to rein in their users, the consensus went, but not *that*. "I fucked up," Huffman wrote in a public apology the following week. "More than anything, I want Reddit to heal, and I want our country to heal." His actions had laid bare a fact that most social media companies went to great lengths to conceal: that ultimately, no matter how neutral a platform may seem, there are always people behind the curtain.

His apology post received more than thirty-six thousand comments.

"ya big dummy," one commenter wrote. "didn't no one tell you to not feed the trolls?"

"I know, I know," Huffman responded. "I honestly thought they might see some humor in it."

"I like Reddit," another commenter wrote. "You can do whatever you want and I won't stop coming here."

"Appreciate the sentiment," Huffman replied.

"Does the outside perception of this site concern you at all?" another commenter wrote. "It seems to be seeping into pop culture that the site is a favorite of the alt-right."

Huffman didn't respond to that.

Three days after Trump was elected, Paul Graham gave an interview to the *Los Angeles Times*. "Back when Reddit was first started, I thought their cheeky tag line 'freedom from the press' was all to the good," he said. "Now I worry about where we're headed." He hadn't quite abandoned his techno-optimism, but his shell of blithe self-assurance had been punctured. "Often when technology causes a problem, it also hands you a solution," he said. "I'm hoping that will be the case here. But I'm damned if I know what it is."

PART FOUR

The Swamp

Shame gets a bad rap these days. I think it's quite a useful emotion.

Zadie Smith, 2017

CHAPTER TWENTY-ONE

The News of the Future

When I first met Lucian Wintrich, at one of the DeploraBall's two open bars, he leaned in close, sloshing a bit of his gin and tonic onto my shoes. "I think you're gonna be very interested in what I'm about to announce," he said.

Whatever he was selling, I was determined not to buy it. He had recently given interviews to *The Atlantic* and *The Daily Beast*, and that night he was being trailed by a crew from Viceland (not to be confused with the Vice News crew that was downstairs trailing Roger Stone). Like any journalist, I'd heard plenty of desperate pitches, but I'd never met anyone so insatiably thirsty for media attention—or, it seemed, for attention of any kind—as Lucian Wintrich.* The last thing I wanted to do was give him more of it.

"You *must* come to one of my dinner parties sometime," he said. "Top-notch food, scintillating discussion, the bourbon flows like water." He was about to start his next sentence when Mike Cernovich called him up to the lectern. Wintrich left his drink on the bar and found the shortest path to the stage, as if pulled there by the spotlight's beam.

He stood next to Jim Hoft, his boss at *The Gateway Pundit*. The site was a font of viral misinformation, half-baked hypotheses, and the sort of cloddish race-baiting that was beneath even *Breitbart*'s standards; and yet, during the 2016 campaign, *The Gateway Pundit* received more than a million pageviews a day, roughly on par with *The Weekly Standard*. "We've been talking to the Trump administration," Hoft said. "We've got their word that *The Gateway Pundit* is gonna have a

---

*I hadn't yet met Milo Yiannopoulos.

White House correspondent this year—and his name is Lucian Wintrich." The crowd erupted in applause, and Wintrich basked in it. He flashed the hand gesture that Richard Nixon had used before leaving the White House lawn, for good, in a helicopter: shoulders hunched forward, first and middle fingers spread into Vs. "I'm going to be," he promised, "the youngest, gayest correspondent in the White House in history."*

He returned to the bar, picked up his half-finished drink, turned toward me, and arched an eyebrow. "So?" he said. "What do you think?"

Three weeks later, Wintrich was in his studio apartment in the East Village, washing down a mouthful of vitamins with a lukewarm take-out latte. He was leaving for Washington, D.C., within the hour. "I'm a bit hungover, I'm sorry to report," he said. "Hardly the ideal way to make my grand D.C. entrance, but so be it." He'd booked a thirty-five-dollar ticket on Megabus. As a fiscal conservative, he explained, he couldn't bring himself to support Amtrak. "It's literally five times the cost," he said. "Yet another thing I can't wait for Trump to fix."

He sent a text to his boyfriend, lit a cigarette, and started to pack. On his computer, he switched from late 1970s postpunk to a BBC news roundup. His walls were covered with framed art: a collage featuring a man, nude except for Nazi combat boots, aiming a rifle; a pill, half red and half blue, mounted and signed by Martin Shkreli; several large prints from the Twinks4Trump series. "Good art should be transgressive," Wintrich said. "These days, it seems, the best way to be transgressive is simply to be a white, male, proudly pro-American conservative."

When he first enrolled at Bard College, he recalled, he was a standard-issue liberal-arts progressive. By his sophomore year, he had become a Reaganite. "I was incredibly annoyed by the PC culture on campus, being told what not to say," he said. "I've always had a contrarian streak." He packed a Saint Laurent blazer, three Hermès ties, and a bottle of Dior Eau Sauvage. "I've got my first few outfits all lined up, and, I have to say, they're extremely cute," he said. He picked up the book on his nightstand (*Coming Apart*, by Charles Murray), weighed it in his hand, and decided to leave it behind.

---

*This received some titters and a few groans. The MAGA coalition of gay libertarians and homophobic social conservatives was still new, and tenuous. The latter's attitude toward the former, so far, seemed to be something like: *Use gay stuff to trigger the libs, if you must, but don't press your luck.*

Hoft sent him a contract formalizing his employment with *The Gateway Pundit*, and Wintrich reviewed it on his phone. In a previous version, he said, "there was a sentence about 'Employee must maintain professional behavior at all times.' I called Jim and asked, 'Does this mean I shouldn't troll liberals anymore?' and he went, 'Oh, we'd better just take that line out.'" The plan was for Wintrich to move to D.C. as soon as he found an apartment there. "I find the city dreadfully boring, honestly," he said, "but I'll make it work."

Hoft, who lived in St. Louis, started *The Gateway Pundit* in 2004. After the party he hosted at the RNC, he and Wintrich became friends, and Wintrich started writing for the site. His beat there could be described, generously, as media criticism—or less generously, as a series of amoral broadsides in an Andrew Breitbart–style culture war. After *BuzzFeed* ran a story accusing *The Gateway Pundit*, among other sites, of publishing "alternative facts," Wintrich wrote a post with the misleading headline "Buzzfeed Admits Liberal 'Fake News' No Longer Works—Points to Gateway Pundit as News of Future."

Wintrich was heading to Washington in the first month of the first reality-show presidency, and the drama inside the White House was already at midseason-cliffhanger levels. "We are fighting the fake news," Trump said in a speech. "It's fake, phony, fake." He added, "And I love the First Amendment. Nobody loves it better than me."

For a few months, the phrase "fake news" had been used, usually by authority figures on the left, to discredit outlets like *Liberty Writers* and *The Gateway Pundit*. Definitions varied. Techno-utopians, many of whom had a strong financial interest in downplaying the problem, tended to define it as narrowly as possible: the work of a few mischievous teenagers in Macedonia out to make a quick euro. Other people, such as Democratic Party flacks hoping to blame Clinton's loss on factors outside her control, interpreted the phrase too broadly. Still, the meaning was clear enough: a fake-news outlet was one that had little interest in getting the facts right, or that thought of inaccuracies as a feature, not a bug.*

---

*Some people contend that "fake news" was never a useful term, because it never had a universally agreed-upon definition. But many abstract concepts are at least as difficult to define as "fake news," if not more so. Consider "media." Or "health." Or "addiction," or "unconstitutional," or "terrorism," or "freedom." Few important words have uncontroversial definitions. We muddle through. Arguing about the definitions can be useful in itself.

Shortly after the election, Trump and his online army started to turn "fake news" to their advantage. They used an elementary technique, the same one they'd used with "deplorable," and "woke," and "based": through sheer repetition, they forced the meme to evolve until it meant more or less the opposite of what it used to mean. Why ask your opponent to drop a cudgel when you could simply use it to return the beating? From the time "fake news" entered the popular lexicon until the time it was rendered effectively meaningless, the phrase had a lifespan of about four months.

Wintrich planned to spend the bus ride to D.C. catching up on recent news and drafting questions for his first press briefing. Instead, he opened his laptop, which was decorated with a Barry Goldwater sticker, and binge-watched several episodes of the animated sitcom *King of the Hill*. He didn't seem to take the news-gathering aspect of his new job all that seriously; more to the point, he didn't seem to consider taking the news seriously to be part of his job.

He shut his laptop and looked out the window. The traditional media, he said, "lambasts Trump no matter what he does. Everyone knows Obama had a bigger crowd at his inauguration. Literally, who gives a shit? It's just pretension and con-descension, on the media's part, to make a big deal of it." His job would be to fight back. He relayed what a prominent pro-Trump conservative had told him: "You were brought in to troll the press corps, and you'd better troll hard." For a mo-ment, Wintrich looked overwhelmed. Then he opened his eyes wide, took a deep breath, and said, "Let's see what happens."

• • •

In normal times, White House press briefings make for boring television. Robert Gibbs, Jay Carney, and Josh Earnest, the three generic-looking white guys who served as successive press secretaries under Barack Obama, could walk through most American cities without being recognized. Only rarely was a clip from one of their briefings—for example, a testy exchange between Carney and Jonathan Karl of ABC News debating the logistics of Obamacare enrollment—remarkable enough to make headlines.

Then came Donald Trump, a man with little tolerance for boring television. The daily press briefings were suddenly among the most highly rated programs on daytime TV, beating out *General Hospital* and *The Bold and the Beautiful*. Trump's press secretary, Sean Spicer, became a recurring character on *Saturday Night Live*, portrayed by Melissa McCarthy. Spicer, whose job was to speak extemporaneously on behalf of the president, was remarkably bad at extemporaneous speaking; the sketches highlighted his propensity to become tongue-tied, flushed with rage, or both at once.*

Major news networks devoted hours to nightly exegeses of Spicer's serial self-contradictions, and to Sunday-morning sermons about how he was imperiling the First Amendment by withholding access from journalists he didn't like. On You-Tube, fan accounts with names such as Trump Mafia and Based Patriot reposted Spicer's briefings, and other conservative outlets posted exultant compilations of his "spiciest" moments, overlaying his rebukes of reporters with images of flames and chili peppers. Depending on your definition of "news," you could say that Spicer made news several times in every briefing, because so much of what he said was astonishing, or that he rarely made news, because so much of what he said was either garbled or obviously wrong.

Previous presidents were too busy with matters of state to obsess over the minutiae of public relations. This is why press briefings exist. In the nineteenth century, presidents could brief reporters themselves, on an infrequent, ad-hoc basis; by the 1920s, doling out information had become a full-time job, and Herbert Hoover became the first president to hire a spokesperson. Mike McCurry, appointed by Bill Clinton, was the first press secretary to allow the briefings to be aired on live TV, a decision he later called a "fatal mistake."

President Trump apparently had plenty of time to watch TV—especially when the voices on the screen were talking about him, which they almost always were. "Look at his daily schedule, and you'll notice how few events are held between 1:00 and 2:00 P.M.," a White House radio correspondent told me. This was when Spicer usually held his briefings. "I sometimes feel like I'm too busy to go to the briefings, and going to them is my job," the correspondent continued. "The thought that the president of the United States might take the time to sit through an entire briefing, much less all of them, is frankly mind boggling." Another correspondent pointed

---

*As soon as Spicer became a household name, Twitter sleuths started to dig up his most cantankerous old tweets—including a few, spread across several years, in which he revealed his unbridled contempt for Dippin' Dots, a dessert made of tiny, flash-frozen balls of ice cream. "Dippin dots is NOT the ice cream of the future," Spicer tweeted, in 2010. Then, a year and a half later: "I think I have said this before but Dippin Dots are notthe ice cream of the future."

out how often press aides delivered notes to Spicer while he was at the lectern, and how obediently Spicer seemed to respond to the notes' directives, cutting a response short or abruptly ending a briefing. The reigning theory was that the notes, which appeared to be written in Sharpie, were messages from the president, watching live from elsewhere in the building.

A few months into his presidency, while flying on Air Force One, Trump paid a visit to the reporters in the main cabin. "I don't get to watch much television, primarily because of documents," he said. "I'm reading documents. A lot."

This was weird, even by Trump's standards. For one thing, no one on the plane had said anything about television. For another, "reading documents a lot" is high on the list of activities it's nearly impossible to imagine Trump doing, along with foraging, Pilates, and deep introspection. It later became clear that the impetus for Trump's outburst was an email he'd just received from *The New York Times*—a list of fifty-one fact-checking questions for an article about him. When the piece came out, it reported that Trump began his days by watching TV in bed, where he sometimes "tweets while propped on his pillow." (Trump, on Twitter: "Wrong!")

Trump had built a career on the understanding that there was no such thing as too much media exposure. He kept picking fights, especially with reporters, in part because fights were good for ratings; he changed his mind about almost everything, but he always maintained that unfriendly journalists were scum. In May 2016, he held a press conference in Trump Tower. He spent much of the time upbraiding the assembled reporters, calling them "sleazy" and "dishonest."

"I think you've set a new bar today for being contentious with the press corps, kind of calling us losers to our faces and all that," David Martosko of the *Daily Mail* said. "Is this what it's going to be like covering you if you're president?"

"Yeah, it is," Trump responded.

He seemed to be operating on several overlapping assumptions: that an arbitrary exercise of power would make him look strong; that it would behoove him to treat the mainstream media, one of the most disliked institutions in the country, as his foil; that he would have wider latitude to lie if he continued to assail the very notion of facticity; and that conflict is attention, and attention is influence.

———

In Washington, Wintrich took a cab to the Hay-Adams hotel—a former mansion a block north of the White House, all decorative moldings and wall sconces. While he waited to check in, two men stepped up to the counter.

"It says here that *The Wall Street Journal* is your preferred publication, Mr. Schwartz," the receptionist said. "Is that correct?"

"Maybe you should get the *National Enquirer* instead," Mr. Schwartz's friend said. "That's what real Americans read."

"Oh, is *The Wall Street Journal* fake news now?" Mr. Schwartz said.

"They're globalist cucks, aren't they?" his friend said.

The receptionist paused, her face neutral, her hands frozen on the computer keyboard.

Mr. Schwartz turned to her and smiled. "We'll take the *Journal*, and also the *Times* and the *Post* if you've got 'em," he said. She chuckled with relief.

I glanced at Wintrich to see whether he was offended or flattered by this exchange, but he wasn't paying attention. A reporter from *Politico* had just emailed him asking for an interview, and he was crafting his reply.

Wintrich met up with Hoft, who would accompany him to his first briefing the next day. "I hate traveling, but I had to be here for this," Hoft said. "*The Gateway Pundit*, this blog I started in my basement, made it all the way to the fucking White House? Are you kidding me? This is gonna be so epic!"

Shortly after the election, Hoft said, he emailed "Trump's people" to ask about press credentials "and they encouraged us to apply." He wouldn't say which people, but he had known Steve Bannon, then Trump's top strategist, for many years, and Sean Spicer had been aware of Hoft's work since at least 2012, when Spicer tweeted a link to a *Gateway Pundit* story about voter fraud. (The story turned out to be false.) While Hoft spoke, Wintrich emailed Hope Hicks, then Trump's director of strategic communications, asking a logistical question; she replied within three minutes. "She's incredible," Wintrich said. "And gorgeous, obviously. I hope I can convince her to be my friend."

Over dinner at a nearby steakhouse, Hoft and Wintrich brainstormed questions they might ask the next day. They were joined by two conservative filmmakers from Chicago who would document their arrival at the White House. "Just make sure everything has 'fake news' in it, Lucian," Hoft said, passing him a Hay-Adams notepad. "Every question you ask with the words 'fake news,' you get a ten-dollar bonus. We'll add that to your contract."

Wintrich sipped a martini and jotted a few notes. "Sean! Over here, Sean!" he said, pretending to raise his hand. "In the last month alone, there have been at least twenty fake news stories in the failing *New York Times*. Does fake news like this get in the way of the president's ability to proceed on policy?"

Hoft cackled loudly enough to startle a woman at a nearby table. "That's fucking hilarious," he said. "Should we do something about *SNL*, maybe?"

"A follow-up, Sean, if I may?" Lucian said. "Do you think the failing show *Saturday Night Live* will be canceled, or can it be made great again?"

"That's hard-core," Jeremy Segal, one of the filmmakers, said.

"Genius," Hoft said.

Andrew Marcus, the other filmmaker, had directed *Hating Breitbart*, a flattering feature documentary about Andrew Breitbart. "I was with him pretty much every minute from 2009 until shortly before he passed," Marcus said. "Remarkable man. Prophetic man."*

For a moment, Wintrich seemed to get cold feet. "Should we have a couple of backup questions that are specifically about policy?" he asked.

"Policy schmolicy," Hoft said.

Segal agreed: "Fuck policy. Politics is downstream from culture. That's what I learned from A.B." These, of course, were the initials of his departed role model, Andrew Breitbart.

• • •

The next morning, in a room at the Hay-Adams, Marcus pulled back the drapes to reveal a perfectly framed view of the White House, with the Washington Monument in the background. "So awesome," Marcus said. "I want my deathbed to be

---

*Marcus's film includes the six-second clip in which Andrew Breitbart most fully embodies the role of Andrew Breitbart. Slowly and clearly, glaring directly into the camera, he pronounces two words: "Fuck. You." He pauses for four seconds, his jaw set, his pale eyes sparkling with rage. Then, in a near whisper, as if blowing the seeds off a dandelion: "War." The object of the "fuck you" was clear enough: the liberals, the media, the cultural Marxists, and so on. The "war" was meant to be a jihad of the spirit, not of the flesh. Breitbart saw evil everywhere—in public universities, in Disney movies, on the evening news—and he considered it his duty, as a cultural revolutionary, to eradicate it. Like most revolutionaries, he was far less articulate about what would come next.

in this room." While Segal filmed, Hoft and Wintrich discussed their plan for the day. They had just received an email informing them that Spicer's daily briefing had been canceled; instead, President Trump would host a joint press conference with the Canadian prime minister, Justin Trudeau, who was at the White House for a state visit. They scrapped their questions from dinner and started to research Trudeau instead.

Wintrich's bravado had returned. His hair was fashionably mussed, and he wore a tie printed with elephants in pastel colors. Skimming an article on his phone, he said that Trudeau "apparently loved Castro. *Fawned* over him."

Hoft, wearing a black suit and a yellow Trump-brand tie, improvised a few questions. "What appeals to you about Communist dictators, Mr. Trudeau?" he said. "What offends you about freedom?"

Wintrich thought the attack could be sharper. "Not to use the gay angle right out of the gate," he said, "but we could say, 'You've voiced support for Castro, who imprisoned gays, and for Muslims, who kill gays—what do you have against gay people?'"

"That's epic," Hoft said.

"I think it's trollier, from a trolling perspective," Wintrich said.

"Love it," Hoft said. "Google 'Castro jails gays' or something, see what you find." Sitting at an antique wooden desk before an open laptop, Hoft clicked on a headline: "Trump Claims America Should Never Have Given Canada Its Independence." The post, on a site called the Burrard Street Journal, quoted a Trump tweet with the hashtag #MakeCanadaAmericanAgain. "Is this real?" Hoft said. "I follow the news. I feel like I would have heard about this." It seemed obvious that the Burrard Street Journal—whose logo was "BS Journal," and whose other top headlines included "Alex Jones Selected to Host Next White House Correspondents' Dinner"—was a news parody site. But Hoft spent several minutes vacillating. He googled "Make Canada American Again" and saw that no mainstream newspapers—the kind that he and the president had taken to calling "fake news"—had picked up the story. "It must be bullshit," he concluded. "God, I hate bullshit sites."

*   *   *

Outside the hotel, Wintrich lit a cigarette for the three-minute walk to the White House. Four days earlier, *The Washington Post* had reported that General Michael

Flynn, before being sworn in as Trump's national security adviser, had discussed sanctions with Russian officials, and had subsequently lied to cover up those conversations. As we crossed Lafayette Park, I asked Wintrich what he thought about the many allegations of coordination between the Trump campaign and the Russian government.

"You mean the pee tape?" he said.

"I mean the whole thing," I said. "Manafort's visits to Ukraine. The timing of Kislyak's meetings. Apparently Rex Tillerson, before he got the Order of Friendship medal, traveled to—"

"It's all a media hoax," Wintrich said. He declined to elaborate. I'd expected, if not something more plausible, then at least something trollier, from a trolling perspective. But his heart wasn't in it. "I keep trying to read up on Russia stuff and I always get bored," he said. Just as Cernovich had dismissed birtherism as old news, Wintrich didn't try to rebut accusations of Russian collusion; he simply dismissed it as a played-out narrative, which was, by his lights, an even more stinging rebuke.

We lined up outside the northwest gate of the White House, waiting to be issued gray temporary passes. The long-serving correspondents with red "hard passes" were waved to the front of the line. April Ryan, the White House correspondent for American Urban Radio Networks, made small talk with the guards while placing her purse and keys on a conveyor belt.

"Hoft? Wintrich?" A Secret Service agent slapped two gray passes on the desk. Hoft and Wintrich took the passes, making gleeful, surreptitious eye contact. They walked through the metal detectors, and a White House aide led them through a door at the back of the shed. They were inside the gates.

CHAPTER TWENTY-TWO

The Narrative of Public Life

The White House briefing room has seven rows of seven seats—tattered blue folding chairs without much legroom. The ceilings are low. The carpets are stained. A narrow hallway leads out of the briefing room, past a row of tiny edit bays, and toward a kitchenette, where there's a lunch table bolted to the floor and a vending machine that sells Snyder's pretzels, Rice Krispies Treats, and cans of Bumble Bee tuna. ("Who would be tempted by vending-machine tuna?" I heard someone ask.)

The front row of seats is reserved for the Associated Press, Reuters, and the biggest TV networks; reporters from *Politico* and *Real Clear Politics* sit near the middle; *BuzzFeed* and the BBC are in the back. The seating chart is the purview of the White House Correspondents' Association, an independent board of journalists who, with the somber secrecy of a papal conclave, assess news organizations according to a number of objective and subjective factors—circulation, regularity of coverage, centrality to the national discourse. There are also correspondents who might be called floaters—those who have White House credentials but no assigned place in the seating chart. In normal times, when press briefings are half empty, floaters can find vacant seats. In the early days of the Trump administration, when each day's briefing was oversubscribed, floaters packed the aisles, angling for a spot with a sight line to the podium.

The paradigmatic floater was Raghubir Goyal, a cordial, absentminded man in his sixties. Goyal claimed to be the White House correspondent for the *India Globe*, a newspaper that, as far as anyone can tell, was either defunct or had never existed at all. Nevertheless, he had attended briefings since the Carter administration, and had asked so many questions about Indo-American relations that his name had become a verb. "To Goyal": to call on a reporter who is likely to provide an innocuous question, or a moment of comic relief. All press secretaries got cornered, and all of them, on occasion, had to Goyal their way out. But no one Goyaled like Spicer.

For years, by tradition, the first question of each briefing had gone to the Associated Press. At Spicer's first briefing, his first question went to the *New York Post*, a conservative tabloid whose reporter, sitting in the fifth row, was clearly surprised. "When will you commence the building of the border wall?" he asked. In Spicer's next briefing, his first question went to a reporter from *LifeZette*, who asked why the administration hadn't taken a harder line on immigration.*

Calling on the reporters in the front row wasn't only about appealing to their egos, a longtime TV correspondent told me. "It's also about maintaining a sense of predictability, a sense that eventually the substantive questions will be answered," he said. "Throwing that into chaos—'Maybe you'll get a question, if you shout loud enough, who knows?'—makes everyone desperate and competitive and makes us look like a bunch of braying jackals. Which I don't think is an accident." Another reporter, a former White House correspondent from a major TV network, claimed that he didn't mind the Trump administration "bringing in conservative voices. Personally, I don't even mind them fucking with the front-row guys, the Jonathan Karls of the world. Those guys are a smug little cartel, and it's fun to watch them squirm, at least for a little while. But at what point does it start to delegitimize the whole idea of what happens in that room? When does it cross the line into pure trolling?"

In 1988, Joan Didion wrote a long and forceful essay decrying groupthink in political journalism. She aligned herself with normal Americans and against the slick media shills—"a self-created and self-referring class, a new kind of managerial elite . . . who invent, year in and year out, the narrative of public life." This was before Twitter, before MAGA, when the worst that could happen to the country was either Michael Dukakis or George H. W. Bush.

When I read Didion's essay, nearly two decades after it first ran, I nodded

---

*The *New York Post* was owned by Rupert Murdoch; *LifeZette* was a right-wing web tabloid cofounded in 2015 by Laura Ingraham, a Trump ally who would go on to become a Fox News host. Other outlets that became newly prominent under the Trump administration included One America News Network, founded in 2013 as a right-wing alternative to Fox News; *The Daily Caller*, cofounded in 2010 by Tucker Carlson, who also went on to become a Fox News host; *Townhall*, a conservative site started by the Heritage Foundation; and the openly pro-Trump *Breitbart*.

along, scribbling my passionate assent in the margins. All things being equal, it's cooler to be a rebel than a conformist, and the twerps on the TV news were conformists of the worst kind. They were like haughty distant relatives—except that, instead of enduring them once a year at Thanksgiving, you had to listen to them every day, and you never got to talk back.

Then came Trump. Twerp bashing was still good fun, but it now raised an urgent and vertiginous set of questions. TV news—especially the postlapsarian twenty-four-hour version, dominated by horse-race politics and missing planes and viral outrage—was bad enough. What if it was replaced by something incomparably worse?

* * *

After they cleared security, Hoft and Wintrich walked past the North Lawn and into the briefing room and gave each other a high five. That they had actually made it inside seemed incredible even to them. Hoft, sitting in a blue folding chair, sent a message to his niece: "This is your favorite uncle texting you from the White House!!!!" followed by a string of emoji hearts and kisses.

When the president hosts a visiting head of state for a bilateral press conference, the event is often held not in the briefing room but in the East Room, the closest thing the White House has to a Versailles-style ballroom. Today, the briefing room was being used as a holding pen, essentially, a place for the reporters to gather until the staff was ready to escort them to the main event. The podium was empty. Hoft and Wintrich stepped behind the lectern, with the official White House seal in the background. They posed for a furtive photo, grinning and making the "OK" hand gesture—thumb and forefinger forming a circle, three fingers in the air. When they sat down again, Wintrich posted the photo on Facebook, captioning it with two emojis, an American flag and a frog.

Like Pepe the Frog, with which it was sometimes associated, the OK hand gesture was a meme that had mutated quickly. Around that time, anonymous posters on 4chan were spreading the rumor that the gesture was an obscure symbol for white power. This was later revealed to be a hoax.* The channers went on to pull the same trick with a series of other signifiers—the peace sign, Facebook's

---

*The channers who started the hoax, which they called Operation O-KKK, were apparently just trolling, trying to see whether the normies in the mainstream media would bite. (They did.) But other channers, presumably, were genuine white supremacists, perpetuating the meme in earnest.

thumbs-up icon, glasses of milk. Part of the goal was to gaslight the normies, to make them doubt even their simplest perceptions. Everything was open to interpretation. Even what looked like clear evidence of avowed hatred could turn out to be a deepfake, or an in-joke shrouded in endless layers of ambiguity.

The news story of the day was Flynn's alleged ties to Russia. So far, Trump had said nothing about it, not even on Twitter. In a few minutes, he would face the White House press corps on live TV. It was a scenario out of a journalism textbook: an opportunity to hold the president's feet to the fire, to ask what the scandal indicated about his administration.

Hoft and Wintrich, oblivious of the mounting tension, continued to hone their questions about Castro. Hoft chatted amiably with a French correspondent, who asked which organization he was with. "A big website in the Midwest called *The Gateway Pundit*," he said. "Very, very large."

"Oh, you're from the Midwest—that's why you're so friendly," she said.

The reporters were escorted down a white marble hallway lined with oil portraits of recent presidents and first ladies. "Holy shit, Lucian, look at this," Hoft said, standing in front of a portrait of Hillary Clinton. Hoft and Wintrich posed in front of the portrait, making the OK gesture. Then they proceeded down the hallway, passing a marble bust of Abraham Lincoln and a grand piano inlaid with gold leaf. "Amazing," Hoft said, under his breath. For the moment, he seemed sincere.

In the East Room, unlike in the briefing room, the White House dictates the seating arrangement for the American press. On each gold-colored chair was a piece of printer paper bearing the name of an outlet: *The New York Times* next to the Christian Broadcasting Network, the AP next to *Breitbart*. Hoft and Wintrich couldn't find any seats for *The Gateway Pundit*, so they took the ones reserved for Al Jazeera, which is funded by the Qatari government, and RT, which is funded by the Russian government. "Everyone calls us Putin's puppets anyway, so we might as well embrace it," Hoft said.

Six TV correspondents—Kristen Welker of NBC News, and five broad-shouldered men—stood on wooden risers, their backs to the podium, waiting to go live. The room got quiet as the president's arrival drew near. The correspondents faced their respective cameras and began to speak—first, one at a time, then all at once, like an orchestra tuning up before a concert:

". . . I would be surprised if he doesn't get some questions about . . ."

". . . does the president still have confidence in his national security adviser . . ."

". . . apparently had discussions with the Russian ambassador . . ."

". . . Flynn is in hot water . . ."

The first journalist Trump called on was Scott Thuman, of the right-leaning Sinclair Broadcast Group. He asked a softball question about Trump's relationship with Trudeau, given their "philosophical differences." Trump's second and final question went to Kaitlan Collins, a 24-year-old reporter with *The Daily Caller*. This was the press corps's last chance to bring up the Flynn scandal. Instead, Collins asked, "What do you see as the most important national security matters facing us?" In person, some of the correspondents were unable to mask their displeasure; on Twitter, the reactions were even stronger. Hunter Walker, of *Yahoo News*, tweeted, from inside the East Room, "Hearing reporters gripe about the lack of Flynn questions now: 'I'm just embarrassed for us.'" For a little while, Collins and Walker engaged in a brief public spat, tweeting barbed remarks at each other from different parts of the White House. Later that day, one of Collins's colleagues at *The Daily Caller* compiled Walker's comments, and those of other correspondents, in a post headlined "7 Butthurt Reporters Who Should Be Deported."

• • •

Back in his room at the Hay-Adams, Hoft was having a conversation, on speaker-phone, with a *Gateway Pundit* staffer who was pitching a story: "I'm hearing that either Priebus or Spicer could be the next to hear 'You're fired.'"

Hoft wasn't interested. "Unless you can frame it as 'Media Sharks Circling for Blood,' some angle like that," he said.

Wintrich was curled up on the bed with his laptop, in a swoon of self-googling. Media Matters, a left-wing nonprofit, had published the photo of Hoft and Wintrich behind the lectern, along with a lengthy blog post headlined "A Dangerous Troll Is Now Reporting from the White House." Wintrich had since received offers to appear on *Tipping Point with Liz Wheeler* and *Full Frontal with Samantha Bee*. The *New York Times* published a piece about him—"White House Grants Press Credentials to a Pro-Trump Blog"—and a few hours later Wintrich filed his rebuttal: "Carlos Slim's Anti-Trump Blog, 'The New York Times,' Attacks Gateway Pundit."

Hoft and Wintrich took an elevator to the basement of the Hay-Adams, where there was a bar called Off the Record, a hangout for White House staffers and political reporters. Hoft ran into an old acquaintance, Sam Nunberg, a former employee of the Trump campaign. "I'm going to see Steve later," Nunberg boasted. He meant Bannon. "I've got some Israel policy guys I want him to meet."

"Oh, neat, I was just talking to Steve," Hoft countered. "He's been reading our stuff, says it's better than ever." They parted, their status competition having reached an impasse. Hoft ordered a lemonade and took a phone call from Julia Hahn, who had been Bannon's protégée at *Breitbart* before going to work with him in the White House. "Jim's a kooky guy, but he does have influence, you can't argue with that," Nunberg said. "Just look at how many times Trump's tweeted out a *Gateway* link, or referenced them in his speeches."

That night, Flynn resigned, resulting in a blizzard of headlines. Neither Hoft nor Wintrich noticed right away—Hoft was on a flight back to St. Louis, and Wintrich was engaged in a Twitter battle with a left-wing reporter at *Mic*. Before Hoft left for the airport, I told him that he should expect to hear from one of *The New Yorker*'s eighteen full-time fact-checkers. "Oh yeah, just like at *The Gateway Pundit*," Hoft said. "We've got a huge department of full-time fact-checkers." He laughed so hard at his own joke that he nearly spilled his lemonade.

After Hoft and Wintrich left, I spent a while at the bar with Nunberg. He wore a pocket square and gold skull-shaped cufflinks; his hair was slicked back; his suit, shirt, and tie all had pinstripes in clashing colors and sizes. He looked like a well-fed bar mitzvah boy whose reception theme was *The Wolf of Wall Street*. Nunberg, who described Roger Stone as his political mentor and "surrogate father," had been fired by the Trump campaign in 2015, when it emerged that Nunberg had once written Facebook posts in which he referred to Obama as a "Socialist Marxist Islamo Fascist Nazi Appeaser," and to Al Sharpton's daughter as a "N---!"*

Off the Record's leather-bound menu included a list of special election-themed cocktails: the Kainehattan, the Pence's Tea Party, the Hillary's Last Word, the Trumpy Sour. Each cocktail cost eighteen dollars or more. This was insane,

---

Sic.

considering that journalism was a dying industry; still, it was the going rate for insider gossip, and everyone paid it. For the previous hour, Nunberg had been talking, loquaciously and at an indiscreet volume, to a local reporter while drinking on her tab. When she got up to leave, he started drinking on mine. During the handoff, Nunberg excused himself to "take a leak." "Have fun with him," the reporter said. "He's a weirdo and a hopeless exaggerator, but he'll tell you whatever you want to hear."

This air of world-weariness was as much a part of the place as the sconces and the moldings. The prevailing attitude was that D.C. was a swamp, a clusterfuck, a clown car inching through gridlock; you were expected to roll your eyes at the situation, make a cynical joke about it, and get on with your business. You couldn't, without being a buzzkill, express too much earnest curiosity as to where the clown car was headed, or whether it might one day hurtle off a cliff. Trump was just another lout, another grifter—in other words, another politician. His caricature was already framed and hanging on the wall, near a scowling Dick Cheney and a jug-eared Obama—all of them, side by side, on the same plane.

Nunberg returned to his barstool, ordered another drink, and introduced himself to me for the third time. "So whaddaya wanna know?" he said. He gave me a preview of his wares. He could offer salacious rumors about which White House staffer was "next on the chopping block," or about whether Bannon and Preibus were allies or nemeses, or about what Jared and Ivanka were really after. "This one you can use on deep background," he kept saying, or, "That'll have to be from 'a source familiar.'"

He was doling out information that was supposed to be valuable, but I couldn't make any use of it. I felt like I was being led into a bank vault full of a foreign currency that I had no way to exchange. For one thing, very little of what Nunberg said would be relevant in a month or two, after the allegiances in the White House had shifted and many of the current staffers had been fired. For another thing, Nunberg was plainly willing to flatter, to self-contradict, to stretch the limits of credulity—he seemed more interested in bad-mouthing his rivals, or in keeping himself entertained, than in any consistent version of the truth. At one point, I mentioned a telling detail I'd just read in a magazine profile of a Trump administration official; Nunberg strongly hinted that he'd been the source for the detail, and that he'd made it up, for fun. I felt confident that, given enough time and a profligate enough bar tab, I could get him to say anything about anyone. It was like a Zen koan: If a source familiar says something patently false, but it's true that he said it, is the quote worth writing down?*

• • •

The day after Kaitlan Collins and Hunter Walker's Twitter feud, they sat near the back of the briefing room, chatting nonchalantly. April Ryan arrived fashionably late, removing her sunglasses, and people stood to let her get to her seat. Just before the briefing was to begin, a short nineteen-year-old named Kyle Mazza darted across the room, staking out a prime position in an aisle near the front. Mazza was a new-media Goyal, a floater among floaters. He was the sole employee of a network he called UNF News, or Universal News Forever (News), which owned no bandwidth on TV or radio—just a skeletal, sporadically updated website.

A sliding door opened, and Spicer approached the lectern. Apart from camera shutters, the room fell silent. "Happy Valentine's Day," he said. "I can sense the love in the room."

He called on Jonathan Karl of ABC. "Can you still say definitively that nobody on the Trump campaign, not even General Flynn, had any contact with the Russians before the election?" Karl asked.

"I don't have any—there's nothing that would conclude me that anything different has changed with respect to that time period," Spicer said.

The next day, the podium in the briefing room was cordoned off with a velvet rope and a placard: "Photos may be taken at ground level only." Evidently,

---

*A year later, Special Counsel Robert Mueller served Nunberg with a subpoena requiring him to turn over his email correspondence with Roger Stone, Steve Bannon, and other Trump associates. Nunberg reacted to the subpoena with a televised meltdown, crisscrossing Manhattan to give five hours of bizarre live interviews in various cable-news studios. "Isn't this ridiculous?" he asked a legal analyst on MSNBC, waving a copy of his subpoena in the air. His facial expression was that of a toddler who threatens to run into the street, then glances up to gauge his parents' reaction.

"No, it's not ridiculous, Sam," she said. "It's *so* not ridiculous."

"I'm not going to jail," he said. "You think I'm going to jail?"

Was it appropriate for MSNBC's bookers, and all the other TV bookers, to let Sam Nunberg on air? Was it proper for dozens of American news outlets to use Roger Stone, for decades, as a source of insider political information? Was it right for Steve Bannon to be invited, in 2018, to appear onstage at The New Yorker Festival? Should journalists continue to amplify the noxious rhetoric of President Donald Trump?

These men are all known liars; they might also be, depending on how literally or seriously one takes their assorted bloviations, racist demagogues spoiling for violence. Still, they have real power, and one function of journalism is to chronicle and confront those in power. Trolls may be puerile, odious, or dangerous, but they set an ingenious trap. By responding to their provocations, you amplify their message. And yet, if no one ever rebuked the trolls, they would run the internet, and perhaps the world.

someone in the White House press office had noticed the photo of Hoft and Wintrich behind the lectern. I took a picture of the placard and texted it to both of them.

"HAHAHAHAHAHA," Wintrich texted back.

"Is that photoshopped?" Hoft responded. "Real?"

CHAPTER TWENTY-THREE

Very Professional and Very Good

The other Deplorables noticed what an impression Wintrich was making in Washington, and the White House briefing room soon became a fire hydrant that no alt-light figurehead could resist marking. Mike Cernovich and Cassandra Fairbanks got temporary passes; they took a photo of themselves behind the lectern, making the OK hand gesture. Afterward, they stood in the aisle to watch that day's briefing. For half an hour, live on Periscope, Fairbanks filmed Cernovich trying and failing to ask Spicer a question. When Spicer finished and left the podium, Cernovich shouted after him, "What about violence against Trump supporters?" Spicer kept walking out of the room. Cernovich turned and repeated his question, now directing it to the correspondents in the blue folding seats. "Why will nobody here cover the violence against Trump supporters?" he said. "This is being completely covered up."

Most of the correspondents ignored him, the way they might ignore a stranger shouting obscenities on the Metro. "Are you a reporter, sir?" April Ryan asked.

"I am, madam," Cernovich responded. "I'm a reporter, I'm a documentary filmmaker."

He and Fairbanks filed out of the room, brushing past Jonathan Karl. Fairbanks kept streaming, and Cernovich kept narrating for the camera. "Let 'em get mad," he said. "I definitely just had a question. Definitely had a question. Journalism. So this is good."

A few weeks later, Jack Posobiec, then the sole employee of the Rebel's D.C. bureau, got a White House press pass. "We've just come through security," Posobiec announced as he walked toward the West Wing. "This is truly hallowed ground we're walking on right now." When he reached the briefing room, he posed for a photo while making the OK hand gesture.

Jerome Corsi, the bestselling author of *Where's the Birth Certificate?*, had since left *WND* for Infowars—the tinfoil-hat equivalent of a star *Time* reporter being poached by *Newsweek*. During a lull in activity, Corsi stood on the podium in the briefing room, livestreaming from an iPad. "Very compact facility," he told an Infowars anchor filling in for Alex Jones. "We're going to be here on a regular basis."*

The substitute anchor, live on air, started interviewing Corsi in the usual Infowars style, stipulating the importance of "defeating the Deep State coup d'état, silencing the mainstream media."

Corsi, obviously uncomfortable, tried to cut the interview short. Apparently, everyone could hear both sides of this conversation as it blared over his iPad. He asked to continue the interview another time, "so we don't have to broadcast everything we're saying to the entire press room."

The first alt-light figure to make news simply by entering the briefing room was Milo Yiannopoulos, who attended a press briefing in 2016, near the end of the Obama administration. Briefings then were so sparsely attended that he was able to sit, flanked by two *Breitbart* reporters. He even got to ask a question. "It's becoming very clear that Twitter and Facebook, in particular, are censoring and punishing conservative and libertarian points of view," Yiannopoulos said. "Is there anything the president can do to encourage Silicon Valley—to remind them of the importance, the critical importance, of open, free speech in our society?"†

Eight weeks earlier, Twitter had deverified Yiannopoulos's account. The company wouldn't say why it took this disciplinary action, but it happened shortly

---

*He wasn't. Corsi had been granted a day pass, but he would never get another one. In 2018, Robert Mueller brought Corsi in for a series of interviews, during which he appeared to perjure himself several times. Mueller later offered Corsi a plea deal, which Corsi refused. "I consider this entire investigation to be fraudulent," he said.
†Many so-called conservatives—including Yiannopoulos and his boss at *Breitbart*, Steve Bannon—were starting to push the idea that Twitter and Facebook and Google were monopolies, and that the government should consider breaking them up. This idea spread across the Overton window from both directions until, in 2017 and 2018, it became one of the rare talking points to gain traction on both Democracy Now! and Fox News. "Google's existence, Google's power, raises real questions about whether you can have an actual democracy," Tucker Carlson said in September 2018. "This is not the capitalism I signed up for."

after Yiannopoulos tweeted, to one of his many antagonists, "You deserve to be harassed you social justice loser." Yiannopoulos engaged in this sort of discourse constantly, and social networks rarely reprimanded him. When they did, it had less to do with the First Amendment per se than with the fact that all social networks have rules, and that Yiannopoulos repeatedly violated them.

For three minutes, Yiannopoulos and Josh Earnest, Obama's press secretary, engaged in a civil debate. By the standards of a press briefing, it was almost scholarly. Yiannopoulos insisted that speech rights must be protected above all else, which had been his hobbyhorse for years. Whenever I was tempted to conclude that he was a nihilistic troll with no core beliefs, I had to correct myself: he did seem to have at least one. "All I care about is free speech and free expression," he said. "I want people to be able to be, do, and say anything."

Then I found a column from 2012, before Yiannopoulos became Twitter famous. The headline was "The Internet Is Turning Us All into Sociopaths." "Social media," he wrote, was encouraging people "to write unspeakable things to other human beings that we would never dream of saying in person. . . . It's as if a psychological norm is being established whereby comments left online are part of a video game and not real life." The Yiannopoulos of 2012, it turned out, was far from a free-speech absolutist. "It's clear that existing hate speech laws are inadequate for the social media era," he wrote. "We ban drunks from driving because they're a danger to others," he wrote. "Isn't it time we did the same to trolls?"

•   •   •

Wintrich sublet his apartment in the East Village and rented a place in D.C., near Logan Square—"a bit characterless," he said, "but I consider it a personal challenge to make it cute." He bought a vintage Louis Vuitton steamer trunk on eBay to use as a coffee table, and flanked his TV with wall-mounted busts of a gazelle and a gemsbok. Most nights, he could be found mixing bourbon cocktails for some anarcho-capitalists he'd met at CPAC, or serving rare flank steak to a group of graphic designers and Instagram models. Occasionally, if the mood struck, he'd shush his guests and start a Periscope video to analyze the news of the day, by which he usually meant his most recent Twitter spat. Once, when I arrived at Wintrich's place in D.C., he told me that I'd just missed Chelsea Manning. I found this hard to believe; since her release from prison, Manning had become a prominent Antifa activist. "Fine, think whatever you want," Wintrich said.*

One night, he looked up from writing a text. "What's the name of that gay island?" he asked the room.

"Lesbos?" one of his guests, a tech correspondent for *Breitbart*, suggested.

"Fire Island," Wintrich said, and went back to typing. The room fell quiet, and people started to look bored. Wintrich, ever the assiduous host, put on some music, poured prosecco, and started a round of Cards Against Humanity, which its creators describe as "a party game for horrible people."

Mainstream reporters kept getting triggered whenever Wintrich appeared in the briefing room, so he kept showing up. He was a floater. Most days, he didn't prepare any questions. Spicer never called on him anyway. Still, his mere presence was an effective act of trolling. "The Aryan Trump twink photo guy, now reporting—in a suit, thank God—from the White House," Rachel Maddow said on MSNBC.

One Friday morning, before the press briefing started, Jon Decker, a White House correspondent from Fox News Radio, saw Wintrich standing across the briefing room. "*Gateway Pundit* is here," Decker warned, sharing his opinion of the site with anyone who cared to listen. The upshot was that Wintrich was an avowed white nationalist (false) who lacked journalistic integrity (true). Wintrich took advantage of the moment, tweeting falsely that Decker had "assaulted" him. *Conflict is attention.*

The fracas spilled outside. At the O.K. Corral, a verbal dispute is liable to become a gunfight; at the White House, a verbal dispute is likely to stay a verbal dispute, with a bunch of reporters crowding around and filming it on their phones. Snow was falling. Wintrich, cheating toward the cameras, put on a pair of sunglasses and lit a cigarette.

April Ryan approached, holding her iPhone in front of her like a talisman, and asked Wintrich to state his political beliefs.

"Um, small government? Personal freedom?" he said. "Half my family died in the Holocaust. To call me a Nazi or whatever else is wildly—it's disgusting."

---

*"I get along with everyone," Wintrich once told me. I'm very open minded." This turned out to be an understatement. He was the kind of person a teacher of mine once warned me about—once warned me, in fact, not to become: a person so open minded that his brain could fall out.

"OK," she said. "Are you a racist?"

"No, of course not."

"What are your views when it comes to integration?"

"I'm all for it."

"Races mingling?"

Wintrich smirked. "My boyfriend's Colombian, so we tend to mingle," he said.

The blows weren't landing. This was Ryan's chance—a spontaneous solo press conference with the infamous briefing-room troll—but she didn't know enough about Wintrich to catch him red-handed.

For months, the Deplorables had been derided for their many obvious transgressions: their dishonesty, their xenophobia, their misogyny. Recently, though, the range of concerns had rapidly narrowed. In many leftist circles, both on social media and in real life, the Deplorables were coming to be defined in a single, simple way: they were all Nazis. Or, at the very least, they were committed white supremacists. To call them anything less was considered a cowardly form of soft-pedaling.

This was an understandable response to a profoundly vexing problem. Since World War II, the lunatic fringe in the United States had always included a few hundred freaks with swastika tattoos; now there was an increasingly organized white-supremacist movement in America, one that had several points of contiguity with both Congress and the White House. This was novel, and terrifying; yet it was often referred to in the mainstream press as merely "edgy" or "controversial." I understood, given the state of things, the longing for clarity. Why not speak plainly about what was happening in front of our eyes? Could we not break the habit of false equivalence even when it came to literal Nazis?

Yet it also didn't make sense to insist that every bad guy on the internet was bad in exactly the same way. This was both a logical mistake and a tactical mistake. For one thing, focusing exclusively on one kind of badness risked leaving every other avenue of badness unchecked.* If Wintrich's critics wanted to make the case that he didn't deserve to work in the White House, there were plenty of good arguments to choose from. But if the only way to discredit a Deplorable was to call him a Nazi, then the charge could be falsified easily—"I'm Jewish" seemed

---

*It also seemed strangely, even insultingly hierarchical. Was it really soft-pedaling to call someone a misogynist or an Islamophobe rather than a racist? Was it so self-evident that one form of bigotry was more unacceptable than another?

to do the trick. The critic would be left with nothing, and the Deplorable would be left with a talking point.

I have agreed with Gavin McInnes exactly once. He was being interviewed by Milo Yiannopoulos, on the latter's YouTube channel. They were both mocking the mainstream media's habit of asking them, in essence, the same question, again and again: "Are you a white nationalist?"

"I did an interview with NBC yesterday," McInnes said. According to him, the NBC journalist was single-mindedly determined to expose him as a textbook white supremacist. He told her that, if that's what she was after, "then your bad guys are everywhere . . . the alt-right would be happy to talk to you, and they say what they mean." Still, he went on, if she wanted to impugn him, she should already have more than enough material to work with, even without broaching the subject of white nationalism. "I'm an Islamophobe, I'm a xenophobe, I'm pretty darn sexist," he said. "Go jump on that!"

•   •   •

I kept getting swept up in the ongoing drama of the news narrative. How could I resist? Every headline—"Trump Campaign Aides Had Repeated Contacts with Russian Intelligence"; "Trump Turns Mar-a-Lago Club Terrace into Open-air Situation Room"—was enough to spark half a dozen activating emotions at once. And yet a small, naïve part of me was still surprised that any newspaper headline or TV chyron could say anything other than "White House Currently Occupied by Donald Trump, Other Assorted Goons and Frauds." Traditional reporters were facing essentially the same dilemma they'd faced when covering online troll raids, only on a far larger scale. They could be evenhanded, or they could tell the truth. It was impossible to do both. The big newspapers couldn't quite bring themselves to adopt a strident, *Gawker*-esque tone, but they were edging closer to it, especially online. The urgency of the national situation seemed to demand a strident response. Besides, audiences loved it—this much was clear to anyone who so much as glanced at the social analytics. The stridency, in turn, only heightened Trump's sense that the press was the enemy of the people—or, at least, the enemy of him, the only person he seemed to care about.

One morning, while Wintrich was out of town, I went to the briefing room by myself. When I arrived, around 11:00 A.M., the reporters were in a frenzy.

"The president just said he was gonna do a press conference!" someone announced. It would be his first solo press conference since taking office.

"He is? When?"

"In an hour, I think? He just said it, out of nowhere."

"*What?*"

"Does he know that 'press conference' means he has to take questions? Like, from multiple people?"

"How should I know what he knows?"

Kyle Mazza strolled by, carrying two cans of vending-machine tuna.

Ostensibly, Trump was going to announce his new pick for secretary of labor. But the hope was that he would also take questions on other subjects, including the Russia scandal. The reporters lined up, waiting to be escorted into the East Room. Normally, a seating plan is drawn up in advance; this press conference, organized on a presidential whim, would be a free-for-all. A few correspondents tried to elbow their way toward the front of the pack.

"OK, guys, nice and orderly," a press aide said.

"We'll get orderly when you're orderly," a TV correspondent muttered under his breath.

The reporters were led down the marble hallway and into the ballroom. They fanned out across several rows of seats: *The Huffington Post* near the front, *Newsmax* in the middle, NPR near the back. Kyle Mazza pushed through the pack and dove into a third-row seat.

Jim Acosta, CNN's White House correspondent, walked toward the front of the room and stood on a wooden riser, facing a camera. He had a conversation, via earpiece, with the anchor Jake Tapper; the rest of the room listened, in tense silence, to Acosta's side of the conversation. "That's right, Jake," Acosta said. "I sure hope this is not fake news." The reporters in the room laughed; the White House staffers did not.

When the TV hit was over, a White House staffer named Boris Epshteyn said, "Jim's trying to get on *SNL*."

"Did that work?" Acosta asked, playing along.

"Nope," Epshteyn responded, stone-faced.

Trump entered twenty minutes late, spent less than a minute discussing his secretary of labor pick, and then got down to business. It became clear that he intended to deliver not so much a press conference as an antipress conference.

"I'm making this presentation directly to the American people, with the media present—which is an honor, to have you this morning—because many of our nation's reporters and folks will not tell you the truth," he said. This sentence contained a misstatement—it was actually afternoon—which was the first of dozens of misstatements, ranging from the trivial to the risible to the potentially impeachable. He was asked repeatedly whether his campaign had any links to Russian officials. He denied the charge succinctly—"Russia is fake news"—and then again at more length: "Russia is a ruse. I have nothing to do with Russia. Haven't made a phone call to Russia in years. Don't speak to people from Russia. Not that I wouldn't, but I just have nobody to speak to. I spoke to Putin twice."

It went on like this for more than an hour. "I do get good ratings, you have to admit that," the president said. As reporters asked questions, he assessed their performances in real time, pitted them against one another, and, like a power-drunk Merlin, ordered them to stand or sit, speak or go silent. I'd seen the most outrageous highlights from Trump's campaign rallies, of course, but most of those were held in airplane hangars or football stadiums. In such venues, Trump did what any stadium act would do: cranked up the volume and played the hits. This press conference was his solo acoustic set. Judging it purely as a technical performance, I found it far more impressive. He had such a limited rhetorical toolkit—a meager lexicon, a warped memory, a weirdly specific kind of monotonal charisma—and yet, with those rudimentary implements, he was able to do so much. He was a vocalist with a raspy timbre and a half-octave range, but he sang with feeling.

At one point, Trump called on April Ryan, who is African American. "This is going to be a bad question," he said. "But that's OK."

Ryan asked a question about Trump's "urban agenda."

"That was very professional and very good," the president said, as if speaking to a child.

Ryan, who had been a White House correspondent for twenty years, said, "I'm very professional."

Trump rambled for a while, likening the city of Chicago to Hell, before asking Ryan if the members of the Congressional Black Caucus were "friends of yours."

"No, no," Ryan answered. "I'm just a reporter."

During a moment of crosstalk, Kyle Mazza stood and asked a question about Melania Trump. "She does a lot of great work for the country," Mazza said. "Can you talk a little bit about what First Lady Melania Trump does for the country?"

"Now *that's* what I call a nice question," Trump said, jabbing a finger in Mazza's direction. "Who are you with?"

"UNF News," Mazza said.

"Good," Trump said. "I'm going to start watching."

The reporters were escorted back to the briefing room, where they exchanged shell-shocked smiles. "Did he literally say 'Russia is fake news'?" one reporter asked another, checking his notes. A correspondent who had covered Latin American dictatorships said, "Who's the banana republic now?" Another journalist kept repeating the word "surreal" more than a dozen times, under his breath.

When Ryan walked in, several people looked up at her with wry sympathy.

"Do you know every black person in the country, April?"

"April, I have a black friend in Cleveland—could you send him a message for me?"

Ryan shook her head and smiled. "I mean, I can't even," she said, and left it at that.

The reporters dispersed to file their stories. They were trying to use the tools at their disposal—asking pointed questions, highlighting contradictory answers—to challenge Trump's mendacity, his volatility, his thinly veiled racism. They were also, simply by doing their jobs as they'd been trained to do them, legitimizing and disseminating Trump's message. He had invited the press corps into an elegant ballroom in order to debase them, and they had broadcast their debasement live, on TV and on Twitter. It was the metamedia equivalent of the schoolyard bully tactic known as "Why are you hitting yourself?" To some viewers, Trump came off as childish and incompetent, and the press seemed diligent, perhaps even heroic. To other viewers, Trump looked like their embattled, stalwart president, and the press looked like a bunch of braying jackals. Either way, the ratings were terrific.

I texted Wintrich to ask if he'd been watching. "SO FUCKING GOOD," he replied. "Incredibly disappointed I wasn't there for it." Even if he had been there, though, his skills would have been superfluous. The press conference had been handled by the world's most gifted media troll, the president of the United States.

CHAPTER TWENTY-FOUR

Success and Empire

A month and a half after the DeploraBall, one of the party's co-organizers, Jeff Giesea, invited a few friends to meet for drinks in the lobby of the Trump International Hotel on Pennsylvania Avenue. "This is an informal 'MAGA meetup,'" he wrote in an email. He wanted to keep up the momentum he'd felt on inauguration weekend, to continue building a grassroots movement. "It's up to us to redefine conservatism for the next generation," Giesea told me—by which he meant the alt-light, or the New Right, or whatever the non-white-nationalist half of the movement was calling itself.

MAGA Meetups became a monthly affair. Whenever I was in D.C., I spent time in the lobby of the Trump Hotel; even on nights when no official meetup was scheduled, I always ran into a few familiar Deplorables. One night, Wintrich and Cassandra Fairbanks were sitting on an overstuffed velvet couch with Yoni and Mary Clare Amselem, who'd hosted the pregame party before the DeploraBall.*

"I'm thinking of starting a podcast," Yoni said. "Everyone's so *safe* and *boring* these days. I wanna invite Louis Farrakhan to debate a white nationalist from Sweden—you know, provocative stuff. Provocative is fun, right?"

The lobby was nine stories high and covered with a glass ceiling, like a gigantic greenhouse or the interior of a cruise ship. Liveried employees stood at attention against every wall. "This is my safe space," Fairbanks said. "I have to worry about

---

*The four of them had met for the first time on inauguration weekend, but they'd since become fast friends; when the Amselems got married a few months later, Wintrich and Fairbanks attended the wedding.

getting harassed by Antifa everywhere else. Here, people leave me the fuck alone. Plus, my daughter loves it—she calls it Trump's Palace.''

Corey Lewandowski stood in the middle of the lobby, backslapping with a few bros and granting the occasional selfie to an admirer. The volatile first manager of Trump's 2016 campaign, Lewandowski was fired for various indiscretions that may or may not have included assaulting a female reporter. He then became a freelance political consultant, and, for a while, one of the token pro-Trump commentators on CNN.

"Were you on good terms with anyone there?" an admirer asked.

Lewandowski made a sour face. "I talked to Jeff Lord, Kayleigh, and Jason Miller," he said—three of the other Trumpists on the network. "The rest of 'em can kiss my ass, honestly."

The music was insipid EDM played at low volume. The scent was Ivanka Trump by Ivanka Trump. (Men's fragrances—Success by Trump, Empire by Trump—were available for sale in the gift shop.) Donald Trump Jr. sat a few feet away, drinking wine with a retinue, while a Secret Service agent stood watch nearby. Kellyanne Conway and Anthony Scaramucci, two of the president's favorite TV surrogates of the moment, had been spotted eating dinner, at separate tables, in the steakhouse adjacent to the lobby.

Entering the Trump Hotel felt like visiting an exclusive club in a fledgling autocracy—a society where all power flows from a single source, and where the only way to get ahead is to put your body and your cash as close to that source as possible. A huge inert American flag hung from the rafters, perpendicular to the floor; the stripes pointed down at the bar, with its backlit imperial bottles of Trump Blanc de Blanc and its bank of four huge flatscreens (Fox News, Bloomberg, CNN, ESPN). I met Brad Parscale, the Trump campaign's digital strategist, who told me that he'd be happy to talk anytime, then ignored my subsequent emails. I met Katrina Pierson, a talking head and Trump booster for hire, who told me that she loved my work, although she clearly said that to everyone. I met irate soccer moms, bow-tie-wearing libertarians, tatted-up Proud Boys, and 4chan shitlords who seemed flummoxed by the mechanics of face-to-face conversation. I met a former Marine wearing a hunting vest, a wealthy deaconess from Nigeria wearing a gaudy church hat, and several young bureaucrats who had just joined the State Department. The lobby was the embodiment of the MAGA coalition— a big tent stretched across a motley swamp. Trump had won. The libs had been triggered. Now the Deplorables drank together in the same glassed-in atrium, listening to the same elevator music, trying to figure out what they actually had in common.

•   •   •

Most of the organizational duties for MAGA Meetups fell to Will Chamberlain, a lawyer in his thirties, and to Jane Ruby, a health economist in her sixties. Whenever I was around, Ruby took on the demeanor of a combative den mother. "So you're, like, embedded behind enemy lines, is that the deal?" she asked me.

"Pretty much," I replied.

"And why should we let you do that?" she said.

"Jane, come on," Fairbanks said, giggling to relieve the tension.

Every time I showed up, Ruby's defenses softened a bit. She kept asking me why I was drawn to the movement, and I told her: I wanted to listen, I wanted to learn, I wanted to understand where my country was headed. This was true, but it left out a lot.

Whenever one of the Deplorables asked why I was always hanging around, I said, "I'm writing a book." Much of the time, the response was, "Oh, cool, me too." Jack Posobiec's book was called *Citizens for Trump: The Inside Story of the People's Movement to Take Back America.* Lauren Southern's book was called *Barbarians: How Baby Boomers, Immigrants, and Islam Screwed My Generation.* Jane Ruby's book was called *A Sea of New Media,* a title she took from a 2010 speech by Andrew Breitbart. "There's room in my mind for the possibility that he was murdered," she told me, referring to a conspiracy theory that Breitbart had been assassinated, possibly by either Putin or Obama.

Will Chamberlain was a Trumpist and a nationalist, but he didn't indulge in urban-legend paranoia. When I brought up Alex Jones, he rolled his eyes and said, "No comment." Many alt-light figureheads, when confronted with the overt racism and anti-Semitism espoused by the alt-right, acted coy, or resorted to false-equivalence dodges. When I asked Chamberlain about the alt-right's bigotry, he said, "It's appalling and contemptible, and it's our job to expel it from our side."*

---

*"My mom happens to be Jewish," Chamberlain added. "Even if she weren't, though, I'd like to think that being anti-anti-Semitic would still be an easy call." Yet he remained a steadfast champion of the alt-light, despite its repeated lapses into nativism and misogyny and xenophobia. "I try to look at how persuasion actually works in the world," Chamberlain told me. "Ted Cruz wins on purely logocentric terms, but Trump outpersuades him every time." Talking to Chamberlain about politics felt a bit like talking to a young-earth creationist about

Chamberlain was an anomaly among his circle in that he seemed to have genuine beliefs—or to have, at least, enough pride to be embarrassed by wanton hypocrisy. It was fascinating to watch him interact with people like Wintrich, who exhibited no such hang-ups. Once, during a cocktail party in his living room, Wintrich dismissed the White House scandal of the day by saying, "Honestly, I think the real problem here is the Deep State media."

"Is it, though?" Chamberlain asked. He straightened in his chair: this was a debate he could surely win. "Does the administration's incompetence not make more sense, as an Occam's razor explanation?" Then he paused and took a sip of bourbon. As much as he enjoyed arguing, his larger goal was to build bridges within the movement, not to burn them.

Fairbanks, playing peacemaker, said, "Whatever happens, we all know the Clintons and the McCains of this world would be a whole lot worse."

Chamberlain reclined and lifted his glass. "I'll drink to that," he said.

---

dinosaurs. I considered some of his core beliefs (for example, that Donald Trump should be trusted with a nuclear arsenal) to be irrational almost to the point of incomprehensibility; but once we agreed to disagree on a few core premises, we could start to have a conversation. Ultimately, I thought of him as a hypercontrarian—the kind of guy who was so eager to be red-pilled that he would swallow any capsule with a pinkish hue, without first bothering to check whether it was laced with hemlock. In the 1950s, the psychologist Leon Festinger coined the phrase "cognitive dissonance" to describe a mental state caused by trying to hold two or more irreconcilable beliefs simultaneously. The more obviously the beliefs clash, Festinger posited, the greater the believer's need for "social support." Thus, the more time passed without Jesus returning to Earth (or without Trump starting to act "presidential"), the more loudly and desperately the millennialist Christian (or the ardent Trumpist) could be expected to proselytize to the unconverted.

CHAPTER TWENTY-FIVE

The Bright Day That Brings Forth the Adder

On April 29, 2017, at the Washington Hilton, the White House Correspondents' Association held its annual banquet. Trump declined to attend, the first time a sitting president had done so in more than a quarter century. (The last president to miss the dinner, Ronald Reagan, had a good excuse: he'd just been shot.)

By way of counterprogramming, the Deplorables hosted a party at Shelly's Back Room, the cigar bar across the street from the National Press Club. "Those people who are meeting across town, at the White House Correspondents' Dinner—those people are not the ones who are telling the truth," Jim Hoft, who had flown in from St. Louis, said over a PA system. The Deplorables were calling their party the Real News Gala. The theme was the 1980s, presumably the decade when America was most recently great.

There were about a hundred guests scattered throughout the bar. Gavin McInnes wore a studded denim vest, and his face was smeared with dirt. "This is how I dressed in the eighties," he said. "I was an anarchist punk then, and I think in many ways I still am." Mike Flynn Jr., smoking a cigar and wearing a *Golden Girls* T-shirt, looked up at a TV that was tuned to Fox News. A photo of his father, who was under investigation for having failed to disclose payments from Russia, flashed on the screen.

Between speeches, Jim Hoft stood in a corner interviewing Cassandra Fairbanks about her recent visit to the White House briefing room. She live-tweeted their conversation, he filmed it on his phone, and Jeremy Segal, one of the documentarians from Chicago, filmed them both. I stood nearby, taking notes. Turtles all the way down.

When dinner was served, the Deplorables split into tables. The sorting seemed to happen automatically, by unconscious simian logic: one table for A-list demicelebrities, other tables for B-listers, C-listers, and so on.* I maneuvered my way toward the A-list table and pulled up a chair.

Cernovich sized me up. "You look bigger, bro," he said. "You been lifting?"

"He's sitting with us?" McInnes said.

"Let him do his thing, man," Cernovich said. "He doesn't put us on a pedestal, but he doesn't lie about us."

"He's the fucking media!" McInnes said. "Why do we keep talking about them being the enemy and then letting them eavesdrop on our conversations?" I had no intention of saying so, but I thought that McInnes made a good point.

Hoft ordered appetizers, and I spooned some hummus onto my plate. McInnes stared at me. "Are you a *Jew*?" he asked. "I've never seen a *Jew* use a spoon like that. They usually just pick up the pita and dive in with their hands."†

The B-listers kept fleeing the relative stigma of their table to hover near the A-listers. "It's just a meme!" Laura Loomer said to McInnes, making the OK hand gesture. "I swear, the media has zero chill." Since leaving Project Veritas, Loomer had started specializing in street confrontations, the more confrontational the better. She filmed them all, of course, posting the footage to multiple social networks with the hashtag #Loomered. These encounters—most of them with Democratic politicians or mainstream journalists, such as CNN anchors—never yielded anything newsworthy, but they were spectacularly uncomfortable to watch. If shows like *Curb Your Enthusiasm* were cringe comedy, then Loomer's Loomerings could be called cringe viral content.

"We have a surprise for you," Hoft announced after dinner. "We have a Thrilla in . . . wherever we're at." It was an eighties-themed dance-off: Gavin McInnes versus James O'Keefe of Project Veritas. McInnes went first, shimmying to "Let's Go Crazy," by Prince, and ending his routine with the Worm. Then O'Keefe, in a fedora, performed Michael Jackson's choreography to "Billie Jean," including

---

*The simplest metric, as usual, was the size of each demicelebrity's Twitter following—most of the A-listers had follower counts in the six figures—but there were other metrics as well. Jeff Giesea qualified for the A-list table not because of his social media following but because of his wealth, and because he was an effective behind-the-scenes organizer. Jack Posobiec, who had more than a hundred thousand Twitter followers, was shunted to the B-list table, perhaps because he was too young and overbearing.

†In 2017, Cynthia Baker, a professor of religious studies at Bates College, wrote a book called *Jew*, about the contested history of the word. "Jew, for some, is a term of deep pride," she wrote; "for others, it is a term of deep loathing."

some tightly controlled spins and a passable moonwalk. As measured by crowd applause, O'Keefe was the clear winner. "Fuck that guy," McInnes said. "He just memorized a bunch of moves. I was dancing from the heart."

•   •   •

A few weeks later, I was in Fairbanks's living room in the D.C. suburbs, watching her try halfheartedly to write a blog post. She had just left Sputnik to join a new media start-up called *Big League Politics*. On the back of her laptop was a decal with an image of Andrew Breitbart, his eyes shut tight with rage, next to the word #WAR.

She got a text. "Roger Stone's speaking at the Young Republican Club in D.C. in an hour," she told me. "Wanna come with?"

Stone stood before a poorly ventilated room full of Capitol staffers. "A feature documentary about me recently appeared on Netflix," he said. "Even though the film was made by two leftist elitist maggots, it's still worth watching." In the audience were Wintrich, Posobiec, and Jane Ruby, who had taken to calling me the Embed. She was hosting a MAGA Meetup that night, at the Trump Hotel, and she'd just asked Stone to make a guest appearance. "The whole time I was asking him, he was staring at my chest," she said. "So I think that's a sign he might actually show up."

Posobiec was exuding even more manic intensity than usual. Recently, in Poland, Trump had delivered a speech that was rife with hypernationalist rhetoric. The decision to give the address in Poland, one of the European countries where nationalist sentiment was most resurgent, was as symbolically significant, in its way, as Ronald Reagan's decision to give a stump speech in Neshoba County, Mississippi. "I did *not* have anything to do with drafting the Poland speech," Posobiec stage-whispered, glancing in my direction to make sure I was listening. "I just somehow knew all the talking points on my Periscope the day before."

On one of my previous trips to D.C., Fairbanks had texted me a YouTube link. "I keep thinking of this scene when you come to stuff," she wrote, "because everyone is so determined to get you to switch." It was a clip from the 1932 film *Freaks*: a group of sideshow performers attempting to initiate a "normal" woman into their clique.

"I hear you're placing bets on who can convert him," Ruby said.

"I'm going to red-pill him first," Wintrich said.

"We've already red-pilled him," Posobiec said. "He just doesn't know it yet." I didn't bother responding to this. They were probably just trolling anyway.

In the clip, the sideshow performers grow increasingly excited at the prospect of the woman's impending conversion. Their anticipation crescendos in a group chant—"One of us! One of us!"—until the woman breaks the spell by throwing a drink on one of the circus performers, causing them all to slink away in shame. That movie was made a long time ago. These days, shame, like so much else, isn't what it used to be.

•   •   •

For a while, I'd been wondering when I would be done with the Deplorables. I'd had my fill of interminable nights beneath Wintrich's gemsbok, making spur-of-the-moment decisions about whether to appear in another Periscope or whether to interrupt another awful joke. I was so familiar with their favorite talking points that I could practically transcribe their spin in my notebook before they spun it. Maybe it was time for us to part ways.

My son was born. I spent hours watching his eyes widen, watching his eyelids flutter closed, watching his chest rise and fall as he slept—the precise karmic antithesis of all the hours I'd spent wading through the muck of the neofascist internet. "You're in for quite a ride," Mike Cernovich told me in a congratulatory voice message. "The first three months suck—anyone who tells you otherwise is giving you fake news—but after that it's amazing." Maybe now I could stop returning Cernovich's calls. Maybe, instead of tracking the minutiae of the Seth Rich murder investigation or the Uranium One deal, I could use that brain space to think about art, or cooking, or politicians who fell within the normal range of mendacity and moral rot.

My wife and I split each night into two shifts, one of us staying on child-care duty while the other slept. One night, at around ten, I fed the kid a bottle and he fell asleep on my shoulder. With my free hand, only half conscious of what I was doing, I grabbed my phone, untangled a pair of earbuds, and opened Periscope.

"Shame on the New York Public Theater for doing this!" Laura Loomer was shouting. She was in Central Park, crashing the stage during an outdoor performance of *Julius Caesar*. In this production, Caesar was dressed as Donald Trump; Loomer resented this attempt at dramatic catharsis, so she'd decided to #Loomer

Shakespeare. "Stop the normalization of political violence against the right!" she was shouting. "You guys are ISIS! CNN is ISIS!" (The latter was a non sequitur, but she couldn't help it.)

She was dragged offstage and arrested. Then Jack Posobiec, who was also in the audience, stood up and shouted, "Goebbels would be proud!" He, too, was removed, and the show went on. "Liberty! Freedom! Tyranny is dead!" an actor declared. "Run hence, proclaim, cry it about the streets."

Posobiec texted to tell me that he was in the lobby of a police station on East Sixty-seventh Street. He was waiting for Loomer to be released, at which point they would head to a late-night burger joint nearby.

Around midnight, I roused my wife as gently as possible. "Sorry, honey," I said. "Kid's asleep in the bassinet. I've gotta go to the Upper East Side and have a burger with some Deplorables."

"A . . . burger?" she said, still half asleep.

Franklin Wright, a burly Proud Boy, was accompanying Loomer for the night, acting as her Periscope cameraman and security detail. He and Posobiec ordered cheeseburgers; Loomer ordered a bowl of chili. They looked at their phones in silence for a while. Loomer had been released with a ticket for misdemeanor trespassing; as we ate, #FreeLaura picked up momentum on Twitter, even though she was already free. "It's more in the metaphorical sense," she explained. "Helping with my legal fees, that sort of thing."

"You're the number four trending hashtag right now," Posobiec said.

"Amazing," Loomer said. "Can you screenshot that and send it to me?"

Laura Ingraham and Sean Hannity tweeted their support of Loomer, and she booked an appearance on Hannity's show the next day.

David French, an anti-Trump Republican, tweeted criticism of Loomer: "Which conservative principle does the heckler's veto advance?"

"Who is this guy French?" Loomer said. "Is he a liberal?"

"He's *National Review*," Posobiec said.

"Oh," Loomer said, rolling her eyes. "Who gives a shit about him?"

"They're just jealous, man," Posobiec said.

Richard Spencer disparaged Loomer, also on free-speech grounds, and suggested a counter-hashtag: #LockUpLaura.

"Fucking Spencer," Posobiec said.

Loomer workshopped several possible rejoinders to Spencer, tweeting the ones that got the best response at the table. "You can't stand the fact that a Jew is in the spotlight," she tweeted. "Oh and by the way, it's (((LAURA)))." Looking up, she said, "I'm thinking of saying '1939 much?' Or should I go with 1945?"

I signaled for the check.

"Andrew! Almost forgot," Posobiec said. "We're doing a rally next weekend in front of the White House. You *gotta* be there."

The Deplorables held rallies all the time. But this one would be different, Posobiec promised, because the leading figures of the alt-right—Mike Enoch, Nathan Damigo, Richard Spencer—would be at the Lincoln Memorial, a mile away, hosting their own competing rally. "It's a line in the sand," Posobiec said. "American nationalists over here, white nationalists over there."

"There's a battle right now for the soul of the movement," Loomer said, putting her phone down and looking me in the eye. "We're done with the Nazi bullshit. You can be a cuckservative, you can go be a Nazi, or you can be on our side, the reasonable side."*

I texted Cernovich to ask whether he'd be speaking at the White House rally. He replied that he would—the media kept calling him alt-right, and he was at pains to leave the label behind. "I want the separation to be clear," he wrote. "Alt-right is a toxic brand now, and it's only going to get worse."

•   •   •

A cab dropped me off outside the Hay-Adams hotel. As I walked, I listened to the civic-nationalist rally on Fairbanks's Periscope feed; two minutes later, when I got close enough to hear the rally in real life, I took out my earbuds and put my phone in my pocket.

A crowd of a few dozen people stood around a portable stage. All the core members of MAGA Meetups were in attendance, either as speakers or as supporters. Jack Posobiec emceed the event. Wintrich and Fairbanks gave a joint speech about leftist violence. I spotted Jeff Giesea and Jack Murphy, who were about to walk to the Lincoln Memorial to check out the alt-right rally. They invited me to tag along.

Murphy was the tall, bearded blogger who had nearly come to blows with Richard Spencer after the DeploraBall. "I would have beaten the shit out of him if

---

*Loomer, on Twitter, had once inaccurately quoted Winston Churchill—"Islam is as dangerous in a man as rabies in a dog"—and then added, "When a dog has rabies, you have to kill it."

Cernovich hadn't broken it up," Murphy told me as we walked toward the National Mall. "I would have been happy to, because conflict is attention, and also because I would have enjoyed it." Murphy was at work on a book called *Democrat to Deplorable.* "I was an Obama voter," he said, "but I took one look at intersectional feminism and went, 'Nope. If that's the left, I'm out.'" He added that he was equally opposed to the ethnonationalism of the alt-right. "Maybe it's because I'm half Jewish," he said. "But I don't think you need to know the difference between nova and belly lox to be able to figure out that an ethnostate in America makes absolutely no fucking sense."

"I still talk with some of the alt-right guys," Giesea said quietly. "I can see how some of their grievances might be legitimate."

When we got to the steps of the Lincoln Memorial, Chris Cantwell, a thick-necked man with a honking Long Island accent, was in the middle of a speech. "At what point do we begin physically removing Democrats and Communists to establish and maintain the libertarian social order necessary for our desired meritocracy?" he shouted. He was paraphrasing an argument by Hans-Hermann Hoppe, a hard-right political philosopher whose work seemed to justify preemptive murder. "Nonwhite immigration and breeding alone are rapidly diminishing what electoral majorities we have remaining," Cantwell continued. "Jewish influence disarms us."

Murphy raised his eyebrows. "Looks like we've found their rally," he said.

There was no stage, no lectern, just a granite landing with two loudspeakers and a handheld microphone. The alt-right leaders stood in a small semicircle, vaping and checking their phones, before stepping forward, one by one, to speak. On the stairs behind them stood a row of young men holding flags: the American flag, the Confederate flag, the teal-and-white flag of an American white-nationalist organization called Identity Evropa. "America was founded by white people," Nathan Damigo, the founder of Identity Evropa, had said during his speech. "It was founded *for* white people. America was not founded to be a multiracial, multicultural society."

The penultimate speaker was the founder of *The Right Stuff*, Mike Enoch—tall and stout, with a grim, downturned mouth. "Let's be honest," Enoch said. "What's really facing our country today is systematic elimination of white people—the displacement and genocide of the white race."

A tourist, riding by on a rented bike, shouted, "Where's your common sense at, though?"

———

Having spent so much time straining to hear dog whistles, I was surprised by how surprising it was to be face-to-face with the dog itself. Yet again, I felt forced into the role of the pearl-clutching traditionalist. The white nationalists had chosen this location on purpose: holding their march on the National Mall, where Martin Luther King had spoken fifty-four years earlier, was part of the troll. All day long, Richard Spencer had been live-tweeting the event with the hashtag #IHaveAMeme. The whole point was to upset the normies.

Well, they got me. I was upset. I just didn't know what to do with that feeling.

I got back to the alt-light rally shortly after it ended. A vaporwave instrumental was playing on someone's Bluetooth stereo. Posobiec and Mike Flynn Jr., who had been sitting on the portable stage, had to get down to let the rental company cart it away.

Jane Ruby led the way to a rooftop bar, and about a dozen Deplorables sat at a banquette with a view of the Washington Monument, discussing their branding strategy. "The alt-right keeps labeling us alt-light, but I don't think we should give in to that," Loomer said.

"Yeah, you don't want to define yourself as the absence of something," Cernovich said. "Although there is precedent for it—7UP, the uncola. So it has worked at least once."

"I think New Right is the best of the ones I've heard so far," Chamberlain said. Cernovich nodded. "New Right is my favorite," he said.

The sun shifted so that it hit the back of Chamberlain's neck. "I should move before I burn up," he said, adding, "How could white supremacy be true if I can't even sit in the sun for five minutes?"

The group ended up, inevitably, in the lobby of the Trump Hotel. Corey Stewart, a revanchist Republican and an unsuccessful candidate for governor of Virginia, sat on a divan explaining why Confederate monuments must be preserved. Stewart—a son of Duluth, Minnesota, who now lived in a restored plantation house in Virginia—had clearly made the calculation that the best way to advance his political career in Trump's America was to pander to racists, more or less openly. It was the Southern Strategy: Post-Subtlety Edition. Earlier that day, he had spoken at the alt-light rally, proclaiming, "We need to stand up to the politically correct madness that is destroying our history." I asked him how far he was willing to extend that sentiment. Why, for example, had he chosen to join the alt-light speakers in front of the White House instead of the alt-right history buffs denouncing Jewish influence from the steps of the Lincoln Memorial? Didn't they, too, claim to be custodians of the Founders' legacy?

"I don't like getting into all that," Stewart replied. "I don't choose sides. I just know there's a kind of energy on the New Right, or alternative right, or whatever you want to call it, and I'm trying to plug into that."

In 2018, Stewart ran for U.S. Senate from Virginia, beating two challengers to secure the Republican nomination. He lost the general election, but he won a majority of the white vote.

●   ●   ●

"It looks like those alt-right guys you saw in D.C. are planning another rally," my wife told me over dinner a few nights later. "In Charlottesville, Virginia. I just saw something on Facebook about it."

"They're always planning another rally," I said. They'd already been to Charlottesville once before, in May. A few dozen of them had stood around a statue of Robert E. Lee, carrying Tiki torches, without attracting much interest. Before that, it was Pikeville, Kentucky. "It's just gonna be some sad, LARP-y dudes doing Nazi salutes," I said. "I'd rather not take the bait."

"Up to you," she said. "Seems like this one's gonna be a big deal."

"I don't want to blow them out of proportion," I said. "They're on the margins, which is where they belong." In a narrow sense, I was right. In a broader, more important sense, I was wrong.

The Past Is Absolute

> **August 12, 2017, 1:40 P.M.**
> Charlottesville, Virginia
> www.periscope.tv/FaithGoldy
> #Charlottesville DOUBLE STANDARD: antifa allowed to march!!!

Wearing a black baseball cap and carrying a selfie stick, Faith Goldy joins a crowd of counterprotesters as they march through downtown Charlottesville. It's a warm, sunny day. The mood is jubilant. The crowd is diverse in every way: black, white; old, young; crust-punk, normie. For some reason, a few of the counterprotesters are dressed as clowns. Some carry Antifa flags, some carry American flags; one sign reads END WHITE SUPREMACY, another sign reads LOVE REIGNS. Goldy speaks into her phone, narrating the scene.

> Goldy: There's a full-on demonstration now going on in the streets. Hundreds and hundreds of Antifa . . . There's freedom of assembly for one group, but not another.

A white-supremacist rally had been scheduled to take place a mile away, near a statue of Robert E. Lee, but it ended before it began. Protesters and counterprotesters clashed with growing ferocity; the governor declared a state of emergency, and the crowd was ordered to disperse. Now the racists are in retreat and the counterprotesters are triumphant. A chant goes up: "Black lives matter! Black lives matter!"

> Goldy: Imagine. There's no permit for this, guys. They're declaring this a victory.

Onlookers lean out of redbrick buildings, cheering on the marchers as they pass. The crowd chants: "Whose streets? Our streets!"

Goldy: These *are* your streets. Unbelievable. OK, I'm a little bit trapped in here. One second, let me get out to the periphery.

A middle-aged African American woman in a Black Lives Matter T-shirt approaches Goldy and confronts her: "Are you with the alt-right? If you're with the alt-right, get away from here!"

Goldy: I'm just looking to learn about inclusion and diversity. I'm here to learn about multiculturalism, and I'm here to learn about how diverse groups lead to very high-trust societies.

The woman has stopped listening, but Goldy wasn't really talking to her anyway. She glances at the camera, raising her eyebrows sarcastically toward her fans. Then she presses a button, flipping the camera from selfie mode to forward-facing mode.

Goldy: All right, there you go. It's the full-on demonstra—oh, shit! Oh shit. Holy shit. Holy shit. Holy shit. Oh God. Oh God. Oh God.

Visceral screams. Crunching metal, thumping sounds, shattering glass. Piles of mangled bodies. "Go go go go!" "Don't trample people—" "What the fuck?" "Move!" A gray Dodge squeals into reverse. The camera tilts and bobs up toward the sky.

Goldy: I'm gonna find a safe space, guys. Let me find a safe space.

She ducks into an alcove and turns the camera back toward herself—short of breath, covering her mouth with one hand, eyes wide with fear.

Goldy: A lot of people got hit. A lot of people got hit. That does not look good.

She walks back to the street corner and surveys the damage. People standing around dazed, people running in all directions, people screaming for medics. American carnage. Commenters keep typing the license plate of the gray Dodge, hoping that Goldy will see it and report it to the police: GVF 1111. On the ground near Goldy's feet, a woman is bleeding.

Goldy: She's badly hurt. . . . We need medics here right away! . . . There's someone who looks like they're in very bad shape over there.

Nearby, two more women lie on the sidewalk, unmoving. Counterprotesters kneel around them, applying pressure to open wounds, waiting for an ambulance to make its way through the crowd. Goldy speaks to one of the injured women, or tries to.

Goldy: You're gonna be OK, ma'am. You're gonna be OK.

Within the hour, the woman, Heather Heyer, will be confirmed dead.

Interview with Faith Goldy

I was there as a reporter for the Rebel, and I was also streaming on my own Periscope, tweeting on my own feed. It's always sort of intertwined.

My first thought, honestly, was that it was a drum, someone leading a drum line. So I turned, and my camera naturally followed my eyes, and the next thing I saw was the car attack—the, or, the car crash—and I went, Holy hell, this was not what I was expecting to cover. Immediately, after that moment, the city became a very charged environment.

Night falls, and I'm a single white woman on my own—no camera crew, no entourage. I'm six feet tall. I stick out. I don't know who recognizes me in this town, or who has it in for me. A lot of the alt-right guys—Spencer, Enoch—those guys had targets on their backs, too, but there's a lot of them, and there's only one so-called Nazi Barbie. So I stuck to places where I felt safe.

A lot of the spaces—sure, you'd describe them as alt-right spaces. Some of the doors you'd knock on, they wouldn't let you in unless you said the Fourteen Words. I don't consider myself alt-right. I think that term has become toxic. But I get where those guys are coming from, I understand what they're trying to do. And they know me, and I felt that they would protect me.

I walked into one of these—safe houses, I guess you'd call them. There were a bunch of guys there, and they were recording a podcast. I guess in retrospect it was a Nazi podcast or whatever—something called the Krypto Report. They invite me on, and, on the spot, I go, "Yep, sure, of course." Why not? What's wrong with having a conversation?

The Krypto Report, a podcast by the Daily Stormer
Episode XXII: The Charlottesville Putsch
August 12, 2017
Recorded after the rally, at "a super-secret after-party," in front of a live audience

---

Robert Warren Ray, a neo-Nazi who goes by the pseudonym Azzmador, is the host of the podcast. Scraggly gray beard, rattail, East Texas drawl.

> Ray: Now, we have a guest that's probably going to surprise everyone—
> that this guest is coming on an alt-right podcast—but we are cer-
> tainly thrilled to have her. Right here we have Faith Goldy of
> Rebel Media.
>
> Goldy: Thanks for having me on. I'm thrilled.

Goldy doesn't declare allegiance to the neo-Nazis, but she doesn't try to establish much distance, either.

> Goldy: You guys came, you had your permits, and you showed up in
> hordes, and I salute you all for doing just that. Not a Roman
> salute, guys, sorry.

"Roman salute" is alt-right slang for a Hitler salute. The crowd laughs at Goldy's inside joke, and Goldy laughs along with them.

> Goldy: What you have is a bunch of young white men who have been
> completely drenched in nonwhite identity politics. And any-
> time that their own race has been brought up, they're told, "It's
> your fault, you're culpable, and you basically amount to
> zero." . . . And when you tell them that, on top of everything,
> now that they've got this revelation, this sort of enlightenment,
> this renaissance that is occurring, that they can't speak—well,

guess what happens, historically, when you shut people's mouths? They start to resort to fists.

Ray: We can either lay down and allow ourselves to basically be stomped to death by the Orwellian boot standing on your face forever, or we can stand up and oppose it.

Ray goes on a short rant: the violence in Charlottesville was instigated by the left, but the mainstream media will never report it that way. As Ray has explained in many other podcasts and other blog posts, there's a simple reason for this: the Jews control the media, and they don't want the masses thinking for themselves.

Goldy: Context is irrelevant in today's media, right? All that matters is narrative. We know that the cultural Marxists own the media, we know that they own academia, et cetera, and they're pushing a particular narrative. . . . I do not think it is outside of the realm of what's possible that within the next five or ten years, probably closer to five, we will have alt-right men and women running for political office.

The audience erupts in raucous applause.

Later that week, after this podcast episode is released, the Rebel fires Faith Goldy. Her fans are outraged—they don't agree with the Nazis' arguments, necessarily, but they believe in free speech. A comment on YouTube: "Will Rebel Media be changing their name to Conformists Media?"

---

www.reddit.com/r/physical_removal
The #1 place to go on the internet to discuss Hans-Hermann Hoppe's idea of "physical removal."
Other recommended subreddits: r/Anarcho_Capitalism, r/The_Donald, r/Nationalism, r/Guns
Moderators: u/Pinochet-Heli-Tours, u/CapitalJusticeWarrior, u/WhiteSissMail, u/ChrisCantwell
Accessed on August 13, 2017

The background image on the home page is a drawing of a fleet of helicopters riding into the sunset. This is an alt-right meme, a reference to the rumor that Augusto Pinochet used to kill Communists, homosexuals, and other subversives by throwing them out of helicopters. From the About Us page:

> This subreddit is for people who wish to preserve and defend the concepts of free markets, private property, free speech, meritocracy, liberty, and freedom. Those who wish to see the death of any of these ideals qualify to get a helicopter ride as they are a danger to individuals, society, and western culture at large.

The page is full of memes about the Charlottesville march. There are many jubilant jokes about the gray Dodge with the license plate GVF 1111, the car that killed Heather Heyer. The most upvoted post on the page, with dozens of karma points, is called "What happened today with the dead antifa was ethical." From the post:

> Details still remain to be known, as well as motives, but we have at least one dead antifa and 19 others injured. This is a good thing. They are mockeries of life and need to fucking go.

The Daily Shoah 179: Episode #GVF1111
The death panel do a special Charlottesville After Action Report!
Podcast recorded on August 13, 2017
Cohosts: Mike Enoch, Sven, Alex McNabb, Jayoh, Richard Spencer, Eli Mosley

---

Opening sequence: a mash-up of 1980s synth music and an old recording of George W. Bush: "If you don't like what we tell you to believe in, we'll kill you."

> Sven: The big C'ville thing finally happened. . . . Lotta action out there, brought to you by Dodge.

Heather Heyer was a real person, but already her death has become a meme. The cohosts segue to one of their favorite talking points: that Antifa protesters may feel like rebels standing up to the Man, but they're actually just unwitting pawns of the establishment.

Mike Enoch: A lot of our guys were interested in the radical left in their youth, myself included.

Sven: Sure. It's exciting, it's fun.

Mike Enoch: I'm not embarrassed to say that, because it's a common story amongst alt-righters.

Sven: Well, yeah. Who doesn't want to be the cool guy fighting the power?

Mike Enoch: And then you realize you're not the cool guy fighting the power. And you're like, Eh, I'm not interested anymore.

A red pill is a dose of truth; a black pill is a reason to succumb to nihilistic depression; a white pill is a reason to be optimistic. The cohosts explain that, before yesterday's rally, the governor of Virginia declared a state of emergency, ordering law-enforcement officers to forcibly prevent the alt-right from speaking.

Mike Enoch: Now, that's a black pill and a white pill. A black pill because it shows you what we're up against, and a white pill because it shows you that they fear us.

Eli Mosley, the president of Identity Evropa, claims that any alt-right violence was perpetrated in self-defense. The media is reporting that the driver of the Dodge was named James Alex Fields, and that Fields was a member of an alt-right group. But that's fine, the cohosts insist, because the evidence isn't in yet. Maybe his car was being attacked by an Antifa mob. Maybe he panicked and his foot slipped onto the gas pedal. That's for a jury to decide.

Richard Spencer: Stop watching CNN. Stop watching Cernovich. . . . We need to be very strong and put forward this narrative. Mistakes were made, we're gonna learn from this, but, morally speaking, no one did anything wrong.

Mike Enoch: We know the media is going to put a narrative out there. We know they're gonna call us KKK, we know they're gonna call us Nazis. . . . Your job, particularly if you have a presence, if you have a lot of followers, if you're somebody with a voice that is heard, even if you're somebody with only a hundred Twitter followers—put out our narrative, because every little bit helps.

Sven: We have gotten this far just letting people know and showing the hypocrisy and the lies of the media. And, every time, something like this gives these nervous Nellies an opportunity—

Mike Enoch: If CNN is black-pilling you, kill yourself!

Sven: Yes! People don't believe CNN.

Mike Enoch: *Normies* don't believe CNN!

Sven These people are operating under the fucking assumption that it's, like, 1975 and CNN is—well, CNN didn't exist then, but you know what I mean—that CBS is all there is, and everybody believes whatever they say.

Mike Enoch: Wolf Blitzer is not Walter Cronkite.

Closing sequence: a recording of Richard Nixon's farewell address—"Always give your best, never get discouraged, never be petty"—played over the song "Adiós, Mi General," an ode to Augusto Pinochet.

Interview with Faith Goldy

After Charlottesville, I spent a lot of time reading philosophy, getting down to first principles. There's something amazing that happens when all the chattering classes are piling on you—"You're a racist, you're a neo-Nazi, you're this, you're that." The result, in my case at least, is that you start to feel more emboldened. If that's gonna be my reputation no matter what, maybe I should be less ambiguous about what I actually believe.

I think we're at a juncture in our history where the West is going through an ideological crisis. My guess is that the dissident right, if you will, will continue to grow in numbers. You might see it publicly or it might happen behind the scenes, but I don't think it can be contained once it's started. Because what you have is an awakening of racial consciousness among white people. For some people, it's going to lead to a place of white guilt. For others, it's gonna be more like, "Hang on, what the hell do I have to feel guilty about?"

———

In the summer of 2018, Goldy announces her candidacy for mayor of Toronto. Out of thirty-five candidates, she finishes third, with 3.4 percent of the vote. The day she loses the election, she changes her Twitter bio from "Next Mayor of Toronto" to "Next Prime Minister of Canada."

Interviews shortly after Charlottesville

Cassandra Fairbanks:

I refused to report from Charlottesville. Refused to go. Now, seeing what a mess it was, I clearly made the right call. People walking around with swastikas? Are you fucking kidding me? And that woman who died— I retweeted the GoFundMe campaign to raise money for her. It's heartbreaking. At the same time, it's also—I do think the media oversimplifies things. I'm sure there were people there, naïve teenagers or whoever, who didn't necessarily know what they were getting into. 'Cause I'm seeing estimates that there were fifteen hundred people marching? I don't think there are fifteen hundred actual Nazis in this country, I really don't.

Jack Posobiec:

I thought the president got it exactly right. Two fringe groups, on both sides. The alt-left and the alt-right, both pushing their extreme racial identity politics. Except I don't even consider those alt-right guys to be right wing, actually. Because what National Socialists ultimately want is big government, right?

Laura Loomer:

Honestly, we need to destroy the alt-right. I'm telling everyone else in the New Right, or the alt-light, or whatever we are: no more fence sitting. We need to get rid of these people. There are leftists on Twitter trying to dox anyone who showed their face in Charlottesville, and I fully support that. I don't want anything violent to happen to them, but if their families find out? If their employers find out? Look, if you don't want that to happen to you, maybe don't show up at Nazi rallies.

Jeff Giesea:

The rally we saw at the Lincoln Memorial, whatever you might think of it, was at least fairly well staged. They got some iconic memes out of it, at least. The images I'm seeing from this just make them look like idiots.

Jack Murphy:

This is their downfall. They can't recover from this.

Mike Cernovich:

If you study humanity, if you study patterns, none of this is surprising. All signs point toward further polarization. Hard left, hard right. I've been anticipating blood in the streets—not wanting it, but ready for it. To me, I'd be tempted to turn this into a narrative of "To what extent is the mainstream hoaxing fake-news media responsible for creating this atmosphere? You've got a few hundred of these idiots out there, and CNN's making them famous—why, just to stoke racial tension?" So that's maybe how I would spin it.

Will Chamberlain:

Appalling. Disgusting. Frightening. Contemptible.*

---

*As I compiled my notes from these conversations, it struck me that the alt-light demicelebrities who expressed the most shock and outrage about the neo-Nazis were also the ones who happened to be Jewish. I wasn't sure what to make of this—small sample size, and correlation doesn't prove causation—but I couldn't help noticing the pattern.

———

I watched the images spread across Twitter: hundreds of torches winding through the University of Virginia's campus, the flames leaping into the night sky. It was late. I tried half sleeping, not sleeping, half reading, not reading. I opened my laptop in the middle of the night, pulled up a blank Word document, sat for a while in the pallid light of the screen. Closed the laptop. The same distended febrile feeling, suddenly unignorable again.

Was the Charlottesville rally newsworthy, in some objective sense, or would it have been better if the media and everyone else had looked the other way? This wasn't a question with an answer; it wasn't even really a question, not anymore. Was the abduction of Charles Lindbergh's baby intrinsically newsworthy? What about O.J.'s car chase in the white Bronco, or Monica's blue dress, or Obama's birth certificate? Once something becomes an ur-text that the whole nation is reading simultaneously, the conversation shifts. It's past time to wonder whether to say something. You just have to figure out what to say.

PART FIVE

The American Berserk

. . . into the indigenous American berserk . . . the
acculturating back-and-forth that all of us here grew up with,
the ritual postimmigrant struggle for success turning
pathological . . .

Philip Roth, 1997

CHAPTER TWENTY-SIX

The Emptiness

I was on a southbound Amtrak, heading to D.C. to cover the DeploraBall, when I learned that Mike Enoch had been doxed.

The name was unfamiliar to most Americans, MSNBC viewers and Fox News viewers alike; but to an inner cadre of web-fluent neofascists, Enoch was an influential and divisive figure. An article on AltRight.com once lauded his "superlative talent as both an orator and a philosopher." "Hate him or love him," David Duke tweeted, "Mike Enoch is someone to pay close attention to."

Just three years prior, Enoch could be heard mocking the likes of Duke and Richard Spencer, criticizing their ideologies as too extreme. But that was before Enoch's radicalization was complete. By the time Trump started running for president, Enoch was openly advocating for a white ethnostate, expressing "skepticism" about how many Jews had died in the Holocaust, and referring to African Americans as "chimps" and "savages." Liberals who claimed to have compassion for undocumented children were "full of shit," Enoch explained, "particularly when it's coming out of the mouths of these smarmy Jews. You're not a compassionate group of people. You're one of the most selfish, vindictive groups of people on the face of the fucking planet." He didn't self-identify as a neo-Nazi, but not because he saw anything wrong with it. "LARPing like it's 1940s Germany isn't my thing," he said at one point. "I think we need a nationalism that's symbolically in line with our time and place. But if one of our guys wants to do the swastika bit, whatever, I'm not gonna countersignal that."

He granted interviews to alt-right-friendly outlets but eschewed encounters with the mainstream media, or tried to turn those encounters to his advantage. When a CNN reporter called him to ask for an on-camera interview, he recorded the phone call, subjecting her to several minutes of painfully awkward banter, before rejecting her request: "Why would I let somebody else twist my words when I am fully capable of getting my message out myself?" He preferred to speak—volubly, articulately, vindictively—on his own podcast, *The Daily Shoah*. The title was a pun about the Holocaust by way of Comedy Central. Like much of Enoch's material, the pun could be interpreted either as a breathtakingly repugnant affront or simply as an edgy meme.

The Daily Shoah had a rotating cast of cohosts, most of whom used pseudonyms: Sven, Toilet Law, Ebolamericana, Death. "Mike Enoch" was a pseudonym, too. Over the years, he occasionally dropped hints about his identity, although he was careful not to reveal too much. He said that he lived with his wife in New York City—"which narrows it down to me and eight million other people"—and that he worked at a normie day job, which he would surely lose if his employers ever learned of his alter ego. His parents were "shitlibs," and they'd trained him to be one, too; as a child, they'd sent him to church camps and public schools, where he'd been "programmed" to believe in racial equality and the brotherhood of man. "If you're a liberal, you've never thought twice, you've never reconsidered, you've absorbed what you were taught in the government schools and by the TV," he wrote. But he was one of the few who'd been able to subvert the programming. After years of struggle, he had learned how to think his way out of the Narrative.

When Enoch's identity was revealed, *Salon* posted an article about it. I tried to open the article on my laptop, but the wi-fi on the train was painfully slow, and the article was laden with pop-up ads and autoplay videos, so it took several minutes to load. While I waited, I tried to open Enoch's blog, *The Right Stuff*, in another tab. I was in a window seat; sitting in the aisle seat next to me was a middle-aged woman. Sweater, reading glasses, bangs: a suburban professional, if I had to guess, maybe an optometrist from Bethesda or a professor at a local college. I angled my screen toward the window, a movement I now made so often, in so many public places, that I often did it without thinking.

The wi-fi went out. I started streaming an episode of *The Daily Shoah* on my phone instead. The suburban professional was reading a paperback novel about a beach house, several generations of women, and whether the mistakes of the past can ever be forgiven. Two feet away from her, in my earbuds, Mike Enoch was talking about gassing the kikes and turning their skin into lampshades.

He was joking. Was he joking? Clearly, he was not issuing an imminent and credible threat to put specific Jews inside an extant gas chamber. Still, it felt like a stretch to call it a joke, not only because it wasn't funny but also because it didn't have the structure of a joke. It was more like a meme. "How long have we been shitposting for at this point?" one of the cohosts asked.

That's precisely what it was: shitposting. The podcast was a 4chan board come to life, full of naughty words and obscure allusions and meta-ironic gas-chamber memes. The purpose of all the shitposting, beyond the usual trolling and triggering of the libs, seemed to be to desensitize the listener over time—to say the unsayable again and again, until grisly hatred came to seem like just another thing on the internet.

The wi-fi came back on, stronger this time, and the *Salon* article finally finished loading. A group of Antifa-affiliated vigilante journalists, possibly working in collaboration with disgruntled alt-right tipsters, had revealed that Mike Enoch was actually Michael Enoch Isaac Peinovich, a computer programmer who worked at a New York e-publishing company and lived on the Upper East Side. As predicted, he lost his job. Someone printed out color photographs of his face and pasted them to telephone poles on the corner of Eighty-second Street and York Avenue with the caption "Say Hi to Your Neo-Nazi Neighbor, Mike Peinovich!" The dox revealed that he had an older sister, a social worker who treated traumatized children, and an adopted younger brother, who was biracial. Of all the details included in the dox, perhaps the most baffling of all was that Mike's wife was Jewish.

The Antifa vigilantes had published two email addresses, both purportedly belonging to Peinovich. Antifa activists often argue that doxing is a legitimate response to an inherently violent ideology, that by espousing fascist views one effectively forfeits the right to privacy. I am opposed to doxing in most cases—I worry about false positives, slippery slopes, the pernicious allure of retributivism—but not opposed enough, apparently, to overcome my journalistic curiosity. I emailed both addresses.

Peinovich responded right away. He said that he didn't want to talk—"I have a platform to tell my story that is bigger than yours"—and yet, every time I sent another email, he answered it almost immediately. I made no secret of the fact that I found his views repugnant, but I added, truthfully, that I wanted to know how he'd ended up in his predicament and what he planned to do next. He replied with memes or flippant one-liners.* I drafted a long, intricate note, trying to persuade him to talk to me for a magazine piece. His entire response was, "You seem kinda mad." We went back and forth like that for a while, but I had no real success in drawing him out, and eventually we both lost interest.

A few days later, he read our full exchange on *The Daily Shoah*. To his credit, he didn't edit his responses to make them sound smarter. But he didn't have to. According to the rules of online debate as explained in *The Essential TRS Troll Guide*, which I hadn't read at the time, Peinovich had won by default, simply by writing fewer words and maintaining his ironic detachment, while I had made a rookie mistake: letting myself get triggered into displaying emotion. After the podcast aired, I got a few nasty Twitter messages from alt-right trolls with names like Helicopter Pilot and The G0yim Kn0w, which was unpleasant but hardly unprecedented. I figured that was the end of it.

Then I heard back from the other email address. "I am not the Mike Peinovich to whom you addressed this email, but I am his father," it read. "My son has distanced himself from our family over the last few years, and, until two days ago, I was totally unaware of his 'alt-right' activities. . . . I am struggling to understand how Mike E. (which is what we call him to distinguish him from me and my father who was also Mike Peinovich) could have said, posted or tweeted the things that are attributed to him."

I called Mike Sr. and we talked for a long time. It was the week of Donald Trump's inauguration, and he sounded weary and a bit dazed, the way a lot of liberals did in those days. "Our family is pretty well integrated into the normal American stream," he said. "We tried to give our kids good values. Mike E. went to good schools, and he loved being part of his church youth group." The Peinoviches lived in Montclair, an upper-middle-class New Jersey suburb that was often listed among the most progressive towns in the country. "We knew that he was an outspoken Trump supporter, and he was very much the only one in the family," Mike Sr. went on, "so we agreed, at a certain point, not to talk about politics."

After the dox, he tried listening to *The Daily Shoah*. He lasted a few minutes, long enough to recognize his son's voice and profane sense of humor, before

---

*"What's your plan now?" I wrote. He responded with a link to a three-second YouTube clip of Bane, the villain from *The Dark Knight*: "Crashing this plane with no survivors!"

turning it off. "The Mike E. I know is a thoughtful guy, a moral guy," he said. "But I guess I don't know him like I thought I did." He was reticent to say more. For a few months, we left it at that.

• • •

I added *The Daily Shoah* to my regular podcast rotation. The internet was teeming with weirdos and extremists; I tried to keep up with most of them, or as many as I could, given that they each seemed to produce about forty-five minutes of content for every waking hour. I watched Jack Posobiec on Periscope speaking mediocre Mandarin while noodling on his bass. I watched Laura Loomer on YouTube protesting sharia law by covering the Fearless Girl statue with a burqa. Once, when I was getting ready to wash some dishes, I saw a push notification on my phone: Will Chamberlain was starting a Periscope. I clicked the link, put the phone in my pocket, and began scrubbing. "Hey, Marantz is watching!" I heard Chamberlain say through my earbuds. "Haven't seen you in a while. What's new?" He and his thousands of viewers waited in silence as I rushed around my kitchen looking for a hand towel. Finally, I managed to type something in the comments, and he moved on. I made a mental note: from now on, watch Periscopes only after they're finished.

While taking out the recycling, I watched Tim Pool searching for nonexistent "no-go zones" in Sweden. While biking laps around Prospect Park, I listened to Mike Cernovich explaining why he'd granted *60 Minutes* an interview, and how he'd been shrewd enough to turn an attempted gotcha piece on its head. I tried to click on most of Alex Jones's push alerts, but his relentless wolf-crying—"Breaking! Plan to Assassinate Trump Leaked"—was hell on my phone's feeble battery.

I also listened to the prolific podcaster Stefan Molyneux, who called himself a "philosopher in the tradition of Socrates." (The Southern Poverty Law Center described him as an "alleged cult leader.") Like Lauren Southern and Gavin McInnes, Molyneux was careful to avoid open endorsements of white nationalism, but he was constantly creeping up to the line. He didn't shout; he didn't use racist slurs; he simply explained, in an imperious, pan-Anglophonic accent, how Europeans had evolved to be more intelligent than Africans, and why it was such a shame that the world wouldn't give white people a fair shake.*

---

*"I think this guy, of all of them, is the one I find the most infuriating," my wife said one morning. She had left the house, realized that she'd forgotten her wallet, and come back inside to hear Molyneux's voice emanating from my laptop. "It's not just the racist pseudoscience. I mean, the racist pseudoscience is bad, obviously, but I think

I only listened to *The Daily Shoah* on headphones. There was a child in the house, after all.

After Mike Enoch got doxed and lost his source of income, he doubled down on white nationalism. He spoke at almost every public alt-right event—the April rally in Pikeville, the May rally in Charlottesville, the June rally in D.C. On August 12, when the big Charlottesville rally was shut down, a few of the people who'd planned to speak reconvened in another park, two miles away. Enoch stood on a wooden riser in the shade of a dogwood tree, surrounded by small concentric circles of reporters, protesters, and counterprotesters. He wore aviator sunglasses, a slight beard, and the unofficial uniform of the day: khakis and a white polo shirt. "Have we heard this conspiracy theory of white privilege?" he said. "This is a concept that was brought to us by Jewish intellectuals, to undermine our confidence in ourselves." He finished his remarks and introduced the next speaker, David Duke. An hour later, James Alex Fields, wearing khakis and a white polo, drove a car into a crowd of people.

Mike Peinovich Sr. spent that Saturday at home. He made breakfast and mowed the lawn. At some point, as he did every day, he sat down to read *The New York Times*. On page A12 was a photograph of a torch-wielding mob, taken in Charlottesville the previous night. He looked at the picture for a long time, but he didn't see Mike E. anywhere. "Thank God," he said, and went about his day.

The next day, when he got home from church, he opened his email and saw that a relative had sent him a YouTube link. He clicked on it: his son and David Duke, standing shoulder to shoulder beneath a dogwood tree. That night, he called me again and asked if I still wanted to talk.

• • •

Three days later, I took a train to visit Mike Sr. and his wife, Billie, in Montclair. They lived in an Arts and Crafts house on a tree-lined block near the center of town. As I walked there from the train station, I saw, through the window of a

what gets me more is his *priorities*. The guy claims to be Mr. Rational Philosopher, and yet every single day he looks around and goes, 'Yep, the most important injustice today is still the fact that white people don't have enough power.' Seriously? Is everything not enough?" She was running late for work, but she had been holding this back for a while, apparently. "California is on fire," she said. It was one of the times that California was on fire. "The ice caps are melting. This dude can't think of a *single* better way to occupy his time?"

restaurant, a TV tuned to CNN. The chyron read, "Cities Bracing for Rallies; White Nationalists Emboldened After Trump Remarks." Two blocks later, I passed a young couple, a pregnant woman in a sundress and a guy with a man bun. "So let me get this straight," the woman was saying. "The police didn't have riot gear, but the fucking hate groups did?"

Mike Sr. answered the door. He was taller and thinner than his son, with gray hair and rimless glasses, but I saw the resemblance right away: the square jaw, the downturned mouth. I also noticed an unfortunate coincidence, which I didn't have the temerity to mention: he was wearing khakis and a white polo, the same clothes that the white supremacists in Charlottesville had worn in order to look like normal, nonthreatening Americans.

Billie and Mike were retired, and they spent several months a year traveling. They gave me a tour of the house, telling stories about items they'd collected: Persian rugs, Mexican pottery, a floor-mounted globe. Mike was once a professor of Old English at the University of Pennsylvania, and his study contained several dictionaries and translations of *Beowulf*, along with contemporary books such as Ta-Nehisi Coates's *Between the World and Me*. We sat in leather armchairs in the living room, and he talked at length about his ancestors. "My grandfather helped drive the KKK out of North Dakota," he said. "My other grandfather came from Yugoslavia, fleeing religious persecution. My dad was a fighter pilot during World War II." At first this seemed like an icebreaker—an amateur genealogist sharing his findings. But as he repeated these facts several times throughout our conversation, I realized that he was trying to clear his family name.

Mike E.'s parents split up when he was three, and Billie married into the family a few years later. As far as she was concerned, she was as much Mike E.'s parent as anyone. She was a psychiatric social worker for many years, and she spoke in the language of therapy. "I feel shock and anger," she said. "I also feel shame, which is irrational, because I don't think I've done anything wrong. I think he brought this on himself because he wants to distance himself from us, from everyone, as a form of self-protection." Then, more quietly, she said, "He must be so lonely."

They still weren't sure how to explain the situation to their friends and family. "What do you do?" Billie said. "Send a letter to your cousins—'Haven't spoken to you in twenty years, hope you're doing well, and, oh, P.S., our son's a Nazi now'?" She worried that people would wonder how she and Mike Sr. had failed as parents. "Everyone wants it to be simple, to know who to blame," one of Mike E.'s relatives told me later. "But lots of kids have parents who get divorced when they're young. Lots of white kids have difficult personalities. They don't all become Nazis."

A few people around town had already heard the news, mostly through Facebook, and some of them were talking about Mike E. as if he had been abducted by a cult, or tied down and injected with a serum of pure hatred. Other people assumed that there must be some key biographical fact—a history of abuse, a chemical imbalance—that would neatly unlock the mystery. But his conversion was more quotidian than that, and therefore more unsettling. Somehow, he had fallen into a particularly dark rabbit hole, where many of the worst ideas in modern history were repackaged as the solution to twenty-first-century malaise.

• • •

As a child, Mike E. suffered from severe eczema and asthma. In most old photographs, his face is red and swollen and his shoulders are hunched, a sign that he is straining to catch his breath. The Peinoviches spent one summer at a lake house in Ohio, where the air was fresh and Mike E. found it easier to breathe. Still, he went swimming with his shirt on, because his skin was covered with scratches and open sores. "When we walked through an airport or a mall with our younger son, we would get stopped and told what a beautiful child we had," Billie said. "Not with Mike E." He was so allergic to so many things—dust, pollen, nuts, shellfish—that he carried an EpiPen almost everywhere he went. At birthday parties, while the other children ate ice cream and cake, he ate saltines.*

In 1980, Mike E.'s mother left Mike Sr. for a family friend, and she later moved out of state. The divorce was ugly, and for many years she rarely saw the children. Mike E. was sent to a series of therapists, who mentioned potential disorders but nothing definitive. One therapist, instead of giving a diagnosis, said that Mike E. was "as vulnerable as a peeled grape."

Gradually, he learned to insulate himself with jokes and insults. He was witty and clever—everyone agreed that he was the smartest person in the family—and he found strength in contrarianism. His ideology shifted over time, but his approach was always the same: exposing and attacking the flaws in consensus thinking, often without any sense of proportion. "He strikes me as someone without a core," one of

---

*When 4chan turned drinking milk into an alt-right meme, Mike Enoch added "Lactose tolerant" to his Twitter bio. Someone who knew him as a child told me, "The funny thing was, anyone who knew him knew that any exposure to dairy would make him sick."

his relatives told me, "who only knows how to oppose and who chooses his positions based on what will be most upsetting to people around him." When he was in fifth grade, his class was asked to wear red, white, and blue in honor of Memorial Day. Mike E. made a point of wearing orange and green instead. "It wasn't a political statement," Billie said. "He was expressing contempt for their rules."

He grew up listening to the Jerky Boys, virtuosos of the scatological prank call, and to Opie and Anthony, a pair of bawdy afternoon-radio comedians who always seemed to be daring their station managers to fire them. Opie and Anthony, in particular, reveled in boundary pushing for its own sake. For several years, they held a Most Offensive Song Contest; crowd favorites included "Baby Raper" and "Stuck in an Oven with Jews." Anyone who didn't enjoy the joke was urged to grow a thicker skin. When the internet came along, most of the shock jocks migrated online, where they no longer had station managers who could fire them; the gatekeepers were more distant, and more permissive. If "Stuck in an Oven with Jews" was shocking prior to social media, the race to the bottom would soon accelerate into free fall.*

Mike E. went to a public high school that was academically rigorous and ethnically diverse—mostly African American kids and white kids, and some whose parents had emigrated from Asia or South America. He had the sort of grades that are common among smart but disobedient kids: As in classes that interested him, Ds and Fs when he was bored or felt that the teacher didn't deserve his respect. He smoked a lot of weed and went to a lot of Phish shows. Once, he and a friend got pulled over while hotboxing a car, and the friend was arrested for marijuana possession; but his father was a big-shot lawyer, and he pulled some strings to get his son's case thrown out. Mike E. knew that the system was unfair, but he was still shocked at how clear-cut the inequity was: a poor black kid, or even a middle-class biracial kid like his brother, probably would have been treated far worse. He complained about this to his parents, who were heartened to see that he was developing a sense of social justice.

He went to Ohio University to study graphic design, but dropped out after the

---

*Anthony Cumia, one half of Opie and Anthony, was fired by his radio bosses in 2014, after he posted pictures of a black woman on Twitter and called her an "animal pig face worthless meat sack." In a Fox News appearance, Cumia explained that "there is a huge violence problem in the black community," and added, "I will never apologize for this . . . this is exactly who I am." The following month, he founded his own online streaming network featuring audio and video talk shows hosted by edgy comedians. One of the network's most popular shows was *The Gavin McInnes Show*.

first quarter. He transferred to the main campus of Rutgers, and then to the Newark campus, but he hated it—the professors were tyrants who demanded blind obedience even when they didn't know what they were talking about—and he spent most of his free time in his dorm room, alone, eating fast food and messing around on his computer. After leaving Rutgers, he took a few computer-programming classes at Pace University, but left without a degree. "Mike E. took his fourth run at college and finally faced the fact that he is not suited to academic life," the family's 2006 Christmas letter read. He moved to Bushwick, in Brooklyn, where he lived in a shared apartment with a bunch of struggling musicians and artists and activists. By default, they all considered themselves somewhere to the left of liberal, maybe closer to anarchist—but they spent most of their free time going to dive bars or house parties, not talking about politics.

Using tutorials online, he taught himself to code. Eventually, he was hired as a back-end programmer at AOL. "Though he commutes into Manhattan to a corporate job," the family Christmas letter continued, "he's still the non-conformist that he always was."

●　●　●

His supervisor at AOL was a blonde woman from the Midwest, an amateur musician and photographer who shared many of his interests—sci-fi movies, medieval history, recondite internet humor. They started dating. She kept an active Flickr account, posting impressionistic nature photos and live-action shots from local rock shows, and she often talked about a fantasy novel she hoped to write one day. Her father was born Jewish and her mother had converted to Judaism, but Mike E. hardly found this remarkable. Half the people he grew up with were Jewish, including his high-school girlfriend.

He and the supervisor got married. (Their wedding ceremony was mostly secular, but they acknowledged their Episcopalian and Jewish roots by reciting an ecumenical prayer and stomping on a glass.) They moved to a one-bedroom apartment on the Upper East Side. To get his eczema under control, Mike E. ordered large doses of prednisone, a prescription steroid, from an Indian website, and took it without medical supervision. He gained so much weight that he was almost unrecognizable, and he went temporarily blind in one eye, necessitating emergency cataract surgery. In addition to weight gain and vision problems, the side effects were supposed to include depression and agitation. People told him to be careful, but he felt no more or less agitated than usual. He didn't love being fat, but it was worth it. The pills were the only thing that made him feel better, so he took the pills.

They knew no one in their new neighborhood. They sometimes went back to Bushwick to see their old friends on the weekends, but not often. Eventually, they stopped going out much at all. Bars were too loud and expensive, and no one had anything interesting to say anyway. Instead, they stayed home, playing video games or reading separately on their laptops. Mike E. spent hours in political-debate forums on Facebook, letting his contrarian side run wild. No one was keeping track of what he said. No one even knew his name, or what he looked like. He might test out a whole range of opinions on a given topic, not yet sure which one he actually believed. Other times, for fun, he would stake out a seemingly indefensible position, then see if he could invent an argument to back it up. It felt like another video game.

He would join a debate forum, get banned for stirring up trouble, and then find a new one. The internet was full of them: subreddits like r/PoliticalDiscussion, Facebook groups like Atheism+ and Left vs. Right. Whatever people were arguing about, he'd find a way to insinuate himself into the argument. He loved good-faith debates: if you won, it was intrinsically gratifying, and if you lost, your ideas got sharper. He loved bad-faith debates, too: once you learned to read people, it wasn't hard to predict which arguments (or shitposts, or non-sequitur memes) were most likely to infuriate them. When you made your opponents so flustered that they had to leave the forum, that was called a rage-quit. Mike E. started racking up rage-quits the way other people collected hunting trophies. Sometimes, in the shower, he would act out some made-up debate without even realizing what he was doing. "Who were you talking to in there?" his wife would ask when he got out.

"For a while, before the internet, liberals just had mainstream TV and newspaper news," he said later. This led to groupthink just as surely as Coke and Taco Bell led to obesity. "It kind of came to a head during the Bush years," he continued. "The feedback loop of liberal outrage—like, they were collectively driven insane." He didn't know the right way to talk about politics, but this facile water-cooler consensus was clearly the wrong way. If he wanted to find something better, he would have to do what he had always done in the past: throw out everything he'd been taught and start from scratch.

Everyone in the normal world seemed paralyzed by a desire for social acceptance. They weren't really trying to pursue the truth, because there were so many thoughts they wouldn't even allow themselves to think. At home with his wife, or on the debate forums, he was free to argue from first principles. It was obvious to him that the country was profoundly off track, and that both major political parties were morally and intellectually bankrupt. The only question was which utopian system should replace the current one.

He read books by Noam Chomsky and articles on Antiwar.com, which published critiques of American foreign policy from the far left and the far right. He dabbled in leftist anarchism for a while, and then in revolutionary Trotskyism. One Saturday, he later wrote, he found himself at a meeting "in a rundown YMCA in Brooklyn with a group of middle-aged Jewish public-school teachers." They were discussing what stance to take on Islamic terrorism—it was awful, but at least it was anti-imperialist. "An overwhelming sense of loathing washed over me like an awesome wave," he wrote. "The people I was around suddenly seemed twisted and horrible. A revelatory religious experience is the closest thing I can compare this experience to."

He set out to find the "direct opposite" of Marxism, whatever that was. He remembered that a member of his Trotskyist group had described a trio of mid-century libertarian writers—Ayn Rand, Murray Rothbard, and Ludwig von Mises—as particularly "dangerous," so Mike E. downloaded some of their books online to see what they were about.* "I tore through Mises's tome 'Socialism' in about a week," he wrote later. "And every one of those words rang true like it was written in my soul." Mises wrote in a dense academic style, but his underlying premise was simple enough: only the free market could provide prosperity and freedom. His students later fleshed out the premise, arguing that government regulations and entitlement programs were almost always counterproductive.

For a few years, Mike E. was a doctrinaire libertarian. He started a blog called *The Emptiness*, where he wrote posts such as "Socialism Is Selfish" and "Taxation Is Theft." His wife kept up her own blog, where she wrote reviews of local concerts and drag shows, but she always made time to support her husband's autodidactic pursuits. When he changed the background of *The Emptiness* to a stock image of a gray funnel cloud, she commented, "Love the new tornado photo! This site is now a swirling vortex of emptiness!" In 2008, he got swept up in the excitement of

---

*He didn't notice it at the time, but he would later note sardonically that all three of those writers happened to be Jewish.

Ron Paul's presidential campaign. Paul was just a protest candidate, but he still received millions of dollars in small donations and won far more votes than anyone predicted. Maybe what seemed like third-rail issues weren't so untouchable after all.

Sometimes, when Mike E. saw his dad and stepmom in New Jersey, he tried to engage them in political debates. Did they really think that the Federal Reserve, an unelected group of plutocrats, deserved to dictate the fiscal policy of the world's largest economy? He would grow adamant, pitching himself forward on the couch and raising his voice, but then his wife would touch him gently on the arm, and he would sit back and let his eyes go blank. "People often tell me that I'm too extreme," he wrote on *The Emptiness*, in 2011. "This is all very conventional and sounds very nice, but quite often it is actually a load of crap and a form of bullying. People tend to get nervous and upset when you take an absolute moral stand on something. They do not like moral certainty, and they particularly do not like it when it can be backed up with logic and evidence."

After a while, he began to wonder whether libertarianism was too tepid. Its own premises, after all, pointed toward a starker conclusion: if the state was nothing but a hindrance to freedom, why not abolish the state altogether, leaving only the unfettered market? He began to call himself an anarcho-capitalist. One of the leading anarcho-capitalist thinkers was the German-born philosopher Hans-Hermann Hoppe, a former Murray Rothbard protégé who argued that government was not just a hindrance to freedom but "an institution run by gangs of murderers, plunderers and thieves, surrounded by willing executioners, propagandists, sycophants, crooks, liars, clowns, charlatans, dupes and useful idiots." *The New York Times* referred to Milton Friedman, the libertarian economist, as "the grandmaster of free-market economic theory"; Hoppe referred to Friedman as "a socialist."

Many mainstream libertarians were so opposed to any kind of coercion that they thought of libertarianism as synonymous with social liberalism, requiring a live-and-let-live approach to all kinds of behavior. Not so, Hoppe insisted. Even in the absence of a state, citizens could still use their freedom of association to form private covenants, and those covenants could implement whatever rules they saw fit. Hoppe even maintained that, if some subgroup of the population posed an inherent threat to the social order, then the troublemakers ought to be physically removed. This was about as far from live-and-let-live as you could get.*

Mises and Rothbard were trained as economists, and most economists assumed that people were basically fungible. According to their mathematical models, whether Product X will be purchased at Price Y should have nothing to do with who's doing the purchasing. But what if people weren't all the same? What if you couldn't account for people's behavior without considering their psychological traits, their cultural background, even their genetic makeup? "Slapped in the face by the reality of human bio-diversity," Mike E. later wrote, "I had to come to grips with the fact that libertarianism isn't going to work for everyone, and the people that it isn't going to work for are going to ruin it for everyone else." If HBD was true—if some groups of people were inherently more capable than others—then maybe multicultural democracy was an experiment that was bound to fail.

He thought he had already examined each of his beliefs, reducing them to their most fundamental axioms. But here was an axiom so fundamental that he hadn't even articulated it to himself, much less subjected it to logical scrutiny. Now that he thought about it, he wasn't sure why he should assume that all people were equal. Maybe they weren't. If this was a textbook definition of racism, then so be it—maybe racism was true. "They're fucking religious fanatics," he wrote later, of liberals like his former self. "They believe in the equality of human beings like a Muslim believes that he has to pray five times facing Mecca, or like a Southern Baptist hates the devil."

His previous radical philosophies had fallen short, he now believed, not because they had failed to account for the world's complexity, but because they hadn't been radical enough. His family, his teachers, his pastors, his peers—they had all recoiled from the reality of European superiority not because the notion was demonstrably incorrect or morally repugnant, but because they were too afraid to think for themselves. After arguing himself out of every previous position, he had finally found the perfect ideology for an inveterate contrarian—one that presented such an elemental challenge to the underlying tenets of his society that he would never run out of enemies.

---

*"In a covenant concluded among proprietor and community tenants for the purpose of protecting their private property, no such thing as a right to free (unlimited) speech exists," Hoppe wrote. "There can be no tolerance toward democrats and communists in a libertarian social order. They will have to be physically separated and expelled from society."

• • •

The idea of racial hierarchy seemed to hold great explanatory power. As a liberal, he had dealt with troubling facts—the achievement gap between black students and white students, say—by invoking the history of racial oppression, or by explaining why the data was more complex than it appeared at first glance. As a Marxist, he had attributed unpleasant facts to capitalist exploitation; as a libertarian, he had blamed the state. But those explanations were abstract at best, muddled at worst, and they required levels of context that were impossible to convey in a Facebook post. Now he was free to revert to a far simpler explanation: maybe white people had more wealth and power because white people were superior. "Libertarian ideals are great, but they can only work in a white country," he said. "All the Edmund Burke shit, all the Russell Kirk shit, all the William F. Buckley shit—if your country's 45 percent white, you can kiss that right the fuck goodbye."

In the debate forums, people loved to rebut arguments by calling them racist. In the past, he'd always had to look for ways to deny this; now he could simply respond by saying, in essence, So what? "All they really have is this underlying moral premise that they expect you to share," he said later. "If you just question that premise, they have no idea what to do next." He couldn't understand why Republican politicians never tried this. Instead of living in fear that someone might accuse them of racism, why not advocate unapologetically for white interests? White people were the only ones who reliably voted Republican anyway.

He felt the urge to explain what he was learning online to people in the real world, but he knew that they wouldn't understand. He stopped haranguing his family about tax policy and the Federal Reserve. They assumed he had lost interest in politics, and he didn't bother correcting them. He imagined telling them everything; he could predict what their responses would be, if they ever got over their initial shock. *This isn't how we raised you!* Yeah, well, maybe you should have raised me differently. *Your brother isn't of pure European stock—does that make him bad?* It's not about good and bad, necessarily—the idea is voluntary separation, not death camps. Mike E.'s brother was a sweet kid, probably his favorite person to hang out with in the whole family. But facts are still facts. A guilt trip might be enough to deter some people, but it wasn't going to work on him.

He was willing to be proved wrong, of course. But when he went looking for counterarguments he never seemed to find anything direct and thorough—just the Democrat narrative that every problem could be solved by spending, and the Republican narrative that everything could be solved by tax cuts, and the History Channel narrative that Hitler was Lucifer and Martin Luther King was the Messiah, and the social-justice-Twitter narrative that white men were the root of all evil. Those were all forms of emotional badgering, not rational debate. When he googled race and crime, he found Jared Taylor. When he googled race and IQ, he found Steve Sailer. He also found the mainstream media warning the normies not to look at the crimethinkers' sites, but those warnings never seemed to include point-by-point refutations of the actual arguments. There were red pills everywhere if you knew where to look.

Mike E. was still frequenting open debate forums, unleashing his fury on liberals and left-libertarians and neocons. Through these forums, he met a few like-minded friends—a painting contractor from Dutchess County, New York; a devout Christian from Tennessee; a philosophy student at the University of Nebraska; an EMT from Virginia. They'd all been Ron Paul supporters before that movement dissipated. Now they called themselves postlibertarians, although they weren't sure what would come next. They started a private Facebook group, where they sent one another essays and video clips by up-and-coming dissidents such as Richard Spencer and Chris Cantwell, also former Ron Paul supporters who were looking for something new. The private Facebook group turned into a sprawling continuous conversation, an ongoing debate about the merits of various micro-ideologies (paleoconservatism, radical traditionalism, neoreaction) mixed with plenty of shitposts and 4chan references and offensive jokes. When they came up with a good talking point, they'd A/B test it on Reddit or Twitter, honing it to see which version would most efficiently drive the shitlibs insane. Together they were inventing a way of thinking, a new way of talking, a new way of seeing the world.

In mid-2012, Mike E. put up a message on *The Emptiness*: "This is an archive of my anti-statist site content from 2010–2012. Those were fun days but not really what I am interested in writing about or pursuing right now." That December, with his new friends from the postlibertarian Facebook group, he started *The Right Stuff*. "We're right wingers," the About Us page read, "but we welcome comments from intelligent and civil people across the political spectrum." A few months later, the About Us page was amended: "While unabashedly authoritarian, fash-ist, and theocratic, we welcome comments from intelligent and civil people across the political spectrum." In 2016, the page was edited yet again:

"Even though you are wrong, we are open to outside opinions. . . . Also we're white and we're not sorry."

• • •

The Right Stuff published blog posts such as "Right Wing Trolls Can Win," "The Rational Racist," and "The Trans*valuation of All Values," a Nietzschean critique of Caitlyn Jenner's gender transition.* One page of the site was set up to accept donations, in dollars or bitcoin. The site also hosted several podcasts, each with its own parody logo: *Fash the Nation, Nationalist Public Radio, Good Morning White America*. *The Right Stuff*'s landing page featured a rotation of paired photos and phrases, each pair designed to be maximally jarring: a smiling photo of Joseph McCarthy with the text "Your rational world is a circle jerk"; a squadron of Italian Fascisti overlaid with the message "Democracy is an interracial porno." The fashy memes were an in-joke for the site's regular visitors, but they were also supposed to be exported to the wider world. Mike E. built freshrarememes.com, a site with step-by-step instructions that made it easy for his followers to combine images and text in provocative new ways. Another *TRS* blogger set up a Facebook page, Fashy Memes, which spawned dozens of imitators: Lazer-Beamed Memes with Fashy Themes, Alt-Right Memes for Fashy Teens, Counter-signal Memes for Fashy Goys.

The idea was to make the memes subversive enough to plant doubt in the normies' minds, but not overt enough that they'd be detected by Facebook's content moderators. It was a difficult balance to get right. The best way to learn was through trial and error. You could tell whether you were succeeding because the results were immediate and objective—you just needed to look at the engagement statistics at the bottom of each post. If you went too far, your whole page might get shut down; but this almost never happened. For the most part, Facebook's content moderators seemed to be looking for nudity, profanity, direct threats, or overt ISIS propaganda. Even if an alt-right propaganda page did get flagged for review, the memes were usually oblique enough that the moderators wouldn't understand what they were looking at. And, if your Facebook page did get shut down, you could always start a new one.

By the time *The Daily Shoah* launched, in 2014, Enoch had grown confident in

---

*"Protagoras said man is the measure of all things. He was an old white cis-sexist shitlord."

his white-nationalist views, but he was not particularly anti-Semitic. The goal of the podcast was to shock both liberals and "basic-bitch conservatives," and the show's name was an efficient way to achieve that goal. "At first, it was a joke," Mike E. explained on Chris Cantwell's podcast. "It was a funny pun. But we kinda put ourselves in a box."

On certain parts of 4chan—especially /pol/, the message board for "politically incorrect" conversation—people gave each other kudos for coming up with new racist slurs, the more shameless the better.* The standard epithets showed up often, but people got more points for calling women "skags" or "trollops," or for calling black criminals "dindus."† People on /pol/ also talked incessantly about the Jews: They're devious shape-shifters! They *look* white, but they're not! Mike E. didn't understand the obsession. Either Jews were white or they weren't. If the white nationalists in America ever successfully established an ethnostate, and if they didn't want Jews to be a part of it, then the Jews could go live in their own ethnostate, the one that the UN had already established for them. This would present problems for his marriage, obviously, but he would cross that bridge when he came to it. Frankly, he knew from years of involvement with radical politics that you don't start packing your bags for the utopia right away. You lay out your vision of an ideal society; you start making it seem conceivable, even plausible; you gradually broaden the Overton window; and maybe, one day, the world starts to inch closer to your vision.

The Daily Shoah came out weekly, at first, despite the name. The cohosts were the core members of the postlibertarian Facebook group: Jesse Dunstan, the contractor from upstate New York, who called himself Sven; Cooper Ward, the Nebraska philosophy student, who went by Ghoul; and the EMT from Virginia, Alex McNabb, who never bothered to use a pseudonym. ("My family knows about this," he said. "They don't really give a shit.") Some episodes featured other

---

*One of *The Right Stuff*'s prominent allies was Andrew Anglin, the publisher of the neo-Nazi site the *Daily Stormer*. In late 2017, the *Daily Stormer*'s style guide, which also served as a propaganda manifesto for the alt-right movement, was leaked to a reporter at *The Huffington Post*. "The reader is at first drawn in by curiosity or the naughty humor, and is slowly awakened to reality," Anglin wrote. "Dehumanization is extremely important, but it must be done within the confines of lulz," or laughs. Anglin didn't put much stock in originality. "The basic propaganda doctrine of the site is based on Hitler's doctrine of war propaganda outlined in *Mein Kampf*," he wrote, including a link to the book. "All enemies should be combined into one enemy, which is the Jews."
†This slur, popular on *The Daily Shoah*, derived from the cohosts' habit of saying the phrase "I didn't do nothin'!" in dialect reminiscent of a minstrel show.

alt-right guests, six or eight of them at a time, all talking over one another on an unsteady Skype connection. The tone of an episode could swing, sometimes within a single sentence, from sincerity to sarcasm to reverse sarcasm. The distinctions were so subtle and ever-shifting that the cohosts sometimes had to tell each other, on air, "I actually meant that," or "I was just doing a bit."

The show aimed to be a full-throated defense of white nationalism that didn't take itself too seriously. It followed the old drive-time shock-jock format, with recurring comedy bits such as prank calls, interviews with notable 4channers, and a news-analysis segment called the Shitlord Report. Dunstan, who had played guitar in a prog-metal band before getting married and having kids, recorded parody songs in his basement and inserted them between segments. He rewrote the lyrics to Danzig's "Dirty Black Summer," turning it into a commentary on the unrest in Ferguson, Missouri. "I Need to Know," by Tom Petty, became the anxious inner monologue of a would-be white nationalist awaiting his 23andMe results. ("I need to know / I need to know / If I'm 3 percent Heeb then it better say so.")

The cohosts ribbed each other with constant banter, or "bantz": McNabb was an interrupter, Dunstan was always out of the loop, Enoch kept starting long monologues with "Here's the thing." *The Right Stuff* blog was so rife with acronyms, abbreviations, and multivalent memes that they posted a "TRS Lexicon" on the site for the uninitiated. "People criticize us for doing too many in-jokes," Enoch said on the podcast. "It's on purpose, to create a feeling of in-group cohesion. We're giving you real narratives, but we're also creating a sense of community." And it *was* a community—not just for the listeners, but also for Mike E., their de facto leader. Some weekends, he took the train up to Dunstan's house in Dutchess County, where they hosted cookouts for the show's cohosts and core fans. The gatherings were small, to ensure everyone's safety and anonymity. Sometimes people would ask Mike to give an impromptu speech about current events; other times, the gatherings weren't all that political, just a chance for like-minded guys to have a beer and enjoy being part of something real.

"Our society is constantly sending us the message: 'You're born into this situation of rootlessness and ennui, and there's nothing you can do about it,'" Enoch said on the show. "'Don't try to recapture roots by going out and engaging in activities that build camaraderie with people you can relate to. Just stay online and be an urbanite who consumes media through a screen in a small apartment.'" *TRS* was a way out of the postmodern hamster wheel, a way to live with purpose. He told his parents, without going into much detail, that he had a new group of friends now. Sometimes, instead of calling them his friends, he used the word "brothers." He said that they were building something constructive, helping young men find their way in the world. When his parents asked more specific questions, he didn't answer. Still, it was clear that he had found his people.

The cohosts of *The Daily Shoah* all agreed that mainstream culture was beyond repair. It almost went without saying. Instead, they spent most of their time differentiating themselves from their ideological neighbors, mocking the cranks and yokels of the far-right internet—anime fanboys, 9/11 truthers, Alex Jones fans, manosphere goons like Roosh V and Mike Cernovich. One target of frequent mockery was the group of alt-right losers who blamed all their personal shortcomings on a shadowy Zionist conspiracy. "There's definitely overrepresentation of Jews in high finance," Enoch said in an early episode. "But that's not really where you need to be pointing fingers, 'cause that's not actually the issue."

In January 2015, he downloaded a PDF of a book by Kevin MacDonald, a former psychology professor at California State, Long Beach, called *The Culture of Critique: An Evolutionary Analysis of Jewish Involvement in Twentieth-Century Political Movements*. People on 4chan were always posting about it, and Enoch wanted to see what the fuss was about. Three hundred pages long and heavily footnoted, the book, published in 1998, was a touchstone of contemporary intellectual anti-Semitism.* MacDonald called himself an evolutionary psychologist, and his argument was that the best way to understand Judaism was not as a religion but as a "group evolutionary strategy." Over millennia, he argued, Jews had developed distinct traits: ambition; high verbal intelligence; loyalty to insiders; wariness of outsiders; a fierce instinct for self-preservation, even at the expense of their host society. The result of all this, in the twentieth century, was that American Jews were prepared to undermine their own country by diluting its traditional heritage. They were doing this, in part, by using their disproportionate influence as cultural

---

*Democritus, in ancient Greece, had an intuition that the world was made up of homogenous, indivisible atoms; 2,400 years later, Rutherford and Bohr expanded this intuition into a proper scientific theory. This was roughly the way the contemporary anti-Semites of the alt-right thought of MacDonald's work. For thousands of years, from the Seleucid empire to *The Protocols of the Elders of Zion*, people had sensed that the Jews were not to be trusted; MacDonald had finally fleshed out this intuition, demonstrating "scientifically" that anti-Semitism had been justified all along.

gatekeepers to promote lax immigration policies, decoupling the United States from its history as a majority-white nation. (MacDonald seemed to assume, like Peter Brimelow and other paleoconservatives, that the United States would be less likely to thrive without a white majority.) Like so much of what the Jews did, MacDonald wrote, their quest to undermine white hegemony was an attempt, either conscious or unconscious, at self-preservation. A cohesive white majority might expel the Jewish nuisance from its midst, as so many nations had done in the past. Therefore, it was in Jews' interest to keep white Americans divided and demoralized, allowing a coalition of ethnic minorities, Jews among them, to rise to power.*

"In science there are a thousand bad ideas for every good one," Steven Pinker, the Harvard cognitive scientist and bestselling author, wrote. He had read a summary of MacDonald's argument and found that it "fails two basic tests of scientific credibility"; therefore, he indicated that he wouldn't deign to read MacDonald's book. "In the marketplace of ideas, a proposal has to have enough initial credibility, and enough signs of adherence to the ground rules of scientific debate, to earn the precious currency of the attention of one's peers." Other prominent scientists either trounced MacDonald's arguments or, more often, ignored them.

Enoch read some of the rebuttals, but they all seemed pretty weak. It made sense, of course, that Jewish academics would reject MacDonald's hypothesis—he was advocating for his ethnic group's self-interest, and they were advocating for theirs. They could dismiss him as a pariah, or declare his work unworthy of "normalization," but this just seemed like name-calling. "I'm not seeing three-hundred-page refutations with footnotes, that's for sure," Enoch said. "I'm seeing 'Wow just wow' and 'I can't even'—a lot of status signaling, basically." What if the normies couldn't refute *The Culture of Critique* more convincingly because, deep down, they sensed that the argument was right?

On *The Daily Shoah*, he called the book "important and devastating, something I urge all of you to read." Then he offered even higher praise: "It triggered me so hard." His whole life, his liberal teachers, many of them Jewish, had taught him to question authority, to defy convention, to follow the facts wherever they led. Well, now he had found a set of facts that they were desperate to keep hidden.

---

*This was why the protesters in Charlottesville had chanted, interchangeably, "You will not replace us!" and "Jews will not replace us!" According to alt-right dogma, which had been heavily influenced by Kevin MacDonald, white genocide—also known as the Great Replacement—was already happening, and not by accident. It was a grand conspiracy being perpetrated against white people by the Jews.

Normies freaked out at the mere mention of the JQ, which only confirmed that he was onto something.

The anti-Semitism on the podcast grew more pointed and more frequent. Allusions to gas chambers and ovens became almost a verbal tic.* Dunstan made a parody ad for the Hans-Hermann Hoppe Physical Removal Company, and the meme got passed around on r/Physical_Removal and on Facebook groups like Based God Hoppe. The gatherings at Dunstan's house started to include book burnings: someone would build a bonfire, people would gather around it, and a guest of honor, such as Enoch or Richard Spencer or the comedian Sam Hyde, would give a short speech and then incinerate a book by a Jew or a Communist. Afterward, people might shout "Hail Victory!" or do a Roman salute. It was sort of like a troll, a way to trigger the normies, except that there were, by design, no normies around.

Mike had no idea what any of this would mean for his marriage. That part seemed almost like a Greek tragedy: his wife was the only person in the world who truly understood him, and somehow he had stumbled onto the one thing that risked driving them apart. For a while, he tried to keep his marriage private while building a public career, under a pseudonym, as an anti-Semitic propagandist. The more rational side of him knew that the contradiction would catch up to him one day, but he tried to focus on the present.

There wasn't one official group called the alt-right—just a disparate alliance of smaller organizations, each with its own hierarchy and internal rules. The leaders of the groups all knew each other, but they operated independently. Unlike some of the other groups, *TRS* had no application process and no formal membership roll. "I'm not a political leader," Dunstan said. "I make funny songs and memes and stuff. My job is to get you in the door. The army recruiter guy standing in the mall, trying to get you to sign up—that's me."

The Hammerskins and the Alt-Knights were into violent street confrontations. The Nationalist Front were straight-up neo-Nazis; the Traditionalist Workers Party didn't call themselves neo-Nazis, but they were pretty close. Then there

---

*Enoch's extended monologues were called "ovenside chats"; the upper-middle class was the "oven-middle class"; a series of interviews with fellow white nationalists was called "Between Two Lampshades." On CafePress, a site that lets you custom-print any logo you want on a piece of merchandise, they ordered a box of *Daily Shoah* oven mitts—"Pop 'em in!"—and sold them for $14.88 apiece, or the cryptocurrency equivalent.

were groups like Identity Evropa, whose members wore preppy clothes and discouraged visible tattoos. IE's leaders were fully red-pilled, but, for strategic reasons, they used normie-friendly rhetoric. Every few weeks they would engage in a public demonstration, hoping to draw attention to their cause on social media and in the mainstream press. They might hang a huge banner from a highway overpass, fly a drone overhead to film it, then add swelling string music to the footage and post it on YouTube. The banners bore messages like "End Immigration" and "You Will Not Replace Us"—not completely outside the Overton window, but provocative enough to get people thinking, and googling.*

David Duke and Stormfront had a stiff, predictable style—the *Daily Shoah* hosts called it White Nationalism 1.0—which caused their best arguments to get lost in a fog of tedium and boomerposting. Richard Spencer specialized in dense philosophical essays, not dank memes. Gavin McInnes and Stefan Molyneux were useful entry points—"a lot of our guys started their journeys by finding one of those shows," Enoch said—but ultimately the alt-light was inadequate as long as they refused to address the Jewish Question. Only *TRS* had figured out the perfect combination of levity and red pills, an aesthetic that could draw in new listeners and then, over time, lower their resistance to the truth. Their podcasts were not available on iTunes, Spotify, or any other major platform, and yet collectively they draw tens of thousands of listeners a week.

In D.C., during a panel discussion with Enoch and other alt-right leaders, Richard Spencer said, "There's something interesting about our movement, something new, and I think *The Right Stuff* probably deserves more credit for it than anyone. There's this trollish hilarity that's almost become inseparable from our movement."

"I believe the term the left used for this, in the sixties, was 'culture jamming,'" Enoch said.

The focus of *The Daily Shoah* broadened with time. The cohosts started critiquing "leftist culture," by which they meant all of mainstream culture—everyone who opposed the alt-right's pro-white advocacy. By attacking leftist and centrist arguments relentlessly, both in good faith and in bad faith, Enoch hoped to

---

*IE also put up posters on college campuses, featuring the group's URL and its cleanly designed teal-and-white logo. "Our postering campaign is the beginning of a long term cultural war of attrition against academia's Cultural Marxist narrative," the group's site read. "As students begin to realize that the direction their lectures take them is based upon false assumptions by their instructors, they will begin rejecting the false narratives and begin looking to us for answers."

convert those opponents who were open to conversion and to sap the morale of those who weren't. "The left—they don't know how fucking predictable they are," he said on the podcast. "I hear one thing about you, I can predict ten other things." Most leftists were too mortified by the alt-right's arguments to examine them in much detail, and Enoch used this information asymmetry to his advantage. "We understand your narratives better than you do," he said.

In July 2015, a group of *TRS* contributors worked together for several days to propel the word "cuckservative" from the fringes to the mainstream. Erick Erickson, a prominent Never Trump conservative, complained on Twitter that trolls were pestering him with the epithet. *The Daily Caller* followed up with an explainer piece called "What's Behind the 'Cuckservative' Slur? (NSFW)." After that, a *Daily Shoah* cohost recounted, the word "cuckservative" reached a mainstream audience, just as the alt-right had hoped. "It went viral," the cohost said. "It reached all the way to *BuzzFeed*."

TRS trolls used the same tactics to promote other hashtags—such as #NRO Revolt, about how "the *National Review* version of conservatism has totally failed America." They explained on the podcast how the trolling campaigns worked: by creating a surplus of activating emotion in neocons and SJWs on social media, the trolls were able to turn their enemies into host organisms, spreading the alt-right's message for free. "When a hashtag gets a lot of action, it trends on Twitter, and it shows up in important people's feeds," a guest on the podcast explained. "The 'cuckservative' Twitter campaign really got us on the map. Now the *National Review*'s writing articles about us."

"We hit them at emotional flashpoints that they cannot ignore, and we get them to promote our narrative," Enoch said. "But be smart. If you start posting, like, Hitler or Confederate Flag avatars, it's not gonna work. . . . Remember, this is a psyop. We are engaged in a psychological operation against them."

On the show, whenever the cohosts mentioned a Jewish journalist or politician, they would emphasize the name, pronouncing it in a whiny, nasal accent and adding a reverb effect. This innovation—the Echo, they called it—became one of their signature memes. On 4chan and 8chan and Twitter, *TRS*'s followers approximated the Echo in writing, surrounding Jewish names with triple parentheses. This seemed at first like just another distasteful joke, but its deeper purpose was to "name the Jew"—to show how many there were, how many positions of authority they occupied—with the ultimate goal of rousing white people out of their complacency. "You'll talk to white Americans today, and they don't actually know if someone's Jewish or not," Enoch said on the podcast. This allowed Jews to operate in plain sight, using ambiguous-sounding names like Miller or Kahn, presenting as white one minute and then as oppressed minorities the next. Enoch spun his northeastern upbringing as an advantage: having grown up around Jews, he understood the enemy. "I have very honed Jewdar," he said on the podcast. "I can tell. And they get very nervous about it, because historically, when gentiles, en masse, start noticing, it means something's up."

Enoch recorded his part of *The Daily Shoah* from his one-bedroom apartment on the Upper East Side. After the dox, his wife told her friends and family that, although she had been aware that he hosted a podcast, she didn't know anything about its contents. This was false. Sometimes, when the cohosts were shitposting about sci-fi movies or bad nineties fashion, Mike's wife, in the background, would add a joke to the conversation. A few minutes later, presumably while she was still in the room, the conversation would drift, as it always did, to jokes about dindus and lampshades.

On December 22, 2015, Mike's wife appeared on a special Christmas episode of *The Daily Shoah* to recite a poem, a parody of "A Visit from St. Nicholas." "She wrote this," Enoch said, "and she's really proud of it." The poem demonstrated a deep familiarity with the show's tone, and with several of its inside jokes:

> 'Twas a TRS *Christmas, and all through the house,*
> *Not a creature was stirring, not even my spouse*
> *The cucks were all prepped for the ovens with care,*
> *Just waiting for morning to pop 'em in there. . . .*
> *Out Communists, out Socialists, out left-libertarians!*
> *Out betas, out allies, SJW contrarians*
> *Out beaners and dindus and Muslim jihadists*
> *Spare us your Syrian-refugee problems*
> *Just fash away, fash away, fash away all!*

Elsewhere in the poem, she referred to herself as a troll. She was an aspiring writer, and presumably she wanted to demonstrate to her husband and his friends that she, too, could excel at their game. Maybe she convinced herself that the words she was repeating were empty signifiers. Under the cloak of anonymity, writing for a receptive audience, she may have imagined that the poem was just another thing on the internet, just an edgy joke that went a bit too far.

• • •

During one of my visits to Mike Sr. and Billie's house in New Jersey, I met their other son, who asked to go by Jay. He worked at a local multiplex; when I met him, he was just getting home from a shift and was still in his work uniform. Before the dox, he and Mike E. had maintained a good relationship. Every few weeks, Jay would take a train to New York. They would see a movie together, usually the latest superhero franchise, and Jay would sleep over.

After Mike E. was doxed, Jay said, "I was a big target." Some of Mike E.'s followers, apparently upset that he had a nonwhite family member, found Jay's Facebook page and defaced it, sending him threats and vile images. "I just deleted them, just blocked the people," Jay said. "I didn't even want to acknowledge it." The two brothers hadn't spoken since. After Charlottesville, whenever Jay was asked to explain his relationship to Mike E., he would respond, "He used to be my brother."

"I think he still thinks he's trolling," Jay continued. "I also like to troll online, so I sort of get it. I learned it from him, I guess." Even though Jay loved heavy metal, he said, "I'll go online and push people's buttons—'Dude, Danzig sucks'— even though Danzig's one of my favorite bands. It's funny sometimes. But you also have to know when to stop."

While we talked, Jay scrolled through Facebook on his phone. "There's all this stuff about white nationalists on Facebook right now," he said, clicking on a video from Charlottesville. "This is weird. There's even footage of the car driving through people."

Mike Sr. leaned forward on the couch: "Don't look at that. You don't wanna see that."

"Yeah, probably not," Jay said, moving on to the next story in his feed.

Between January, when Mike Sr. found out about his son's online persona, and August, when the name Mike Peinovich began to appear in national newspapers, the two Mikes saw each other just once, in the lobby of a Manhattan bank. "My mother left each of her grandkids, including Mike E., a small inheritance," Mike Sr. said. "I couldn't bear the thought of any of that money falling into the hands of these hate groups, so I set up a trust, and I got the paperwork together, and I just prayed that he would sign it." Mike E. deliberated for a few minutes, then signed the documents.

As they waited for the paperwork to be processed, they made labored small talk. "He told me he'd been going to the gym and not eating carbs," Mike Sr. said. "He didn't say where he was living, or what he was doing with his days. It felt like talking to someone I hardly knew." Before he left, Mike Sr. made one last request. He asked his son to legally change his last name. He could change it to Enoch, or Paine, or anything, really, other than Peinovich. Mike E. agreed.

The day after the rally in Charlottesville—on what happened to be Mike Sr.'s seventy-third birthday—he texted Mike E., reminding him of his promise. "Please change your name," he wrote. "You have abandoned your heritage, your ideals and your family."

He waited a few minutes. The text bubble with three dots appeared on the screen. Then came Mike E.'s response: "Whatever."

He was going back on his promise. "I've thought about it and decided not to do it," he wrote. "It's my name." He insisted that any angst his family was experiencing was not his fault but the fault of the media: "You're being gaslit by CNN. I can advocate whatever I want, I'm an American citizen with rights." Mike Sr. didn't respond right away. His son kept typing: "You can believe the media if you want, but that's pathetic, tbh. You should be more open-minded."

Mike Sr. thought of a few potential responses to this, but nothing that seemed likely to have any effect. Instead, he repeated his request: "Change your name."

Mike E. refused. "Perhaps if you had shown more sympathy and interest in fairness," he wrote, "my decision would be different."

"Thanks for the birthday present," Mike Sr. wrote. That was the last time they communicated.

•   •   •

On a Friday afternoon, a month after I started visiting the Peinoviches at their home, Mike Enoch called my cell phone. "I hear you've been talking to my family," he said. I told him that I'd been hoping to speak to him, but that it would have to wait; I was in the middle of lunch. "What are you having?" he asked. I didn't want to tell him the real answer—a bagel and lox—so I lied and said I was eating a salad. As if we were on his podcast, he went on a comedic riff about a take-out

chain called Just Salad: "I've always thought that that was a nice little double en-
tendre, to appeal to social-justice-minded white people." He was about to board a
train to Washington, D.C., so we agreed to talk again that night. I assumed that he
would record the call, troll me for a few minutes, and then play the audio on his
show, as he'd done with other reporters.

In the end, we spoke for more than two hours. He was surprisingly forthcoming. Many of the earliest English-language novels, such as *Tristram Shandy* and
Robinson Crusoe, start with a recitation of the protagonist's family lineage, and
Michael Enoch Peinovich began his narrative that way, too. "My family always
LARPed as WASPs, even though we're not Anglo-Saxon," he said. "My dad wore
tweed jackets, that whole thing." His biological mother, he said later, "was always
a bit of a race realist on this point. She's completely Norwegian, while my dad is
half Norwegian and half Serbian." She was a committed liberal, but on this point,
at least, they seemed to find some common ground. "My mother always said,
'Your temper comes from your Serbian side,'" he added. "I'm quite sure she meant
that in a racial sense. And I think there's something to that."

Every journalist develops a technique to keep people talking. Nodding and
rapt eye contact work well in person, but not over the phone. One of my techniques, which I wasn't aware of at the time, was to repeat the word "Right," even
when my interview subject was saying something horribly wrong. Midway
through my conversation with Enoch, my wife popped her head into the room,
signaled for my attention, and mouthed the words "Is he recording?"

I muted the phone and said, "I think so."

"Well then stop agreeing with him!" she said.

In hindsight, Enoch told me, he was always more wary of African Americans
and Jews than he let on. "I noticed these differences, even when I didn't necessarily
put emphasis on them or think that they were socially deterministic," he said. He
now spoke freely about his "intense, personal antipathy for Jews," but insisted that
he did not hate black people: "I just feel sorry for them and see them as a social
problem." I asked how to square this with the fact that he had a black brother. "He's
only a quarter black," he responded, and that was all he would say on the record.

A few times, I tried to ask another obvious question: If you never liked Jews,
why did you marry one? The first time I asked, he sighed and said, "I don't really
know." The next time, he said, "She's only half Jewish, for one thing. And Jews
have certain physical features that I don't think are particularly attractive. She

didn't have those. I thought she was very pretty." Nor did she exhibit what he considered typical Jewish traits: "The pushiness, this absolute inability to empathize with others, an exploitative personality. She didn't have any of that."

For a while, he hoped that his podcast and his marriage could coexist. "I wanted to have it both ways," he said. "But then we got popular." In 2015, when his identity was still secret, he attended a conference hosted by Richard Spencer's think tank. Most people in the room recognized his voice, and several told him that they'd bought tickets to the event specifically in order to meet him. "At that point, it was, like, OK, this is getting out of control," he told me. "I kept saying, 'It'll be fine, it'll be fine,' but I knew I was just delaying the inevitable."

We talked about *The Culture of Critique*, the anti-Semitic book that he'd found so formative, and I mentioned that I'd just ordered a copy on Amazon. "Well, don't red-pill yourself too hard," he said. Then he paused: "You're not Jewish, are you?" he asked.

I am. I don't put triple parentheses around my name on Twitter, as some Jews do, in defiance of *TRS*'s Echo. But I have never made a secret of my identity. I have written for Jewish magazines. My face looks Jewish. My name sounds Jewish. All of this information was readily available on the internet.

"Yep," I said.

"Interesting," he said, sounding a bit flustered. "Fully Jewish, or half Jewish?"

"Fully," I said. "Your Jewdar must be broken."

"Yeah, well, you've got red hair," he said. "That threw me." He encouraged me to read MacDonald's book nonetheless. "I would hope that you would be able to look past any dissonance and at least examine the argument," he said. "Maybe do some internal—not that I expect you to hate yourself . . ." He trailed off.

At one point, without prompting, he said, "You wanna know the first thing my dad asked me after Charlottesville? He didn't say, 'Are you OK?' or 'How are you?' He said, 'Change your name.'" His mother had asked about his safety—"Mothers are mothers," he explained—but not his stepmother, and not his father. "He didn't care about that," he said. "All he cared about was his *good name*." I couldn't be sure, over the phone, but it sounded like he was crying.

• • •

For a few days after he was doxed, Mike Enoch tried to insist that he wasn't Mike Peinovich, but he soon posted a confession on *The Right Stuff*. "Yes my wife is who they say she is," he wrote. "I could try to explain my whole life for the last ten years to you but what difference at this point would it make. Life isn't perfect." In his absence, Dunstan and McNabb convened an emergency recording of *The Daily Shoah*, in which they attempted to address the controversy without fully explaining it. "I don't know what kind of cognitive dissonance Mike had to live with to be in that situation," McNabb said. It wasn't clear that there would ever be another episode of the show.

On white-supremacist forums across the internet, including on *The Right Stuff* itself, opinions were divided. Some commenters vowed to boycott the site until Enoch divorced his wife ("I can't believe all you fags still support this jew fucker!"), or accused him of being "controlled opposition." Some held out for more information ("how Jewish? Because if 1/4 or less, I don't give a shit"). Others made non-sequitur observations ("I'm more disappointed by how fat he is than anything").

"Wow just wow," Andrew Anglin wrote on the *Daily Stormer*. "This may be the first time I've ever said 'wow just wow' with 100% deadly seriousness. This was definitely not expected." Although Anglin understood why many in the movement felt betrayed by the news—"Really, he should have gotten a divorce. I think that's reasonable"—he argued that Enoch deserved a second chance. "I don't think that Mike is a shill," he wrote. "Tens of thousands—maybe even hundreds of thousands—of men have been brought into the movement through *TRS* and Mike's work, and nothing can or will change that."*

Immediately after the dox, Enoch told people, in private, that he was done with white nationalism. Dunstan and McNabb could continue the show without him, or they could end it; either way, his plan was to leave the alt-right, disappear from the internet for a while, and try to mend his relationship with his wife. But it soon became clear that, no matter what Mike did, it wouldn't be enough to save his marriage. His wife was leaving. She moved out of New York and went to stay with her parents. Mike stayed behind in the apartment on the Upper East Side, unsure what to do next.

Six days after the dox, he started telling people that he'd changed his mind. The movement was all he had left. He and his cohosts recorded an episode of *The Daily Shoah* announcing Enoch's triumphant return. "We're not letting this thing beat us," Dunstan said. "We're not going anywhere."

---

*From the *Daily Stormer*'s style guide: "The site continues to grow month by month, indicating that there is no ceiling on this." Also from the style guide: "We should always claim we are winning, and should celebrate any wins with extreme exaggeration."

A propagandist with enough time and talent can explain away even the most glaring contradiction, and Enoch had spent years developing an intimate bond with his fans. "I appreciate everyone's support," he said. On the air, Dunstan read dozens of notes from listeners who, despite the news about Enoch's wife, were remaining loyal to the show. Some had donated hundreds or thousands of dollars to Enoch in his time of need. "My heart goes out to his wife," wrote one fan, a long-distance trucker who listened to *The Daily Shoah* on cross-country drives. "I imagine she is getting a huge amount of shit from her family and the larger community. If she is married to Mike, she must be a good individual."

"That is a really nice thing to say," Enoch responded on the air. "I'm sure she'll appreciate that." He didn't mention that she was living in the Midwest, trying to lie low, doing her best to stay off the internet.

•   •   •

I visited Enoch's mother, a retired president of a small college, in her tidy, sun-filled apartment in New York City. She sat in one upholstered armchair and I sat in another; nearby, on a love seat, was a throw pillow embroidered with a few flying angels and the words of the Serenity Prayer. "Mike E. knows what I think about his politics," she said. "I was very active in Hillary's campaign, and I do a lot of pro-immigrant volunteering at my church—I'm being trained to accompany people to their ICE hearings—so I'd say we disagree very strongly."

"And you consider it a political disagreement?" I said. "Or does it go beyond politics?"

"He's my son," she responded. "It doesn't matter what it is. I'm not going to stop loving him, or talking to him."

She told me about a time a few months earlier, when he'd asked to bring some friends over for dinner. "I was annoyed. I said, 'Mike E., dinner's in three hours—I don't know if I have enough chicken!' But he said, 'I would think that you'd at least want to meet my friends,' and I went, 'You know what, that's a good point. Why shouldn't I want to meet your friends?'"

He'd brought over two burly men, one of whom was a member of the Alabama National Guard. "They introduced themselves as Richard Spencer's personal bodyguards," she told me. "I thought, Well, I certainly wasn't bargaining for this. But they turned out to be polite young men, I have to say. At one point they started getting into it, about diversity this and Judaism that, and I said, 'Look, I don't think we should argue.' So I changed the subject: 'Is it your first time in New York City? How are you enjoying it?' And after that the evening went smoothly."

She'd always liked Enoch's wife—"ex-wife, I guess I should say"—and had recently sent her a birthday card. The ex-wife, in her response, wrote, "I wish I could push a reset button on my life."

"The last time Mike E. was here, I told him about that note," his mother said. "He was sitting at the dining-room table, right over there, and when I told him those words he just burst into tears."

On her phone, she showed me text messages that she and her son had exchanged while he was at the Charlottesville rally.

Her: "I just want to remind you that you do not have health insurance."

Him: "We're safe. We just want to express ideas. The ACLU is supporting our right to speak."

Reading this, she glanced up at me. "He knows I'm a big supporter of the ACLU," she said. "So I'm sure he thought that would soften me up."

"And did it?" I asked.

"Oh, probably," she said.

She showed me another text exchange, also from when he was in Charlottesville, in which she asked if he'd received the package she'd sent in the mail. She explained to me that the package was full of new shirts. "The ones he had at the time were too big and billowy," she said. "I figured, if he was going to be on TV, I wanted him to have something that fit better." I didn't know what to say to that. My first thought was, If my son ever tells me that he's planning to speak at a white-supremacist rally, I hope my reaction is not to go shopping. But my second thought was, Honestly, I have no idea what I would do in that situation.*

Near the end of our conversation, I asked Enoch's mother if she could think of anything unusual about his childhood, anything that might have steered him toward the path he was on. She answered by talking about his "heritage." "I believe that Serbs and Croatians are a hateful, vengeful people," she said. "He has that vengeful blood running through his veins. He doesn't just have that Scandinavian blood, that pure Norwegian blood."

---

*My wife worked as a public defender for several years. Some of her clients were accused of crimes that were horrifically violent or deeply shameful, but their parents' reactions, which ranged from permanent ostracism to total forgiveness, didn't correspond neatly with the gravity of the accusations. "You can never predict what anyone's response is going to be," my wife told me. "But it's usually a good bet, in my experience, that a mother is going to try to be there for her son, pretty much no matter what."

Once again, I didn't know what to say. A comment about pure blood would have been off-putting in any context; in this context, I found it stupefying. In the twenty-first-century United States, we sometimes tell ourselves that racial essentialism is a rare and inexplicable defect, but in fact it doesn't come from nowhere. When I was a child, my grandmother told me, sternly and repeatedly, that every person on Earth was a unique miracle, equally worthy of dignity and opportunity and respect. "You don't need to believe in God to know that," she said. "You know it because that's what it means to be human—seeing the humanity in everyone else." She also told me, when I was seven years old, that I'd done well on a math test because of my "Yiddishe kop"—my Jewish brain. Even now, I can't imagine how my younger self reconciled those two apparently contradictory ideas.

●   ●   ●

On my last visit to the Peinoviches' house in New Jersey, Mike Sr. flipped through a photo album that Billie had brought up from the basement. One photo sparked a pleasant memory: a twenty-fifth-anniversary trip to Hawaii, in 2008, with the three children. "We were all in good spirits that week, even Mike E.," he said. "We went out to these long dinners and ordered a bunch of cocktails, which probably helped. Mike E. had brought along this computer program he'd made—"

"The Bergman Plot Generator," Billie said.

"He somehow figured out how to randomly generate plots of Ingmar Bergman films—"

"'A dark knight encounters death on a lonely road,' that kind of thing—"

"And he left it running, in the condo we were renting, and all day it would be spitting out plots," Mike Sr. said, chuckling. "We'd come back inside and read them out to one another, and we'd fall down laughing."

His smile faded. "I still love him, in spite of everything," he said, his voice catching. The sun started to set, casting shadows across the living room, and he went into the kitchen to open a bottle of wine. Billie said, "All I keep thinking is that, if we were Jewish, we'd be sitting shiva right now."

Earlier in our conversation, Mike and Billie had asked me a series of questions about the alt-right. They seemed like attempts to understand Mike E.'s personal motives, although they were phrased as broader questions about the movement. Was the extreme rhetoric just a sick joke, or did they actually mean it? How did they decide when to be outrageously provocative and when to hold back? Instead of answering categorically, I mentioned a specific example: the response to the killing of Heather Heyer, which had caused a rhetorical schism within the movement. A few alt-right leaders, hoping to give their movement a sheen of respectability, had been relatively restrained.* Others reacted with vicious cruelty. "Heather Heyer was a fat, disgusting Communist," Jason Kessler, the organizer of the Charlottesville rally, tweeted. "Looks like it was payback time."

When I first mentioned this rhetorical schism, Mike Sr. started to ask me which side his son had fallen on. But then he caught himself: "You know what, forget it. I don't need to know."

Now, reentering the room with the wine in his hand, he changed his mind. "I think I actually do want to know," he said. "About how Mike E.—whether he said anything about that poor girl."

I didn't give him any of his son's direct quotes. I didn't have to. As soon as I hesitated, he knew enough.

"Oh," he said, his face twisted in sharp, silent agony. "Oh, no."

• • •

I handed in a piece about Enoch. I had made mistakes, as always, and the fact-checker corrected them. The pottery in the Peinoviches' house came from Mexico, not New Mexico; Kevin MacDonald spelled his name with a capital D. When the fact-checker called Enoch, he said that he considered himself a white nationalist, not a white supremacist, but that we could print whatever we wanted. He denied having stomped on a glass at his wedding; but I'd seen the wedding album with my own eyes, so the fact stayed in. Enoch also used the fact-checking process to take a few more vicarious swipes at his parents. "If my dad told you some shit about how my grandpa fought the Nazis during World War Two, I'm gonna have to preemptively correct that," he said. "I understand why that has nice rhetorical resonance and all, but my grandfather fought in the Pacific Theater." I considered running this by Mike Sr., but concluded that I'd already put him through enough.

Several of Mike E.'s relatives had told me, independently, that they'd always considered him "the smartest one in the family." The fact-checker disputed this. He didn't doubt that they'd said it, but he was also responsible for verifying

---

*Richard Spencer, for example, tweeted, "Heyer's death was deeply saddening." (The next day, however, when Spencer appeared on *The Daily Shoah*, his comments about Heyer's death were far less diplomatic.)

the content and context of each quote, and this one seemed like it risked convey-
ing a false impression. "He has certain intelligent instincts related to aesthetics
and communication," the checker said, "but beyond that—well, I worry that his
family, and now us, are trying to see a silver lining where there is none." Understandably, the checker was wary of overemphasizing the intelligence of a person
who had reached such colossally stupid conclusions. We had a long discussion
about it, in which I countered that intelligence and morality were independent
variables—that a lot of bright people held reprehensible beliefs, and that the fact
that an otherwise smart person could succumb to internet neofascism was part of
what made internet neofascism so terrifying. After a while, the checker and I
agreed that we wouldn't be able to settle on a mutually satisfactory definition of
intelligence by press time, and we left it to the editor of the piece to cast the tie-
breaking vote. She decided that we should describe Enoch not as "smart" but as
"clever."

Next, we had to pick a rubric. Annals of Activism? The Political Scene? Enoch
wasn't exactly a political theorist, and *The Right Stuff* wasn't a political-action
committee or a think tank. It was a content farm producing an endless supply of
blog posts and podcasts and memes. Its goal was not to organize congressional
campaigns or to write draft legislation but to nudge the Overton window.

We went with Annals of Media.

Enoch called me several more times. I knew that he was recording our conversations, probably hoping to generate material for his podcast; but the calls were useful for my purposes, too, so I kept taking them.

I assumed that his minions would descend on me after the piece came out. It
occurred to me that, if Enoch had met me in person, he might be more likely to
order his troll army to stand down, should the need arise. Shortly before the piece
was published, I texted him to ask if we could meet for a drink.

"Sure why not," he texted. "Let's go to Heidelberg. Good beer and brats."

It was a German beer hall on the Upper East Side. "You know, this whole part
of Manhattan used to be a German neighborhood," Enoch said, as we were led to
a table by a hostess wearing a dirndl. We sat across from one another, and he
stared at me for a long moment.

Having familiarized myself with the *TRS Troll Guide*, I knew that my only job was to remain unruffled. "This place is pretty LARP-y, don't you think?" I said, ordering a Lowenbrau and a platter of bauernwurst.

"You eat pork?" he said.

"We're sneaky like that," I said.

He asked me what I thought of *The Culture of Critique* now that I'd read it. I answered as forthrightly as possible. "Whatever I say, you'll argue that I can't be objective," I began. "Which, fine, maybe no one can be objective about anything." But my honest opinion, leaving aside whether I found the book offensive, was that MacDonald's argument made no sense. There were a hundred things wrong with it. I picked one. "He says that Jews are overrepresented in leftist movements," I said. "Fine. Jews are also overrepresented in right-wing movements. Jews are over-represented in centrist movements. Jews are overrepresented in physics depart-ments. Jews are overrepresented in circuses." Steve Bannon had recently been fired, due in part to post-Charlottesville blowback, leaving Stephen Miller as the chief architect of Trump's most draconian anti-immigrant policies. Jews were even overrepresented in Trumpist nativism! The phenomenon of Jewish over-representation was a curious one, I conceded, but MacDonald's gloss did nothing to explain it.

"I can dispute some of your points," Enoch said. "The Stephen Miller thing—I will admit, I actually can't figure that one out. I'm thrilled about it, don't get me wrong, but I don't know what to make of it."

We talked about Israel for a while. Or rather, he talked and I listened. He seemed to assume that I was a center-left Zionist (against settlements, in favor of everything else), although I'd given him no indication one way or another. Zion-ism is one of the alt-right's favorite talking points—*If they get to have an ethno-state, why don't we?*—and Enoch followed Israeli news far more closely than I did. "The Chief Rabbinate requires proof that someone is Jewish—racially Jewish, mind you—before they can get married in the state of Israel," he said. "Some rab-binical rulings even suggest using DNA tests for this purpose. What's your take on that?" I stayed quiet and ate my wurst. Even good-faith discussions about Zion-ism, among family or friends, often grew heated. What was the point of debating *halachah* with a professional anti-Semite?

He invited me on *The Daily Shoah* for a discussion about MacDonald's book and the JQ.

"I don't think that's gonna happen, man," I said. Philip Roth once wrote about how nothing could make an ambivalent Jew feel more unambivalently Jewish than sitting in a church, but Philip Roth never sat in a beer hall with a not-quite-Nazi.

When it was over, we lingered outside on the street corner. I was eager to get home, and I kept looking for natural ways to end the conversation, but Enoch seemed to be in no rush at all. He puffed on his vape pen, which was shaped not like a pen but like a first-generation Walkman brimming with liquid glycerine. Smoking is a bad idea, but at least it looks cool; this clunky piece of plastic, filling up his entire fist, reminded me of what child-development experts call a transitional object. "I'm getting the fuck out of this city," he said. "There's nothing for me here anyway."

A few weeks later, he moved to Dutchess County to be closer to Dunstan. Most days, they recorded the podcast from Dunstan's man cave, which was full of microphones, weight lifting equipment, and merchandise bearing *The Right Stuff*'s logo. They set up a paywall on their site; subscribers, in addition to the usual audio, got to watch a video feed of the cohosts holding forth, for hours, while sitting on reclining office chairs. Snippets of the video feed sometimes surfaced on YouTube, and whenever I watched one I found it overwhelmingly boring and sad. Dunstan had tacked a *TRS* flag to the wall behind him, but the upper corners kept drooping to reveal the Iron Maiden poster beneath it. Every few minutes, Enoch would put on reading glasses, scroll to a new headline that he considered worthy of mockery, then take off his glasses and rub his eyes.

• • •

When my piece about Enoch came out, the trolling was milder than I expected. The following episode of *The Daily Shoah* included a twenty-one-minute response segment—"This Freudian bullshit is how Jews approach everything"—and then an abrupt segue to some shitposting about Charlottesville. On Twitter, Enoch wrote a mock confession ("I admit it fam: I was red-pilled by childhood allergies"). He also released "The Marantz Tapes," two lengthy compilations of excerpts from our phone calls.

The "tapes" were mostly banal bits of conversation interspersed with *Seinfeld*-style theme music. The audio was selectively edited, of course, but then so were the quotations I'd used in my piece. The next time we talked on the phone, Enoch brought up the tapes and asked what I thought of them. "You know, I'm a journalist, too, in my own way," he said. "Or, not a journalist, but an opinion maker or whatever the hell you wanna call it."

Near the end of 2017, Roy Moore, a far-right extremist, state judge, and alleged pedophile, ran for U.S. Senate in Alabama. A few days before the election, at a campaign event, one of the few African Americans in the audience asked Moore when America had last been great. "I think it was great at the time when families were united," Moore said. "Even though we had slavery, they cared for one another. . . . Our families were strong, our country had a direction." Obviously, in this context, "our families" meant "white families."

Alt-right talking points kept drifting toward the center of the national vocabulary. They were repeated again and again—by YouTubers, by talk-radio hosts, even by sitting members of Congress.* "Virginia has transformed politically because it has been transformed demographically," Tucker Carlson, the most popular cable anchor in his time slot, said in November 2017. "Twelve percent of Virginia is foreign-born, and that has made all the difference. . . . They've replaced you." Like Moore, Carlson was making a naked appeal to white racial grievance. The word "you" could only have referred to white people; the word "replaced" seemed like a clear allusion to the alt-right's Great Replacement theory, the substance of many of the slogans and chants in Charlottesville.

Laura Ingraham, another Fox News host with an immense platform, invoked race even more overtly: "The Democrats mostly want to replace those old, white, yahoo conservatives with a new group of people who might be a little bit more amenable to big government." Some nights, instead of haranguing the Democrats, Ingraham used more specific dog whistles, railing against "globalists," or "elites," or George Soros. I texted Enoch, asking him whether he thought that Ingraham was nodding toward the JQ. "There is always the likelihood that she is aware," he replied. "Nixon was. Billy Graham was. Tucker most certainly is."

I asked Enoch, "Have you been surprised by how many mainstream figures, elected officials, etc. have recently started to dog-whistle in a more overtly white-nationalist direction?"

---

*In 2017, on Twitter, Iowa congressman Steve King wrote that "culture and demographics are our destiny. We can't restore our civilization with somebody else's babies."

"I find it odd that this country ever stopped being white nationalist," he responded. Still, he marveled at how quickly the unsayable had been made sayable: "It shows that our strategy of widening the Overton window is working."

In 2018, Enoch and Dunstan rebranded *The Daily Shoah* as *TDS*, an initialism that now purportedly stood for nothing. ("Tedious," they often pronounced it.)* They made an effort to refrain from egregious racial slurs or explicit glorification of violence. They were trying to creep toward the outer edge of the mainstream—or, at least, trying to avoid the kind of viral attention that might cause their domain server to notice their site and ban it. "It is a meme war," Enoch said on TDS. "We've managed to stay alive, and to punch way above our weight."

Longtime fans noticed the show's new tone. On 4chan, opinion was divided:

No naming the jew. entire conversation feels tense. What aren't they telling us? If there are any people in the world that need to be careful it's these guys because the jews will assfuck them into oblivion at the drop of a shekel. (((peinovich)))

They kept A/B testing, trying to continue dropping red pills without getting deplatformed. Instead of fantasizing about physically removing all liberals from society, the cohosts alluded more obliquely to "urbanites" and "bugmen"; instead of assailing the Jewish agenda by name, they referred to "cultural Marxism" and "the J-left"; instead of joking about turning George Soros into a lampshade, they simply maintained that, like any plutocrat with an international reach, Soros was a fair target for political critique. It was a new version of the Southern Strategy—what might be called the Soros Strategy. "Our role is to be the intellectual vanguard," Enoch said. "We have almost a direct alt-right-to-Tucker pipeline. He waters the narratives down somewhat, makes them acceptable so he won't get kicked off of Fox News, and then he puts them out there."[†]

---

*After the mass murder at the Tree of Life synagogue in Pittsburgh, I wrote a short blog post about Kevin MacDonald, internet radicalization, and why the alt-right was so hung up on the Jews. The next day, Enoch read the headline of my piece on the air. "'The Dark, Specific Logic of Online Hatred,'" he said sardonically. "Maybe that's what TDS should stand for. 'The Dark Specific.'"

[†]"Tucker Carlson is basically 'Daily Stormer: The Show,'" Andrew Anglin, the publisher of the Daily Stormer, wrote, in a tone of grateful disbelief. "Other than the language used, he is covering all of our talking points."

In September 2018, on his prime-time show, Carlson asked, "How, precisely, is diversity our strength?" A few weeks later, he declared that immigration "makes our country poorer and dirtier and more divided." A guest on Fox Business referred to the "Soros-occupied State Department." In advance of the midterm elections, the National Republican Congressional Committee released an ad in which George Soros sat with hands folded ominously, his image crudely Photoshopped next to stacks of cash. The ad looked like something that Mike Cernovich might have tweeted in 2016 to promote one of his trending hashtags. At the time, such a tweet would have been seen as bizarre, negligible, unthinkably fringe. Two years later, it was merely controversial.

•   •   •

I was at a coffee shop in my neighborhood when I saw a Periscope notification. Will Chamberlain was filming a new video, a discussion of my recent article on "Mike Enoch and the anti-Semitic rabbit hole." That was a tough one to avoid clicking on right away, but I managed to wait, per my new rule, until the stream was over.

"The intellectual path that Mike Enoch went down, at least at the start, was really similar to the intellectual path that I went down," Chamberlain said. "It's interesting to see why he went all the way down the rabbit hole to white supremacy and why I feel like I didn't."

"Mike Enoch nearly destroyed my life," a commenter wrote. "Daily Shoah drew me in, nearly caused me to abandon everything."

"Can we just ignore them and maybe they'll go away?" another commenter wrote.

A commenter called @ActualRacist tried to say something, but Chamberlain blocked the comment before it showed up.

Enoch's path, Chamberlain said, was not mere fodder for intellectual curiosity. It also raised a more practical question: "How to change it, how to bring people back from the brink." There were still untold numbers of aimless young people on Twitter, many of whom should have been intelligent enough to know better, who nevertheless remained susceptible to the allure of white-nationalist propaganda. "These are kids that need to be deradicalized," he said.

The American Berserk II

CHAPTER TWENTY-SEVEN

The Mountain

When Samantha was halfway through high school, her family moved to a featureless cul-de-sac in a drab Florida suburb: Orange Julius, Cracker Barrel, highway, strip mall. As soon as she got there, she wanted to leave. Her parents were fighting all the time; it seemed to her that she was expected to fix their relationship, but she had no idea where to start. She had a younger brother, and they were extremely close—"codependent" was the word she used, half ironically, although it was a precocious word for her to know, much less to know how to use half ironically. She was like that, though. She would surprise her teachers by remembering some offhand comment, verbatim, months later; then, on other days, she'd skip school and drive around aimlessly, smoking weed and listening to Joy Division. She sometimes tried to justify her behavior by referring to that old Mark Twain line about how you shouldn't let your schooling get in the way of your education, but maybe a more honest explanation would have been good old teenage nihilism.

Somehow, the two books that made the most sense to her were *Fight Club* and *The Sayings of the Buddha*. The first step toward true liberation was recognizing that the world you saw around you was actually an illusion, a thin veneer over a vast, howling void. (*Fight Club*: "I am so ZEN. This is BLOOD. This is NOTHING.") There was an old Buddhist parable about a man walking down a long path. At first, he looks up and sees a mountain in the distance. Then, when he's farther along on the path, he looks up again and sees a void where the mountain used to be. Only much later, near the end of his journey, does he fully understand the truth—that all is emptiness, including the mountain—at which point he is suddenly able to see the mountain again. This was the kind of thing that Samantha liked to think about while the rest of her classmates were hanging out at the mall, smoking cloves, and debating whether the Rays were going to win the pennant. No wonder she hated high school.

Before her family moved to Florida, she'd spent her entire childhood in a rural town in central New Jersey, a few miles inland from the Shore. She'd always been too passive, too pliable about defining herself; instead, she let other people define her. They called her Stargirl, a reference to a young-adult novel about a quirky kid who gets kicked off the cross-country team because she refuses to follow the marked path. Samantha was fine with that reputation. She leaned into being Stargirl, wearing flowy skirts and quoting weird indie movies. Now, in Florida, she was nothing. "sometimes i think about disappearing," she wrote on her Tumblr. "it feels like nothing to wake up. there is no home to return to." At every summer job, on every family vacation, she would meet some guy who claimed to love her, but it never turned out to be the kind of love that involved paying attention to what she actually said or who she actually was.

She was a senior in high school when Obama ran for president, and she volunteered to canvass for him on the weekends. Politics didn't generally appeal to her, but everyone seemed to agree that the Bush era had been a total disaster, and Obama seemed like a smart guy with a good heart. Still, although she didn't mention it to anyone, she was a bit jealous that he got to be so many things at once— Hawaiian, Kansan, Kenyan, Indonesian—while she was still nothing. In New Jersey, she'd spent weekends hanging out with her friend Rowena, whose mom served ackee and saltfish and told stories about growing up in Jamaica, or with her friend Sơn, who taught her the occasional funny phrase in Vietnamese. What did Samantha have to offer her friends? "Come over this weekend, we can help my grandma cook spaetzle." "Cool, where'd she learn that?" "Oh, you know, when she was growing up in Germany in the thirties." That was not a conversation anyone wanted to get into. Instead, Samantha stuck to the occasional self-deprecating joke on behalf of all white people: we have no rhythm, our food has no flavor, we ruin everything we touch.

On one level, it was legitimately true that white people had fucked over the rest of the world for centuries; if it made her friends feel better to hear her acknowledge this fact, then she was down to do her part. On another level—a more mystical, beneath-the-veneer-of-illusion level—wasn't race ultimately just a distraction? Every few days, it seemed, one of her friends, white or nonwhite, would post a link to some *BuzzFeed* listicle about the 12 Worst Things White People Did This Month. Samantha sometimes felt like sticking up for herself, but she worried that if she did, even in a quippy way, she would get called out for her white fragility. One of Samantha's black friends posted an article on Facebook about some jackass at a college in Maryland who had recently formed a White Student Union. The post racked up comments:

Ugh.
Fuck this dude and his privilege.
White people gonna white people.

Samantha was the only white person her friend had tagged in the post, so she tried to do her part: she typed a comment about how, as an unelected representative of Caucasians everywhere, she condemned the actions of this garbage human. Again, fair enough. Either the guy was being a dumb troll or he was an actual racist; either way, he did sound like an asshole. Still, though, what did it mean that her friend had tagged her in the post at all?

After high school, she started working at a Chipotle in town, dating anyone who seemed interesting, trying to figure out what might come next. For some reason, she was fixated on the idea of applying to mortuary school, which seemed like something that Margot Tenenbaum, her favorite movie character, would do. But then Chipotle offered her a job managing a new location in another state. It was an opportunity to get away, and she took it.

The job was about halfway between Florida and New Jersey, in one of those small Southern cities that was always showing up on Top-10 lists of the most underrated places to visit for a weekend. She knew no one there, which suited her fine. There were a few colleges nearby, and some microbreweries, and a walkable Main Street with brick buildings that were about half a century less old than they looked. A few weeks after moving, she quit the Chipotle job to work at a café and bar downtown—morning shifts as a barista, night shifts as a bartender. She was good at service, not only because she knew a lot about coffee and beer and wine but because she knew how to connect with people. You could call it flirting, and sure, sometimes it was flirting. Other times, though, it was more about being who the customer wanted you to be—coming across as quick and witty, or intuiting that the customer wanted to be slightly quicker and wittier than you and toning it down accordingly. It was just a sense. Some people had it, and she was one of those people. At first there was nothing, the usual emptiness, two lonely strangers in a bar. Then: a spark, a fleeting mutual secret, a wisp of intimacy. She'd tried all the drugs, or most of them, and intimacy was her favorite one.

She wore ballet flats to hide how tall she was. She could never tell if she was wearing too much or too little makeup. Was she pretty? Pretty was the opposite of how she felt, but then again self-esteem had never been one of her specialties. Still, it was an observable fact that she did not have trouble attracting men's attention. People were drawn to her. It wasn't good or bad; it just was. Except, if you wanted to overthink it—and overthinking was quite high on her list of specialties—people weren't really drawn to *her*, per se, because she was just anticipating what they were likely to want and then mirroring it back to them. Laid out coldly like that, it could sound manipulative, but she wasn't interested in manipulation. She was interested in connection.

People were always telling you to follow your bliss, which sounded nice in theory, but in practice they only seemed to respect one particular kind of bliss-following. In books and movies, the Serious Man who wanted to discover his true identity was always going on a solitary quest, or hiding away in a cabin to write the Great American Novel. Well, she had tried being alone with her own brain, and it never went smoothly. It wasn't as if she wanted to be a conformist shill—whatever the establishment consensus was, she'd always positioned herself as far from it as possible. Still, when she tried to consider what her true identity might be, or what having a true identity even meant, she could only approximate the concept by imagining herself from the outside in, through the eyes of other people.

She didn't follow political news very closely, but as far as she could tell Obama's presidency was turning out to be a dud. The grand changes he'd promised were not materializing—or, if they were, she wasn't seeing it. The Republicans were in charge for a few years, then the Democrats took over for a few years; either way, the world kept on looking basically the same. At least, that was the sense she got whenever she turned on CNN or the *Today* show. Could everything really be as monotonous and predictable as it seemed, or was that also part of the illusion? Late one night, she called her brother, who'd been spending a lot of time watching YouTube videos. He told her about a theory he'd been learning about: that there was a maze of secret underground bunkers below Denver International Airport, and that it might be the global headquarters of the Illuminati. Samantha didn't even know what that meant, exactly, but the idea freaked her out so much that she kept thinking about it for days afterward. It almost certainly wasn't true. If anything remotely like that was actually real, she would have heard about it. Right? Unless of course the elites really were powerful enough to keep the whole thing a secret. In which case—well, whatever. What impact did it have on her life? She wasn't in Denver. She had no way to judge any of these assertions for herself. Lies, damned lies, and statistics: you could comfort yourself by finding articles claiming the bunkers didn't exist, or you could freak yourself out by looking for evidence that they did. Ultimately it just came down to which sources you chose to reject and which ones you chose to believe.

Her original plan was to stay in the small Southern city for a few months before going back to school. But she was often too passive when it came to big life decisions, and a few months ended up turning into a few years. The café where she worked was a social hub; local activists and poets would spread their stuff across tables and hang around all day, shooting the shit, working on their laptops or pretending to work.

She got to know the master roaster at the café, and they started dating. At night, he'd take her out drinking with the other baristas and line cooks: girls with half-shaved heads and piercings, vegan punks, guys who played in noise-rock bands. Everybody had a thing. Samantha cycled in and out of phases, perennially unsure of what her thing should be. In middle school, her favorite movie had been *Empire Records*, about a bunch of bighearted misfit kids trying to save their local independent record store. ("Damn the Man! Save the Empire!") She'd identified so strongly with Lucas, a brooding clerk at the store, that she wore his signature outfit—black sweater, jeans, Pumas—every day for six months. During another phase, which lasted several weeks, she'd refused all sustenance except for saltines, baby carrots, and cranberry juice. Her friends in New Jersey liked to joke that Samantha was always getting into something new and weird, and that she never got in halfway. Samantha thought of her phases as experiments in ascetic discipline, sort of like Steve Jobs's signature black turtleneck—by paring down your wardrobe and other trivial decisions, you could free up mental space for something more meaningful. She just had to figure out what that something else would be.

In the summer of 2014, when she was twenty-four, she met Richie. She forgot about the master roaster right away. Richie could cook and dance and play the guitar; he was assertive and nurturing and humble all at once. She was always falling for some new guy—that was another of her friends' running jokes about her—but the connection with Richie was stronger than anything she'd felt before. When he walked into a house party, the room tilted slightly on its axis, everyone unconsciously orbiting a bit closer to him. The first time she went to his place, they stayed up and talked all night. She started to imagine that as long as they kept talking, as long as they didn't fall asleep, the sun would never have to rise.

There was no way to refer to her feelings, or even to think about them, without resorting to cliché. This only made her appreciate, whenever a pop song came on in the coffee shop (*love is a battlefield*; *love is like a flame*) why those radio clichés were so popular in the first place: as trite as they were, they described something irreducibly real. When you were reading Jane Austen in your bedroom, if you came across a description of the heath or the seaside, you just had to take Jane's word for it. Once you'd seen the south of England for yourself, you could verify: Yes, the hills really are that green. The sea really does roar. Can confirm.

Socrates was a man; men are mortal; therefore Socrates was mortal. Richie was an American male below the age of thirty; it was the twenty-first century; therefore Richie derived much of his sense of humor—much of his understanding of the world—from the internet. Whenever he or Samantha did something stereotypically American, he would say, "We're such fucking burgers." This was a 4chan thing: Americans were burgers, Canadians were leafs. He showed 4chan to Samantha a few times, but she could never get through more than a page or two before wrinkling up her nose and closing the tab. Burger and leaf were the least of it—every other post was faggot this or kike that or kill yourself, slut. She had no problem with dark humor when it served a purpose, but this seemed gratuitous and exhausting.

"Not for me," she told Richie.

"Fine, but you're not gonna get half my jokes," he said.

They broke up a few times, unprepared to handle the intensity of their feelings, but they always got back together. It went on like that for months. When the Academy Award nominations were announced in early 2016, there were, for the second year in a row, no people of color among the twenty acting nominees. The hashtag #OscarsSoWhite trended on Twitter, or at least on woke Twitter.

"If they were truly woke, their hashtag would be #HollywoodSoJewish," Richie said.

"Well," Samantha said, "Jewish people *are* white, so . . ."

He gave her a Meaningful Look whose meaning she could not begin to fathom. "Yeah," he said. "Sure they are."

In November of that year, Samantha told her friends that she was planning to vote for Hillary, but she didn't end up voting at all. Richie voted for Trump. He drove around town on Election Night, elated, a victory party of one. He'd never been overtly political before, but when he talked about Trump—the God-Emperor, as 4channers called him—Richie sounded like an ardent nativist. This made him an outlier in Samantha's circle of friends, but she was in no mood to pick a fight with him, at least not about politics. He was entitled to his opinion.

Everyone began to notice that Richie was changing somehow. It was as if his personality was a faint pencil sketch that was now being traced over in charcoal. He grew a beard. He started powerlifting. Instead of playing the guitar at house parties, he stayed home and played chess online. The first few times she asked what was going on with him, he stared at her and said nothing. When he did finally answer, all he would say was that he'd been reading a lot of new blogs and subreddits, and that they were teaching him how to become a better man.

She became a manager at an upscale bar in town. Some mornings, when she was hungover, she would vow never to drink again. Then she would drink again, and Richie would give her shit for it. "If you keep acting like such a degenerate," he'd say, "then I won't be able to defend you on the Day of the Rope." She didn't get the joke. It must have been another 4chan thing. She asked what it meant, but he just laughed and changed the subject.

One night, standing outside the bar on a cigarette break, she googled "day of the rope" on her phone. She opened a thread on a subreddit called r/OutOfThe Loop, and she felt queasy and lightheaded as soon as she saw the words, even before their meaning reached her brain.

"What is the 'day of the rope'?" the original post read.

"It is pure unfiltered hate," the top answer read. "As I understand it, the original concept of the day of the rope was aimed purely towards racial purification." The phrase came from *The Turner Diaries*, a 1978 novel that was found in Timothy McVeigh's car after the Oklahoma City bombing. In the book, an underground syndicate of white Americans starts stockpiling weapons, scheming to take their country back. When the uprising happens, the syndicate's first move is to execute all nonwhites, including Jews. This sparks a civil war that culminates in a mass public hanging of all white "race traitors"—judges, journalists, anyone with mixed-race children. That's the Day of the Rope.

Samantha drove to Richie's house and barged into the living room. "What the fuck is this about?" she asked, showing him her phone, her hand trembling. He sat silently on the couch. She paced around the room, terrified, alternately yelling and going silent.

After a while, he looked up at her and started talking in an eerily calm voice. "I'm a fascist," he said. "I've been reading a lot about this, and I've come to the conclusion that the white race will not survive unless we stand up for our interests."

The Turner Diaries was fiction, he explained. The revolution wouldn't have to be violent, necessarily; that part was just an edgy meme. Still, edgy memes served an important purpose—they shocked white people out of their complacency. That was what had happened to him. From there, he had moved on to the more academically rigorous alt-right sites: *Radix Journal, VDARE, American Renaissance, The Right Stuff.* Of course he was put off by the arguments at first—everyone was—but that was just a vestige of social conditioning, an irrational fear response that kicked in whenever you started to look too closely at the evidence. The mainstream media elites had trained everyone to be uncomfortable with any information that hadn't been prevetted. But the media elites were just trying to sell you their own narrative, and there were some questions that they never seemed to raise. Why, for example, had the United States suddenly been flooded with nonwhite immigrants—59 million of them since 1965—after being a majority-white nation for centuries? Were the immigration statistics and the crime statistics and the IQ statistics all just a coincidence, or were they part of some larger scheme?

She didn't have the data to rebut his talking points, and he knew it. She stood there in silence, letting him say whatever he was going to say. "You might hate me after this," he concluded, "but at least I respect you enough to tell you the truth."

She gathered her things to leave. There was no point in responding. He didn't try to stop her; he just walked out to the front porch, lit a cigarette, and watched her car pull away.

On the drive home, she was crying so hard that she could barely see the road. She would never talk to Richie again, that much was clear. The only real question was what this indicated about herself. They'd been together, off and on, for more than two years. How had she missed the warning signs? Was she just a gullible idiot? Or was she, deep down, a monster like him?

She walked inside and opened her laptop on the kitchen counter. Before ending this chapter in her life, she decided, she owed it to herself to understand, if only in an anthropological way, how Richie had gone so horribly wrong. She decided to look at some of the sites he'd mentioned, the ones he'd called "academically rigorous." She was a curious person, and she liked to think that she had enough integrity not to flinch in the face of any idea, no matter how unpalatable it seemed.

Five days later, after reading every alt-right article and watching every alt-right video she could find, she called Richie. She had looked into it, she said. He was right. She wanted to become an advocate for the white race, too.

It actually did feel a bit like watching the Matrix dissolve into a green curtain of digits. Or like stepping through a looking glass, or emerging from Plato's cave, or staring up at a mountain and seeing only emptiness. She finally understood why those allegorical tropes were so enduring across centuries. Just like the love songs on the radio, the clichés were cliché for a good reason, but you could only appreciate it by experiencing it for yourself. She still saw her coworkers every day, and they still saw her; but in a way they couldn't really see her, because she had been transformed.

When you looked at the alt-right's actual posts and videos—not at how they were portrayed on CNN or Wikipedia or *BuzzFeed*, but at the content itself—it was often fairly polished, even cerebral. The caustic LARP-y memes, like the ones on 4chan, still rubbed Samantha the wrong way; but those were just a small part of the movement. Jared Taylor was a Yale graduate with a gentle Southern baritone and the demeanor of a sweater-wearing dad. Richard Spencer was supposed to be some super-Nazi boogeyman, but when she looked at his YouTube channel she didn't see a sputtering maniac; she saw hour-long lectures about politics and race and opera and Romantic poetry. All day, in her car or through her earbuds, she listened to alt-right podcasts and videos and livestreams. At first she found them shocking; then she found them engrossing; eventually, the dialogue started to merge with her internal monologue, until she could hardly tell the difference between what they said and what she thought.

Becoming a member of the alt-right, it turned out, wasn't exactly a process of logical persuasion. It was more like a gradual shift in your mental vocabulary. Before, she had spent her morning commute listening to NPR, or to Dan Savage's sex-advice podcast. It suddenly seemed bizarre that nobody had had a problem with her spending her mornings learning all the details of fisting and "water sports," but that, if any of her coworkers ever heard the words "survival of the white race" playing over her car stereo, she would probably have to flee the state. Why the hostility? Were white people really so problematic that they weren't even allowed to survive?

She kept watching alt-right videos, waiting for the mask to slip—for some leader of the movement to reveal overt hatred or obvious hypocrisy—but she couldn't honestly say that she ever saw it. "Look at Japan," Nathan Damigo, an alt-right activist, said in one YouTube video. He mentioned that the country was 99 percent ethnically Japanese, which seemed impossible. Samantha paused the video to look it up. Accurate. "Is anyone demonizing them, saying that they want to do horrible things to other people?" Damigo continued. His point was that racially homogenous societies were not inherently hateful—that, in fact, they led to higher trust, lower crime, and more social stability.

He wore a fitted gray suit, slicked-back hair, and a teal-and-white lapel pin in the shape of a triangle. He didn't sneer or use ethnic slurs. He was patient, almost academic. The way Damigo told it, he just wanted white people to be able to thrive without having to apologize constantly for their own existence. Listening to him, Samantha remembered something her grandmother had told her when she was younger: "Never, ever apologize for who you are."

The normal world kept running its tired old script, but she wasn't buying it anymore. Once, for a second, she turned on a comedy game show on NPR; the announcer made some awkward joke about how Trump was a dimwit, and she turned it right back off. NPR was supposed to be neutral, objective journalism, yet they couldn't even hide their contempt for the man half the country had just entrusted with the presidency. Her normie friends on social media, instead of making arguments against the alt-right, mostly resorted to dismissive jokes, or conjectures about what the alt-right's words might secretly be implying. Samantha couldn't believe how easy it was to tune it all out.

She moved in with Richie, and the alt-right internet became their world. "Let's do an experiment," he said one night, opening a bottle of wine and sitting next to her on the living-room couch. She listed all the people she'd been learning about—Damigo, Spencer, Kevin MacDonald—and they looked them up, one by one, on the normie internet. She knew what they'd find, of course: Nazi this, white supremacist that. But she had *just* heard Damigo explain, in his own words, why he was *not* a supremacist, merely a separatist. "This is what I tried to warn you about," Richie said. "The media's always trying to sell you something."

He introduced her to *The Daily Shoah*, and they played a drinking game: chug whenever Sven can't keep up with the conversation, or whenever Enoch starts one of his rants with "Here's the thing." The podcast was about politics, sort of, but it was also about instilling a sense of community. The cohosts could turn any banal phrase into an inside joke or a non-sequitur riff. The memes about dindus and ovens and helicopters were still too much for Samantha's taste, but ultimately Mike and Sven seemed like smart guys who had thought hard about the underlying philosophical arguments. If they needed to be edgy to prove their shitlord bona fides, she could live with that.

The symbol from Nathan Damigo's lapel pin, the teal-and-white triangle, popped up again and again on the internet. She started to recognize it as the logo of Identity Evropa. "We are a generation of awakened Europeans who have discovered that we are part of the great peoples, history, and civilization that flower from the European Continent," their website read. "We oppose those who would defame our history and rich cultural heritage." She examined the whole site and couldn't find a single word she objected to. Every other ethnic group was allowed to express its identity and advocate for its beliefs. Why shouldn't European-Americans have a seat at the table? "Join us," the site read. "Become part of something bigger than yourself."

The application took about thirty seconds.

"Are you of European, non-Semitic heritage?" Yes.

"Have you ever been convicted of a felony?" No.

"Do you have any visible tattoos?" Um . . . define visible.

One of IE's leaders interviewed Samantha over Skype. He assured her that her tattoos wouldn't be disqualifying—the main purpose of the question was to rule out anyone with tattoos of SS bolts or swastikas, and also to keep track of members' identifying markings in case they ever got doxed. She and the interviewer developed an instant rapport. She knew enough about the alt-right, at this point, to intuit how he'd want her to come across: a strong woman, but still feminine; confident enough to keep up with the guys, but subservient enough to know her place. Within a few minutes, she could tell that it was working—that this was a game she would be able to win. The conversation went for much longer than the scheduled half-hour, and he accepted her into IE on the spot.

They gave her the passwords to IE's private servers on Discord. There were about two hundred people in IE at the time, and only a handful of them were women. Samantha gave out her phone number and told people in the movement, especially women, to text her if they ever needed anything. If a woman was having relationship problems, Samantha would give advice; if a woman got doxed and needed to lie low for a while, Samantha would offer her a couch to crash on. When people were preparing to break the news to their normie relatives that they were alt-right, Samantha would coach them through it: *Make sure they know that you don't hate anyone else, you're just pro-yourself.* One minute, she'd be at work, mixing a drink, listening to the locals talk about the latest boneheaded Trump tweet; the next minute she'd be outside, on her break, scrolling through a hundred notifications on her phone, typing in ten Discord chats at once, helping to build the underground movement that would restore her people to honor and dignity. If she went an hour without checking her phone, hundreds of people noticed. Before, what was the most important decision she'd made in a given day? What to wear? What music to play? Now she typed things and it actually changed what people did in the world.

It took only about two months for Samantha to become the women's coordinator of IE. Her new friends told her how impressive it was that she'd reached the upper echelons so quickly, but it seemed as if all you had to do to distinguish yourself was have a modicum of competence and actually do what you said you were going to do. The organization was full of guys who would make ambitious plans and then drop the ball. Samantha underpromised and overdelivered. The guys still took most of the credit, but she tried not to worry about that.

She used a pseudonym—everyone in the movement did, except for those who'd already been doxed and had no choice but to use their real names. If the normie world ever figured out how to match her online persona to her real-life identity, she'd surely get fired; her family might disown her; angry mobs could even show up at her house. Everyone in the movement lived with the constant threat of doxing. This was why, even though the movement was full of fleeting alliances and fake signs of intimacy, the best way to tell if someone really trusted you was to see whether they were willing to tell you their real name. Once you knew that, you held their life in your hands.

Richie had joined IE, too, on her recommendation, but he wasn't advancing as quickly as she was. He would never admit it, of course, but he seemed resentful. The alt-right had been his thing, and now she was taking it over. They started to grow apart. Eventually, he moved out. She still felt that cliché fluttery-stomach feeling whenever she thought about the guy who used to play the guitar at house parties; but, for better or worse, that guy didn't exist anymore.

She still kept in touch with her brother. They talked on the phone several times a week. She didn't tell him everything, but she revealed enough—allusions to memes, or to her new "political" friends—that he started to piece it together. Whenever she dropped similar hints around her coworkers, they tended to ignore them or treat them as jokes. But her brother spent a lot of time on the internet; he knew how deep the rabbit hole could go. He started calling her by a new nickname, which he meant both ironically and unironically: Vanilla ISIS. "I know you have a good heart," he told her. "Just don't forget who you are."

She moved to another Southern city, near where several other alt-right leaders lived. She got another bartending job, and she also spent hours every week, sometimes hours a day, doing volunteer work for IE. She used Google Maps to scout locations for future marches and protests. She moderated various Discord and Slack channels, trying to keep the conversation within bounds. One time, in a Discord chat, a guy posted a meme of a fried chicken leg hanging from a noose. Samantha, the moderator, put the guy in Discord "jail," meaning that he could read posts but couldn't like or comment on them. He went over her head, complaining to the top leadership that she had stifled his free speech. But the leaders backed Samantha: even though she was a girl, she was still above him in the hierarchy, and in this case she was right. You might think you were just posting an edgy meme, but you never knew when Antifa or the feds might be watching.

Her favorite task was interviewing new applicants to IE, sometimes two or three dozen of them a week. A few times, in the background of a Skype call, she'd see a Gestapo helmet on a bedroom shelf, or the person would mention wanting to fight in the imminent Racial Holy War. Those were automatic rejections. But most people seemed pretty down to earth. She would start by asking them about how they first got red-pilled, or about their favorite movies—anything to put them at ease. "What do you like to cook?" she asked one woman. The answer was pad thai, but the woman was hesitant to say so because she thought it wouldn't sound European enough. "Oh, please, you do not have to worry about that," Samantha said.

In truth, though, sometimes a face would pop up on Skype, and within seconds Samantha would know that the person was too dark to qualify. One woman was half Indian, half white, but she swore that she only felt a connection to her European side. Another guy was Latino, but he said, "I'm American. My kids are American. I want to fight for the survival of this country." In those moments, Samantha felt a mix of pity and distress. Couldn't the guy just join La Raza or something? Why was he applying to IE, anyway?

She sent him a form rejection email.

"Is it because I'm not white enough?" he wrote back. "Do you think I should join the Proud Boys instead?"

She didn't respond.

In the spring of 2017, a leader within IE started a new invite-only Discord channel. He was organizing a rally in Charlottesville, Virginia, in mid-May, to protest the removal of a Robert E. Lee statue. Samantha decided that this would be a good time to meet her new community in real life. She rented an Airbnb, bought a new white swing dress, and drove for most of a day to get there.

Before the march, everyone gathered in a nearby park to go over the route. The guest list was small—about a hundred people, mostly IE members, all fully vetted. She was prepared to stand inconspicuously on the sidelines, but people kept approaching her and treating her like a celebrity: "Oh, my gosh, you were my interviewer!" "Thank you so much for bringing me into this thing." Some asked for selfies. A lot of the younger guys tried to hit on her—incompetently, but still, it was kind of sweet. The movement felt real and robust, and she was at the center of it.

After the rally, there was a big banquet under a frame tent. The leaders stood at the front, where there was a PA system, giving speeches—Nathan Damigo; Mike Enoch from *The Right Stuff*; Jason Kessler, who'd helped organize the event; even the Based Emperor himself, Richard Spencer. All the people she'd spent hours watching on screens or listening to through earbuds, suddenly come to life. Sam Dickson, a seventy-year-old "racial communitarian activist" and the man Richard Spencer called "my greatest influence," recalled his childhood in Jim Crow South Carolina, and his ancestors' experience in post-Reconstruction South Carolina. "I asked my grandmother, 'How were the whites able to take the state back when the blacks were the majority of the population?'" Dickson recalled. "She said, 'We had to get all the white people in line.'" Since then, Dickson said, getting white people in line had been his life's work. In an avuncular tone—acknowledging that it was cheesy to do the back-in-my-day shtick, but doing it anyway—he said, "I urge you to be happy and joyous warriors, because the setup today is so much better than it was back then. It's a hackneyed cliché that the internet has opened up sources of information that weren't available, but I don't think those of you who are young have any idea how difficult it was . . . to make contact with other people. Now you have all these social networks."

When Spencer took the microphone, he said, "I was going to talk about mind-set." The crowd giggled—everyone associated that word with Mike Cernovich, whom they considered a preposterous alt-light huckster. Lisping, Spencer pretended to hawk "my ebooks and nutritional supplements." Then, in his real voice, he gave an expansive speech about the thing that made him feel most hopeful about the future: the indomitable red-pilled fervor of Generation Z. "I feel like a cynic among fanatics when I meet young people," he said.

That night, there was a big house party at a local Airbnb where some of the rally's organizers were staying. The basement, the kitchen, the hallways, the living room—every space was crammed with guys in white polos, jacked up on adrenaline. They had showed up in force and exercised their First Amendment right to protest. Nobody had dared stand in their way. They had nothing to apologize for. Who knew what else this movement could achieve?

In the backyard, Samantha struck up a conversation with Richard Spencer, the man of the hour. He touched her arm and offered her a drag of his cigarette. Everyone else was focused intently on him—the young guys were practically forming rope lines to ask him about Žižek, or memetics, or the categorical imperative—but he kept ignoring them and talking to Samantha instead. She willed her facial muscles to stay neutral, trying not to seem like a fangirl.

"Do you get off on the fact that these kids treat you like a god?" she asked.

"I gave a speech today, and it changed the way you view the world," he responded. "Isn't that a bit godlike?"

She went inside to get another drink. A few minutes later, Spencer walked into the room. As soon as he entered, a skinny kid—couldn't have been much older than eighteen—raised a glass in Richard's direction. "Sieg!" the kid shouted.

A few other boys snapped to attention and shouted, "Heil!"

They did the call-and-response a few times, more and more energetically, until everyone in the room was either watching or joining in with stiff-armed salutes. She'd heard stories about this, she knew about the memes, but it was different to see it all around her—to feel the hot breath of the boys, to see their eyes go wide with a kind of ferocious ecstasy.

Richard drank it in. He smiled as wide as she'd ever seen a person smile. The saluting went on and on; the kids were high on the pure energy of it, sloshing their beer onto the floor, rocking onto the balls of their feet. Richard, from across the room, looked straight at Samantha and raised one eyebrow. He didn't have to do more than that. His meaning was unambiguous: *So? You're too good to do it, too?*

She had already told everyone that the Nazi stuff was not for her. She knew in her heart that it was wrong. This whole thing was supposed to be about pride and self-love, not about hate, not about violence. He kept looking her dead in the eye, unflinching, the internationally famous super-Nazi, calling her bluff. Her arm went up. She did it. God help her, she did it.

Another guy she'd met in Charlottesville was an emerging leader in the movement—not one of the speakers at the banquet, but someone who was starting to ascend to that top tier. There were rumors that he might be the next leader of IE. Not long after the rally, he got doxed. The dox included his home address, and he announced on Discord that he needed to get out of town for a while. He and Samantha talked over Skype, and although she'd only intended to comfort him, she found herself offering him a place to crash for a little while. This was what you were expected to do within the movement: when one of your people was in need, you offered help.

He showed up at her apartment a few days later and came on strong. He was very convinced that they should be together. She wasn't, but he wore her down, and she decided to give it a shot. The guy was obviously in a fragile state. She tried to have compassion. But it was never a good fit, and, after a few weeks, she asked him to start sleeping on the couch.

Things went downhill quickly after that. He agreed to move out of her bedroom, but he wouldn't look for a new place or help with the rent. He didn't cook or do dishes. He barely even went outside. If she tried to ask when he was planning to move out, he would get angry, the conversation would escalate, and he'd end up calling her a whore, or warning her that, when he was in charge of the ethnostate, she would be sent to a breeding camp. Later he would apologize and say that it was just a joke. But he would also mention that he knew her real name and where she lived, and that he could release that information whenever he wanted.

He didn't hit her, and he didn't rape her. But she didn't feel like she was in control of the situation, either. What was she supposed to do, call the cops on one of the leaders of her own underground movement? When the cops came, what would she tell them—"This creep won't leave my apartment"? Was that even a crime? Besides, as soon as he found out that she'd betrayed him, he would dox her and ruin her life—or, at the very least, no one in the movement would ever trust her again, and the movement was all she had. No, it was impossible. She'd always prided herself on being an easygoing person, socially astute enough to adapt to any situation. So she adapted.

They could be platonic roommates in private, he told her, but in public she was to keep up the ruse that they were a couple. He was going to be a power player in the alt-right, and as far as "movement optics" were concerned, Samantha was going to be his First Lady. He introduced her to everyone as his girlfriend—the new IE power couple. He kept climbing through the ranks of the organization, taking on more projects and then blowing his deadlines. Sometimes he would guilt Samantha into doing his work for him; then she'd hear him on a conference call in the other room, accepting praise for a spreadsheet he'd barely glanced at.

At one point, they spent a weekend in New York City hanging out with a bunch of inner-circle movement leaders, drinking bourbon and joking about the impending race war. They took a train upstate, to Sven's house, for one of *TRS*'s famous book burnings. She stayed quiet most of the time; she was a girl, so it was easy to disguise sulking as submissiveness. Then Monday came, and they went home and took a break from the ruse. She went back to work, and he went back to calling in to alt-right podcasts over Skype, or playing video games on the couch.

Along with Jason Kessler and a few other people, he started planning another Charlottesville rally, in August. It would be a bigger one this time, a triumphant return—Charlottesville 2.0, they called it. She could hear him through the walls, screaming over his headset about supply routes into town and escape plans in case things turned ugly. The demonstrators would march through the University of Virginia with torches and then gather in Robert E. Lee Park, demanding that their European American heritage be treated with respect. White people around the country, seeing this valiant display, would be roused from their apathy and join the movement. Samantha helped with the logistics here and there—when David Duke had trouble getting a hotel room under his name, she booked one for him, posing as his granddaughter—but mostly she tried to stay out of it.

She didn't dare tell anyone, not even her brother, but she was starting to wonder whether joining the alt-right had been a terrible mistake all along. The more helpless and angry she felt about her domestic situation, the less she felt like making excuses for the rest of the movement. If this was how one of the alt-right's most exalted leaders behaved behind closed doors, then what other blatant hypocrisies were being overlooked? She'd spent months convincing her friends, and herself, that the movement was more innocuous than it seemed, that their fears were misplaced. But what if the ironic racism really was just racism? What if white separatism and white nationalism and racial realism were all epithets for the same old-fashioned violent impulse? What if the alt-right was basically what the normies said it was?

Once she saw this possibility, she couldn't unsee it. On the Discord channels, the grisly memes kept coming: helicopter rides, gas chambers, "John Deere's new multi-lane protester digestor." When she was first starting to get red-pilled, she'd told herself that she was waiting for the mask to slip and reveal actual hatred; by the time the hatred was there in plain sight, she'd been so turned around by movement propaganda that she somehow made herself look past it, or convinced herself that it was all just harmless shitposting. Now, as quickly as she'd tumbled down the rabbit hole, she could feel herself drifting back up toward the surface. It felt a little bit ridiculous that, after coming this far, all it took to make her reconsider everything was a world-class nightmare of a roommate. Then again, maybe it was no more ridiculous than all the other circumstances that had led her into this mess.

She had requested a day off from work to attend the second Charlottesville rally, but she canceled the request at the last minute and went to work instead. All day, she tried to avoid looking at the TVs hanging above the bar. When she heard that someone had been killed in a car crash, her reaction was a mixture of panic and a kind of immediate, disembodied clarity. *There's no way to justify any of this,* she thought. *I need to find a way out.*

It wasn't easy to quit the alt-right, but it was possible. She remembered a few people who had seemed totally ensconced in the movement until one day they went dark and you never heard from them again. Instead, you heard rumors: This guy moved to a new state. That guy got a new phone number, met a new woman, started a new life as a normie. Samantha was still in her twenties. It wasn't too late to get a college degree. Maybe she could even have a family one day, after she figured out how to deal with her own issues.

Had she really been so goddamn weak that all they had to do was charm her, make her feel pretty and popular and needed, and she would drop everything else in her life to chase that feeling? All the warning signs came back to her in a sickening montage. That drive home from Richie's house, blinking to see the road through tears; setting up her laptop on the kitchen counter. *Am I an idiot?* she'd asked herself then. *Or am I a monster like him?* Both, apparently. On some level she'd always known the truth, but it was almost too obvious. Instead of letting herself see it for what it was, she had tried to embellish it into some profound, complicated mystery. First you see the mountain. Then you see that there is no mountain. Then, finally, you start to see the mountain again.

The following August, the one-year anniversary of the infamous Charlottesville rally fell on a Sunday. She was scheduled to work an all-day shift. That was for the best, she decided: it was better to be around people, even people she couldn't really open up to, than to be alone. She had moved to a suburb in the northeast, staying with her aunt and working at a café that served homemade quiches and jams. Jason Kessler was marking the anniversary by holding a rally in D.C., but nobody in the movement trusted Kessler anymore. Any alt-right group that still had a shred of self-respect, including IE, ordered its members to stay away; Kessler invited Richard Spencer, Chris Cantwell, and David Duke to join him, but they all declined. In the end, Kessler marched with about two dozen misfits and literal Nazis, including a guy with the number 14 tattooed on his face. Samantha checked her phone anxiously throughout the day, but her normie friends were posting about Omarosa and the Space Force and a guy who'd stolen a plane and crashed it off the coast of Seattle. It was as if the anniversary rally wasn't even happening.

She'd been dating someone for a month and a half, and he seemed to like her so far. "I was mixed up in some pretty extreme political stuff," she'd told him on their second date.

"Well, whatever it was, it couldn't have been so bad," he'd replied. "I know you now, and you're clearly a good person."

Was she, though? What about her was good? Some days, she thought, *I went through a terrible phase, I made some really inexplicable choices, but I'm still the person I always was.* Other days, she thought, *Anyone who was smart enough to understand what Richie was saying that night but too spineless to leave him is not a person who will ever deserve forgiveness.* She watched *Sharp Objects*, a show on HBO, and thought about cutting herself; but if she bled enough to make a mess then someone would call an ambulance, and it would turn into a whole thing, and she already had enough reasons to feel ashamed.

She got back in touch with some of her closest childhood friends from New Jersey, people she hadn't talked to in a long time. She tried to explain where she'd been and what she'd seen, but she could never strike the right tone. When one of them asked her a question, she responded with a self-deprecating joke about her lost year as a secret hipster Nazi, and her friend accused her of making light of the situation: "Why are you always deflecting responsibility?" Samantha rewatched the Nathan Damigo interview on YouTube, the one that had struck her as so polished and eloquent. Now she could only react with rueful laughter and a full-body cringe. But maybe cringing was also a deflection of responsibility? Fuck, man. She couldn't even do shame right.

Most days, on her way to work, she tried to listen to podcasts that were informative but not at all political. One was an interview with a philosopher named Martha Nussbaum, who talked about moral stigma and the social value of regret. Another was a series about the complex personal lives of the worst people in history, people like King Leopold II and Muammar Qaddafi. Apparently, even if you'd ruined an entire country for generations, or forced multiple young girls to "marry" you, or done other unimaginably heinous things, there were still plenty of people who would be willing to say, after you were gone, "You know, his ideas about health care weren't all bad" or "Actually, he was always sweet to me." Did that mean that irredeemable monsters were just effective brainwashers? Or did it mean that even monsters could still have redeemable qualities?

Her friends kept asking her about the alt-right, claiming that they wanted to understand everything, but ultimately they seemed to be looking for reassurance, not understanding. They wanted to know that they were immune—that it had happened to Samantha, but that it could never happen to them, or their husbands, or their brothers, or anyone else they knew. *Well,* Samantha thought, *maybe some of you are immune, but not all of you. Maybe not even most of you.*

People acted as if her descent into the alt-right had been caused by something discrete and tangible—that some magic switch had been flipped in her, causing racist propaganda to resonate with her soul in a sinister and specific way. Or maybe they imagined that the magic switch inside her had always been flipped on, that her innate bigotry had always been waiting to rise to the surface. The scarier and more mundane fact was that there was no magic switch. Whenever she tried to examine her most fundamental beliefs and desires—before the movement, during, and after—she didn't find rage or self-love or a death wish or a lust for power. She found nothing solid at all.

•   •   •

When I got an email from a woman saying that she had just left Identity Evropa and wanted to talk to a journalist about it, I was in the conference room on the thirty-eighth floor of the World Trade Center. It was late, and the building was nearly empty, so I had exchanged my cramped office for a room with a view. I called her on Skype. She hadn't yet told her story to anyone, and saying it out loud made her anxious, so she paced up and down a flight of stairs while she talked, burning off some of her anxiety. Our conversation lasted more than three hours. Every so often, as I took notes, I glanced across the river at the glowing red dial of the Colgate Clock.

It all seemed a bit too pat to be true: damsel in distress climbs to the upper echelons of the organized white supremacy movement, then absconds and tells a Jewish journalist how the whole thing operates. I wondered if she was a plant sent by Project Veritas, or a troll trying to send me on a wild goose chase. Or maybe her story was true but she was telling a sanitized version of it, portraying herself as a hapless victim.

Over the next year and a half, we talked for hundreds of hours, both on the phone and in person. I talked to her relatives and friends. She showed me screenshots and photographs and played me audio recordings. She wasn't a plant. At first, though, she did try to sanitize her story. It took her a long time to tell me about the Nazi salutes, for example, and then a long time after that to admit that she'd joined in. She kept insisting that she'd never wanted violence to befall anyone for any reason, that she'd never had hate in her heart. I had no way of knowing whether that was true.

Again and again, she asked different versions of the same question: "Do you think I'm a bad person?" I tried answering in several ways, but in truth I thought that the question missed the point. She had obviously made tragically, pathologically bad decisions; and yet I also believe that it's possible for people who have made terrible decisions to work toward redemption. In the end, it didn't seem useful to worry about whether she was Bad or Good. Those are permanent metaphysical attributes, and I didn't think metaphysics had much to do with it.

Sometimes, in the course of my alt-right reporting, I would find myself in the company of someone gleefully, unrepentantly Bad—Milo Yiannopoulos, say, or Richard Spencer—and a familiar feeling would come over me. Around the twentieth time I felt it, I realized what it was: a longing for the same cheap catharsis that I'd experienced when I was nine years old, on my couch, watching Ricki Lake. Where are the bad people? They are on the stage, under the bright lights. Racism does not reside among us, the audience; you can tell because they are the ones being pointed at, and we are the ones doing the pointing.

I don't mean to imply that there is no moral distance between me and Richard Spencer. What I mean is that white supremacy is not so superficial a problem that it can be solved by getting rid of a few bad apples. You can't eradicate crime by sending people to jail. You can't fix the opiate crisis by bombing poppy fields. It's tempting, but far too facile, to imagine that the way to end racism is to identify the racists, to shame them on Twitter, to punch them in the streets. That may, in some cases, be clarifying; it may produce a temporary victory, or a moment of catharsis; but it doesn't address the roots of the affliction. What we need, and urgently, is a new moral vocabulary.

In the meantime, what should social networks do about the surfeit of hazard-ous memes floating around the internet? Let's say you're hosting a party in a ware-house. You can't eradicate all pathogens from the air. You don't know how many of your guests are sick, and you don't want to stand outside the front door holding a thermometer and a stethoscope. The best you can do is plan for contingencies. You can ventilate the room, and put Purell on the tables, and install a carbon monoxide detector. If some idiot is going around sneezing in people's faces, you can ask him to stop, or you can kick him out of the party. You won't eradicate all disease, but you can keep it from reaching an epidemic threshold.

Some types of people seem to be particularly susceptible to extremist online propaganda: people with weak real-world social ties; people with unstable senses of self; people with too much verbal intelligence and not enough emotional intel-ligence; people who prize idiosyncrasy over logical consistency, or flashy contrar-ianism over humble moral dignity. Still, there is no formula that can predict exactly who will succumb to fascism and who will not.* People act the way they do for a million contingent reasons. Nature matters and nurture matters. Some peo-ple seem strong but turn out to be weak; some people bear opaque trauma, invis-ible even to themselves; some people are desperately lonely; some people just want to watch the world burn. We would like to imagine that, in the current year, the United States has developed a moral vocabulary that is robust and widespread enough to inoculate almost all of us against raw bigotry and malign propaganda. We would like to imagine that, but it would be wishful thinking.

---

*Researchers have been trying to develop such a formula at least since 1947, when Theodor Adorno and three psychologists published a personality test called the F-scale. It remains, as they say, more an art than a science.

PART SIX

A Night for Freedom

Where everybody lies about everything of importance, the truthteller, whether he knows it or not, has begun to act; he, too, has engaged himself in political business, for, in the unlikely event that he survives, he has made a start toward changing the world.

Hannah Arendt, 1967

CHAPTER TWENTY-EIGHT

Common Sense

A year to the day after Donald Trump was sworn in as president, Cassandra Fairbanks was in New York, taking an Uber toward Hell's Kitchen, on her way to a party called A Night for Freedom. "The venue is called Freq," she told the driver. "F-R-E-Q. Some kind of nightclub, I guess." Next to her in the backseat was Lucian Wintrich, who was clutching a book of philosophical essays by Frank Meyer, a founding editor of *National Review*. "I get motion sick if I actually read in a car," he told me. "But I wanted to bring something impressive to fake-read, just in case you'd be around."

Fairbanks had left *Big League Politics* to take over Wintrich's job as the Washington bureau chief of *The Gateway Pundit*. Wintrich was back in New York, blogging sporadically. "D.C. is *exhausting*," Wintrich said. "I can't tell you how many rooms I'd walk into where people would immediately start testing boundaries: 'Since it's just us in here, we can agree, can't we, that America would be safer and more prosperous as a white country?' At first you think they're just being transgressive, until it sets in how many of them are not at all joking." Almost as confusing as the duplicity of the crypto–white nationalists, Wintrich said, was the erratic behavior of the president. "Where does the political theater stop and the sincerity begin?" he went on. "Sometimes he'll do something so absurd that I'll catch myself thinking, Should I try a complete public reversal where I denounce Trump, maybe say the whole thing was a troll all along? Because I do think Trump sycophancy is a sinking ship. But then I think, That would be too much of a stretch, even for me. I do believe most of what I say. About seventy percent."*

---

*After he appeared on an alt-light podcast that veered a bit too close to outright white nationalism, Wintrich was fired from *The Gateway Pundit*. With his newfound free time, he planned to start working on a book. "I'm still in

I asked Fairbanks how long she planned to stay on the sinking ship, but she wasn't listening. Julian Assange had invited her, via direct message on Twitter, to visit him at the Ecuadorian Embassy in London, and she was busy making travel arrangements.

A Night for Freedom had been organized by Mike Cernovich, who billed it on Facebook as "an environment where free speech and open inquiry are welcome." He would use it as an opportunity to plug his next project, a documentary called *Hoaxed: The Media's War on Truth*. There would also be speeches by Gavin McInnes and Stefan Molyneux, and a DJ duo playing EDM, and a well-stocked bar. "It's important for our movement that we keep getting together in the same room, keep our momentum going," Cernovich told me. "Our people should be vibing with each other about art, culture, fitness. Not everything has to be so political."

For the past few months, he'd been trying to pivot his personal brand away from deplorability. "I don't want people to think of me as a pro-Trump guy anymore," he said on Periscope. "I want people to think of me as a mind-set guy, a journalist, a commentator, a social media personality, a filmmaker, an author." MAGA was a good way to trigger the libs for a while, but all memes eventually outlast their utility.*

As part of his pivot, Cernovich had been sifting through his old tweets and blog posts, culling the most egregious ones.† Finally, he'd deleted his old blog

---

the research phase," he told me. "I recently came across this wonderful essay, I'm sure you've heard of it—'The Paranoid Style in American Politics'? I just adored it. It's so old, and yet still so wildly relevant."

*Cernovich had long worried about Trump's capriciousness—"Why is it in anyone's self-interest to stay loyal to a guy who shows zero loyalty to anyone?" he once asked, in private—but he'd tried to keep his frustrations to himself. The final straw was the precipitous rise and fall of Anthony Scaramucci, the investment banker and smooth-talking media operator who became the shortest-serving White House communications director in history, serving for a total of eleven days. In July 2017, the day Scaramucci was fired, Cernovich told me, "The Mooch is one of the only people around Trump, except for Don Jr. and one or two others, who actually use social media the way it's supposed to be used. If they're throwing him under the bus, then they truly have no plan at all." A few weeks later, Cernovich went to Manhattan to interview Scaramucci for *Hoaxed*, and I tagged along. We sat in the opulent basement of the Hunt & Fish Club, a Midtown steakhouse of which Scaramucci was part owner, waiting for the cameras to be set up. "Ask me whatever you want," Scaramucci told me. "Trump Organization finances? Kushner's deals in China? Let's chop it up." I made sure he knew that I was a journalist from *The New Yorker*, and that we were on the record. "No problem!" he said. "Come on, I'm a front-stabbing motherfucker, everyone knows that." This surprised me, seeing as Scaramucci's recent comments to another *New Yorker* reporter ("I'm not Steve Bannon, I'm not trying to suck my own cock") had cost him his job in the White House. Nevertheless, Scaramucci proceeded to dispense his gossip, and I dutifully wrote it down. (I looked into it later, and little of it checked out.) "Want more?" he said. "I'll tell you whatever you're interested in. I get along great with reporters, you know." Ten minutes later, he sat in front of the camera for his interview. "The media has destroyed itself in an effort to remain profitable," he said.

†This made them harder to find, but not impossible. Nothing ever truly disappears from the internet. Then again, as Cernovich was happy to admit, "People can keep bringing up old screencaps of this or that tweet, and I can just keep brushing it aside. 'Nah, that looks forged.' 'That's taken out of context.' 'Maybe I got hacked.' Some people won't believe you, but some people will. It's all in how you sell it. Meanwhile, I keep moving forward, and the old stuff keeps receding further into the past."

entirely, migrating some of the archives to Cernovich.com, where he also sold Gorilla Mind herbal supplements and a new line of skincare products. The name *Danger & Play* had invoked nihilism, sadism, misogyny. But Cernovich.com could, in theory, expand in almost any direction.

He got to the venue two hours early and paid the deposit in cash. The previous venue had reneged that morning, and he didn't want to take any chances. "Welcome to life as a crimethinker, dude," he said. "I don't even say very edgy stuff anymore, but this still happens whenever I book anything. Venue gets calls from Antifa, venue owner googles my name, and then it's, 'Nope, no freedom of association for you.'" This was another reason for his attempted pivot: life as a dissident was starting to be a drag. Still, whatever happened tonight, he was confident that he'd be able to spin it as a victory. "If we get to have our dance party here, then great. If this venue bails on us, I'll head over to the Algonquin and do a more exclusive thing, and maybe I'll do a Periscope—'See how we're being persecuted, we need to hang together in these trying times.' Either way, I'll find a narrative that works."

They got to have their dance party. The venue was less than half full, and most of the guests were oddly overdressed. Compared to the exuberant energy of the DeploraBall, the atmosphere now felt sad and stilted, like a wedding reception for an unhappy couple. The DJ duo played a dance remix of "All I Do Is Win," and a few men in suits bopped rigidly to the music, holding bottles of beer in one hand and checking their phones with the other. Onstage, in front of the DJ booth, two blonde dancers gyrated in sneakers and American-flag leotards.

While waiting in line for a drink, I overheard three separate conversations about the price of bitcoin. I ran into Colin Flaherty, the surly racist from Delaware whom I'd interviewed long ago, in City Hall Park. "YouTube keeps taking down my pages, but my fans keep putting bootlegs of my videos back up," he told me. "I guess you can only keep the truth hidden for so long."

Cassandra Fairbanks found me at the bar. "I brought a guest you might want to meet," she said, introducing me to Chelsea Manning.

"What are you doing here?" I asked Manning. She couldn't really say. She used the words "infiltrate" and "confront" and "prove that I can enter their spaces." When she walked away, I asked Fairbanks, Jack Posobiec, and Will

Chamberlain what she'd meant. "No idea!" Posobiec said. "I'm pretty sure she's just our friend."

Stefan Molyneux took the stage and started giving a spirited speech about his hopes for the future. "I would like to wake up in the morning without feeling like I'm being replaced," he said. Yoni and Mary Clare, the couple who'd hosted the pre-party before the DeploraBall, found me in the crowd. "When I heard that Molyneux was gonna be here, I bought a ticket right away," Mary Clare said. "Isn't he such a brilliant philosophical mind?" Molyneux was trying to articulate the movement's utopian vision, but his meaning was mostly lost on me. "Virtue is the price you pay to get to the cathedral called love!" he shouted. "They don't want us to know the truth, they don't want us to have virtue, so that we never know love!"

Cernovich wrapped up the night's entertainment by projecting a trailer for *Hoaxed*. There were urgent, glitchy effects, and an ominous synthesized score in the style of *The Matrix*. "All media is narrative, and we are in a war of narratives," Cernovich's voice narrated. A few frames later, Stefan Molyneux stepped out of a cave and into the light. Title cards:

EVERYTHING

THEY TOLD YOU

IS A LIE.

The next day, Cernovich wrote a post on Cernovich.com called "How A Night for Freedom Changed History."

Cernovich had bet his career on the assumption that he could say almost anything—that he could use the macrotargeting techniques of shitposting and rage-bait to make himself too big to ignore—and that all would eventually be forgiven. This was the plan underlying much of the Deplorable movement, to the extent that there had ever been a coherent plan. The ranking algorithms on social media laid out clear incentives: provoke as many activating emotions as possible; lie, spin, dog-whistle; drop red pill after red pill; step up to the line repeatedly, in creative new ways. Even if you crossed the line and got banned from one social network or another, there would always be more platforms.

These assumptions turned out to be partially correct. New platforms would continue to emerge (BitChute, Rokfin, Parler), but not every platform has an equal impact on the national discourse. The biggest social networks, such as Facebook and Twitter and Reddit, had been founded by brash young disrupters with plenty of capital, a high tolerance for risk, and a naïve faith in techno-utopianism. They had left their gatehouses mostly unguarded, a freedom that the amateur propagandists quickly learned how to exploit. Now the free-for-all days were starting to come to a close.

After more than a decade of invoking vague "free-speech principles," the new gatekeepers, now businessmen in their thirties, were trying to flesh out exactly what those principles were. It was too little, too late, but it was something. They finally understood—or, at least, were starting to seem to understand—that their imagined utopia was never going to materialize. This realization may have been a sign of maturity; it may have been a calculated response to internal pressure from investors, or a strategy to stave off government regulation; or it may have been a simple defense mechanism, a reaction to being socially shamed. Within a few short years, the general public's attitude toward social media had swerved from widespread veneration to viral fury.* The disrupters had no choice but to respond somehow. After all, they believed in the wisdom of crowds.

In November 2018, Mark Zuckerberg posted a note to his Facebook profile. "Many of us got into technology because we believe it can be a democratizing force for putting power in people's hands," he wrote. "I believe the world is better when more people have a voice to share their experiences, and when traditional gatekeepers like governments and media companies don't control what ideas can be expressed." He hadn't abandoned his techno-optimism—he still asserted, in the present tense, that the postdisruption world "is better," which was at best an arguable claim—but his self-assurance had clearly been punctured. "The past two years have shown that without sufficient safeguards, people will misuse these tools to interfere in elections, spread misinformation, and incite violence," he continued. "One of the most painful lessons I've learned is that when you connect two billion people, you will see all the beauty and ugliness of humanity."

The note received 41,000 likes, 4,000 loves, 852 surprised emojis, 160 angry emojis, 81 crying emojis, and almost 8,000 comments.

---

*When historians look back on the Trump era, they may see this as one of its few silver linings. If Hillary Clinton had been elected president, as everyone expected, it's unlikely that public opinion would have turned so swiftly against the social media tycoons, forcing them to reckon with what they had wrought.

"Keep up the good work!" a stock trader from Michigan wrote. "Ignore the media, keep on improving."

"do you think hell exist?" a Congolese Evangelical pastor wrote.

"yes, right here on earth," an American woman wrote.

"Suckerberg," a British woman wrote.

"let me guess," a woman from Washington State wrote, "you guys never really thought of how explosive free speech really was did ya??"

• • •

On August 12, 2017, the Saturday of the deadly rally in Charlottesville, Steve Huffman, the CEO of Reddit, spent most of the day on a plane. He kept refreshing r/Politics and r/News on his laptop, looking at image after image of his alma mater's campus as it was overrun with torch-wielding white supremacists. "I got really emotional," he said. "I wish I could say I reacted calmly and rationally, but it hit me in a pretty personal way." He found the images disturbing not only as an American, a Virginian, and a University of Virginia alumnus, but also as the inventor of one of the most powerful memetic petri dishes in history. Just as Yishan Wong had hoped five years earlier, Reddit had indeed become a universal platform for open human discourse. Huffman knew that his platform's openness had been exploited— was likely still being exploited at that very moment—by neofascist activists, maybe even by some of the ones who had brought the violence to Charlottesville. When his plane landed, he got on a call with a few of his top employees. "If any of these people are on Reddit, I want them gone," he said. "Nuke 'em."

This felt cathartic, but personal catharsis is not a good way to make policy. "Steve, you're pissed off right now," one of his employees told him. "Let's talk about it more rationally on Monday."

When they got back to the office, the first thing they did was decide to delete r/Physical_Removal. At the time, the most upvoted post on the subreddit was a celebration of Heather Heyer's death; Reddit had a rule against content that "encourages or incites violence," and the post violated that rule. By midday on Tuesday, r/Physical_Removal was gone, its frenzied memes and images of helicopters replaced by a scrubbed white page, an image of a gavel, and the words "This community has been banned."

Already, this was more than the old Reddit would have done. r/Physical _Removal claimed to be a place for philosophical discussion. Hans-Hermann

Hoppe was hardly Steve Huffman's favorite philosopher, but in theory that wasn't supposed to matter. The twenty-one-year-old Huffman might have worried about a slippery slope: if redditors weren't allowed to discuss texts that endorsed violence under certain circumstances, then would Reddit have to start censoring all mention of *Fight Club*, and *Common Sense*, and the Bhagavad Gita, and the Bible? But the thirty-three-year-old Huffman was no longer paralyzed by such scenarios. "Communities like Physical_Removal are just bad for Reddit, and they're bad for the world," he said. "Every call involving free-speech issues is difficult, but this is a difficult call I am fine with making." If you're throwing a warehouse party, and one room of the warehouse is packed with bloodthirsty weirdos, you may have to kick them out.* Huffman was coming to accept his role as a gatekeeper; he wasn't even all that reluctant about it anymore.

"It felt good to get rid of them, I have to say," Huffman continued. "But it still didn't feel like enough." r/Physical_Removal was just one subreddit, after all. The site now had more than a million subreddits—an endless hallway of rooms in need of inspection. Over the next few weeks, Huffman had a series of conversations with his general counsel, his top engineers, and his head of policy. "We all had the same goal: We don't want Reddit to be an incubator for horrible stuff," he said. "The only question was how to do it in a way that didn't cause more problems than it solved." First they would start getting rid of the unapologetic neofascists; after that, they could start dealing with more ambiguous cases.

"Encouraging or inciting violence" was a narrow standard, and Huffman and his team decided to expand it. Four words would become thirty-six: "Do not post content that encourages, glorifies, incites, or calls for violence or physical harm against an individual or a group of people; likewise, do not post content that glorifies or encourages the abuse of animals." The new rule raised new questions, and the team drafted a nonexhaustive list of exceptions ("newsworthy, artistic, satire, documentary").

---

*In 2016, a group of computer scientists at three universities published a study called "You Can't Stay Here: The Efficacy of Reddit's 2015 Ban Examined Through Hate Speech." Did shutting down a few toxic subreddits, such as r/FatPeopleHate and r/Coontown, "diminish hateful behavior" overall, or did it merely "relocate such behavior to different parts of the site"? Using regression analysis to interpret a data set of 100 million Reddit posts, the researchers concluded that the ban had worked: "Users participating in the banned subreddits either left the site or (for those who remained) dramatically reduced their hate speech usage." (Eshwar Chandrasekharan et al., "You Can't Stay Here: The Efficacy of Reddit's 2015 Ban Examined Through Hate Speech," *Proceedings of the ACM on Human-Computer Interaction* 1, no. 2 (November 2017): http://comp.social.gatech.edu/papers/cscw18-chand -hate.pdf.)

Jessica Ashooh, the company's head of policy, has a doctorate in international relations, and she'd spent four years as a policy consultant in Abu Dhabi. "I know what it's like to live under censorship," she said. "My internal check, when I'm arguing for a restrictive policy on the site, is, Do I sound like an Arab government? If so, maybe I should scale it back." One high-ranking Reddit employee, who grew up in Communist Eastern Europe before making his way to the United States, said, "You don't want to be so in love with oversight that you become the Stasi, and you don't want to be so terrified of oversight that you become a breeding ground for Nazis. It sounds simple, but it's unbelievably hard to get right."

They decided to announce the site's new antiviolence policy on a Wednesday in October. "We'll probably hear from a few of the free-speech, how-dare-you-ban-anything-ever people," Huffman said. "But honestly I wouldn't be surprised if the more common reaction is, 'What took you so long?'"

On the morning of the announcement, Ashooh sat at a long conference table with a dozen other employees. Before each of them was a laptop, a mug of coffee, and a few hours' worth of snacks. "Welcome to the Policy Update War Room," Ashooh said. "And, yes, I'm aware of the irony of calling it a War Room when the point is to make Reddit less violent, but it's too late to change the name."

She went over the plan for the day. All at once, they would swap out the old policy for the new policy, post an announcement explaining the change, and take action against a few hundred subreddits. Some of these were borderline cases, subreddits that were probably in violation of the new policy; their moderators would receive a warning and be given a second chance. Others were subreddits that were flagrantly, irredeemably in violation; these would be banned immediately. "Today we're focusing on a lot of Nazi stuff and bestiality stuff," Ashooh said. "Context matters, of course, and you shouldn't get in trouble for posting a swastika if it's a historical photo from the 1936 Olympics, or if you're using it as a Hindu symbol. But, even so, there's a lot that's clear-cut." I asked whether the same logic—that the Nazi flag was inherently a glorification of violence—would apply to the Confederate flag, or the Soviet flag, or the flag under which King Richard fought the Crusades, or the flag of the U.S. Marine Corps. "We can have those conversations in the future," Ashooh said. "But we have to start somewhere."

I glanced at a spreadsheet on an employee's laptop: an alphabetical list of the 109 subreddits that were being banned (r/KKK, r/KillAllJews, r/KilltheJews, r/KilltheJoos), along with the reason for each ban ("mostly just swastikas?") and the name of the employee who would carry it out. r/The_Donald was not on the list. "The_Donald's mods know we're keeping an eye on them, and they've gotten very careful about playing by the rules," Huffman said. Besides, "their anger comes from feeling like they don't have a voice, so it won't solve anything if I take away their voice. That's the call I've made, at least so far. I know some people feel strongly that it's the wrong call, because I hear from those people a lot—including people in my personal life." This, too, was part of being a gatekeeper.

At about 10:00 A.M., the purge began. "Thank you for letting me do Dylann RoofInnocent," one engineer said. "That was one of the ones I really wanted." He obliterated the subreddit with the push of a button.

"What is ReallyWackyTicTacs?" another engineer asked.

"Trust me, you don't want to know," Ashooh said. "That was the most unpleasant shit I've ever seen, and I've spent a lot of time looking into Syrian war crimes."*

The new antiviolence policy was posted, and a few hundred redditors commented on it. The comments included sarcasm ("this'll work out swell"), cynicism ("If you think this is anything more than theatre I've got a bridge to sell you"), and several requests to ban r/The_Donald, which were ignored. One employee, a young woman wearing a leather jacket and a yacht cap, was in charge of monitoring the comments and responding to the most relevant ones. "Everyone seems to be taking it pretty well so far," she said. "There's one guy, freespeechwarrior, who seems very pissed, but I guess that makes sense given his username."

"People are making lists of all the Nazi subs getting banned, but nobody has noticed that we're banning bestiality ones at the same time," Ashooh said.

Or maybe people had seen it, an engineer suggested, but "no one wants to admit it. 'Guys, I was just browsing r/HorseCock and I couldn't help but notice . . . '"

The woman in the yacht cap said, "OK, someone just asked, 'How will the exact phrase "kill yourself" be handled?'"

"It all depends on context," Ashooh said. "They're going to get tired of hearing that, but it's true."

"Uh-oh, looks like we missed a bestiality sub," the woman in the yacht cap said. "Apparently, SexWithDogs was on our list, but DogSex was not."

---

*"I don't even understand these two," someone said, glancing at two of the subreddits on the list. "One is called DinduNuffin and the other is DidntDoNuffin. Is that a meme I don't know?" No one in the room could explain it, so the job fell to me.

"Did you go to DogSex?" Ashooh said.

"Yep."

"And what's on it?"

"I mean . . ."

"Are there people having sex with dogs?"

"Oh yes, very much."

"Yeah, ban it."

"I'm going to get more cheese sticks," the woman in the yacht cap said, standing up. "How many cheese sticks is too many in one day? At what point am I encouraging or glorifying violence against my own body?"

"It all depends on context," Ashooh said.

I understood why other social media companies had been loath to let me see something like this. Never again would I be able to hear a lofty phrase about a platform's shift in policy—"open and connected," or "optimize for user value," or "modern public square"—without imagining a group of people sitting around a conference room, eating free snacks and making fallible decisions. Social networks, no matter how big they get or how familiar they seem, are not ineluctable forces but experimental technologies built by human beings.*

Once, Steve Huffman and I had dinner in New York. He wore a T-shirt, jeans, and Adidas indoor-soccer shoes. I asked him about his response to the violence in Charlottesville: Was he spurred into action, at least in part, by his personal connection to the place?

"I'm sure that was part of it," he said. "And I can see how somebody, even a former version of myself, would be creeped out by that." He took a sip of beer. "Honestly, all I can say is, I don't see a way around it. Is it better if I see a Nazi rally and go, 'I have no feeling about this, I leave it all up to the algorithm'?" A few minutes later, he thought of something else to say, but decided against it. Then he took another swig of beer and said it anyway. "I'm confident that Reddit could sway elections," he said. "We wouldn't do it, of course. And I don't know how many times we could get away with it. But if we really wanted to, I'm sure Reddit could have swayed at least this election, this once."

---

*"I don't think I'm going to leave the office one Friday and go, 'Mission accomplished—we fixed the internet,'" Huffman once told me. "Every day, you keep visiting different parts of the site, opening this random door or that random door—'What's it like in here? Does this feel like a shitty place to be? No, people are generally having a good time, nobody's hatching any evil plots, nobody's crying. OK, great.' And you move on to the next room."

In a perfect world, of course, no one person, much less a thirty-three-year-old computer programmer in soccer shoes, would have the power to manipulate a presidential election. And yet this is the world we live in. For too long, the gatekeepers who ran the most powerful information-spreading systems in human history were able to pretend that they weren't gatekeepers at all. *Information wants to be free; besides, people who take offense should blame the author, not the messenger; anyway, the ultimate responsibility lies with each consumer.* Now, instead of imagining that we occupy a postgatekeeper utopia, it might make more sense—in the short term, at least—to demand better, more thoughtful gatekeepers.

•   •   •

In the fall of 2017, I landed in Chicago, rented a midsize car, and started driving west toward Kewanee, Mike Cernovich's hometown. I asked Google to send me on the most efficient route, because there was nothing to see along the way—or so I thought, until I noticed a sign for a small town called Tampico, the birthplace of Ronald Reagan. I pulled off the highway. On Main Street—next to a bank, a funeral parlor, and a general store, all closed in the middle of the afternoon—was a metal plaque bearing Reagan's face, and his words: "Whatever else history may say about me when I'm gone, I hope it will record that I appealed to your best hopes, not your worst fears."*

When I got to Kewanee, the light was starting to fade. Mike Cernovich was sitting on a porch with his father and grandfather, both of whom are also named Mike. Mike's father had silver hair and a beard, and he wore work boots and a Carhartt T-shirt. A TV, audible through a screen door, was tuned to CNN. "He's always listening to this liberal stuff," Mike's father said of his father, without a trace of rancor. "Even Fox is too liberal for me. I'd rather go watch one of Mike's videos on Facebook or wherever, or some Bible-believing videos." He'd just come from a twelve-hour shift operating a crane at a local junkyard. "At work, when I'm baling cars or whatever, I'll put in my headphones all afternoon and listen to Infowars," he said. Like his son, Mike's father considered himself a freethinker; unlike

---

*This was a quote from Reagan's address to the 1992 Republican National Convention. In that speech, as in so many similar speeches by Kennedys and Clintons and Bushes and Obamas, Reagan expressed his faith in the basic munificence of the American national character, his foundational belief that We Are Good. "My fellow citizens," he said, "I have always had the highest respect for you, for your common sense and intelligence and for your decency. . . . May all of you as Americans never forget your heroic origins, never fail to seek divine guidance, and never lose your natural, God-given optimism."

his son, he was irrepressibly cheerful. "I don't get mad when people believe different," he said, smiling. "They can do what they want."

Shauna walked outside holding Cyra, who was almost ten months old. "Andrew!" she said. "How've you been? Michael, did you ask Andrew how his flight was?"

"Yeah, babe," he said, falsely, looking down at his phone.

"Michael," Shauna said, adopting a chiding tone that was roughly half sincere. "Remember what he wrote in that article about you. He said you don't make enough eye contact. Which wasn't wrong."

"He said 'less eye contact than on camera,'" Mike said. "I didn't mind that, though. The low blow was 'fleshy.'" He kept his eyes trained on his phone while he talked.

The Cernoviches decided to meet for dinner at a chain restaurant called Happy Joe's. Mike's father went to pick up Mike's mother and younger brother; I got a ride in Mike's rented minivan. I sat in the back with Cyra, who was watching a Persian music video on an iPad. "Mike tells me you've got a kid now!" Shauna said. "That's so awesome. I'm gonna need to see some pictures." I handed over my phone, and she oohed and aahed. It was one of the ten days between Rosh Hashanah and Yom Kippur, a period traditionally devoted to repentance and reflection. The whole way to Happy Joe's, I had a silent argument with the God I don't believe in, justifying my decision to spend this time with Mike Cernovich's family instead of my own.

Mike's father ordered for the table: hot wings, garlic bread, a couple of pizzas. Mike ordered a salad with dressing on the side. "Sit next to your mom," Shauna whispered, but Mike sat next to me instead.*

"Michael, I've been meaning to ask you about this Cathy O'Brien woman," Mike's mother said. "Is it true what she talks about?"

"I don't know who that is, Mom, but it's probably bullshit," Mike said.

"The government put her under mind control, and the Clintons raped her when she was a child."

"Bill *and* Hillary raped her?"

---

*"I know how to *talk* to him," Mike told Shauna, in my presence, in the car after dinner. "He's read the books I've read. He knows the media gossip I know about. What am I gonna talk about with my mom? The sweet mercy of Jesus?"

"That's what she says."

"Geez, Mom, where do you even find this stuff?"

"It's all over the internet, Michael!"

Mike's father watched this exchange with an equanimous smile, his arms folded on the table. Then, without segue, he turned to me. "I know you probably think I'm crazy," he said. "I believe in Noah's Ark, and I believe carbon isn't gonna ruin the climate, and I believe we've never been to the moon—we'd be there if we'd been there. That's just what I believe. Now that don't make it true, but I can still believe it, right?" He looked around the table. "This could all be a dream, for all I know," he continued. "But the food tastes good. We're together. Michael brought his baby home for a visit. We could be slaves in North Korea, or worms sitting on a log, but we're here instead." He took a bite of pizza, his blue eyes sparkling.

Mike wasn't listening; he was distracted by a video on his phone. "This is savage, dude," he said. "This is actually uncomfortable to watch." It was a video on the Cernovich Media Facebook page, which was managed by two employees in Florida and Washington State. "We split the profits, and I let them post whatever they want as long as the numbers are good," he said. "I don't even see what's on there unless people start texting me about it, like now." Hillary Clinton had just published a memoir about the 2016 campaign, and she was promoting it with a cross-country book tour. Laura Loomer was bird-dogging Clinton, selling the resulting footage to Cernovich Media. Tonight, while Clinton signed books in Brooklyn, her top aide, Huma Abedin, walked outside and immediately got #Loomered.

"When will you divorce Anthony Weiner?" Loomer, filming, shouted at Abedin. "Why are you protecting a man who was sexting underage girls?" Abedin kept walking, poker-faced, trying to ignore Loomer, who was just inches away from her on the narrow sidewalk.

"This is *brutal*," Cernovich said. "She has no security or anything. I feel awful for her." He meant Abedin. "But this is the future of media, bro, for better or worse. Everyone will be in everyone's face like this." His tone was world weary, almost forlorn, as if he were merely an objective spectator, not a media entrepreneur choosing to disseminate this footage for profit.

As we left the restaurant, Mike's father shook my hand and grinned affably. "You can say I'm crazy in your book if you want to," he said. "It don't matter to me. Say what you believe. I'm not gonna read it anyway."

———

Back when Milo Yiannopoulos was still too big to ignore, I emailed him to ask about an event he was putting together at the University of California, Berkeley. The event seemed to be falling apart, and I wanted to know whether he still planned to make the trip. "I'd be happy to consider having you embedded with us," he responded, although I hadn't suggested it. I repeated my question. He refused to answer it, and he wouldn't let anyone on his staff answer it, either. Yiannopoulos had about a dozen employees, but when it came to any important task he trusted only himself. And no task was as important to him as media relations.

"Turns out I'll be in NYC for 24 hours," he wrote. "Why don't we meet in person instead?"

We had breakfast at the Trump Soho Hotel. He wore the designer sunglasses of a lesser Kardashian, the bleached and artfully tousled hairdo of a K-pop star, and an outfit that landed somewhere between bouncer at a Reno pool party and admiral in the Franco-Prussian War. "I swear by Mariah Carey, these Berkeley administrators are being such cunts," he said as he sat down. He whistled involuntarily when he talked, the result of a new and ill-fitting set of prosthetic teeth.

He told me that, while he was staying at the Trump Soho, he was also paying for a room at the Trump International Hotel, in D.C., in case he needed to schedule any last-minute meetings near the White House. At the time, Yiannopoulos's bills were being paid by Robert Mercer, the far-right billionaire who had also been the biggest donor both to the Trump campaign and to *Breitbart*. Yiannopoulos constantly flaunted his unearned wealth on Instagram: Louis Vuitton luggage, Balmain boots, Perrier-Jouët champagne. "I'm probably being kicked off another social platform now, as we speak," he said. "This is what it means to be dangerous, darling. This is how the system treats you. But we persevere, we persevere."

I ordered. Yiannopoulos, texting, said, "I'll have whatever he's having, plus a side of bacon."

The server brought us coffee, and I asked for soy milk on the side.

Yiannopoulos looked up. "You know, don't you," he said, "that the edgelords have coined a new term for geeky, bespectacled New York journalists who drink soy milk?" I did, and we said it in unison: "Soy boy." Then Yiannopoulos picked up his coffee and sipped it through a straw.

"Just to be clear," I said, "you're using a straw to drink hot coffee, and you're the one making fun of me?"

"These teeth were fucking expensive, I'm not staining them," he said. "Besides, I'm fabulous, I do what I want."

Yiannopoulos's lifestyle was growing less fabulous by the day. He had risen to fame as the tech editor of *Breitbart*, but, after a video surfaced in which he made light of pederasty, he was pressured to leave *Breitbart*. A few months later, *BuzzFeed* published private emails revealing Yiannopoulos's extensive flirtation with neo-Nazism, and Robert Mercer publicly disavowed him as well. Yiannopoulos was soon banned from Venmo and PayPal; he'd sold a book proposal to Simon & Schuster, but the book's publication was later canceled;* he dissolved Milo Entertainment Inc. and laid off the staff. In late 2018, millions of dollars in debt, Yiannopoulos opened a Patreon account, attempting to crowdfund his "magnificent 2019 comeback." The following day, he was banned from Patreon. A few months later, "on character grounds," he was banned from the country of Australia.

After Charlottesville, many alt-right organizations were banished from most major social networks. Mike Enoch kept trying to open new Twitter accounts, and the company kept deleting them. A few Proud Boys were filmed beating up Antifa protesters in New York; after footage of the incident went viral, Gavin McInnes was banned from Facebook, Twitter, Instagram, and Amazon. Laura Loomer was forbidden from using Lyft and Uber after complaining about an "Islamic immigrant driver"; after she was banned from Twitter for a different Islamophobic outburst, she handcuffed herself to the front door of the company's New York headquarters, creating yet another cringeworthy video. Alex Jones was banned from all major platforms, decimating his revenue stream and forcing him to crash congressional hearings to get his name back in the headlines.

The Deplorables held fast to the dogma of free-speech absolutism, accusing tech executives of draconian censorship whenever they made a serious attempt to

---

*Yiannopoulos attempted to sue Simon & Schuster for breach of contract. The lawsuit was unsuccessful, but it did allow the book editor's comments on Yiannopoulos's manuscript ("gratuitous"; "irrelevant"; "a sea of self-aggrandisement and scattershot thinking"; "let's leave 'cuck' out of it"; "DELETE UGH") to be added to the public record.

moderate the content on their networks. The prevailing sentiment among the Deplorables seemed to be that, short of yelling fire in a crowded theater, anyone should be able to say anything in any venue. But thinking before you speak is not repression, and censure is not censorship. The Constitution guarantees that Congress shall make no law abridging freedom of speech; it does not guarantee anyone's right to threaten strangers in the public square, or to shout obscenities on TV, or to use a social media platform to agitate for the physical removal of your fellow citizens, or to promote racist ideas without being made to feel like a racist.

In the end, the Deplorables were not able to widen the Overton window so drastically that they could fit inside it. They did, however, score some even larger victories. They helped propel their man into the presidency. They helped normalize flagrant mendacity and open racism. In many circles—circles that currently extend as far as the White House—jocular contempt for women has been brought back into fashion, as have overt Islamophobia, raw nativism, and the theory of human biodiversity. As the late philosopher Richard Rorty presciently noted, the academic left spent decades trying to make nativism and bigotry unacceptable. But acceptability is merely a social norm, and, according to some anonymous accounts on social media, academic leftists are nothing more than cultural-Marxist traitors anyway.

The American popular vocabulary is in a period of deep dysfunction. Jordan Peterson—by some measures, the most popular public intellectual of this decade*—is not a white supremacist, but his rhetoric on the subject can be disturbingly fuzzy. He has been asked many times whether he is alt-right, and his standard answer is that he isn't—not because the delusion of white superiority is a deep and abiding scourge that must be uprooted in order to save Western civilization from itself, but simply because "identity politics" is misguided, both when the left does it and when the right does it.† This is the sort of false equivalence that would have been staggering just a few years ago. Now it barely registers.

---

*Peterson's book *12 Rules for Life*, a hodgepodge of clinical psychology, Jungian mythology, and self-help, sold three million copies in its first year, an unprecedented level of viral success for a previously unknown writer.
†"If you're playing a collectivist game, I don't give a damn if you're playing it on the left or the right. It's a bad game." This was how Peterson put it in May 2018, speaking before a crowd of thirty-six hundred people at an amphitheater in London, but he has reiterated the same sentiment dozens of times. His disavowals of the alt-right sometimes sound uncomfortably close to Mike Cernovich's disavowal, on his blog, in the summer of 2016. Peterson is a contrarian, and it's possible that he simply resents being asked to repeat anything so dully conformist as the truism that Nazis are uniquely despicable. But some truisms are worth repeating, and some questions have only one right answer.

On the most popular cable-news network in the country, prime-time hosts often deliver racist messages that hardly qualify as dog whistles, so clear are they even to a casual listener. Questions that have rightly been considered closed for decades are now treated as open once again. "White nationalist, white supremacist, Western civilization—how did that language become offensive?" Steve King, a congressman from Iowa, said in an interview with *The New York Times* in January 2019. At some point, the broken American vocabulary will be replaced by a new one. But whatever comes next will bear the scars of the current disruption.

"The world does not speak," Richard Rorty wrote. "Only we do." If Rorty is right that a transition to a new moral vocabulary is analogous to a paradigm shift in science, then we could be in for a rough few years. Before Copernicus, most Europeans believed that the sun revolved around the Earth. After Copernicus, most Europeans came to believe the opposite. But the change was neither sudden nor tidy; people didn't learn of the new astronomical findings in 1543 and accept them all at once. "Rather," Rorty wrote, "after a hundred years of inconclusive muddle, the Europeans found themselves speaking in a way which took these interlocked theses for granted." When Rorty made this argument, he was drawing on the philosopher Thomas Kuhn, who invented the concept of the paradigm shift. Kuhn argued that revolutions in human thought progress through five stages. It's no accident that the word Kuhn used for the inconclusive-muddle stage—a stage that can last for decades, even centuries—was "crisis."*

To change how we talk is to change who we are. More and more every day, how we talk is a function of how we talk on the internet. The bigoted propagandists of the alt-right are wrong about almost everything, but they are correct about this much: the United States of America was founded by white men, for white men. The problem with the bigots is not that they acknowledge this aspect of the country's history; the problem is that they cling to it, doing their utmost to revive the horrors of the past, instead of taking up the more difficult task of piecing together the future. The bigots are not destined to win. Nor are they destined to lose. The ending is not yet written. The blithely optimistic view—the view that still infuses far too many op-eds and Silicon Valley pitch meetings and political stump

---

*After "crisis," according to Kuhn, comes "revolution," and with it the emergence of a new paradigm. Kuhn was writing about science—the book in which he laid out his theory was called *The Structure of Scientific Revolutions*— but his central metaphor came from politics. "In both political and scientific development," he wrote, "the sense of malfunction that can lead to crisis is prerequisite to revolution."

speeches—is that the basic good sense of the American people will prevail, that the good stuff will spread, that if we just hold fast we will surely end up in the right place. But the vehicle doesn't drive itself. Getting to the right place takes work. Copernicus was not the first astronomer to suggest that the Earth revolved around the sun. Aristarchus of Samos proposed the same idea in the third century B.C., but Aristotle convinced everyone that the idea was wrong. Overcoming Aristotle's mistake took almost two thousand years, and even then it required a struggle.

The United States was founded on lofty theoretical principles and a reality of brutal conquest. The country went to war with itself over the question of whether all of its residents deserved to be treated as people, and then, long after the war ended, continued to answer that question in the negative. As immigration has proliferated in recent decades, so has a tide of xenophobia. The ideal of a true multi-ethnic democracy—a society rooted in pluralism and dignity and meaningful, lasting equality—is a noble and necessary goal, one that this country has never come close to reaching. "If we," James Baldwin wrote, "do not falter in our duty now, we may be able, handful that we are, to end the racial nightmare, and achieve our country, and change the history of the world." We must achieve our country; we will not be forgiven if we fail; and yet our success is hardly guaranteed. True multiethnic democracies are historically rare. They have tended to balkanize, or to descend into sustained conflict. If our union is to succeed at drawing itself closer to perfection, then we will first need a new set of questions, a new way of talking, a new way of thinking—a new moral, social, and political vocabulary.

Maybe one day Americans will find themselves speaking and acting in a way that takes real justice and solidarity for granted. Maybe. But the sun did not reach into the brains of Renaissance Europeans to make them accept the scientific truth of planetary motion, and the universe will not reach into our brains now to make us accept the moral truth of equality. The arc of history may bend in that direction, but the arc of history is not bent inexorably or automatically. It does not bend itself. We bend it.

Epilogue

It has become a tradition for big tech companies to release elaborate, self-referential jokes every April Fools' Day. The point is to generate some free publicity, to make the company seem quirky and relatable; but it can also have the opposite effect, especially when the premise of the joke is Silicon Valley's unprecedented power. A few years ago, Twitter announced that it would start charging for vowels. More recently, Amazon revealed voice-recognition software that could take commands from pets, and Google shared a mock-up of its new data-storage center on Mars. The companies hadn't actually commissioned any of these projects, but they probably could, one day, if they wanted to. Get it?

In 2017, instead of a parody announcement, Reddit unveiled a genuine social experiment. It was called r/Place, and it was a blank square, a thousand pixels by a thousand pixels. In the beginning, all million pixels were white. Once it started, any Reddit user could change a single pixel, anywhere on the grid, to one of sixteen colors. The only restriction was speed: the algorithm allowed each redditor to alter just one pixel every five minutes. "That way, no one person can take over—it's too slow," Josh Wardle, the Reddit product manager in charge of r/Place, explained. "In order to do anything at scale, they're gonna have to cooperate."

The experiment had been live for about twenty minutes when I found Wardle in the common area, huddled over his laptop, frantically refreshing dozens of tabs. So far, the square was mostly blank, with a few stray dots blinking in and out of existence. But redditors were making plans and, in true Reddit fashion, clinging to those plans with cultish intensity. A new subreddit, r/TheBlueCorner, was conspiring to turn the whole square blue; r/RedCorner was vowing to make it red; already, they were on a war footing. Other groups planned elaborate messages, fractal patterns, and references to various memes. A broad coalition—leftists, Trump supporters, patriotic libertarians, prepolitical teenagers—decided to draw an American flag in the center of the square. They congregated at r/American FlaginPlace, where they hashed out the exact dimensions of the stars and stripes, and shared strategies for repelling potential invaders. Meanwhile, a group of nihilists at r/TheBlackVoid prepared to blot out whatever the other groups created. *Some people just want to watch the world burn.*

Wardle went to great lengths to show me that Place was a pure democracy—the algorithm was designed so that, once it went live, all he could do was watch, along with everyone else. Now, toggling compulsively from tab to tab, he seemed nervous. "The idea was 'Let's put up a very simple microcosm of the internet and just see what happens,'" he said. "Reddit itself is not the most complex idea. It's sort of a blank canvas. The community takes that and does all sorts of creative things with it."

"And some terrible things," I said.

"I'm pretty confident," he said. He paused. "I'd be lying if I said I was a hundred percent confident." Already, one of the top comments on Place read, "I give this an hour until swastikas." One of Wardle's colleagues told me, "That was what kept Josh up at night. Before this went live, he was literally calculating, 'OK, it takes a minimum of seventeen pixels to make a swastika—what if we open this up to the world, and the headline the next day is "Reddit: A Place to Draw Swastikas on the Internet"?'"

The upper-left corner turned a choppy, flickering purple as the "Blue Empire" and the "Red Empire" battled for dominance. A graffiti artist, or artists, wrote "9/11 was an inside job"; a few minutes later, the "was" turned into "wasn't," and the "an" became "anime." Elsewhere, "Dick butt" became "Dick butter," then "Dick buffet"; "Kill me" became "Kill men," then the words disappeared entirely. And then the swastikas arrived—just a few of them, but enough to make Wardle raise the hood of his sweatshirt, retreat into an empty conference room, and shut the door, looking pallid.

In his office, Huffman met with Chris Slowe, Reddit's first employee, who is now the chief technical officer.

"How is Place going?" Huffman asked.

"Pretty much as expected," Slowe said. "A lot of memes, some Pokémon, and a barrage of dicks."

"If there's ever a Reddit musical, that wouldn't be a bad title," Huffman said.

"I have faith in our people," Slowe replied.

People stood in the common area, eating from paper plates, watching a live feed of Place on a wall-mounted TV. One employee, reading the comments, brightened. "A bunch of people are finding swastikas and then telling everyone else where they are, so that people can go get rid of them," she announced.

"I just saw it!" another employee said. He pointed to a section of the screen. As we watched, one swastika was erased, and another was modified to become a Windows '95 logo. After a while, the swastika makers got bored and moved on.

At one point, the American flag was set on fire, its red, white, and blue pixels replaced with orange flames and black smoke. The defenders of the flag, still coordinating the efforts at r/AmericanFlaginPlace, rallied to stamp the fire out, and the Reddit employees cheered.

"Feels like watching a football game in extreme slow motion," one said.

"Or like watching the election results."

"Oh God, don't say that."

Toward the end, the square became a dense, colorful tapestry, chaotic and strangely captivating. It was a collage of hundreds of incongruous images: logos of colleges, sports teams, bands, and video-game companies; a transcribed monologue from *Star Wars*; likenesses of He-Man, David Bowie, the Mona Lisa, and a former prime minister of Finland. In the final hours, shortly before the experiment ended and the image was frozen for posterity, r/TheBlackVoid launched a surprise attack on the American flag. A dark fissure tore at the bottom of the flag, then overtook the whole thing. For a few minutes, the center was enveloped in darkness. Then a coalition of thousands of redditors joined up to beat back the Void; the stars and stripes regained their form, and, in the end, the flag was still there.

The final image contained no visible hate symbols, no violent threats—not even much nudity. Late in the day, Wardle emerged from hiding, poured himself a drink, and pushed back his hood. "It's possible that I will be able to sleep tonight," he said.

I wrote an article about Reddit, ending with the saga of r/Place. Everyone I knew interpreted the final scene differently. My most optimistic friends read it as an affirmation, another reason to keep faith in the basic good sense of the American people. My more pessimistic friends wondered whether I'd gone soft—where was my skepticism, my vigilance, my attunement to humanity's deep deficiencies? I told both camps: the scene doesn't imply that We Are Good or that We Are Bad. All I knew was that, on this particular day, on this particular part of the internet, the hordes had joined together to beat back the darkness. Even better, they'd done it on their own, without the guidance of gatekeepers, relying only on the wisdom of the crowd.

Then I got a direct message on Twitter. "For r/place, Reddit employees had mass white-out tools where they could quickly and easily remove swastikas," the message read. "Those swastikas weren't all replaced by other users." The message came from a Twitter account with a female avatar photo, but the person behind it wouldn't tell me her name. She claimed to be a former Reddit employee. "Heard about the white-out tools from an engineer who still works at Reddit," she continued. "They're probably feeding you quite a bit of propaganda tbh."

I tried to report out the rumor, asking a few former employees who'd recently left the company.

"Totally sounds like something they would do," one former employee said. "Why leave it to chance?"

"Doesn't sound like them," another former employee said. "I think they're too old-school techno-libertarian to try playing tricks like that."

I messaged the woman on Twitter, asking for more information, or for proof of her identity.

She didn't respond.

A few weeks later, I tried again: "Maybe we could talk on the phone?"

No response.

A few weeks after that: "So was this just a troll?"

I never heard from her again.

GLOSSARY

A NOTE ABOUT TERMINOLOGY:

Language evolves constantly, especially on the internet. Affiliations and ideologies can change; words and symbols can be warped until they mean the opposite of what they once meant. As Reddit's head of policy once said, when it comes to thorny questions about online speech, "It all depends on context." The definitions below, then, are not immutable, and the brief character sketches are hardly exhaustive. The purpose of this glossary is more modest: to summarize a few concepts and terms that may be unfamiliar, and to introduce some key characters and their (ever-shifting) allegiances.

PEOPLE (in order of appearance)

Cassandra Fairbanks

> Writer for a variety of outlets including *Sputnik*, *Big League Politics*, and *The Gateway Pundit*; former leftist turned alt-light activist; "I care more about free speech, including for Chelsea Manning and Julian Assange, than almost any other issue"

Jack Posobiec

> Navy veteran; Republican operative turned alt-light activist; co-organizer of the DeploraBall; correspondent for the Rebel and One America News Network

Jeff Giesea

> Digital entrepreneur; former employee of Peter Thiel; co-organizer of the DeploraBall; donor to online trolls and propagandists

Mike Cernovich

> Purveyor of self-help books, herbal supplements, fitness advice, and internet memes; lawyer; former manosphere blogger; prolific tweeter; mottos include "Conflict is attention" and "Attention is influence"

Milo Yiannopoulos

> Social media sophist; former *Breitbart* editor and columnist; peddler of books, T-shirts, coffee mugs, and crypto-fascist memes; self-described as "the most fabulous supervillain on the internet"

Lauren Southern

> Former correspondent for the Rebel; Canadian; anti-immigration activist; "I'm

in this awkward position where the alt-light calls me alt-right and the alt-right calls me alt-light"

Jim Hoft

Founder of *The Gateway Pundit*; "conservative gay activist"; conspiracy theorist

Roger Stone

Longtime Trump associate and campaign consultant; self-described "dirty trick-ster"; motto: "Admit nothing, deny everything, launch counterattack"

Alex Jones

Founder and chief anchor of Infowars; prolific conspiracy theorist

Gavin McInnes

Cofounder of *Vice*; cofounder of the Proud Boys, a "Western chauvinist" street gang; "I'm an Islamophobe, I'm a xenophobe, I'm pretty darn sexist"

Laura Loomer

Freelancer known for staging and livestreaming street confrontations; conspira-cist; Zionist; Islamophobe

Lucian Wintrich

Former White House correspondent for *The Gateway Pundit*; alt-light culture warrior; creator of photography project called Twinks4Trump

Jerome Corsi

Infowars correspondent; prolific conspiracy theorist

Faith Goldy

Canadian; ran unsuccessfully for mayor of Toronto on a nationalist platform; fired by the Rebel after appearing on a neo-Nazi podcast

Will Chamberlain

Co-organizer of MAGA Meetups in D.C.; lawyer; "anti-anti-Semitic"

Jane Ruby

Co-organizer of MAGA Meetups in D.C.; retired health economist and entrepre-neur; red-pilled by Andrew Breitbart

Andrew Breitbart

The John the Baptist of the Deplorables; motto: "Politics is downstream from culture"

Alt-right

Mike Enoch

Founder of the blog *The Right Stuff* and the podcast *The Daily Shoah*; anti-Semite and white supremacist; doxed shortly before Trump's inauguration

Richard Spencer

Anti-Semite and white supremacist; coined the term "alt-right"; publicly toasted Trump's election victory with what appeared to be a Nazi salute; founder of *Radix Journal* and AlternativeRight.com

Nathan Damigo

Founder of Identity Evropa; former U.S. Marine; white nationalist

David Duke

Anti-Semite and white nationalist; founder of the Knights of the Ku Klux Klan; former Louisiana state representative and presidential candidate

Disrupters

Steven Huffman, Alexis Ohanian

Cofounders of Reddit

Emerson Spartz

Founder of Dose, OMGFacts, and GivesMeHope; "viral guy"

Paul Graham

Silicon Valley entrepreneur; "the closest thing the technology community has to either a Bertrand Russell or a P. T. Barnum"

Mark Zuckerberg

Founder of Facebook; "We're a technology company, not a media company"; "When you connect two billion people, you will see all the beauty and ugliness of humanity"

KEY TERMS

Alt-right

Coined in 2008 by Richard Spencer—first as "alternative right," later abbreviated—the term has since been used in a variety of contexts, ranging from the most innocuous (an irreverent, web-savvy alternative to traditional conservatism) to the least (an anonymous swarm perpetrating harassment and bigotry). After the 2016 election, it became universally apparent that, edgy memes aside, the movement had always contained a core of sincere racism and anti-Semitism. Most often, in this book, I use "alt-right" the way Spencer and his acolytes use it—more or less interchangeably with web-savvy white nationalism.

Alt-light (a.k.a. New Right, American nationalism, civic nationalism, or Western chauvinism)

After the 2016 election, what had recently been one movement (the alt-right) split into two: the alt-right and the alt-light. The alt-right was characterized by lurid racism, anti-Semitism, misogyny, Islamophobia, and a tendency to spew disinformation; the alt-light claimed to reject overt racism and anti-Semitism, but seemed fine with the rest. In public, the leaders of the two factions were at pains to highlight their differences. "I'm not alt-right, dude," one alt-light figure said. "They care about the white race. We care about Western values." In private, the lines were often blurrier.

Activating emotions

Emotions—whether positive or negative, prosocial or antisocial—that tend to elicit a given behavior (e.g. clicking or sharing a link). Activating emotions beget engagement, and engagement begets virality.

Charlottesville 1.0

The alt-right's term for their rally on May 13, 2017, in Charlottesville, Virginia. A few dozen white supremacists marched, with torches, around a statue of Robert E. Lee. A few dozen protesters held a candlelight vigil. The whole thing was fairly uneventful.

Charlottesville 2.0

The alt-right's follow-up rally in Charlottesville, Virginia, in August 2017. This rally was far larger and more chaotic, and it culminated in a white supremacist driving his car into a crowd of protesters, killing one of them.

Cuck

A slur, laden with racist and sexist connotations, used by the alt-right and alt-light to denigrate those they see as weak or worthy of contempt. (Also, "cuckservative": an insufficiently zealous conservative.)

Dox (both noun and verb)

To reveal someone's name, address, or other personal information against that person's will, as a form of retribution.

Echo

An anti-Semitic meme invented by bloggers and podcasters affiliated with *The Right Stuff*. The auditory version consists of an echo being added to a Jewish person's name; the written equivalent consists of three parentheses placed around a Jew's name, like so: (((Andrew Marantz))). Later reclaimed by Jewish writers and activists, some of whom wear the mark proudly.

Engagement

Clicks, shares, comments, likes—any metric that enables a social media company to quantify users' response to a piece of content.

Human biodiversity

The hypothesis that people are different, that they differ in predictable ways, and that some groups of people—some races, for example—have drawn stronger cards in the genetic lottery. In other words, a form of intellectualized racism.

Jewish Question (JQ), the

Mild version: "Why are Jews overrepresented in media, academia, and banking?"
More overt version: "Are Jews white?"
Most overt version: "What should we do about the Jews?"
Before it was a topic of discussion among the alt-right, the Jewish Question was a topic of academic discussion in eighteenth- and nineteenth-century Europe (notably in Bruno Bauer's 1843 book *Die Judenfrage*) and in Nazi Germany (where the proposed answer to the question was "the Final Solution," aka genocide).

LARP, LARPing

Live action role-playing. Literally, a kind of fantasy gaming, e.g. Dungeons & Dragons. Figuratively, on the internet, LARPing usually refers to an embarrassing or unconvincing form of pretense—for example, an awkward attempt to act out one's online persona in the real world.

Manosphere

A loose affiliation of blogs and message boards, prominent in the early part of the 2010s, that promoted various forms of antifeminism. Subcultures within the manosphere included pickup artists, men's rights activists, incels, volcels, and MGTOW (men going their own way). Prominent manosphere blogs included *Return of Kings* and *Roissy in D.C.*

Meme

Defined by Richard Dawkins in 1976 as any "unit of cultural transmission" that propagates "by leaping from brain to brain."

Microtargeting

The process by which internet companies analyze user data in order to tailor ads, news stories, and other content to each consumer's preferences.

Narrative, the

A nonnegotiable set of axioms and language rules—one that is, according to some fringe commentators, imposed and enforced by a nefarious cohort of media executives, political donors, and other cultural gatekeepers.

Overton window

The range of socially acceptable opinion, which can shift over time. Originally applied to legislative policy, now applied to matters of cultural or political concern more broadly.

Pepe the Frog

Formerly innocuous cartoon frog coopted by internet racists.

Red pill

A metaphor derived from the 1999 movie *The Matrix*: to take the red pill, or to be red-pilled, is to discover some forbidden truth. On many corners of the fringe internet, the "truth" in question is actually a dangerous lie: white supremacy, male supremacy, etc.

Shitposting

A style of discourse prevalent on some parts of social media (especially certain corners of 4chan, 8chan, Gab, some parts of Reddit). In the best case, the result is absurdist so-bad-it's-good humor; in the worst case, the result is bigotry or incitement to violence.

Troll (both noun and verb)

In the early days of the internet, trolling was akin to a prank, even a kind of performance. To troll people was to get a rise out of them; a troll was an expert at doing this, often anonymously. Over time, trolling took on a darker connotation. These days, what's sometimes called trolling is often more like propaganda, bigotry, or harassment.

Vocabulary

The philosopher Richard Rorty's term for a society's underlying set of assumptions, its way of talking to itself, its way of describing and interpreting the universe.

Acknowledgments

Writing a book is such an exercise in solipsism—for me, anyway—that it feels impossible to express sufficient gratitude to everyone who helped me, encouraged me, or put up with me over the past few years. But I'll try. First, thank you to Rick Kot, who was always able to see the forest for the trees while continuing to perceive each tree in uncanny detail, and whose editorial insights and steady hand made this project possible. I'm also grateful to everyone else at Viking—Norma Barksdale, Diego Nuñez, Kristina Fazzalaro, Andrea Schulz, and Brian Tart—for taking a chance on a first book, and for seeing it through with such grace and aplomb.

Tina Bennett is a trenchant reader, an indomitable hype woman, an engaging polemicist, and the best agent in the business. I'm lucky to be the beneficiary of her talent. Thanks also to Laura Filion, Svetlana Katz, and everyone else at WME.

Many friends read parts of the manuscript, or the whole manuscript, and gave thoughtful comments throughout. My profound thanks go to Vinson Cunningham, Jonathan (Skoal) Gold, Sam Graham-Felsen, Antonia Hitchens, Meechal Hoffman, Patrick Radden Keefe, Gideon Lewis-Kraus, Rob Moor, Emily Nussbaum, Matthew Palevsky, Ari Savitzky, and Alexandra Schwartz. Drinks are on me forever.

I will never stop being amazed that I get to call *The New Yorker* my professional home. I have learned a tremendous amount from my colleagues there—especially the not-sung-enough editorial brain trust, including (but not limited to!) Nimal Eames-Scott, Rob Fischer, Carla Blumenkranz, Eric Lach, Eleanor Martin, Sharan Shetty, Emily Stokes, and Hannah Wilentz. Thanks, in particular, to Henry Finder, Pam McCarthy, Susan Morrison, and Dorothy Wickenden, for making the magazine what it is; to Deirdre Foley-Mendelssohn, a master of the editorial arts of perspicacity, hand-holding, schmoozing when there's time, and working when there isn't; to Daniel Zalewski—a uniquely gifted editor and writer, an attentive mentor, and a generous friend—who improves every piece of writing he touches, including this book; and to David Remnick, who somehow manages to be both a superhero and a mensch, and who gave me the space and encouragement I needed to embark on this project (and then line-edited the thing, incredibly, in no more than forty-eight hours). May you all continue to be exemplars of trustworthiness and taste, even in a postgatekeeper world.

Thank you to Molly Farneth for helping me get my Rorty straight, to Athmeya Jayaram for helping me replace my dead dogmas about J. S. Mill with living truths, and to Daniel May for innumerable conversations about pragmatism, the tragic paradoxes of liberalism, and the best parts of old Uncle Drew videos. Natalie Coleman and Sam Argyle provided invaluable research. I am especially indebted to Tyler Foggatt, a brilliant reporter and a befogged author's secret weapon. Rozina Ali, Ewa Beaujon, Sean Lavery, Talia Lavin, and Nick Niarchos fact-checked this material, either for *The New Yorker* or for the book (or, in Sean's case, both); in addition to saving my ass by correcting my mistakes, their services also included wise editorial counsel, incisive counterarguments, and deft turns of phrase that I was all too happy to steal.

This book would have been worse if not for the conversations I had with Bobby Baird, Zoe Chace, Adrian Chen, Kate Klonick, Robert Krulwich, Courtney Martin, Sruthi Pinnamaneni, and Kevin Roose. Thanks also to everyone at Data & Society, especially Matt Goerzen and Brian Friedberg, who both know more about /pol/ than anyone should.

Thank you to Samantha for trusting me with your story, and for the music recs.

I am grateful to my family for making me who I am—especially to Eric and Emily Marantz, to Dorothy Gray, to Julia Gray and Paul Marantz, and to the memory of Clare Marantz. Rachel, Brian, and Ilana Lustbader felt like family long before they actually became my family. A special shout-out to Kevin Brenner, who paid me to sit in a dumpster while day-dreaming about reportage, and to Robin Marantz Henig, who line-edited this whole book with a keen and sensitive eye—a much better gift than any turquoise-and-purple quilt!

Lastly, thank you to Gideon, my favorite guy in the world, and to Sarah Lustbader, the best person I know. I floated the idea of listing you as a coauthor, and the fact-checkers deemed it misleading but not exactly false, which sounds about right to me. Most of what's good in this book, like most of what's good in my life, is because of you.

Notes

Author's Note: *Antisocial* is a work of reporting. The events described in the book really happened; with rare exceptions, which are noted below, the names are real. When I learned a fact from another reporter's work, I have tried to cite it, either here or in the text; in most other cases, the facts and events recounted in the book are ones that I learned about through interviews, or reconstructed through research, or witnessed firsthand.

Books are copyedited, meticulously polished objects. Tweets are not. Instead of overloading every page with footnotes that say "*sic*," I have used my judgment when quoting online posts, correcting a few obvious but tricky typos and leaving the rest—grammatical errors, self-contradictions, ugly slurs, bad takes—mostly untouched.

Writing about propagandists, bigots, and other bad-faith actors requires vigilance, careful editorial deliberation, and the constant weighing of conflicting values. I did my best to avoid falling into various potential traps: lionizing the bad actors or normalizing their behavior or repeating their talking points uncritically. In the end, my hope is that if diligent reporting can help to illuminate the causes of extremism in Syria or Sri Lanka or Belgium or the Philippines, maybe it can do the same at home.

vii **"Morality, if it is to remain":** James Baldwin, "As Much Truth As One Can Bear," *The New York Times Book Review*, January 14, 1962.

vii **"Under all this dirt":** Lydia Davis, *Can't and Won't* (New York: Farrar, Straus & Giroux, 2014), 90.

PART ONE: DEPLORABALL

9 **"Everyone knows, or ought to know":** George W. S. Trow, "Collapsing Dominant," *Within the Context of No Context* (New York: Atlantic Monthly Press, 1997).

CHAPTER ONE: THIS IS AMERICA

18 For more than two decades: Jones's remarkable conversion from Trump skeptic (July 12, 2015: "I don't trust him as far as I can throw him") to Trump booster (December 30, 2015: "If Trump isn't sincere behind the scenes then I've been fooled") was documented in exhaustive detail by the podcast *Knowledge Fight*, a talmudic, profane, and strangely delightful source of Infowars exegesis.

CHAPTER TWO: PRIDE

24 Zach, a skinny Proud Boy: Zach is an alias.

31 A prepublication copy: Trump, on Twitter, before the book was published: ".@AnnCoulter's new book—'Adios, America! The Left's Plan to Turn Our Country into a Third World Hellhole'—is a great read. Good job!" After the book was published, the leftist magazine *Current Affairs* called it a "vicious, dehumanizing book" that nevertheless made for "effective propaganda."

32 Buchanan never wrote for *National Review*: In subsequent interviews, Buchanan indicated that, if Buckley considered him persona non grata, then the feeling was mutual. But in later years, especially after Buckley's death, the ban seemed to ease: *National Review* covered many of Buchanan's books, sometimes quite positively, and invited him to appear on its podcasts several times.

32 His goal, he told an interviewer: David Corn, "Pat Buchanan, Editor," *The Nation*, October 24, 2002, www.thenation.com/article/pat-buchanan-editor.

CHAPTER THREE: THE CONTRARIAN QUESTION

44 "Who cares if someone is racist?": A year earlier, Cernovich had tweeted, "I went from libertarian to alt-right after realizing tolerance only went one way and diversity is code for white genocide." He never retracted that statement or apologized for it. Apologies, he believed, made him look weak; he preferred to hedge and spin, maintaining as much plausible deniability as possible.

45 Spencer had permitted a Jewish videographer: The videographer's name was Daniel Lombroso. Spencer later told me, "I didn't know he was Jewish at the time."

47 Thiel had a long history: "I no longer believe that freedom and democracy are compatible," he wrote in 2009, on a libertarian blog. "Since 1920, the vast increase in welfare beneficiaries and the extension of the franchise to women—two constituencies that are notoriously tough for libertarians—have rendered the notion of 'capitalist democracy' into an oxymoron." In 2016, he said that colleges were "as corrupt as the Catholic Church was five hundred years ago."

49 Many were blinkered coastal elites: In 1969, several Chicago police officers raided the home of Fred Hampton, the seventeen-year-old deputy chairman of the Black

Panther Party, and Hampton ended up dead. The police officers told the media that they had been under fire and had shot Hampton in self-defense. The media repeated this claim. As Jeff Gottlieb and Jeff Cohen later reported in *The Nation*, much of the contemporaneous press coverage of the incident relied heavily, if not exclusively, on police statements. Police officers reenacted the raid on television for a local CBS affiliate, using a set built solely for this purpose. "*The Chicago Tribune* ran an account drawn from the policemen involved in the assault, and accompanied by a photograph of the apartment on which circles were drawn around what purported to be bullet holes caused by bullets fired at the police," they wrote. The purported bullet holes turned out to be nail heads. *Chicago Sun-Times* reported this detail accurately at the time, but the larger truth—that the police had not acted in self-defense, and that Hampton was likely assassinated by agents of his own government—took years to emerge. Jeff Gottlieb and Jeff Cohen, "Was Fred Hampton Executed?" *The Nation*, December 25, 1976, www.thenation.com/article/was-fred -hampton-executed.

CHAPTER FOUR: TO CHANGE HOW WE TALK IS TO CHANGE WHO WE ARE

52 It seemed that he was earnestly trying: "After the DeploraBall, I found myself in an unpleasant conversation on the sidewalk outside with someone I surmised to be somewhat of a public figure (given the crowd around him), but who I did not recognize," Mary Clare wrote later in an email to me. "I was entirely unaware of his views at the time. Now that I know more about who he is, I find his politics to be in direct conflict with my beliefs as a Catholic and as a conservative. I find his role in public discourse to be entirely unproductive and immoral."

60 Just as Darwin had shown: Rorty used a wide array of canonical texts to bolster this view, citing many of the major Western philosophers of the nineteenth and twentieth centuries—Dewey, Nietzsche, Derrida, Habermas, Sartre, Rawls, and on and on. These philosophers didn't agree on much, but according to Rorty, they all shared a contingent view of history.

INTERLUDE: MOVABLE TYPE

71 In 2013, for the first time: Maureen A. Craig and Jennifer A. Richeson, "On the Precipice of a 'Majority-Minority' America: Perceived Status Threat from the Racial Demographic Shift Affects White Americans' Political Ideology," *Psychological Science* 25, no. 6 (2014): https://doi.org/10.1177/0956797614527113.

PART TWO: A HUMAN SUPERPOWER

73 "The internet is almost the perfect distillation": Interview with Eduardo Lago, conducted March 2000 but unpublished until "A manera de prólogo. Una conversación inédita con David Foster Wallace," *Walt Whitman ya no vive aquí* (Madrid: Editorial Sexto Piso: 2018). First appeared in English as "A Brand New Interview with David Foster Wallace," *Electric Literature*, November 16, 2018, https://electricliterature.com/a-brand-new-interview-with-david-foster-wallace.

CHAPTER FIVE: THE GLEAMING VEHICLE

79 **"Content that evokes high-arousal emotion":** Jonah Berger and Katherine L. Milkman, "What Makes Online Content Viral?," *Journal of Marketing Research* 49, no. 2 (2012): 192–205.

CHAPTER EIGHT: EATING THE WORLD

99 **Peter, Reid, Mark, Marc, Elon:** That would be Thiel, Hoffman, Zuckerberg, Andreessen, and Musk.

103 **Graham, impressed by the young man's display:** This story is recounted in *The Facebook Effect* by David Kirkpatrick, published in 2011. As of this writing, Facebook's market capitalization is $480 billion, ten percent of which would be more than enough to subsidize a few of *The Washington Post*'s foreign bureaus.

CHAPTER NINE: BRAINWRECK POLITICS

111 **As long as these entrepreneurs:** In theory, anyway. In practice, Cambridge Analytica's parent company was found guilty of breaking British campaign-finance law, and was fined £15,000.

CHAPTER ELEVEN: THE INVISIBLE PRIMARY

128 **In 1972, a poll suggested that Walter Cronkite:** As the press critic Jack Shafer noted in *Slate* in 2009, the "Cronkite-equals-trust cliché" was never supported by robust evidence. The poll in question was mainly about politicians; Cronkite, the only newscaster on the list, was deemed only six points more trustworthy than the "average senator." Two years later, when a more apples-to-apples poll compared Cronkite to his rival anchors at NBC and ABC, he ranked fourth in the "best-liked" category.

128 **In 2013, according to a *Reader's Digest* poll:** Courtenay Smith, "Reader's Digest Trust Poll: The 100 Most Trusted People in America," *Reader's Digest*, May 2013, www.rd.com/culture/readers-digest-trust-poll-the-100-most-trusted-people-in-america.

128 **"The extent to which celebrity is prized":** The other three coauthors of *The Party Decides* were David Karol, Hans Noel, and John Zaller (Chicago: University of Chicago Press, 2008).

131 more than fifty percent of American adults: Michael Barthel, "Newspaper Fact Sheet," Pew Research Center, June 13, 2018, www.journalism.org/fact-sheet/news papers; Shannon Greenwood, Andrew Perrin, and Maeve Duggan, "Social Media Up-date 2016," Pew Research Center, November 11, 2016, www.pewinternet.org/2016/11 /11/social-media-update-2016.

PART THREE: TOO BIG TO IGNORE

133 "The desire . . . to make a face": Alice Munro, "The Beggar Maid," *The Beggar Maid: Stories of Flo and Rose* (New York: Alfred A. Knopf, 1979).

CHAPTER TWELVE: BEYOND GOOD AND EVIL

144 *Roissy in D.C.* was a pseudonymous blog: The blog's apparent author, Jim Weid-mann, worked at the Financial Industry Regulatory Authority by day; by night, he was a prolific barfly, picking up women and then blogging about his exploits, as well as his broader theories about gender relations. His pseudonym was an allusion to *Histoire d'O*, a French erotic novel that was published and subsequently banned in the 1950s, in which a woman is brought to a mansion in the Paris suburb of Roissy-en-France, branded, and kept as a sex slave.

144 PUA sites, or "game" sites: PUA bloggers taught that game was a skill, and that, like any skill, it could be mastered with effort. A man's "sexual market value" could be enhanced by obvious factors, such as wealth and attractiveness, and also by less intuitive life hacks, which the bloggers promised to reveal to their readers. Mano-sphere message boards were full of testimonials from anonymous men who pur-ported to have bent the world to their will, running game on attractive women. The skill could also be transferred to other domains: you could run game on your bosses, your enemies, even your friends.

144 "misandry is the new Jim Crow": Roissy went even further on his blog, upending consensus opinions in a tone of pseudopoetic nihilism: "Fuck you and your misplaced empathy. Fuck you and your phonyfuck indignation. Especially fuck you and your happy sappy shifting morality hands across humanity meek shall inherit the karmic magical moral comeuppance excuse mongering rationalizing hypocritical there but for the grace of no one but myself go I virtue on the cheap fantasyland pissant pawn of your selfish gene replicating cog in the bloodsoaked gears of the amoral universal machine bullshit. Stare into the gaping maw of the id monster motherfuckers because I am rubbing your face in its hot stinking breath."

CHAPTER THIRTEEN: A FILTER FOR QUALITY

147 "A squirrel dying": David Kirkpatrick, *The Facebook Effect* (New York: Simon & Schuster, 2010), 181.

148–149 Yet he encouraged everyone to take his advice: In one post, Graham gave advice on "what an essay really is, and how you write one. Or at least, how I write one." It was a piece of writing about how to write, yet it was full of solecisms and mixed metaphors. In one paragraph, an essay was a train, a thread, a foot race, a pencil sketch, and a river, all at once. ("Err on the side of the river.")

149 They approached Graham: This story is recounted in Christine Lagorio-Chafkin, *We Are the Nerds: The Birth and Tumultuous Life of Reddit, the Internet's Culture Laboratory* (New York: Hachette, 2018).

CHAPTER FIFTEEN: REDUCTIO

171 *Justice means obeying the law*: This is Thrasymachus's definition of justice, in Plato's *Republic* (I, 338-c).

171 In early 2016, William Powers: Powers was part of an MIT research group that had a special arrangement with Twitter. The company gave the researchers an unprecedented amount of data—including all the tweets sent on the platform, hundreds of millions of them each day—and the researchers crunched the numbers and published their findings, both in scientific journals and on Medium. William Powers, "Who's Influencing Election 2016?" Medium, February 23, 2016, https://medium.com/@socialmachines/who-s-influencing-election-2016-8bed68ddecc3.

CHAPTER SIXTEEN: THE MEDIA MATRIX

180 In early August, they started to dominate: Matt Drudge made his name in 1998, when he broke the story of the Monica Lewinsky scandal before any other outlet. After that, his site's traffic exploded. In July 2016, Drudge got a billion and a half pageviews—more than *The Washington Post*, *Bloomberg*, *Vice*, and *BuzzFeed* combined. Drudge's politics had always been cartoonishly anti-Democrat. In recent years, he'd grown increasingly fond of unscrupulous right-wing sites such as Infowars and *Gateway Pundit*. Yet mainstream media gatekeepers kept visiting the site, and over time it took on a most-photographed-barn quality: journalists kept looking at Drudge because they knew that other journalists were looking at Drudge, too.

CHAPTER SEVENTEEN: FITNESS AND UNFITNESS

183 Its stories were often featured: A 2008 Nielsen ranking of the "Top 30 News Sites" listed WorldNetDaily.com at number 23, just above WashingtonPost.com. The most popular site on the list was the *Drudge Report*.

CHAPTER NINETEEN: POISE IS A CLUB

201 **After 9/11, though, his rhetoric grew:** In 2007, Dobbs claimed, falsely, that the U.S. had seen a recent spike in leprosy cases due to "unscreened illegal immigrants coming into this country." In 2009, he started suggesting, also falsely, that Barack Obama may have been born abroad.

INTERLUDE: TRUST NOTHING

210 **Facebook's researchers divulged the experiment:** Users were livid, and after that, Facebook either stopped conducting secret experiments or stopped telling the public about them. Adam D. I. Kramer, Jamie E. Guillory, and Jeffrey T. Hancock, "Experimental Evidence of Massive-scale Emotional Contagion through Social Networks," *Proceedings of the National Academy of Sciences of the United States of America*, June 17, 2014, www.pnas.org/content/111/24/8788.

PART FOUR: THE SWAMP

219 **"Shame gets a bad rap these days":** Zadie Smith, "Zadie Smith Interview: On Shame, Rage and Writing," Louisiana Channel, video, April 16, 2018, https://vimeo.com /264942344.

CHAPTER TWENTY-ONE: THE NEWS OF THE FUTURE

225 **Depending on your definition of "news":** In moments of panic, Spicer's instinct was to blame the press, even when the press had nothing to do with the topic being discussed. When Trump signed an executive order banning residents of seven Muslim-majority nations from entering the United States, Spicer denied that the order was a ban. "But the president himself called it a ban," Kristen Welker of NBC News said. "Is he confused, or are you confused?" Spicer replied, "I think that the words that are being used to describe it are derived from what the media is calling this."

CHAPTER TWENTY-THREE: VERY PROFESSIONAL AND VERY GOOD

242 **By the standards of a press briefing:** Earnest, living up to his name, posed gentle Socratic counterpoints. On one hand, "part of what's built into our system is a respect for private companies to put in place their own policies"; on the other hand, social media is "predicated on freedom of expression." This was a tension that free-speech absolutists never quite figured out how to resolve. When discussing their zealous devotion to the First Amendment, they tended to elide the inconvenient fact that Twitter and Facebook also had First Amendment rights, including the right to ban almost anyone from their platforms for almost any reason.

242 **"I want people to be able"**: This iteration is from an interview on *Real Time with Bill Maher*, in 2017, but Yiannopoulos repeated the idea whenever and wherever he could: on Fox News, on local news, on NPR, and on all available social media platforms, until he was banned from them.

245 **"Are you a white nationalist?"**: There was plenty of reason to think that both men were racists. Both of them dog-whistled so constantly that the better metaphor might have been a teakettle over an eternal flame. And, if that wasn't enough, there was also more overt evidence. McInnes, in a 2002 interview with the *New York Press*, was asked whether he was annoyed by his hipster neighbors in Williamsburg. "Well, at least they're not niggers or Puerto Ricans," he replied. "At least they're white." Yiannopoulos, according to reporting in *BuzzFeed*, used email passwords that referred to landmark moments in Nazi history, such as Kristallnacht and the Night of the Long Knives. Whenever he was caught crossing a line, Yiannopoulos claimed that he'd been trolling. But an email password is a strange place to try to shock the normies, given that the whole point of an email password is that no one is supposed to see it. Still, even with all this, it was impossible to make an airtight case that either man was an out-and-out white separatist. McInnes's wife was Native American. Yiannopoulos's husband was African American. An interracial marriage doesn't preclude someone from being a racist, of course, but it does preclude someone from joining most white-nationalist groups, or from gaining their support. Indeed, the hardcore alt-right, even when talking among themselves, did not embrace McInnes and Yiannopoulos; they considered them traitors. If McInnes and Yiannopoulos were white nationalists, they were clearly determined to hide it. Asking the question once again, in a televised interview, was unlikely to crack the case.

CHAPTER TWENTY-FOUR: SUCCESS AND EMPIRE

250 **"Plus, my daughter loves it"**: According to many constitutional scholars, the Trump International Hotel had suddenly transformed, on January 20, 2017, from a flamboyant real-estate investment into a flagrant violation of the emoluments clause. Several of Trump's cronies and business associates stayed at the hotel during inauguration weekend, paying as much as eighteen thousand dollars for a single suite—either a rip-off, a bribe, or both. A lobbying group hired by the Saudi government had been renting rooms in the hotel for months, funneling hundreds of thousands of dollars directly from the Saudi royal family to the Trump Organization.

CHAPTER TWENTY-FIVE: THE BRIGHT DAY THAT BRINGS FORTH THE ADDER

255 **Trump had delivered a speech**: From the speech: "Do we have enough respect for our citizens to protect our borders? Do we have the desire and the courage to preserve our civilization in the face of those who would subvert and destroy it?"

PART FIVE: THE AMERICAN BERSERK

273 **"into the indigenous American berserk":** Philip Roth, *American Pastoral* (New York: Houghton Mifflin Harcourt, 1997), 86.

CHAPTER TWENTY-SIX: THE EMPTINESS

294 **They were doing this:** "The war to disestablish the specifically European nature of the U.S. was fought on several fronts," MacDonald wrote. "The main thrusts of Jewish activism against European ethnic and cultural hegemony have focused on three critical power centers in the United States: The academic world of information in the social sciences and humanities, the political world where public policy on immigration and other ethnic issues is decided, and the mass media where 'ways of seeing' are presented to the public."

295 **"In science there are a thousand bad ideas":** This was part of Pinker's contribution to a forum, on *Slate*, called "How to Deal with Fringe Academics." As it happened, the forum was almost entirely devoted to one academic: MacDonald. "How To Deal With Fringe Academics," *Slate*, February 4, 2000, https://slate.com/news-and-politics/2000/02/how-to-deal-with-fringe-academics-5.html.

298 **surrounding Jewish names with triple parentheses:** Someone uploaded a browser extension to the Google Chrome store called the Coincidence Detector. The purpose of the extension was to automatically add triple parentheses to any Jewish-sounding name. The lead of a 2016 *Forbes* article, as transformed by the Coincidence Detector, reads: "With his blunt remarks on immigration, real estate billionaire and GOP presidential candidate Donald Trump might be leading the Republican race, but his pool of critics grow every single day—and it now includes an increasing number of fellow billionaires. Crossing bipartisan lines, billionaires like (((George Soros))), Rupert Murdoch, (((Larry Ellison))), Bill Gates and (((Mark Zuckerberg))) have all voiced their support for pro-immigration action, and some have even called out Trump."

302 **"I'm quite sure she meant that in a racial sense":** Asked about this later, she claimed she'd meant it "in a cutural sense."

308 **I didn't give him any of his son's direct quotes:** On *The Daily Shoah*, Mike Enoch referred sarcastically to "the cat lady that was killed," and said of James Fields, "He did nothing wrong. Frankly, he should get a medal."

CHAPTER TWENTY-SEVEN: THE MOUNTAIN

317 **her friend Rowena:** Rowena's name has been changed.

317 **her friend Son:** Son's name has been changed.

320 **secret underground bunkers below Denver International Airport:** For more on this conspiracy theory, visit www.flydenver.com/greathall/denfiles.

321 **she met Richie:** Richie is an alias.

PART SIX: A NIGHT FOR FREEDOM

339 **"Where everybody lies about everything":** Hannah Arendt, "Truth and Politics," *The New Yorker*, February 25, 1967, www.newyorker.com/magazine/1967/02/25/truth-and-politics.

CHAPTER TWENTY-EIGHT: COMMON SENSE

347 **The new rule raised new questions:** Some employees argued that the list of exceptions ought to be more comprehensive; others argued, echoing Alexander Hamilton in Federalist 84, that there should be no list of exceptions, lest people infer that the list was meant to be comprehensive.